SOLUTIONS MANUAL

AND

TEACHING NOTES

THE DESIGN
OF
COST MANAGEMENT SYSTEMS
TEXT CASES
AND
READINGS

Robin Cooper
Harvard Business School

Robert S. Kaplan
Harvard Business School

PRENTICE HALL
Englewood Cliffs, New Jersey 07632

Editorial/Production Supervision: *Christine McLaughlin*
Editor in Chief: *Joe Heider*
Pre-press Buyer: *Trudy Pisciotti*
Manufacturing Buyer: *Bob Anderson*

 © 1992 by Prentice-Hall, Inc.
A Simon & Schuster Company
Englewood Cliffs, New Jersey 07632

Printed in the United States of America

10 9 8 7 6 5 4 3 2 1

ISBN 0-13-204132-4

Prentice-Hall International (UK) Limited, *London*
Prentice-Hall of Australia Pty. Limited, *Sydney*
Prentice-Hall Canada Inc., *Toronto*
Prentice-Hall Hispanoamericana, S.A., *Mexico*
Prentice-Hall of India Private Limited, *New Delhi*
Prentice-Hall of Japan, Inc., *Tokyo*
Simon & Schuster Asia Pte. Ltd., *Singapore*
Editora Prentice-Hall do Brasil, Ltda., *Rio de Janeiro*

In appreciation of their outstanding work in formatting, preparing, and assisting with this manual, we dedicate the Instructor's Manual to our secretaries:

Elizabeth Andersen
Judith Ross

Case Errata for the First Printing

<u>Sentry Group</u>

The cost per cost drive unit for sales ($) should be 0.0112 not 0.12 in Exhibit 8.

<u>Hewlett Packard: Queensferry Telecommunications Division</u>

1.	The volume variance on page 429 of the book should be $43,000 unfavorable, not $41,000.

2.	The instrument test driver in Exhibit 2 should be test hours not labor hours.

3.	The budgeted cost of instrument test in Exhibit 6 should be $526.82 not $406.20.

CONTENTS

INTRODUCTION

The Design of Cost Management Systems contains seven years of case-writing, course development, and publication on management accounting systems. The material has been continually introduced in Harvard Business School's MBA and executive programs until the second year MBA elective has become completely transformed. The book enables instructors at other schools to conveniently access this material along with a complete set of teaching notes for each case. Readings have been included either for background reading for students or to allow instructors to devote an entire class to a particular issue and reading (with no case scheduled). Complementary books that could be used in conjunction with this material include:

H. Thomas Johnson and Robert S. Kaplan Relevance Lost: The Rise and Fall of Management Accounting (HBS Press, 1991 (paperback))

R. S. Kaplan and Anthony A. Atkinson, Advanced Management Accounting, Second Edition (Prentice Hall, 1989)

R. S. Kaplan (ed.), Measures for Manufacturing Excellence (HBS Press, 1990)

Brinker, Barry J. Emerging Practices in Cost Management (Warren, Gorham & Lamont, 1990) [a collection of about 50 articles that appeared in the Journal of Cost Management between 1987 and 1990]

Lamont F. Steedly (ed.), World-Class Accounting for World Class Manufacturing (Montvale, NJ: National Association of Accountants, 1991) [a collection of articles on cost management systems that appeared in Management Accounting between 1985 and 1990]

Several supplementary materials are available to be used in conjunction with the book. Prentice-Hall has videotapes that accompany the Ingersoll Milling, Mayers Tap, and Tektronix cases. These tapes can be requested from Prentice-Hall by book adopters. Several of the cases -- Mayers Tap, Fisher Technologies, and Schrader Bellows -- have menu-driven Lotus 1-2-3 (Release 2.01) spreadsheet programs that enable students to manipulate and calculate case data quickly. A video tape, containing several segments with two of the company's cost system designers talking about the design and implementation process, may also be purchased to accompany the Schrader Bellows case series. Schools can purchase the disk for each program and the video from:

Harvard Business School Publishing Division
Operations Department
Boston, MA 02163

Telephone:	(617) 495-6117 or -6192
Telefax:	(617) 495-6985

Order Numbers and Prices

9-088-001	Mayers Tap, Inc.: Designing a Cost System	$250
9-088-002	Fisher Technologies	150
9-088-003	Schrader Bellows: A Strategic Cost Analysis	250
9-886-525	Schrader Bellows (video, VHS)	90

Contents of each software package

one 5.25" disk,

installation directions,

software note on the use of the disk,

a **licensing agreement** which gives the instructor permission to network or reproduce the disk and worksheets for students,

one course module with the cases and worksheets needed for duplication.

Requirements

IBM PC or compatible with 640K memory

IBM PC DOS 2.0 or above

LOTUS 1-2-3, Release 2.01 or above

(All orders must be prepaid, shipping and handling extra.)

Course Organization

Currently, at Harvard, the following cases in the book are taught in the required 1st year MBA course, Financial Reporting and Management Accounting:

Seligram: Electronic Testing Operation
Mayers Tap (A) and (B)
Mueller Lehmkuhl
Destin Brass Products
Siemens Electric Motors Works (A)
Polysar

These materials provide a foundation in cost system design and an introduction to activity-based costing and performance measurement.

The second year elective, taught by Robin Cooper in Spring 1991, had the following case sequence:

1. La Grande Alliance
2. Bridgeton Industries
3. Commonwealth Blood Transfusion Service
4. Mayers Tap (B) and (C)
5. Digital Communications
6. Fisher Technologies
7. Micro Devices Division
8. Schulze Waxed Containers
9. Metabo
10. Texas Eastman
11. Analog Devices
12. Texas Instruments: Cost of Quality (A) and (B)
13. John Deere Component Works (A)
14. John Deere Component Works (B)
15. Schrader Bellows (A) and (B)
16. Schrader Bellows (D-1)
17. Schrader Bellows (E)
18. Tektronix (A)
19. Tektronix (B)
20. Hewlett Packard: RND
21. Zytec
22. Union Pacific (Intro) and (A)
23. Union Pacific (B)
24. American Bank
25. Kanthal (A)
26. Winchell Lighting (A)
27. Manufacturers Hanover Corporation

The Hewlett Packard: Queensferry Telecommunications Division was used as the final examination in May 1991 for this course. In subsequent years, HP:QTD will be part of the main curriculum. In previous years, the Sentry case was used as the final exam. The Bridgeton case was used successfully as the final exam for the first year MBA course, Financial Reporting and Management Accounting in December 1990.

We have used the following sequence of cases when training company teams who would be responsible for designing activity-based cost systems in their companies:

Bridgeton
Seligram
Mayers Tap (A) and (B)
Siemens Electric Motor Works (A)
John Deere Component Works (A) and (B)
Schrader Bellows (all)
Tektronix

When we are teaching ABC concepts to experienced practitioners and consultants, we use:

Siemens Electric Motor Works (A)
John Deere Component Works (A) and (B)
Schrader Bellows (all)
Tektronix (A)
Kanthal (A)

Srikant Datar and George Foster, when teaching a 2nd year MBA elective, "Strategic Control Systems," at Stanford in early 1990, used cases from the book in the following sequence:

Mueller Lemkuhl
Ingersoll Milling Machine
John Deere Component Works (A) and (B)
Kanthal (A)
Siemens Electric Motor Works (A)
Union Pacific (Introduction) (A) and (B)
Texas Eastman
Texas Instruments: Cost of Quality (A) and (B)
Analog Devices

These lists should enable instructors to identify the core cases and to construct their courses around these cases to meet their students' interests and needs.

Assignments

We have deliberately omitted all assignment questions from the cases in the textbook. We usually tailor the questions to the particular audience we are addressing and prefer not to limit our flexibility by having the discussion or assignment questions as part of the case. Also, sometimes our understanding or teaching strategy for the case changes. Assigning questions separately enables the discussion of the case to advance with our understanding or use of the case. With each teaching note in this manual, we have included the assignment questions that we currently use when teaching the cases to MBA students. Instructors are encouraged to use these questios on their first time through the material, but to then modify them in subsequent uses to focus the students on the issues they wish to emphasize. Remember that in a case discussion, we use the advance questions just to guide the students' preparation. We might use quite a different set of questions to generate an active class discussion and to bring out conceptual issues and theory during the class.

If students are unfamiliar with case preparation and discussion, instructors can order from HBS Publishing and distribute with the course outline and syllabus, the following note:

"The Use of Cases in Management Education,"   9-376-240

Instructor Preparation

We have made the cases available in book form, along with this instructors manual, so that the material can be accessed by instructors in schools around the world. But to teach a course from the book will require much more time than just teaching another round from a standard cost or managerial accounting textbook, especially one that an instructor is already familiar with. Instructors who are coming new to this material will discover that they have to make a considerable investment to get comfortable with each case they teach. We have found, however, that instructors at other business schools who have made the investment have found the returns worthwhile. Students become much more interested in and excited by management accounting material. Their employers welcome the new skills they have learned. And the instructors themselves usually find that they can now understand the contemporary dialogue occurring about redesign of cost management systems. We have greatly enjoyed developing and teaching this material during the past seven years. We look forward to welcoming more of our colleagues to this new approach of teaching management accounting, and to engage them in dialogue about the concepts and theories that emerge from study of the material.

Introduction To Cost Systems

The cases in Chapter 1 provide an introduction to existing cost systems: their properties, uses, and limitations. We generally start our courses off with about three cases from this chapter to introduce students to the operation of cost systems in actual organizations (particularly useful for students whose only previous exposure was in a traditional cost accounting course, that stressed analysis of simple problems). There is no particular order in which these cases need to be taught. They each give a glimpse into problems that can occur when designing and implementing cost systems in actual organizations. Recently, we have started the Harvard 2nd year MBA cost management systems course with La Grande Alliance. It is a fun case to teach, taking place in an organization quite different from the usual manufacturing setting of cost accounting. It always generates active student involvement and discussion, and the message is quite different from what students expect in the first case in the course.

Paramount Cycle was placed first in the book, to provide an example of a well-functioning standard cost system. The system described in the case has some interesting features that students may not have seen before (e.g., the scrapped labor and overhead accounts). But Paramount can be used as the metaphor for the entire course. The system accumulates all costs, allocates them to products, and closes variances each period to departments. It functions well for inventory valuation but the overhead applied via the standard product cost system bears no relation to the resources required to build the different bicycles and components. Also, the variance information is reported at the end of the month in aggregate accounts, providing little information for employee learning and improvement. In effect, Paramount is just the kind of cost system -- precise, objective, and adequate for closing the books each period -- that is critiqued in the first three readings at the end of the chapter.

Bridgeton Industries is another excellent case at the start of a course. It demonstrates how allocating overhead based on actual production volumes can lead a division into a death spiral, as high volume products are outsourced and overhead is applied to the remaining products. The cost of excess capacity is revisited in Chapter 3 and instructors have the option of postponing this case until reaching that topic. Bridgeton can also be used to highlight the difference between consumption of a resource and spending on the resource, a theme that will continue throughout the course, as an alternative to thinking narrowly about fixed and variable costs.

Institutional Furniture is a simple case that demonstrates fundamental flaws in cost system design. Students may enjoy seeing how messed up a cost system can get. The basic problem is that the cost system does not recognize all the outputs produced by the company, though failures in internal controls and record-keeping also contribute to the mess.

Stalcup Paper illustrates the dangers of relying upon the product costs produced by a standard cost accounting system to evaluate managerial performance. The product costs are distorted by arbitrary allocations that distort management decision-making and evaluation. It is a simple case designed to warn students about relying blindly on reported product costs.

Commonwealth Blood Transfusion Service is a joint cost case. The case occurs in a non-manufacturing environment but where costing issues are extremely important, at least politically, as the excerpts from the newspapers in the case indicate. This case is intended to show a problem - of allocating joint costs - that is beyond the capacity of any cost system to solve. Some joint costing issues may arise in cases later in the course so that it is useful to treat this problem explicitly, early in the course, so that students learn that this is basically an unsolvable problem. (Some instructors, however, with analytically well-trained students may want to use this opportunity to articulate some of the complex cost allocation procedures [marginal costing from the shadow prices of a nonlinear programming problem, or Shapley values from a game-theoretic solution] that have been proposed to solve the joint costing problem in regulated environments.)

La Grande Alliance presents the link between costing and pricing. The case is set in an exclusive restaurant and is useful in getting students to recognize that elaborate cost determinations are not always that useful. It also focuses the discussion on what the definition of the product is that the company is selling, a particularly important issue for service organizations that do not produce a specific, tangible product.

Ingersoll Milling Machine presents a much more advanced manufacturing environment than the other cases in this chapter. It illustrates a company in transition; major technology changes have been introduced in the factory, but the company's cost system has changed little in the past decade. Students can discuss whether the cost system for machining operations is really critical for the company, and the consequences from continuing with a direct labor based system in what will soon be a lights-out (completely automated) production environment. The case also illustrates the role for project accounting, when a product may take up to 24 months to build. A video tape is available for this case to show students how a flexible machining center operates; this would be worth showing since it is hard to describe in words or pictures the tremendous capabilities of these computer-run machines.

The readings in this chapter provide a good background for the cases. "Yesterday's Accounting Undermines Production," can be used with Paramount, Bridgeton, Institutional Furniture, or Ingersoll. "Accounting Lag," and, particularly "Flexible Manufacturing Systems," would work well with Ingersoll Milling. In fact, a separate class can be devoted to the Foster-Horngren article to discuss what kind of cost management system should be designed for highly automated and flexible environments. "Does Your Company Need a New Cost System?" can be used with Paramount, Bridgeton, or Institutional Furniture, encouraging students to identify the symptoms described in this reading with the situations faced by companies in these cases.

Paramount Cycle Introductory Comments

The Paramount Cycle case was written by Michael Sandretto, and his teaching note follows these introductory comments. The assignment questions he included in the case were:

1. Explain how cost of goods sold is determined.

2. Explain how the overhead spending and volume variances are calculated. How does Paramount develop a standard burden rate?

3. How is the material usage variance calculated?

4. Many companies include labor and overhead from previous departments in the material cost of a piece part of sub-assembly. Why might Paramount prefer to keep those costs separate?

5. Explain how the labor efficiency variance is calculated.

6. Assume that beginning inventory (July 1, 1979) was $6,235,000. Calculate the July 31, 1979 inventory.

7. Where were the major variances incurred during July?

8. How can Paramount's system be used to extimate the cost of a bicycle? Use series FB as an example. Is this a full or a direct cost system?

9. Paramount's standard cost system relies on a rough estimate of the value of in-process inventory. An alternative system would require that a monthly physical inventory be taken, while a second alternative would have the foremen record all material lost on a monthly scrap report. Compare the three methods.

Alternative Teaching Strategies

Paramount can be taught straight as an example of a well-functioning standard cost system. It is more complex than the examples students would have been exposed to in introductory managerial and cost accounting courses, and therefore provides both a good learning experience and a good introduction to cost systems design in complex organizations. Concepts such as keeping labor and overhead costs separate from materials costs as products flow through successive processing stages can be discussed, as well as the role for scrapped labor and overhead accounts. Paramount's well-functioning system contrasts well with the shortcomings of other cases in Chapter 1 such as Bridgeton, Institutional Furniture and Stalcup. Taught in this way, the limitations of the Paramount Cycle system will not start to show up until students reach cases like Metabo in Chapter 4 or Siemens and John Deere in Chapter 5, where the systems are much better designed either for operational control or product costing. When these more recent cases are taught, the instructors can ask students to contrast the new cost systems developed at Metabo, Siemens, and John Deere with Paramount's system to show how even well-designed traditional systems are not timely or accurate for managerial information.

An alternative approach would have students reading "Yesterday's Accounting Undermines Production,"; "Accounting Lag: The Obsolescence of Cost Accounting Systems,"; and/or "Does Your Company Need a New Cost System?" (at the end of the chapter) in conjunction with preparing Paramount Cycle. One could reduce the number of questions asked directly about the calculations in the case (though issues of retaining separate labor and overhead cost accounts as products flow through successive production stages may still be worth discussing) and insert additional questions such as:

1. Are the criticisms made in the assigned readings of conventional cost systems justified for Paramount Cycle?

2. What are the strengths of Paramount Cycle's cost accounting system? What functions does it do well?

3. What are the weaknesses of Paramount Cycle's system? What important functions, if any, are missing from Paramount's system?

The discussion of these questions need not be too extensive or specific since the issues will be revisited in many subsequent cases in Chapters 4-7. Among the highlights to raise:

- Paramount's system provides a systematic and comprehensive method for assigning the costs of materials, labor, and overhead to products. The calculations of cost of goods sold and inventory values would likely meet all reasonable standards for consistency, auditability, and objectivity.

- The system provides a full range of monthly variances on materials price and usage, labor rates and usage, and overhead spending and volume effects. These monthly measures would provide senior management with broad indication as to where purchasing and manufacturing problems might be arising.

- The monthly reports, however, come too late for any corrective action and likely are redundant to the operating information that could be collected by local department managers. Also, the monthly time period is too long and the variety of products manufactured during that period are too broad for the causes of the variances to be attributed unambiguously to their sources. The long time lag between action and feedback information provides little to no chance for operators and managers to learn how to improve manufacturing processes. The standards assume a stable environment, and learning and improvement effects are suppressed.

- No guidance is provided on how departmental variances can be assigned to the variety of products that flow through the department during each monthly period. Materials, labor and overhead variances are measured at the departmental level, not at the job or product level (Paramount is an excellent example of a process costing system for a discrete manufacturing environment). Therefore any allocation of departmental variances to products must be done arbitrarily with no causal relation between different products and the non-standard use of materials, labor, and overhead resources. Thus, Paramount provides a classic example of the problems with traditional cost accounting systems that the activity-based cost systems in Chapters 5-7 were developed to remedy.

Following this alternative teaching strategy enables an early session in the course to connect with the students' training in traditional costing systems (albeit in a more complex setting than they may have been exposed to in the examples used in introductory courses and books). But this exposure also links to the book's (and, we hope, the course's) philosophy to design cost management systems, not to satisfy financial and cost accounting objectives, but to enhance management decisions, control, and learning. With this latter philosophy, it is not enough that the costing system is "correct;" that all numbers are captured and assigned appropriately to the company's chart of accounts. The system must demonstrate that it actively helps operating managers and employees do their jobs better.

Paramount Cycle Company
Teaching Note

Paramount Cycle Company is designed to illustrate a comprehensive cost accounting system. The. case traces variances from the departmental level through the income statement. The system is based upon a cost system used by several firms.

The case was written with four objectives in mind:

1. Show the details of a complete standard cost system.

2. Demonstrate how a system can be designed to somewhat existing manufacturing system.

3. Discuss how such a cost/budgeting system can be used to control a manufacturing operation. This discussion can include numerous management control issues, such as appropriateness of this type of control, desired level of control, and who should receive reports generated by the system.

4. Discuss how standard costs and variances can be used to obtain product costs for product profitability analysis.

For first year MBA students the first objective can be taught in an 80 minute class while the last three objectives can be covered in a second 80 minute class or less. The first day can be highly structured and somewhat of a walk-through, since the system is described in the case. The second day should be more loosely organized since there are numerous points which can be discussed. The case can be used for one 80 minute session with second year MBA students. This note is divided into a general discussion of teaching strategy (A) and answers to questions in the case (B).

Professor Michael Sandretto prepared this teaching note as an aid to instructors in the classroom use of the case, Paramount Cycle Company, No. 180-069.

A. Teaching Strategy

1. Discussion of Overall System   I begin by asking someone to explain how COGS is determined (question 1), and then move to schedule 1. I then have students explain each of the schedules, in order, without discussing how variances might occur (questions 2, 3, 5, and possibly 4).

There are two points which appear in this case which are seldom seen in textbooks or cases. First is the fact that labor and overhead are kept separate from material. Thus, whenever a seat is scrapped there is material scrapped (Schedule 4, part A) and also scrapped labor and overhead (Schedule 4, part B).

A second point is that material usage and labor efficiency variances are calculated by using estimated values for inventory in process. For labor, the estimated value is one-half the standard value of orders in process since orders are, on average, one-half completed.

Since estimated inventories are used for calculating variances, an important question is: how accurate are these variances? The answer is that they are not very accurate for a period of one month, but for a 4-6 month period the variances are reasonable. The auditors (three different companies audited by three different big accounting firms) were satisfied that the inventory numbers for in-process inventory were reasonable. They did not take a physical inventory of in-process inventory; the numbers shown on schedule 3 (or 4) were used for audited financial statements.

The above discussion covers questions 1, 2, 3, and 5, which concern describing the system. Each is covered in the case. Questions 4, 6, and 9 may also arise during a general description of the system.

2. Parallel to Manufacturing System   I ask how the department variances might be used and if it seems that they are useful for controlling operations. I use the following diagram and ask what we can learn about operations in each area:

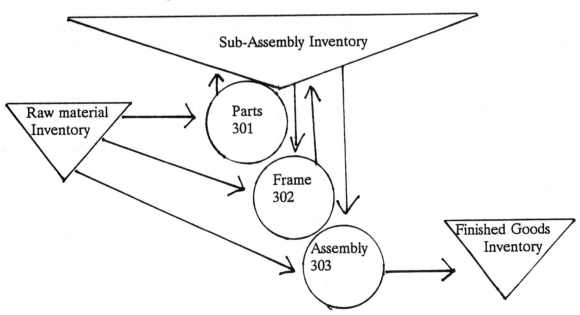

This should quickly lead into the third objective:

3. Control of Operations   Students should consider the various levels of detail and ask who might be interested in each level of detail. The following levels of detail are possible and it is likely that top management would be interested in the first few levels of detail while operating management would be more concerned with the last few levels of detail.

1.   COGS.
2.   Material, labor and overhead.
3.   Standard (M,L & OH) and individual variances (Schedule 9).
4.   Variances by department (Schedule I & 4).
5.   Detailed variances (Schedule 1 and support data from Schedule 4).

I ask how reports should be made if this were a subsidiary or division of a conglomerate.

One point which students may raise is that manufacturing variances by department are of little value since manufacturing knows about variances when they happen, while accounting only knows at the end of the month. Although this may be true in some firms, it is not true in most. In attempting to find significant variances, it is frequently necessary to look at several levels of detail (e.g., total labor efficiency variance, variance by department, then variance by operator) and sometimes over a period of one or more months. Those firms that look only at manufacturing reports tend to get buried in detail since there may be no overall summary which shows how total costs or total variances change overtime.

In discussing which variances are important, I expect students to concentrate on the larger variances. Some of those are discussed in the answer to question 7, Part B.

4. Product Costs   Numerous methods could be used to allocate variances to individual series. See question 8, Part B.

Additional Comments

I tell students that the actual system was actually more complex than in the case. At the middle size of the three firms, among the additional complexities were the following:

1.   20 departments, not 8.

2.   Up to 5 production departments for one product, plus several parts departments.

3.   A variance for receiving either more or fewer parts than ordered and charged for (a very common occurrence).

4.   A variance to record material lost in testing.

5.   A variance to record material lost when sent to outside vendors for processing (e.g. plating).

6.   A variance to record parts salvaged from scrapped subassemblies.

I also tell them that one such system was operated by a 19-year-old high school graduate with 1 college course (basic financial accounting) and by a 24-year-old high school graduate with perhaps 6-8 college courses (4 in accounting). This could raise the issue of how much to spend on a system and who you get to run such a system.

B. Answers to Questions

Question 1   Described in the case (page 4 and Schedule 8).

Question 2   Spending and volume variances are calculated in Schedules 5 and 6.

Question 3   Described in the case (pages 4-5 and Schedules 2-4):

Beginning inventory (estimated as standard cost of units in process)
+ <u>Material issued at standard cost.</u>

= Goods available before variances.
- <u>Goods to stock at standard.</u>

= Estimated ending inventory & material lost.
- <u>Estimated ending inventory.</u>

= Material scrap variance.

Note that whenever material is scrapped, there will normally be labor and overhead scrapped (Schedule 4, Part B). See question 9 for further discussion.

Question 4   Two reasons for preferring material cost only are that it is easier computationally and that people in manufacturing prefer to keep material, labor and overhead costs separate. Otherwise, they treat the material cost as a number dreamed up by accountants.

There are two analytical reasons why Paramount may prefer to keep the three costs separate. First, since this is a full cost system, if costs are kept separate, it is relatively easy to convert the costs to direct cost. All that is required is that material (standard & variances) and labor (standard & variances) are added, then variable overhead (30% of direct labor, for example) can be added to material and labor to obtain direct cost.

A second reason for preferring separate cost categories is that the firm can keep track of value added to a product (labor & overhead). This may be useful in pricing decisions.

Question 5   Described in the case (page 6 and Schedules 2-4):

Beginning inventory (estimated at 50% of standard labor for work in process).
+ <u>Labor paid at standard rates.</u>

= Goods available before variances.

- <u>Goods to stock at standard.</u>

= Estimated ending inventory and variances.
- <u>Estimated ending inventory.</u>

= Labor efficiency variance.

Note that when labor is lost through inefficiency, overhead is also lost (Schedule 4, Part d).

This is clearly a rough estimate and is discussed further in question 9.

Question 6   This is straightforward and can be calculated from schedule 9.

Beginning inventory at standard	$6,235,000.00
+ Purchases	2,120,701.48
- Variances	96,185.00
Goods available for sale at STD.	$8,259,516.48
- Cost of goods sold at STD.	1,896,068.67
Ending inventory at STD.	$6,363,447.81

OR

Beginning inventory at standard	$6,235,000.00
+ Purchases at STD.	2,112,077.48
- Manufacturing variances	87,561.00
Goods available for sale at STD.	$8,259,516.48

Question 7   Several variances were inserted to initiate discussion:

Schedule 1. Purchase price variance may be high in product group 300 because light weight metals may have increased in price or because of changes in exchange rates. Derailleurs, for example, would be purchased in either Japan, Italy or France.

Schedule 4. Material usage variance is high in the precision parts department (301) and the precision frame department (302). Standards may be incorrect or there may be a problem in manufacturing.

Scrapped labor is high in a few departments (103, 302, and 303). That is possible since some parts have a high material content while others have a high labor content. Labor efficiency variance is also high in departments 301 and 302. This may be reasonable since time is probably spent on items which are scrapped.

Schedule 5   The overtime variance is high. This can be expected since the plant is operating above planned capacity (favorable volume variance). A point which can be raised is how valid is the budget for overtime. Whenever the plant operates at greater capacity than planned, there will probably be an unfavorable overtime variance. A favorable overtime variance will occur whenever the plant operates below planned capacity.

Question 8   There are numerous possibilities for calculating cost for a particular series. Any such system will require that variances be allocated on some basis, usually sales or production. The firm allocated variances as the basis of average production over a 4-6 month period and used total variances for that same period.

Separate calculations were made for material and for labor:

	Material			Labor	
	Group 300		FB	Group 300	FB
% of Production	$\frac{13,255}{122,079}$ =		10.9%	$\frac{1,195}{10,837}$ =	11.0%
Purchase Price Variance		$19,020	1,902		
Usage Variance	301	9,547	1,041		
	302	16,174	1,763	287 Hrs.	32
	303	3,154	344	393 Hrs.	43
Labor Eff. Var.	301			562	62
	302			1,263	139
	303			-12	-1
Total			$5,050	275 Hrs.	
+ Units Produced			180	180	
Variance Per Unit			$28.06	1.52 Hrs.	
Standard Cost			73.64	9.31	
Total			$101.70	10.83 Hrs.	

Since the labor rate variance is insignificant, it can be ignored, or else an average wage rate can be calculated for departments 301, 302 and 303. Ignoring that variance, costs are:

Material		$101.70
Labor	10.83 Hrs. x $6.50	70.38

Overhead can then be added in increments:

Variable Overhead ($1.0709/labor, per Schedule 5)	75.37
Total Direct Cost	236.88
+ Nonvariable Overhead (1.50 - 1.0707)	30.20
	$277.65

This compares to a standard cost of:

Material		$73.64
Labor	9.31 x $6.50	60.52
Overhead	$1.50	90.77
		$224.93

Question 9   A monthly inventory of work in process inventory is clearly the most accurate method. That, however, is extremely expensive both in terms of accounting time· and far more importantly, lost manufacturing time. Having foremen turn in scrap reports is far easier and is frequently used in business. On the surface, this seems more accurate than the method used by Paramount. However, there may be a tendency among some foremen to report less scrap than a department actually incurred. · The method used by Paramount is also subject to some manipulation since a line's inventory can be built up or reduced by requisitioning more or fewer additional parts than are required.

Although Paramount's system is relatively inaccurate over a short period of time, it seems reasonable for longer periods. It is relatively inexpensive and is not subject to major manipulation.

Bridgeton Industries

Teaching Note

The Bridgeton Industries case was written as an introductory case for either an introductory or an advanced management accounting course. It was designed to be taught in a sequence that includes Seligram, Inc. Electronic Testing Operations and Mayers Tap, Inc. The case can also be used as the introduction for a module on capacity costing that includes Micro Devices Division, Schulze Waxed Container, and Hewlett Packard: Queensferry Telecommunications Division.

The case introduces students to three major issues:

1) the primary calculations that cost systems use to determine burden rates.

2) the concept of the death spiral: when production volume decreases, the burden rate increases, and hence the reported product costs increase.

3) the concept of fixed and variable costs.

4) the difference between consumption and spending cost models

This teaching note outlines an 80-minute teaching plan.

Suggested Assignments:

1. The overhead allocation rate used in the 1987 model year strategy study at the ACF was 435% of direct labor dollar cost. Calculate the overhead allocation rate using the 1987 model year budget. Why do you get different numbers?

This teaching note was written by Professor Robin Cooper as an aid to instructors using Bridgeton Industries (190-085).

13

2. Calculate the overhead allocation rate for each of the model years, 1988 through 1990. Are the changes since 1987 in overhead allocation rates significant? Why have these changes occurred?

3. Consider two products in the same product line:

	Product 1	Product 2
Expected Selling Price	$62	$54
Standard Material Cost	16	27
Standard Labor Cost	6	3

Calculate the expected gross margins as a percentage of selling price on each product based on the 1988 and 1990 model year budgets assuming selling price and material and labor cost do not change from standard.

4. Are the product costs reported by the cost system appropriate for use in the strategic analysis?

5. Assume that the selling prices, volumes, and material costs for the 1991 model year will not change for fuel tanks and doors produced by the ACF of Bridgeton Industries. Assume also that if manifolds are produced, their selling prices, volume, and material costs will not change either.

   a. Prepare an estimated model year budget for the ACF in 1991,

      (1) if no additional products are dropped.

      (2) if the manifold product line is dropped.

      Explain any additional assumptions you make in preparing your estimated model year budgets.

   b. What will be the overhead allocation rate under the two scenarios?

6. Would you outsource manifolds from the ACF in 1991? Why, or why not? What more information would you want before reaching a final decision?

Class Discussion

Q1. What is the competitive environment for Bridgeton?

The discussion should focus on the fact that Bridgeton is not competitive in many of its products. The discussion of their position in the industry should include:

   a) The fact that the oil crisis initiated major changes in the automotive industry.

b) Bridgeton Industries attempted to adjust to the oil crisis by building two diesel engine plants.

c) After oil prices decreased, the market for diesel cars eroded, forcing the closure of the engine plant.

d) Although cost cutting was attempted, the facility appeared to have entered a destructive cycle of product outsourcing.

Q2. How has Bridgeton reacted to its competitive environment?

Bridgeton has carried out a serious campaign for cost reduction, and outsourced products identified as noncompetitive; it has reduced overhead and become more competitive. Morale is good; there is an abundance of team spirit. Everyone thinks they have their act together; however, something is wrong because the parent company continues to outsource products.

Q3. What did the outside strategic analysis recommend?

The analysis recommended that all products be classified in terms of competitive position and outsource the non-competitive ones. The factors considered when classifying a product included quality, customer service, and technical capability. However, as the system became operationalized, reported product cost became the dominant factor. Evidence for this assertion is provided by the way the classification procedure is described in the case.

- Class I = World-class, i.e. having costs equal to or lower than competitors.
- Class II = Potential World-class, i.e., having costs 5-15% higher than competitors.
- Class III = No hope of becoming World-class, i.e. having costs more than 15% higher than competitors.

Note the focus on cost in the descriptions. Thus, one important outcome of the strategic analysis was to make cost information much more important at Bridgeton.

Q4. What is the structure of Bridgeton's cost system?

The cost system consists of a single cost center containing all of the overhead costs of the facility. These costs are allocated to the products using direct labor dollars.

If Seligram was taught before Bridgeton, then a comparison of the Bridgeton system to the initial Seligram system can be drawn. If Seligram is taught after Bridgeton, then the reverse comparison is useful.

Q5. Calculate the budgeted allocation rate for the 1987 model year.

The answer of 437% ($107,954/$24,682) differs from the official rate of 435% by 2%. This difference is due to roundings. Management decided that the "extra" accuracy from using 437% instead of the easier 435% is either spurious (the budgets are not that accurate) or irrelevant (no decision will change because of the simplification).

Q6. Calculate a burden rate for each of the model years - 1988 through 1990.

	1988	1989	1990
Total Overhead	$109,890	$78,157	$79,393
Total DL $	$ 25,294	$13,537	$14,102
Calculated Burden Rate	434%	577%	563%
Official Burden Rate	435%	575%	565%

There is a 3% difference in the calculated rates for the first two years 1987 and 1988. Notice, however, the rounding process obfuscated this change. Thus, if the 3% reduction represents real savings due to cost reduction, then the effect of rounding is harmful. However, if the 3% is spurious, then rounding is beneficial since it signals that no significant cost reduction has been achieved.

A more significant cost reduction pattern is seen in the model years 1989 and 1990. Here the reduction of 14 percentage points in the burden rate is not masked by rounding, though the reported improvement is reduced to 10 percentage points. Some of this reduction and potentially all of the reduction observed in 1987 to 1988 could be caused by the increase in sales volumes across the two sets of two years. The firm (ignoring outsourcing) is growing at about 5% per annum, and typically, growth will result in slightly lower burden rates as the fixed costs (see later) are spread over a larger direct labor dollar base. The 14% reduction observed across 1989 and 1990 is probably too large to be explained by a 5% sales increase. The more likely explanations include the cost reduction programs and a lag in the ability to avoid costs related to the outsourcing decision.

A very different pattern in burden rate change emerges when the years 1988 and 1989 are compared. The burden rate jumps from 434% to 577%. Clearly, the majority of this jump cannot be explained by anything but the decision to outsource the oil pans and muffler-exhaust systems at the end of 1988. Discussion on the cause of this increase in burden rate should be postponed to later in the class when the concepts of fixed and variable and avoidable and unavoidable costs have been introduced.

Q7. What are the expected gross margins as a percentage of selling price of products 1 and 2 based on the 1988 and 1990 model year budgets?

The purpose of this question is to increase the students' comfort with calculating product costs. The relative simplicity of the cost system at Bridgeton Industries allows the central equation of product costing to be easily understood. Namely:

$$\text{Product Cost} = \begin{array}{c}\text{Direct}\\\text{Material}\end{array} + \begin{array}{c}\text{Direct}\\\text{Labor}\end{array} + \left[\begin{array}{c}\text{Burden}\\\text{Rate}\end{array} \times \begin{array}{c}\text{\# of}\\\text{Allocation units}\end{array}\right]$$

It might be beneficial at this point to explain that as the cost system design becomes more complex, the equation remains structurally unchanged but simply adds terms. That is:

$$\text{Product Cost} = \begin{array}{c}\Sigma\ \text{Direct}\\\text{Material}\end{array} + \begin{array}{c}\Sigma\ \text{Direct}\\\text{Labor}\end{array} + \Sigma\left[\begin{array}{c}\text{Burden}\\\text{Rates}\end{array} \times \begin{array}{c}\text{\# of}\\\text{Allocation units}\end{array}\right]$$

Once the central equation of product costing is understood, then the way products are costed in even the most complex systems can be understood, in principle. For the two products in suggested assignment 3, the calculations are:

1988

	Product 1	Product 2
Expected Selling Price	$62.00	$54.00
Standard Material Cost	$16.00	$27.00
Standard Labor Cost	6.00	3.00
Standard Overhead Cost	26.10	13.05
Total Cost Gross Profit	48.10 13.90	43.05 10.95
Gross Margin %	22%	20%

1989

	Product 1	Product 2
Expected Selling Price	$62.00	$54.00
Standard Material Cost	$16.00	$27.00
Standard Labor Cost	6.00	3.00
Standard Overhead Cost	33.90	16.95
Total Cost Gross Profit	$55.90 7.10	$46.95 7.05
Gross Margin %	10%	13%

Students should be asked to explain the shift in relative gross margin percentage. Product 1 which originally was the more profitable now has a lower reported gross margin percentage. The reason, of course, lies in the relative intensity with which the two products consume direct labor. Product one consumes twice as many direct labor dollars as product two; therefore, it is allocated twice as much overhead. As the direct labor burden rate increases, product one becomes relatively less attractive compared to product two. This discussion should introduce quite naturally the concepts of fixed and variable costs. The next part of the classroom discussion should be dedicated to understanding what these terms mean.

Q8. What are fixed costs?

The traditional definition of fixed costs should be extracted from the students. They should then be asked for examples of costs that would be fixed under the definition they have suggested. Typical examples include: depreciation taxes, insurance, some personnel costs, and the plant manager's salary.

Students should then be directed to Case Exhibit 2 and asked which of the overhead accounts will be primarily fixed. They should be asked what test they would use to identify fixed costs. These might include:

1) Interviewing the managers responsible for the costs to determine how they believe the costs behave

2) Regression analysis of the results over a number of years

3) Common sense

For Bridgeton Industries, Exhibit 2 can be used to explore what costs do not appear to change with normal fluctuations in the level of production. In the context of Bridgeton Industries, it is important to decide if we mean fixed in the normal course of business or in the outsourcing. Most students should vote for the normal course of business. Using Case Exhibit 2 and 3, the behavior of the various overhead cost items can be explored by comparing the individual line items in 1987 with 1988 and 1989 with 1990. Predominantly fixed costs are those that do not change across the two sets of paired years. As can be seen from Teaching Note Exhibit 1, the following accounts appear to be predominantly fixed: 1000, 1500, 4000, 5000, 8000, 9000, and 14000.

Q9. If a cost is not fixed, what is it?

The traditional definition of variable costs should be identified. It is helpful to make students sensitive to the need to specify a timeframe for variable costs, just as is typically the case for fixed costs. A series of questions such as: Does direct labor fit the definition? If you drop production by 10% in one month, will 10% of the direct labor go away? This will help sensitize students to the complexity of variable costs. Students should be asked: do we need to add a time frame to our definition of variable cost? Students should identify one year as the timeframe relevant to the Bridgeton Industries case reflecting the firm's budgeting cycle.

The one-year timeframe that is imbedded in the definition of fixed and variable costs is a natural outcome of the budgeting cycle in most firms. Students should be made to understand that fixed and variable are terms that relate to the budgeting cycle and not product costing. This difference will be explored in more depth later in the class and is a useful way to set the stage for activity-based costing, if this subject is to be addressed later in the course.

Students should again be directed to Case Exhibit 2 and asked which costs are variable. These will be the costs that vary in direct relation with the number of direct labor dollars consumed. These costs can be identified by computing the direct labor burden rates for each overhead account. The predominantly variable costs will be those with approximately the same burden rate in all four years. As can be seen from Teaching Note Exhibit 2, the following accounts appear to be predominantly variable: 2000, 3000, and 12000.

Q10. If a cost is neither fixed nor variable, what is it?

Students will now introduce the concept of semi-fixed or semi-variable costs. Students should be asked why costs behave in this way. There are two possible explanations:

1) It contains some costs that vary with the usage of the machines and some that vary with the passage of time. The first set of costs are eventually variable and the other set is fixed.

2) The costs are lumpy. That is, they have to be acquired in discrete quantities that are large enough to be visible when modeling cost behavior. For example, you cannot buy 10% of an inspector. You have to buy a full inspector who is capable of inspecting about 5000 parts a week. One can argue that direct labor is lumpy--but the number of direct laborers is usually so great that the lumpiness averages out over the one-year horizon.

Q11. Can you describe graphically the cost behavior we associate with fixed, variable, and semi-variable costs?

A student should be asked to "draw" the classical graphs of fixed, variable, and semi-fixed costs (see Teaching Note Figure 1).

Q12. What do we mean by the term "cost" when we draw these graphs?

This question invariably causes the students confusion. They typically have never thought about what they mean by the term "cost" in this context. The level of frustration in the class usually builds to quite high levels before a student, or the instructor, suggests that the graphs describe the **cash flows** anticipated at different production volumes.

Typically, one or more students, particularly those with accounting background, object to the term cash flow. They point out that inventories and depreciation decouple "cost" from cash flow. They are absolutely right and care has to be taken to clarify why this decoupling can be ignored for the purposes of this discussion. For inventories, it is fairly simple to get students to understand that inventories just introduce a delay between spending and consumption and that assuming that the inventory is replaced, spending will rapidly follow consumption. For depreciation, the spending occurs in a large "lump" when the asset is acquired. Depreciation is an attempt to allocate costs (spending) from one time period to another so as to match to consumption. Depreciation is not an attempt to allocate costs to products. Therefore, it can be ignored for the purposes of this discussion.

To capture the above concepts, the instructor should introduce the term resource spending to capture the cash flow orientation behind the graphs of cost behavior. Spending is preferable to cash flow because of inventories and other decoupling mechanisms. Variable costs can now be defined as costs whose level of spending is dependent upon the volume of production, and fixed costs as costs whose level of spending is independent of production volume (with the normal timeframe caveats). Semi-fixed costs are those costs where changes in the level of production result in measurable, discontinuous shifts in the level of spending.

Q13. Is a spending orientation appropriate for budgeting, or for product costing?

Students should identify budgeting as an attempt to estimate future spending levels. The terms fixed and variable costs are appropriate terms to use for budgeting, and operations management control but not for product costing. For example, a flexed budget estimates expected spending levels at different production levels. It is useful to point out the relationship between the budget and the cost system. The budget is used to define the spending levels at the anticipated volume for the period. The cost system uses this spending level to determine the burden rates for the period. Thus, the budget is the starting point from which the cost system's burden rates are derived.

A simple example can be used to illustrate why a consumption model is appropriate for product costing purposes. This example revolves around a semi-fixed cost. Imagine a firm that produces 1,000 units of products a year. It requires an ongoing expenditure of $5,000 per year to maintain this level of production. If the volume of production is to increase the level of expenditure will increase to $10,000 per year. This example can be illustrated by drawing a large diagram of a semi-variable cost on the board (see Teaching Note Exhibit 2 but exclude the dotted line from the origin to the second step point).

Students should be asked to calculate the cost of a unit of product if the plant is producing 1,000 units per year. The answer is $5.00. If the firm achieves a 20% margin the selling price would be $6.00. The instructor can involve students by selling one of them a "piece of chalk" for $6.00. The instructor should then ask students to calculate the cost of each unit of product if the plant is producing at a volume one unit above the step point and has increased spending accordingly. This reported cost is $10.00 (rounded), twice the previous reported cost. If the firm is to maintain its desired 20% margin, the selling price must increase to $12.00. The instructor should return to the student who bought the chalk at $6.00 and try to sell him or her another piece of chalk at $12.00. The student will reject the new price and "go elsewhere".

The instructor can then turn to another student and tell him or her that, "You purchased the extra piece of chalk. This is all your fault, you should pay for the extra $5,000." The student should reject this perspective and be willing to pay only $6.00, the market price of chalk. The instructor can now write the profit and loss statements for the product under the two scenarios. The product has gone from a 20% margin to a heavy loss position ($6.00 -$10.00). Under the Bridgeton strategic analysis, a class I product has just become a class III one. The product should be outsourced.

By this time every student should be aware that all is not well. If we use cost plus pricing, we have very disgruntled customers, if any. If we use market pricing, the product is a loser and should be outsourced. If we try and use a marginal cost approach, the incremental customer never appears. We need a different approach to product costing.

Q14. How can we overcome this problem?

A student should suggest that the cost of the product should not change with the acquisition of the new capacity. The instructor should ask students how they can achieve that objective. Eventually, a student will suggest that we treat the extra cost as excess capacity. The dotted line that connects the origin to the second step point in Teaching Note Figure 2 can now be drawn in. The instructor should inform students that to achieve their objective of having reported costs remain the same, they must cost products according to this dotted line. Students should be asked what this line represents. They will eventually, often painfully, come to understand that this is the resource consumption line. It captures how much of the resources that have been acquired are actually consumed.

Q15. If we use a consumption definition of costs to report product costs can you use those costs to make decisions?

The answer is that you cannot. Cost systems do not report relevant costs. Instead, they report costs that focus managerial attention. To make decisions, you have to shift from a consumption to a spending perspective. The analogy of a geological map can be used to explain the difference between spending and consumption. The instructor can ask a student how he or she would use a geological map to find oil. It is useful to diagram the process that emerges on the board: study map, identify a likely area, undertake a seismic survey, drill for oil, and then discover if oil is present. The instructor should then describe the same process using product costs: Study reported costs and profitability, find a likely product or group of products to analyze, perform special study, reduce consumption of resources (for example, drop products), and then manage spending to match consumption. It is only when spending is managed that profits increase.

Student attention should now be focused on the special study. The instructor should ask the students what kind of model, spending versus consumption, is appropriate for the special study. The answer is necessarily spending. The objective of the special study is to identify the cash flow or spending consequences of an action identified by the consumption model as potentially profitable, say for example to drop 50 low volume products. If the special study identifies that the reduction in spending associated with the decision will be beneficial to the firm, then the next step is to drop the products. Dropping the products will reduce consumption, but it will not automatically reduce spending. To reduce spending, management has to change the level of acquisition of resources. For example, they have to decrease the number of people employed.

To highlight another advantage of adopting a consumption versus spending approach for product costing purposes, the instructor can allow the simple example to become more complicated. A student should be asked whether he or she would automatically buy the extra capacity for the extra order of chalk if they received an order for one additional piece. The answer should be no. The student should then be asked to identify when they would acquire the extra capacity. Typically, the student will take several factors into account, expected future demand, other methods to increase capacity, the ability to buy on the outside, etc. The decision to add capacity is a complex one. A different student can be asked if they can predict when the first student will choose to add capacity. Again, the answer should be no. The instructor by asking several students can build consensus that it is virtually impossible to predict a priori when the additional capacity will be added because there are too many factors to consider.

Students should be asked how they would manufacture the extra volume without first acquiring the extra capacity. There are at least two options, 1) introduce overtime and 2) stop the workforce from performing some discretionary tasks such as preventative maintenance. These techniques work well in the short run, but after a few months the work force will be overworked or the reason for performing the discretionary task will become apparent, for example, when the lack of preventative maintenance leads to an increase in the number of breakdowns. Students should realize that the temporary solutions only postpone the inevitable acquisition of the extra capacity. The instructor can now make a critical observation, the causal event, **the change in the level of consumption caused by the increased volume occurred sometime in the past but the associated change in the level of spending is only just occurring**. This phenomenon can be demonstrated by redrawing the spending curve for the semi-fixed cost in the simple example. The relationship between spending and production volume is it not a single line but a "probability blur" that covers a range of about 100 units (see Teaching Note Figure 3). The discussion to date should have shown the students that a cost system cannot handle such a blur. Cost systems are necessarily deterministic in nature. Adopting a consumption orientation allows cost systems to avoid the "blurs".

Q16. Why don't we simply ignore fixed costs and just use variable costs?

The discussion that is caused by this question is typically unfocused and somewhat confusing. To help the students understand the problem, the simple example can be modified. The firm now produces two products, white and yellow chalk. The two products consume exactly the same amount of material and labor but the yellow product consumes twice the amount of semi-fixed resources as the white one. The market price of the two products is the same. The instructor can pose the following question to students "Which is the most attractive product?" The obvious answer is the white one. Having obtained consensus, students can be asked to use a contribution approach to indicate which of the products is the most attractive. They discover rather rapidly that using a contribution approach (that only considers variable costs) indicates that both products are equally attractive. The contribution approach fails to reflect the consumption of the semi-fixed resource. To differentiate between the two products, the cost system has to include the semi-fixed costs. To do this intelligently, as already demonstrated, it must adopt a consumption approach.

Q17. What are avoidable costs?

These are the costs that can be avoided by outsourcing products. They are different from fixed costs as described above. Case Exhibit 2 gives some insights into which costs are avoidable by comparing the direct labor burden rates for each overhead account in 1988 to 1989. Since the ratio of direct labor dollars in 1988 to 1989 is 1.87, a totally unavoidable cost will have a 1989/1988 burden rate ratio of 1.87, while a totally avoidable cost will have a ratio of 1.00. Teaching Note Exhibit 3 shows the direct labor burden rates for 1989/1988. As can be seen, account numbers 2000, 3000, and 12000 are predominantly avoidable. In contrast, accounts 1500,

4000, 5000, 9000, and 999 are predominantly unavoidable. The remaining accounts are only partially avoidable.

The difference between the concepts of fixed, variable and avoidable costs can now be displayed for Bridgeton Industries.

Account Number	Cost Behavior Normal Conditions	Cost Behavior Outsourcing
1000	F	S
1500	F	U
2000	V	A
3000	V	A
4000	F	U
5000	F	U
8000	F	S
9000	F	U
11000	S	S
12000	V	A
14000	F	S

Legend:	F = Fixed	U = Unavoidable
	V = Variable	A = Avoidable
	S = Semi-variable	S = Semi-avoidable

Note in Bridgeton, all variable costs are avoidable, all semi variable and some fixed are semi avoidable, and some fixed are unavoidable. The two dichotomies fixed/variable and unavoidable/avoidable are not synonymous.

Q18. Are the costs reported by the cost system appropriate for the strategic analysis?

The analysis of cost behavior shows clearly that the costs reported by the existing cost system are not appropriate for use in the strategic analysis. First, they do not differentiate between unavoidable and avoidable costs, and second, it is not clear at the individual product level that they are sufficiently accurate to predict how outsourcing individual products will effect the cost structure of the firm.

Q19. Why did the burden rate increase in 1989?

The inability of the firm to avoid all of the costs that the cost system allocated to each individual product, causes the reported cost of a product to be higher than its avoidable costs. Therefore, as products are outsourced the unavoidable costs are left behind and subsequently allocated to the remaining products. When this condition exists, firms risk entering the death spiral because:

1) The burden rate immediately goes up.

2) The reported costs of the remaining products increase. Therefore, the lowest profitable product stands a risk of being dropped down into Class III.

3) If only reported costs are considered, additional products will appear unprofitable and become candidates for outsourcing.

4) As these additional products are outsourced, the burden rate increases and continues outsourcing until nothing (except unavoidable costs) is left.

Q20. How should we treat the unavoidable costs for the outsourced product?

The unavoidable costs associated with the outsourced products should not be included in the costs allocated to the remaining products. They should be treated as excess capacity costs and written off. The discussion of how to treat excess capacity costs can either be allowed to continue or can be discouraged, if other cases from the capacity costing module are being taught later in the course.

Q21. Prepare an estimated model year budget for the 1991 model year assuming no additional products are dropped.

There are so many different assumptions that can be made for this assignment that it is not clear that providing a solution in the teaching note will be beneficial. Appendix 1 contains several student solutions to this assignment. These solutions were picked to display the range of creativity that can be applied to the assignment.

The simplest approach is to assume that the cost behavior observed in the two-year period 1989 and 1990 will be maintained, and then predict accordingly using a simple linear assumption, i.e., if sales went up by x% from 1989 to 1990 they will increase by a similar amount in 1991. A slightly more complex analysis might run regressions on sales, direct material and direct labor over the four-year period to get a better estimate of the underlying sales growth for the remaining product. Whether a two-year or four-year perspective is better depends upon whether the effort expended on selling the remaining products remained the same across the four-year period. Similar concerns apply to the direct material and direct labor estimates, as it is likely that the effort to become more efficient on the remaining products has intensified.

For overhead, the simplicity of the cost systems limits the sophistication of the analysis undertaken. Any attempt to predict using all four years is virtually going to lead to meaningless estimates. The best one can do is to look at the cost behavior observed across the years and predict accordingly.

One important lesson that students should learn from trying to estimate the 1991 model budget year is how poorly the existing cost system helps in this process. By combining all overhead into a single cost pool, Bridgeton Industries management loses the ability to explore cost behavior at the product and product line levels without first performing a special study. The strategic analysis was such a study, but over time the "official" product costs came to dominate.

Student and managers should not underestimate the importance of the product costs reported by the firm's cost system.

Q22. Prepare an estimated model year budget for the 1991 model year assuming that the manifold product line is dropped.

This assignment is even more difficult than the previous one and requires that the student make assumptions about the avoidability of costs. The insights into avoidability gained by analyzing the 1988 and 1989 budgets should provide some help but it is not clear that the same cost behavior, either by degree or by account type, will be maintained. Appendix 1 contains several student solutions to this assignment. These solutions were picked to display the range of creativity that can be applied to this assignment.

Q23. Would you outsource manifolds in 1991?

This question requires the students to think about all the factors that should be considered in an outsourcing decision. These include:

1. Cost avoidability
2. Estimates of future demands for products
3. The importance of maintaining an independent manufacturing capability.
4. The impact on labor relations, if outsourcing will lead to lay-offs.
5. The reliability of external vendors.
6. Alternate uses of the capacity.

Appendix 1 contains several student solutions to the assignment.

Teaching Note Exhibit 1

Overhead By Individual Account 1987-1990

Overhead By Account #	1987	1988	1989	1990	1987 1988	1989 1990
1000	7,713	7,806	5,572	5,679	0.99	0.98
1500	6,743	6,824	5,883	5,928	0.99	0.99
2000	3,642	3,794	2,031	2,115	0.96	0.96
3000	2,428	2,529	1,354	1,410	0.96	0.96
4000	8,817	8,888	7,360	7,433	0.99	0.99
5000	24,181	24,460	20,063	20,274	0.99	0.99
8000	5,946	5,946	3,744	3,744	1.00	1.00
9000	6,708	6,771	5,948	5,987	0.99	0.99
11000	5,089	5,011	3,150	3,030	1.02	1.04
12000	26,954	28,077	15,027	15,683	0.96	0.96
14000	9,733	9,784	8,025	8,110	0.99	0.99

Teaching Note Exhibit 2
Overhead Direct Labor Burden Rates
By Individual Account 1987-1990

Overhead Account #	1987	1988	1989	1990
1000	$0.312	$0.309	$0.412	$0.403
1500	0.273	0.270	0.435	0.420
2000	0.148	0.150	0.150	0.150
3000	0.098	0.100	0.100	0.100
4000	0.357	0.351	0.544	0.527
5000	0.980	0.967	1.482	1.438
8000	0.241	0.235	0.277	0.265
9000	0.272	0.268	0.439	0.425
11000	0.206	0.198	0.233	0.215
12000	1.092	1.110	1.110	1.112
14000	0.387	0.593	0.575	0.575

Teaching Note Exhibit 3
A Comparison of Three Direct Labor
Burden Rates of 1988 and 1989

Overhead Account #	1989	1988	1989/1988
1000	$0.412	$0.309	1.33
1500	0.435	0.270	1.61
2000	0.150	0.150	1.00
3000	0.100	0.100	1.00
4000	0.544	0.351	1.55
5000	1.482	0.967	1.53
8000	0.277	0.235	1.18
9000	0.439	0.268	1.64
11000	0.233	0.198	1.18
12000	1.110	1.110	1.00
14000	0.593	0.387	1.53

Appendix 1

Question 4

Student A

4. Please refer to Exhibits 1, 2, and 3.

a. Exhibit 1 is my projected MY 1991 budget if all three products are produced. I made the additional assumptions that labor costs and overhead costs are unchanged from 1990 levels. This seems reasonable given that material, sales and volume levels were unchanged, indicating a stable environment with respect to inflation, industry structure, demand, and levels of competition.

In this scenario (produce all three products), the overhead burden rate is unchanged from 1990, that is 563.0%

Exhibit 2 is my projected MY 1991 budget if manifolds are dropped from the product line. It assumes that all direct costs associated with manifolds will thereby go to zero, as we saw in previous product line reductions in 1989. It also assumes a corresponding, though proportionately smaller, reduction in production overhead. This is to be expected: we saw this occur in 1989; also, descriptions of overhead accounts indicate that they contain variable components. However, the size of the variable component differs for the various accounts. The reduction in each account was estimated based on the 1989 reductions. It was assumed that the ratio of the percent overhead reduction to the percent direct cost reduction seen in 1989 would hold for a 1991 drop of manifolds. This incorporates the differing levels of variability in the various overhead accounts, and seems consistent with observation. Changes in $DL or material costs were not used because: percent reduction in these two accounts were approximately the same; certain overhead accounts varied more directly with one, some with the other.

In this scenario (no manifolds produced), the overhead burden rate increases to 753.2% ($56958/$7562). This is to be expected, as we again see $DL decreasing faster than overhead.

Exhibit 1: MY 1991 Budget Producing Manifolds

Sales	1991 Additional Assumptions
Fuel Tanks	$ 83,535
Manifolds	$ 93,120
Doors	$ 49,887
Total	$226,542

Direct Material	
Fuel Tanks	$ 16,996
Manifolds	$ 35,725
Doors	$ 16,825
Total	$69,546

Direct Labor

Fuel Tanks	$ 4,599	Assume Labor Costs
Manifolds	$ 6,540	Also Unchanged
Doors	$ 2,963	
Total	$ 14,102	
Dir. Cost Total	$ 83,648	

Overhead

1000	$ 5,679	Assume overhead costs
1500	$ 5,928	also unchanged
2000	$ 2,115	
3000	$ 1,410	
4000	$ 7,433	
5000	$ 20,274	
8000	$ 3,744	
9000	$ 5,987	
11000	$ 3,744	
12000	$ 15,683	
14000	$ 8,110	
Total	$ 79,393	

Factory Profit (Gross margin)	$ 63,501

Exhibit 2: MY 1991 Budget No Manifolds

Sales	1991	% Drop
Fuel Tanks	$ 83,535	
Manifolds	$ 0	
Doors	$ 49,887	
Total	$133,422	41.1%

Direct Material

Fuel Tanks	$ 16,996	
Manifolds	$ 0	
Doors	$ 16,825	
Total	$33,821	51.4%

Direct Labor

Fuel Tanks	$ 4,599	
Manifolds	$ 0	
Doors	$ 2,963	
Total	$ 7,562	46.4%
Dir. Cost Total	$ 41,383	50.5%

Overhead

1000	$ 3,942	30.6%
1500	$ 5,054	14.7%
2000	$ 1,065	49.7%
3000	$ 710	49.7%
4000	$ 6,067	18.4%
5000	$ 16,379	19.2%
8000	$ 2,262	39.6%
9000	$ 5,209	13.0%
11000	$ 1,827	39.7%
12000	$ 7,892	49.7%
14000	$ 6,552	19.2%
Total	$ 56,958	28.3%

Factory Profit	$ 35,081
(Gross margin)	

See text for explanation of assumptions

Exhibit 3: MY's 1988/1989 Budgets Used to Estimate O/H After Manifolds Dropped

	1988	1989	% Decrease	
Sales	$351,071	$216,338	38.4%	
Dir. Material	$127,363	$ 66,956	47.4%	
Dir. Labor	$ 25,294	$ 13,537	46.5%	
Total Direct	$152,657	$ 80,493	47.3%	
				O/H % Drop/
O/H				Dir. Cost Drop
1000	$ 7,806	$ 5,572	28.6%	0.61
1500	$ 6,824	$ 5,883	13.8%	0.29
2000	$ 3,794	$ 2,031	46.5%	0.98
3000	$ 2,529	$ 1,354	46.5%	0.98
4000	$ 8,888	$ 7,360	17.2%	0.36
5000	$ 24,460	$ 20,063	18.0%	0.38

8000	$ 5,946	$ 3,744	37.0%	0.78
9000	$ 6,771	$ 5,948	12.2%	0.26
11000	$ 5,011	$ 3,150	37.1%	0.79
12000	$ 28,077	$ 15,027	46.5%	0.98
14000	$ 9,784	$ 8,025	18.0%	0.38
Total	$109,890	$ 78,157	28.9%	0.61

The above percent changes are used to estimate the change in O/H resulting from the drop of manifolds. The ratio of O/H drop to direct cost drop is assumed to be the same in 1991 (no manifold) as was seen in 1988-1989.

Student B:

See "Exhibit 2" for calculations.

Assumptions:

The first set of assumptions deal with the 1991 budget dropping no products. I assumed that everything will remain the same as in 1990. Looking at trends from 1988 to 1990, direct material and direct labor costs as a percentage of sales has remained constant. Since the question tells us the price and volume are fixed, and I have these cost trends constant, I left labor and material costs constant. I also said, following this same logic, that the overhead costs were to remain constant, giving me a 1991 budget the same as the 1990. Here, I did not give the plant the benefit of the doubt. The factory profit still was $63,501, but this would be the worst case. What do I mean, "worst case"? The plant is making great strides in cutting cost, improving processes, improving labor relations, etc. (A POM dream). Eventually, that will show up in the bottom line. Personally, I think it will show up in 1991, maybe cutting total costs by 5% or so, improving profits to $71,653, but to be conservative, I held these things constant.

The second set of assumptions deal with the 1991 budget dropping manifolds. Again, I assumed, looking at trends from 1988 to 1990, that direct material and direct labor costs will remain the same for the remaining products (see above for my non-conservative thoughts on the subject). I did not say that the overhead costs would go down proportionally to the direct labor dollar decrease from eliminating manifolds. If I did this I would lower the total direct labor costs by 46.4% (the direct labor $ removed $6,540 divided by the total direct labor $, $14,102). This would give me a factory profit of $48,365. I do not believe this to be the case because I don't think all the overhead costs are avoidable. It wasn't the case when the plant dropped mufflers and oil pans so I don't see it being the case now.

Specifically, I made the following assumptions for overhead:

1000   Lowered those by the percentage decrease in direct labor because I thought need for janitors and truck drivers would be proportionately less. (46.4%, I gave the benefit of the doubt).

1500   I cut by 23.2%. I believe half the salaried non-IEs were probably needed just to keep the plant running (payroll, nurse, plant manager). The foreman (direct supervision) on the manifold line could be cut.

2000   Lowered by 46.4%, same as 1000.

3000   Not cut, the manifold line was automated, so this section should not be affected.

4000   Cut by 23.2%. Still have to heat and light the plant (including the empty space left by the manifold) but the direct power to the manifold machines will be eliminated.

5000   Cut by 23.2%, the line was automated, so the numbers of skilled labor (machinists, repair, tool and die, etc.) probably are used in higher percentages by the other two products (so I cut 1/2 of % of DL$).

8000   Cut by 67%, since the manifolds had the expensive machine (assumed they would sell machines) and a big chunk of the depreciation.

9000   Not cut, stayed constant

11000   Cut by 23.2%, same as 5000

12000   Cut by 46.4%, same as direct labor cut by eliminating the product.

14000   Cut by 23.2%, same as 5000.

The total plant profit in case one, no cuts was $63,501. In case two it became $35,440. The new burden rates would be 563% with no cuts (taking the assumptions I made) and 735% taking the cut.

"Exhibit 2"

MY 1991 Budget

	No Products Dropped	Manifolds Dropped
Sales		
Fuel Tanks	$ 83,535	$ 83,535
Manifolds	$ 93,120	
Doors	$ 49,887	$ 49,887
Total	$225,542	$132,422
Direct Material		
Fuel Tanks	$ 16,996	$ 16,996
Manifolds	$ 35,725	
Doors	$ 16,825	$ 16,825
Total	$ 69,546	$ 33,821
Direct Labor		
Fuel Tanks	$ 4,599	$ 4,599
Manifolds	$ 6,540	
Doors	$ 2,963	$ 2,963
Total	$ 14,102	$ 7,562

Overhead	Keep	Drop Manifolds
1000	5,679	3,045
1500	5,978	4,558
2000	2,115	1,134
3000	1,410	1,410
4000	7,433	5,708
5000	20,274	15,570
8000	3,744	1,235
9000	5,987	5,987
11000	3,030	2,327
12000	15,683	8,400
14000	8,110	6,220
Total	79,303	55,599
Factory Profit	63,501	35,440

Student C:

4) a) (1) No products are dropped.

I will be assuming that the current improvements in efficiency will only offset direct labor costs relative to inflation and labor costs in absolute $ will stay the same.

I will also assume that overhead costs do not go up from 1990 to 1991 (ignoring COLA/S unemployment ins. increases, etc.).

With the above assumption, nothing changes from 1990.

Sales	$226,542
Dir. Material	$ 69,546
Dir. Labor	$ 14,102
Total Overhead	$ 79,393
Factory Profit	$ 63,501

This assumption of no change is simplistic but it makes the analysis cleaner and enhances the contrast w/scenario 2.

2) Manifold Products line is dropped.

The assumption in scenario 1 still holds except that those items impacted by the drop of manifold production will be changed.

Sales		
Fuel Tanks	$ 83,535	
Doors	$ 49,887	
	$133,422	(59%)

Direct Material

Fuel Tanks	$ 16,996	
Doors	$ 16,825	
	$ 33,821	(48%)

Direct Labor

Fuel Tanks	$ 4,599	
Doors	$ 2,963	
	$ 7,562	(54%)

Direct Contribution
before overhead $ 92,039

Overhead

Have to decide for each account how much it will be without manifold production (assuming the same plant is kept for production).

1000   Assuming this varies with volume which can be represented by sales, therefore drops to 59% of old figure. - 3,342

1500   Salaries presumed are mostly a fixed cost dropped very little when muffler and oil pans were dropped. Assuming only 10% drop. - 5,335

2000   Supplies should vary with sales to 59%. - 1,248

3000   Should vary with direct labor drop to 54%. - 761.

4000   Utilities dropped very little in the past. Assuming 15% drop because they are relatively fixed. - 6,318

5000   Again, specialized employees are relatively fixed so I drop them 15% (didn't drop much from 1988 to 1989). - 17,234

8000   Depreciation will be allocated based on materials processed. I am assuming that the manifold machines can be sold at their current book value. But because the process for manifolds is highly automated, I should drop it to more than proportional 48%. Lets say it drops to 35%. - 1,310

9000   Relatively constant personnel cost. Reduced by 10%. - 5,388

11000   Set up costs are very low on manifolds because they are automated in production. Allocated on sales but the drop is not to 59% by to 70% because of automation. - 2,121

12000   Benefits should vary with direct labor drop to 54%. - 8,469

14000   Should drop same as account 5,000 by 15%. - 6,894

Total overhead without manifolds = $58,420

a) The Budget

Contribution before overhead	$92,039
Overhead	$58,420
Factory profit	33,619
Profit with manifolds	63,501

Profit went down because many costs are relatively fixed. Manifold contrib. = 50,855; Overhead = 20,973; drop manifolds lower profit by 50,855-70,973 = 29,882.

b) Overhead allocation

Scenario 1:   563%
Scenario 2: $\dfrac{58,420}{7,562}$ = 773%

This is assuming that the current allocation system is kept. This is undesirable. A move to an activity based system would provide better cost information.

Question 5:

Student A:

I would not outsource manifolds from the ACF in 1991, assuming that performance on the other dimensions of quality, customer service and technical capability were satisfactory.

Looking at Exhibits 1 and 2, the MY 1991 budgets, with and without manifold production, we see that the dropping of manifolds actually reduces factory profit from $63,501 to $35,081. It thus makes no sense to drop the manifolds.

This is because the manifolds were making a positive contribution to ACF's fixed costs. While their production may not have been covering all allocated costs, it was more than covering all variable costs -- including genuinely variable overhead. Below is an analysis of the manifold production cost breakout:

Sales	$93,120
$DL	$ 6,540
Materials	$35,725
Dir. Margin	$50,855

Var O/H $22,455 (Difference between O/H with manifolds - Ex 1 - and without - Ex. 2)

Contrib. $28,400 (30.5%)

This contribution is significantly higher than the one calculated according to the Bridgeton methodology, which allocates overhead according to the 563.9% burden rate ($36,820).

Before reaching a final decision, I would need more information. As already mentioned, I would need evaluations of ACF's performance on the other dimensions: quality, customer service, and technical capability. Even if ACF was cost competitive -- as the above analysis indicates - outsourcing could be justified if performance was deficient on one of these criteria.

I would also need to know precisely how much overhead could be eliminated by dropping manifolds. The analysis I have done is only an approximation. Actual, long-term cost reductions in overhead might be greater or smaller. This depends on the specific requirements of manifold production, and ACF's ability to drive out more cost over periods longer than a few years.

Finally, I would need to know what the outsourcing costs would be. Even if ACF was found to be competitive, a truly outstanding vendor which was world class would be worth pursuing if the terms of a long-term partnership could be established to the satisfaction of all involved.

Student B:

No, not until I know more about the following:

Will I get a replacement product to help cover overhead and make my people (union) happy by keeping them employed?

What are the projections for the increase in manifold prices and sales? These should be calculated before any decisions are made.

I do not know these things. What I do know is productivity and quality are on the rise. If I lose manifolds, I lose bottom line profits. That manifolds could be "Crown Jewels" of the plant in the future if everything pans out. That I'm equipped with automated equipment and a super work force, and capacity to make manifolds a super product. I also know that the competition has changed (Japan) my product mix has changed, but my costs accounting system hasn't. It needs to so I can make proper decisions in the future. Maybe I need to add more costs centers. Before I make any strategic decisions I would fist change my cost structure. See exhibit 3 for changes (old and new).

Student C:

Based on my analysis in question 4, outsourcing manifolds will result in a net reduction of factory profit from $63,501 to $33,619 because the direct contribution from manifolds is greater than the drop in overhead if they are removed. My analysis however makes a plethora of assumptions about the behavior of overhead costs. Indeed they may behave differently, so I would need more precise estimates of their reduction if manifolds are outsourced.

In addition, the analysis assumes that the current plant is kept. Moving to a smaller plant/downsizing, this one to accommodate fuel tanks and doors exclusively may get rid of many of those fixed costs. In fact is seems that this process has not happened yet in regards to the absence of mufflers and oil pan.

Outsourcing implies strategic variables. Are manifolds important to the Bridgeton product line? Can other plants produce them with the same quality, customer service, and technical capability? (The other guidelines in evaluating products according to the analysis study). We need to know the effect on the union. Will more people in the unemployed pool ultimately mean higher wages for current workers? What will the result on improving productivity be?

What will happen to fuel tanks and doors? Will they drop classes as well (They probably would given my analysis of the resulting rise in burden rates to 7.73%). I do not believe that manifolds should be outsourced but admittedly it is a qualified no.

Bridgeton Industries
Figure 1

Three Types of Cost Behavior

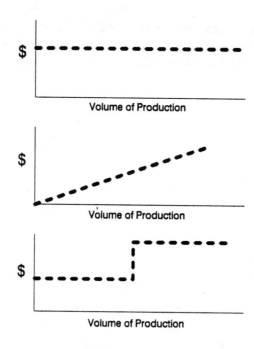

Bridgeton Industries
Figure 2

Semi-Fixed Costs

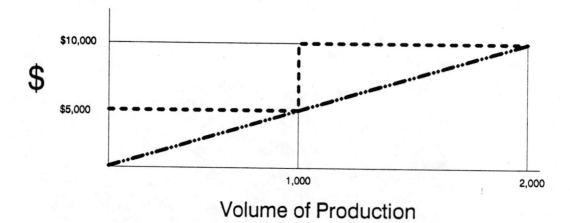

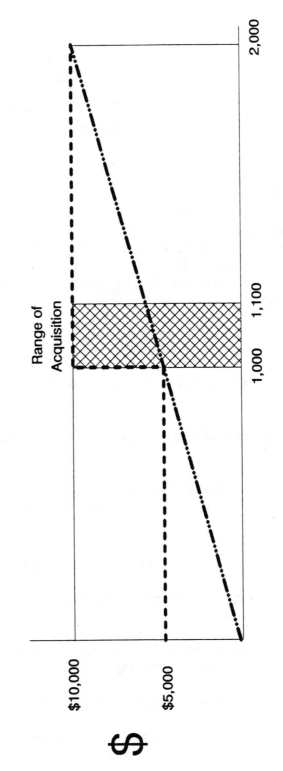

Bridgeton Industries
Figure 3
Semi-Fixed Costs Showing Range of Acquisition of Extra Capacity

Volume of Production

Institutional Furniture[1]

Teaching Note

Institutional Furniture describes a production setting that should be relatively easy for students to understand. They certainly will be familiar with the end products. The case provides a pathological example of how messed up a standard cost system can become. It provides students with an opportunity to identify the critical design weaknesses in a cost system, and to contemplate how these weaknesses can be remedied by rather simple changes to internal processes and the design of the system.

Assignment Questions:

1. What factors contributed to the surprise writedowns and losses at the end of 19x4 and 19x5?

2. What changes should management implement in 19x6 to minimize similar occurrences in the future?

3. Describe the changes you would make to Institutional Furniture's cost accounting system. How should "falldown" and "rework" be accounted for in the revised cost system?

Class Discussion

Q: **What is the nature of the production process?**

The factory has two basic production areas. First, lumber is taken out of inventory and cut into furniture parts, prepared, coated, and placed into WIP inventory. In the second stage, the furniture parts are drawn out of inventory, assembled into finished pieces, and packed into cartons before shipping.

Q: **What is the nature of Institutional's existing cost system?**

Each of the nine production areas has its own standard labor rate. Deviations from the standard labor rate are closed periodically to a labor price variance account. Labor

---

1. This teaching note was prepared by Robert S. Kaplan as an aid to instructors using Institutional Furniture.

costs enter inventory at actual hours but leave inventory at standard hours. Therefore, usage variances, idle time, inaccurate standards, and time worked on reworked and scrapped items are all left in the WIP labor account.

Materials are tracked in eight work-in-process categories. Materials are entered into inventory at standard cost with purchase price variances closed to the income statement at acquisition time. Standard materials costs in the eight categories are updated frequently, based on information provided from the purchasing agent. Thus items can enter and leave WIP and FG inventory with different costs. (Exhibit 2 on page 24 shows the eight materials price and nine labor rate variance accounts for December 19x5 and cumulative year-to-date.)

Overhead is applied at a single plant-wide rate of 165% of direct labor dollars (DL$). All costs are allocated (full costing), with no separation of fixed and variable costs.

The plant operates with a periodic inventory system, checking physical inventory only once a year.

It may be interesting to note that Institutional Furniture has a classic job shop production process but has installed a process cost accounting system, with variances closed to departments and not to individual jobs. Also, the plant is treated as one large cost center with inputs (materials and labor) counted reasonably well, but only one kind of output (good pieces of furniture) counted by the cost system.

Q: **What problems are contributing to the large inventory writedowns at the end of each year?**

Students should be able to have a field day with this question. Among the items they should raise are:

- Materials may be lost because of bad yields from raw materials, especially lumber.

- Items lost during the production process are not charged against WIP; Bad materials, scrap, production errors can all be fed to the "hog" with no accounting for this lost output.

- The frequent change of standards will tend to depress inventory values (especially in finished goods inventory) as items are withdrawn from inventory at higher prices than when they entered. This factor offsets to some degree the overstatement of inventory caused by other factors. Apart from accounting issues, it will be difficult to monitor efficiencies if the standards keep changing.

- There is virtually no control of materials in the plant. Materials are vulnerable to theft, and excessive and sloppy use. The casual control of veneer under consignment could also create problems.

- There is no way to measure labor efficiency. Labor variances could be caused by bad standards, poor efficiency, the failure to record the labor content of items scrapped, and the cost of labor required for rework.

- The costing of modified units (costed at 78% of selling price) seems arbitrary. The costs of modifications could vary by type of product and the percentage of sales estimate can be affected by differential pricing for the modified units. Also the allocation of modification costs to sub-accounts will be inaccurate if the mix percentages applied to the sub-accounts are wrong.

- Falldown (rejects) and rework are not costed properly, especially when bad items are fed to the hog.

- For bid jobs, WIP is relieved based on the estimate of time and materials made for the bid, while actual time and materials would be charged to the inventory accounts. Also, only the estimated costs for the amount requested by the customer are relieved from inventory. The extra units made and shipped are not accounted for so their manufacturing costs remain in inventory.

Q: **Well this is a pretty long list. We have a big task ahead of us? What kind of changes would you recommend that Edwin Nixon make to Institutional's systems?**

For improved physical control, the two production areas can be physically separated, and buffered by a controlled, perpetual physical inventory system. A separate raw materials storage area should be established, with materials issued only with a work order. Lumber should be inspected and graded when it arrives.

For the cost system, if indirect costs vary across the nine work centers, Nixon can consider developing separate overhead rates for each center. Also, scrap, rejects, and rework standards can be established, and actuals measured, for each work center. For the more customized stages of production (such as assembly and finishing), an actual, job-order cost system can be established with actual labor, materials, and work center overhead charged directly to the furniture lot. The costs incurred for modifications and bid items should be tracked with an actual, job-order system.

Standards should be established once a year, based on forecasted average (mid-) year prices. The standards should only be changed if prices vary, unexpectedly. by more than a specified percentage (e.g., 10% of standard). When standards change, don't create an out-of-balance condition by changing inventory values without making the corresponding offsetting entry to an income-statement (or balance sheet contra) account.

Q: **What are the main lessons we learned from Institutional Furniture?**

- Companies can have truly awful cost systems.

- Be sure that, one way or another, all the outputs from the production processes (the consumers or demanders of factory resources) get included in the cost system. This includes prototypes, special items, rework, and scrap.

- The cost system designer had better understand the nature of the production process. Otherwise, the system will produce nonsense.

Stalcup Paper Company

Teaching Note

The Stalcup Paper Company (SPC) case illustrates some important issues in cost accounting. It can be used very early on in a first or second year course to sensitize students to some of the vagaries of cost allocation. I use the case to reinforce the mechanics of cost allocation learned from earlier cases in the course, such as Bridgeton Industries and Seligram. I also use the case to warn students about the differences between responsibility accounting and product costing. The issues covered by this case include:

1. How changes in the mix of products manufactured can result in apparently contradictory changes in reported product costs.

2. The inappropriateness of relying upon arbitrary allocations to evaluate managerial effectiveness.

3. How to use cost information to evaluate managerial performance.

4. The limitations of cost information in evaluating managerial performance.

This case outlines an 80 minute teaching plan.

Suggested Assignments:

1. The existing cost system and the one proposed by the manager will result in different product costs. Discuss the implications to the firm of changing from the existing system to the system of the manager.

This teaching note was written by Professor Robin Cooper as an aid to instructors using Stalcup Paper Company (186-297).

2. How useful are the per-pound costs collected by the cost system to management? In particular, how useful are they:

    a. for setting prices or selecting among products, under current market conditions and at full capacity?

    b. for making purchasing decisions?

3. How useful are Exhibits 3 and 4 in evaluating the manager's performance?

4. Explain why the cost system shows that the unit costs of both old and new rags have increased while the manager shows that they have decreased.

5. How well did the manager perform in 1984 as compared to 1982?

6. What changes would you propose to the cost system? Why?

Classroom Discussion

Q1. What is the competitive environment of Stalcup Paper Company?

The case does not provide us with much information about the firm's competitive environment. However, the following facts are important:

1) The significant change in the percentage of old rags to the total dropped from approximately 80% to approximately 50%.

2) The increase in volume of 25% of pounds produced.

3) Labor is paid on a daily basis and can sort 55 pounds of old rags or 575 pounds of new rags. This difference is caused by the presence of "foreign material" in the old rags such as buttons, rubber, and, metal.

Q2. What is the structure of the existing cost systems?

The cost system at SPC is a typical direct labor hour based system. It has a different burden rate per department. The costs of the firm are broken into two categories, direct labor costs (the case does not mention material costs), and overhead. Overhead is broken into two categories: direct departmental and general factory overhead. The direct departmental overhead contains the salary of the manager and the wages of the employees that support the department. The general factory overhead consists of costs that can not meaningfully be identified by department. These costs include items such as factory-wide waste collection, miscellaneous labor, and executive salaries. In the first stage of the two stage procedure, the direct departmental overhead is directly charged to the departments and the general factory overhead assigned using the direct labor hours consumed in the department. In the second stage, all overhead is assigned using direct labor hours. Figure 1 illustrates the structure of this system.

Q3. What is the relationship between Exhibit 2 and Exhibit 3 for 1982?

Case Exhibit 2 provides a breakdown of the expenses of the rag sorting department. The directly charged overhead is $383,745 and the general factory overhead is $286,920. Dividing these costs by the direct labor costs gives the two burden rates of 122% and 91% respectively. When these percentages are applied to the **total** direct labor hours consumed by the two products, old and new rags, the system reports departmental overhead associated with the old rags of $374,808 and the new rags of $8,991 (These numbers do not reflect a 122% burden rate but a slightly higher one. The source of this inconsistency is not clear). In theory, the sum of the two departmental overheads should equal the departmental total; however, rounding errors are observed and the sum of the old and new rag totals does not equal the departmental total. Such roundings are common. They occur whenever the burden rate is truncated. Students might be asked to comment on whether truncating the burden rate is appropriate. They should be made aware of the inherent level of accuracy in cost systems.

Another important point that should arise is that Exhibit 3 was prepared after the end of the year. Thus, SPC has an **actual** cost system not a standard one. Students should be asked how often it makes sense to run the cost system at SPC. They might decide quarterly or annually. Unless conditions change dramatically, the numbers should be relatively stable.

Q4. What is the system proposed by the manager of the department?

The proposed system changes the second stage from direct labor hours to pounds processed. This seemingly small change causes the reported costs of each pound of new rags produced to shift quite dramatically from $2.85 to $17.55 per pound produced. This shift occurs because the new system assumes that one pound of new rags consumes as much overhead as a pound of old rags. Exhibit 4 shows a per pound charge of $9.52 and $7.12 for both old and new rags for department and general overhead respectively. The old system assumed that each direct labor hour consumed the same amount of overhead.

In addition, the change in the second stage causes the cost per pound in 1984 to be **lower** for **both** old and new rags than in 1982. In contrast, the original system, reports **higher** costs for **both** old and new rags in 1984 compared to 1982. This seemingly impossible result confuses many students. To illustrate its cause, I use a simple example.

A company produces two products, A and B. Product A consumes 10 hours of direct labor to produce while product B only consumes 1 hour. The only variable cost of production is direct labor: all other costs are fixed. Fixed costs amount to $10,000. In 1982, the company produced 80 units of A and 20 units of B. In 1984, the company produced 50 units of A and 50 units of B. Compute the reported product costs using direct labor hours to allocate the fixed costs to products and number of units produced. Direct labor costs $20 per hour.

The reported costs for products A and B in 1982 using a direct labor hour based cost system are:

Direct Labor:

    Product A -- 10 hours @ $20 per hour = $200.00
    Product B -- 1 hour @ $20 per hour = $ 20.00

Overhead:

    Total hours:

        Product A -- 10 hours * 80 units = 800 hours
        Product B -- 1 hour * 20 units = 20 hours
                                        820 hours

    Burden rate:

        $10,000 /820 hours = $12.20 per hour
        Product A -- $12.20 * 10 = $122.00
        Product B -- $12.20 * 1 = $ 12.20

    Total Reported Product Cost:

        Product A -- $200.00 + $122.00 = $322.00
        Product B -- $ 20.00 + $ 12.20 = $ 32.20

and in 1984:

    Direct Labor:

        Product A -- 10 hours @ $20 per hour = $200.00
        Product B -- 1 hour @ $20 per hour = $ 20.00

    Overhead:

        Total hours:

            Product A -- 10 hours * 50 units = 500 hours
           Product B -- 1 hour * 50 units = 50 hours
                                      550 hours

        Burden rate:

           $10,000 /550 hours = $18.18 per hour
           Product A -- $18.18 * 10 = $181.80
           Product B -- $12.20 * 1 = $ 18.18

Total Reported Product Cost:

Product A -- $200.00 + $181.80 = 381.80
Product B -- $ 20.00 + $ 18.18 = $ 38.18$

Thus, the effect of the shift in product mix is to make each product appear more costly to produce. This is caused by the reduction in direct labor hours associated with the shift in product mix. The reduced direct labor hours causes the burden rate to increase and hence the reported unit product costs. The direct labor content of each product remains unchanged.

Q5. What are the product costs reported by a units produced system?

The reported costs for products A and B in 1982 using a number of units based cost systems are:

Direct Labor:

Product A -- 10 hours @ $20 per hour = $200.00
Product B -- 1 hour @ $20 per hour = $ 20.00

Overhead:

Total units:

Product A --	80 units
Product B --	20 units
	100 units

Burden rate:

$10,000 /100 units = $100 per unit

Total Reported Product Cost:

Product A -- $200.00 + $100.00 = 300.00
Product B -- $ 20.00 + $100.00 = 120.00

and in 1984:

Direct Labor:

Product A -- 10 hours @ $20 per hour = $200.00
Product B -- 1 hour @ $20 per hour = $ 20.00

Overhead:

Total units:

Product A --   50 units
Product B --   50 units
                                          100 units

Burden rate:

$10,000 /100 units = $100 per unit

Total Reported Product Cost:

Product A -- $200.00 + $100.00 = $300.00
Product B -- $ 20.00 + $100.00 = $120.00

Under the number of units based system reported costs do not change. This makes sense because the number of units did not change and therefore, the overhead cost per unit remained unchanged. Since the direct labor content also remained the same for both products, so did their reported product costs.

Looking at the two sets of reported product costs, we see part of the apparent discrepancy documented in the SPC case. Namely, under one system, the cost per pound of all products increased while under the other it remained the same.

The central lessons of this simple example are:

1)   When the bases used to assign costs to products is changed, reported product costs will change.

2)   When product mix changes cause the total quantity of the bases used in the second stage to increase (decrease), the reported cost of individual products will decrease (increase) due to fixed costs being allocated over more (less) units of the bases.

3)   These shifts in reported product costs do not necessarily indicate that the production process has become more (less) efficient. Rather, they show that the total number of units of the bases has changed.

4)   Different bases can have different effects. In the simple example, the total number of direct labor hours consumed changed across the two years (in fact, it decreased significantly) while the total number of units processed did not. Therefore, the product reported by the direct labor-based costs increased while the product costs reported by the units processed based system remained unchanged.

Q6. What is the total cost of product produced in both years under the two systems?

At this point, I prove that the two cost systems "work" by multiplying out the reported product costs by the volumes produced. This gives:

Labor hour based system (1982):

Product A	$322.20 per unit * 80 units = $25,776
Product B	$ 32.20 per unit * 20 units = $ 644
	$26,400

Labor hour based system (1984):

Product A	$381.80 per unit * 50 units = $19,090
Product B	$ 38.18 per unit * 50 units = $ 1,090
	$20,999

Note: This is $21,000 when corrected for roundings.

Units produced based system (1982):

Product A	$300 per unit * 80 units = $24,000
Product B	$120 per unit * 20 units = $ 2,400
	$26,400

Units produced based system (1984:

Product A	$300 per unit * 50 units = $15,000
Product B	$120 per unit * 50 units = $ 6,000
	$21,000

These numbers can easily be reconciled to the total expenditures in the two years. It is useful to occasionally demonstrate that systems "work" by proving that the total cost of the resources consumed by the product equals the total reported cost of products. This is particularly true in SPC because of the counter-intuitive effect on reported product costs caused by the shift in bases from direct labor hours to units processed.

Q7. What will the product costs reported by the direct labor hour system be in 1984 if the volume increases 20%?

To complete the simple example, and illustrate SPC completely, I introduce a volume increase of 20% in 1984. This change causes the volume of production of the two products to be 60 units each. The reported product costs become:

Direct labor based system (1984):

Direct Labor:

   Product A -- 10 hours @ $20 per hour = $200.00
   Product B -- 1 hour @ $20 per hour = $ 20.00

Overhead:

Total hours:

   Product A -- 10 hours * 60 units = 600 hours
   Product B -- 1 hour * 60 units = 60 hours
                                       660 hours

Burden rate:

$10,000 /660 hours = $15.15 per hour
Product A -- $15.15 * 10 = $151.50
Product B -- $15.15 * 1 = $ 15.15

Total Reported Product Cost:

Product A -- $200.00 + $151.50 = $351.50
Product B -- $ 20.00 + $ 15.15 = $ 35.15

The two sets of reported product costs for 1984 are:

	A	B
1982 (no increase)	$381.80	$38.18
1984 (increase)	$351.50	$35.15

As can be seen, the increase in volume and hence number of direct labor hours worked causes reported product costs to decrease. The total decrease is equal to 20% of the fixed costs, not 20% of total reported costs because the variable costs (i.e. labor) are still the same per unit.

When compared to 1982 reported costs, we see the increase caused by the mix change dominates the decrease caused by the volume increase. Therefore, reported product costs increase:

	A	B
1982	$322.20	$32.20
1984 (volume increase)	$351.50	$35.15

Q8. What are the product costs reported by the units produced system in 1984?

Units Produced (1984):

Direct Labor:

Product A -- 10 hours @ $20 per hour = $200.00
Product B -- 1 hour @ $20 per hour = $ 20.00

Overhead:

Total units:

Product A --	60 units
Product B --	60 units
	120 units

Burden rate:

$10,000 / 120 units = \$83.33$ per unit

Total Reported Product Cost:

Product A -- $\$200.00 + \$83.33 = \underline{\$283.33}$
Product B -- $\$ 20.00 + \$83.33 = \underline{\$103.33}$

The two sets of reported costs for 1984 are:

	A	B
1984 (no increase)	$300.00	$120.00
1984 (increase)	$283.33	$103.33

As can be seen, the increase in volume and hence the units produced causes the reported products to decrease. The total decrease is again equal to 20% of the fixed costs.

Under the units produced bases system the 1982 and 1986 reported product costs were the same as long as the volume remained constant. Consequently, the produced-based system shows reported costs decreasing from 1982 to 1984 as the volume increases.

The example now shows the reported cost of products A and B **increasing** under the direct labor hour system and **decreasing** under the units produced system. Thus, the simple example mirrors exactly the SPC case. The changes in reported product costs are caused by a shift in product mix (which causes the reported costs under the direct labor hour system to increase) and an increase in volume (which causes the reported product costs under both systems to decrease). The net effect of the two changes causes the apparently contradictory results, where under one system reported product costs go up and in the other they go down.

Q9. Was labor used more efficiently in 1984 than 1982 at SPC?

The process of evaluating performance can now begin. The case does not report the hourly labor rates. However, in 1982 inflation was high so labor rates can be expected to increase. Assuming that the processing times of 55 pounds per hour for old rags and 575 pounds per hour for new rags remains the same in both years, then we can determine the total number of hours worked in the two years:

	1982		1984	
	lbs	Hours	lbs	Hours
Old Rags	3,220,000	58,545	2,460,000	44,727
New Rags	810,000	1,409	2,520,000	4,383
Total Hours		59,954		49,110
Total Wages	$314,475		$257,775	
Wage Rate		$5.25		$5.25

As can be seen, the estimated wage rate remains the same. Either labor efficiency has not changed nor has the wage rate, or any increases in wage rates have been offset by increased efficiency.

Q10. Was indirect labor used more efficiently?

This is a more difficult question to answer. An extra 950,000 lbs of rags were carried. It requires several assumptions to estimate how efficiently the indirect labor force functioned. The indirect labor costs include the salary of the manager and the wages of the individuals who carry the rags to and from the sorters. The number of individuals should be roughly proportional to the number of pounds of material processed. The pounds processed has gone up 23.6%. If we assume all of the change in indirect labor costs is due to the increase of volume then we get 23.6% is equal to $15,105 ($143,100 - $127,995). That gives 100% as $64,000 and the managers salary as $63,995 ($127,995 - $64,000), which is clearly too high. Therefore, it seems likely that the additional 980,000 lbs were moved more efficiently than the average pound in 1982. There is no way to tell whether the increased efficiency was due to economies of scale (the incremental weight required very little additional individuals to move), or more efficient use of the workforce in general (all of the material was moved more efficiently).

Q11. How about the other expenses in the direct departmental overhead?

There is no systematic pattern. Repair labor is lower but repair materials is higher. This pattern could be due to too little repair work followed by a major breakdown or breakdowns or just statistical fluctuations. Alternatively, it could reflect a transfer of effort from repair to moving the material. The change in repair labor however is relatively small at $1,530. The doubling of repair materials should be investigated. The other accounts show virtually no change in the two years.

In general, the direct departmental overhead costs do not appear to be directly proportional to either direct labor hours or weight processed. While direct labor costs and (therefore probably) direct labor hours dropped 12% and the weight processed increased 24%, total departmental overhead increased 3%. The costs are either independent of both factors, the two factors are compensating for each other, or the costs of the department are not being well managed.

Q12. How about the general overhead?

This is a trick question since the general overhead is allocated to the department. The drop in the level of general overhead allocated to the department reflects two separate effects. The first is the drop in the consumption of direct labor in the department. This drop will automatically reduce the total general overhead allocated to the department (assuming the direct labor hours consumed by the other departments remains unchanged). In addition, the burden rate has dropped from 91% to 88% further reducing the charge.

Q13. Is the direct labor hour system better than the per pound system?

This is a difficult question to answer. The cost of moving the material to the sorters is probably roughly proportional to the weight of material moved. However, see the earlier analysis. This proportionality would suggest that the per pound basis is more appropriate in the second stage. The repair costs might also be more proportional to the weight of rags processed, though it might be more sensitive to old rather than new rag weight. The two data points provided do not suggest that a strong short term relationship exists. The power costs similarly might be more related to the weight of material processed than the direct labor hours. However, the drop observed between the two years suggest that it might be related to direct labor hours. If the power is simply to light and heat the facility, then the costs are independent of both the hours worked and the weight processed.

If some costs are related to weight and others to direct labor hours, the system could be redesigned to use two bases in the second stage, direct labor hours, and weight processed. Students should question whether such a system is too elaborate for the rag sorting department of SPC.

Q14. How useful are the per pound costs collected by the cost system to management?

The costs reported by the cost system have little use per se. The company relies upon the market to determine the majority of prices. Thus, reported product costs are of little use for pricing purposes. In times of full capacity, reported costs are used to help maximize the profitability of the firm. However, since many costs are effectively fixed in the short run, only the variable costs need be considered. Currently, the system does not differentiate between fixed and variable costs.

For attention focusing purposes, the cost system is also probably inadequate. The costs of the department do not appear to be driven predominantly by direct labor hours. Therefore, the reported product costs do not reflect accurately the consumption of resources.

Summary

The Stalcup Paper Company case provides a simple example that allows students to explore the vagaries of allocating fixed costs to products and the irrelevance of such allocations to evaluating managerial performance. The primary lessons the students should gain from class are:

1) Reductions in reported fully absorbed product costs do not necessarily signal that resources are being used more efficiently.

2) Changes in product mix can cause reported fully absorbed product costs to change without signalling changes in efficiency.

3) The choice of bases used to assign costs to products can lead to very different swings in reported product costs, caused by changes in product mix.

4) Evaluating managerial efficiency requires decomposing reported product costs into controllable and uncontrollable elements.

Commonwealth Blood Transfusion Service

Teaching Note

The Commonwealth Blood Transfusion Service (CBTS) case was written to illustrate the problems associated with reporting individual product costs for joint products. It was designed to be taught in an advanced course on cost accounting. The joint cost problem posed by the CBTS case is extremely complex. It is necessary to tell students to ignore intermediate products and work-in-progress to be able to draw a solution (alternately, additional information can be provided in the assignments). No solution to the joint cost problem is proposed. The arbitrariness of reporting individual product costs is acknowledged in the opening quotations and should be reinforced throughout the class discussion. The motivation for determining individual product costs is political in nature. Management at CBTS have no choice but to report individual product costs. The case therefore focuses on different methods of allocating the joint costs and the potential reactions of the different constituents to these methods.

The case introduces students to three major issues:

1) The problems associated with allocating joint costs to products.

2) The different methods of allocating joint costs.

3) The reaction of different constituents to these allocation methods.

This teaching note outlines an 80-minute teaching plan.

Suggested Assignments:

This teaching note was written by Senior Lecturer in Accounting, Falconer Mitchell, University of Edinburgh, and Professor Robin Cooper as an aid to instructors using Commonwealth Blood Transfusion Service (191-087).

1. Identify as many approaches as you can to determine product costs for the Plasma Fractionation Plant.

2. Treating the PFP as a single process that costs $32.2 million and produces 17 joint products, use each of the approaches you identified for assignment one to determine reported product costs. You can ignore intermediate products, work-in-process, and other inventory changes.

3. What are the strengths and weaknesses of each approach?

4. Treating the PFP as 9 (A-I) separate processes that together cost $32.2 million and produce 17 joint products, use the approach you think most appropriate to determine reported product costs. You can ignore intermediate product, work-in-process, and inventory changes.

5. How would you have to modify your answer to question 4 to take into account intermediate products, work-in-process and other inventory changes?

6. Which of these approaches would the various constituents prefer?

Class Discussion

Q1. What is the competitive environment of the CBTS?

Students should identify the pressures created by the emergence of a private hospital system with a concomitant demand for blood and a government dedicated to privatization. Together, these factors are creating a pressure towards developing individual product costs despite the joint cost problems. The choice of an allocation scheme is further complicated by the demands of the different constituents. These constituents include the government, the health associations, the donors, and the CBTS staff. Each of these constituents potentially have different beliefs about what represents a "fair" allocation procedure.

Q2. What is a joint cost?

I get the students to discuss the concept of joint costs. I draw the following diagram and talk about the problems associated with joint costs:

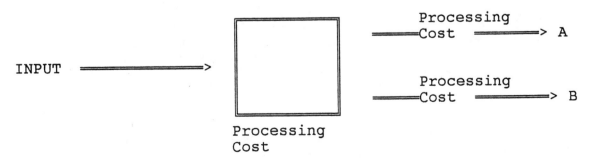

I discuss the terms joint product, by-product, split-off point, and separable costs. I initiate a 5-minute discussion on the whole joint cost issue asking students questions like what differentiates a joint product from a by-product and if there is any way to meaningfully allocate joint costs to products. I ask them if a machine producing different types of widgets is a joint cost problem. I get them to understand that the critical issue is the unavoidability of producing multiple different products from a common resource. My aim is to familiarize the students with the terminology of joint costs and the arbitrary nature of any allocation scheme. I ask them to think of commercial parallels to the CBTS, for example, oil refineries, chemical processing, and meat production, in order to demonstrate the broader significance of the joint cost issue.

Q3. What is the production process at the CBTS and where are the joint costs?

I use a transparency of case Exhibit 2 and show that there are layers of joint costs at CBTS. This layering compounds the problem of allocating the costs but the general principles remain the same.

Q4. What are potential bases for allocating the joint costs to the products?

There are at least six possible bases that can be identified from the case:

- number of units produced
- number of donations
- processing hours
- sales value
- weight
- number of processes

The numerical data for the first four bases is given in Appendix 1A to this note.

Q5. What is the simplest way to allocate the costs at the CBTS?

Treating the CBTS as a black box that consists of a single process that costs $32.2 million and produces 17 joint products is the simplest way to allocate costs at the PFP. This model can be diagrammed as:

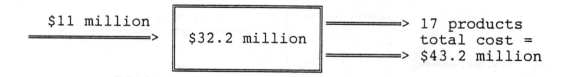

I get a student to demonstrate the calculations for one of the above bases and then ask for the product costs reported by the other bases. I write the solutions on the board so that students can see how they compare. (The individual product costs reported by four bases are shown in Appendix 1B to this note).

Q6. Does the choice of bases make a difference?

The answer is clearly yes. I ask students which makes the most sense. This is in many ways a trick question since the allocations are arbitrary, but some results look more believable than others. For example, using the number of units basis, all products have the same reported cost, which looks less realistic then using sales value.

Q7. What are the fundamental assumptions made by each allocation approach?

To get students to understand the fundamental assumption made by each allocation approach, I write the bases identified on the board and get students to identify the fundamental assumption each makes. I start with the simplest assumptions to understand, and end with the most complex. When I have finished the board looks as follows:

BASES	FUNDAMENTAL ASSUMPTIONS
Number of units produced	Each unit cost the same
Number of donations	Each donation costs the same
Processing hours	Each processing hour costs the same
Weight	Each pound of output costs the same
Number of processes	Each process costs the same
Sales value	Each sales $ costs the same and hence earns the same profit.

I ask students what is different about the sales value approach to all of the others, and I get them to realize this is the only approach that is guaranteed to report product costs below market price for all products.

Q8. What are the advantages and disadvantages of the four different bases?

	Number of Units	Number of Donations	Processing Hours	Market Price
Advantages	Simple to Measure	Captures Inputs	Captures Effort	All products profitable
Disadvantages	All products cost the same regardless of size etc.	Ignores production complexity and is perhaps only suited for the original plasma input	All costs may not be time driven	Prices fluctuate rapidly so reported cost fluctuates
	Mixture of profitable and unprofitable products	Mixture of profitable and unprofitable products	Mixture of profitable and unprofitable products	

Q9. What are the drawbacks of the black box approach?

The black box approach clearly ignores important information about processes and costs inside the PFP. However, I want the students to understand that the PFP is really a series of black boxes that interrelate. Any lesson we learned from the simple approach applies to the mini-black boxes inside the PFP.

Q10. How would you allocate the costs to PFP products using available information about the processes inside the PFP?

I start by focusing student attention on process E. Again, the four different bases can be used to split the costs at each step. I demonstrate the approach by looking at one internal step. I pick step E because it is at the end of the process. I put the following diagram on the board.

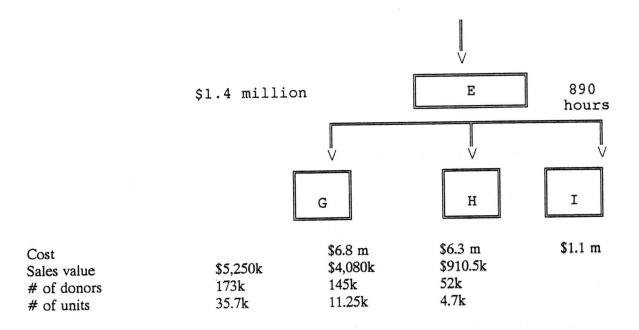

		G	H	I
Cost		$6.8 m	$6.3 m	$1.1 m
Sales value	$5,250k	$4,080k	$910.5k	
# of donors	173k	145k	52k	
# of units	35.7k	11.25k	4.7k	

and get the students to discuss the appropriateness of the various approaches. I demonstrate that this is exactly the same as a simple one stage joint cost problem.

One common approach to the joint cost allocation scheme that is inapplicable at CBTS is "sales value less further separable costs". For CBTS this basis produces negative results:

	G	H	I
Sales Value	$5,280k	$4,080k	$ 910.5k
Separable Costs	$6,800k	$6,300k	$1,100k
NET	($1550k)	($2220k)	($199.5k)

This result should alert management to the potential target areas for cost reduction, i.e. are we inefficient at producing these products.

Q11. How would you handle the cost of step C?

There are several ways to allocate the costs of step C. I draw the following diagram and get the students to discuss the potential allocation approaches:

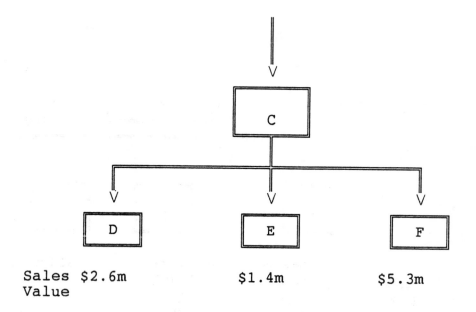

Sales $2.6m $1.4m $5.3m
Value

The simplest alternative Sales Value requires measuring the same attribute of the next processing step or steps and using that attribute as the allocation basis. Potential bases include the weight of each output, the processing hours required in the next or all future steps, or the cost of subsequent processing.

I point out that step C can be treated as a simple one stage joint cost problem. Therefore, the CBTS problem can be viewed as a series of independent joint cost problems. The solution to the joint cost problem for the PFP using sales value is shown in Appendix 2 to this note.

Q12. How would you handle intermediate products and work-in-process approaches?

I focus the students attention on process A. It has both intermediate products and work-in-process. For process A we have enough information to determine an estimate of the value of the incremental work-in-process and intermediate products using the weight of the plasma shipped to the PFP. The incremental work-in-process is 2,000 kg. The increase in weight in the two intermediate products cryoprecipitate and supernatant are 7,000 kg. and 8,000 kg. respectively. Therefore, the total increase in equivalent output for process A is 17,000 kg. Since total input was 110,000kg (ignoring an insignificant change in inventory of frozen plasma of 375 kg), the change in equivalent output stored as work-in-process and intermediate products is 15.5% of total input. Using weight to allocate the costs, the additional inventory has a process value of $325,000 and a raw material value of $1,700,000 ($17,000kg x $25 x 110,000/440,000). These calculations are shown in the following Exhibit:

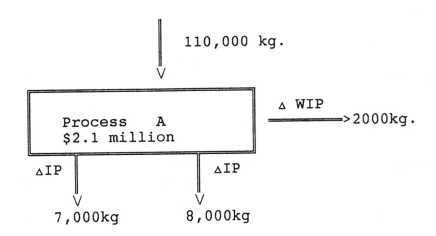

Total ΔWIP + ΔIP = 17,000 kg or 15.5% of input

Conversion Cost =	$ 325,000
Material Cost (17,000kg at $100 per kg.) =	$1,700,000
Total ΔWIP and ΔIP cost =	$2,025,000

A more thorough analysis yields virtually identical results.

	Material	Conv. Cost
Production in Equivalent Units:		
WIP (start)	------	2,000
Processed fully	104,000	104,000
WIP (end)	6,000	3,000
	110,000	109,000
Cost	$11 million	$2.1
Cost per E.U.	$100	$19.27

Δ in WIP and IP

Starting WIP	4,000 x $100 =	400,000
	2,000 x $ 19.27 =	38,540
Starting IP	8,000 x $119.27 =	954,160
	12,000 x $119.27 =	1,431,240 2,823,940
Closing WIP	6,000 x $100 =	600,000
	3,000 x $ 19.27 =	57,810
Closing IP	15,000 x $119.27 =	1,789,050
	20,000 x $119.27 =	2,385,400 4,832,260
Total Δ WIP and Δ IP =		$2,008,320

Q13. If we resolve the inventory problems and choose the best allocation bases we can find, will the reported costs have any meaning?

This question is designed to remind students that joint cost allocations are incorrigible, i.e., no method can be rationally considered correct. This means that the criteria for choice will ultimately be impossible to justify and defend (although some interesting discussion can emerge on trying to do just that). This should bring home to students the flexibility and arbitrariness which joint costs pose for management accounting. Ultimately individual intrinsic product costs remain an unknown despite the most elaborate and time consuming computations.

Q14. Which approach is each of the constituents likely to prefer and why?

It is at this stage that the case discussion will illustrate how cost allocations, in practice are influenced by behavioral as well as technical accounting considerations. Each constituent will view the alternatives from a particular standpoint. Their judgment will be colored by their attitudes to and perceptions of both the process and the end result of the joint costing exercise. For example CBTS staff may, for reasons of job security and renumeration, wish to use the method which makes the service look most efficient. This could be based on the end-result of the allocation, leading to a preference for the method which shows that key products are produced at less cost than the relevant commercial price. Alternatively, if an overall view of the service is taken the method which would result in the greatest total surplus (or lowest deficit) for the service when output is price at prevailing commercial rates. There may also be a perception among managerial staff that product cost changes should reflect operational factors, reflecting changes in performance within the service. This would not be the case if the commercial price basis were used for the joint cost allocations as price fluctuations are frequent and substantial. These prices may also reflect the pricing strategy of firms (e.g. loss leaders) rather than reflecting underlying cost.

On the other hand the Health Association may wish to select the method which will result in the highest cost recovery charges for those products being supplied to the private sector. This choice would safeguard the service from the charge that they (and so the taxpayer) were subsidizing the private firms. For political reasons Government might well endorse this view although they too will have to consider the impact of cost recovery charges to state owned hospitals (where high charges for high usage products may cause adverse political publicity). The chosen method may also have to possess a simplicity and an inherent equity or fairness so that its explanation to donors is facilitated and so that it can be accepted by them that profits are not being made from their donations.

The donors are more difficult to understand. They do not have objectives that can be captured via economics. The simplest most easily defended approach might be the preferred. The selling value approach might be considered too commercial and suggestive that eventually the service will sell its products at a profit. The number of donations approach is in keeping with the spirit of the donors but will create problems if it becomes public knowledge that the service is selling products below cost to the public sector. This will occur if the service sells its products to the public sector but uses any bases but sales value to allocate costs. Selling products below cost will occur since the private sector is unlikely to buy from the service above market price. Thus, the private sector will "cherry pick" the service by buying from the lowest cost source.

The various constituents all have different agendas. Since there is no theoretically sound solution to the joint cost problem, the choice of allocation procedure becomes political. There is no obvious dominant solution to the problem.

Appendix 1A　Basic Methods of Joint Cost Allocation

	Number Produced		Number Donations	
Coagulation Factors				
Factor VIII	50,000	(26.23)	326,000	(34.92)
Factor IX	8,000	(4.20)	68,500	(7.33)
Immunoglobulins				
Intramuscular -				
Normal	5,000	(2.62)	28,000	(3.00)
Normal	15,000	(7.87)	26,000	(2.78)
Rh (D)	6,000	(3.15)	25,500	(2.73)
Rh (D)	4,000	(2.10)	16,500	(1.77)
Tetanus	3,000	(1.57)	15,000	(1.61)
Hepatitis	1,500	(0.79)	42,000	(4.50)
Varicella-Zoster	1,000	(0.52)	13,000	(1.40)
Rubella	200	(0.10)	7,000	(0.75)
Intravenous -				
Normal	10,000	(5.25)	48,000	(5.14)
Tetanus	250	(0.13)	60,000	(6.43)
CMV	1,000	(0.52)	37,000	(3.96)
Albumen Products:				
Human Albumin	4,000	(2.10)	43,500	(4.66)
Human Albumin	700	(0.37)	8,500	(0.91)
Plasma Solution	80,000	(41.96)	168,000	(18.00)
Plasma Solution	1,000	(0.52)	1,000	(0.11)
	190,650		933,500	

Appendix 1A (cont'd) Basic Methods of Joint Cost Allocation

	Processing Hours		Sales Value	
Coagulation Factors				
Factor VIII	6,730	(4.85)	15,000,000	(33.71)
Factor IX	7,930	(5.72)	4,800,000	(10.79)
Immunoglobulins				
Intramuscular -				
Normal	8,510	(6.14)	225,000	(0.51)
Normal	8,490	(6.12)	225,000	(0.51)
Rh (D)	8,250	(5.95)	720,000	(1.62)
Rh (D)	7,960	(5.74)	240,000	(0.54)
Tetanus	8,130	(5.87)	225,000	(0.51)
Hepatitis	8,480	(6.12)	1,575,000	(3.54)
Varicella-Zoster	7,770	(5.60)	750,000	(1.69)
Rubella	7,890	(5.69)	120,000	(0.27)
Intravenous -				
Normal	9,600	(6.92)	3,000,000	(6.74)
Tetanus	8,560	(6.18)	450,000	(1.01)
CMV	7,820	(5.64)	1,800,000	(4.04)
Albumen Products:				
Human Albumin	8,050	(5.81)	900,000	(2.02)
Human Albumin	7,630	(5.50)	10,500	(0.02)
Plasma Solution	10,150	(7.32)	14,400,000	(32.35)
Plasma Solution	6,700	(4.83)	60,000	(0.13)
	138,650		44,500,500	

Appendix 1B Basic Methods of Joint Cost Allocation - Results

	Number Produced		Number Donations	
	Total Cost $	Unit Cost $	Total Cost $	Unit Cost $
Coagulation Factors:				
Factor VIII	11.331	227.00	15.085	301.70
Factor IX	1.814	227.00	3.167	395.88
Immunoglobulins				
Intramuscular -				
Normal	1.132	227.00	1.296	259.20
Normal	3.400	227.00	1.201	80.07
Rh (D)	1.361	227.00	1.179	196.50
Rh (D)	0.907	227.00	0.765	191.25
Tetanus	0.678	227.00	0.696	232.00
Hepatitis	0.341	227.00	1.944	1296.00
Varicella-Zoster	0.225	227.00	0.605	605.00
Rubella	0.043	227.00	0.324	1620.00
Intravenous -				
Normal	2.268	227.00	2.220	222.00
Tetanus	0.056	227.00	2.778	11112.00
CMV	0.225	227.00	1.711	1711.00
Albumen Products:				
Human Albumin	0.907	227.00	2.013	503.25
Human Albumin	0.160	227.00	0.393	561.43
Plasma Solution	18.127	227.00	7.776	97.20
Plasma Solution	0.225	227.00	0.047	47.00
	43.200		43.200	

Appendix 1B (cont'd) Basic Methods of Joint Cost Allocation - Results

	Processing Hours		Sales Value	
	Total Cost $	Unit Cost $	Total Cost $	Unit Cost $
Coagulation Factors:				
Factor VIII	2.095	41.09	14.563	291.26
Factor IX	2.471	308.88	4.661	582.63
Immunoglobulins				
Intramuscular -				
Normal	2.652	530.40	0.220	44.00
Normal	2.644	176.27	0.220	14.67
Rh (D)	2.570	428.33	0.700	116.67
Rh (D)	2.480	620.00	0.233	58.25
Tetanus	2.536	845.33	0.220	73.33
Hepatitis	2.644	1762.67	1.529	1019.33
Varicella-Zoster	2.419	2419.00	0.730	730.00
Rubella	2.460	12300.00	0.117	585.00
Intravenous -				
Normal	2.989	298.90	2.912	291.20
Tetanus	2.670	10680.00	0.437	1748.00
CMV	2.436	2436.00	1.745	1745.00
Albumen Products:				
Human Albumin	2.510	627.50	0.873	218.25
Human Albumin	2.376	3394.29	0.009	12.85
Plasma Solution	3.162	39.53	13.975	174.69
Plasma Solution	2.086	2086.00	0.056	56.00
	43.200		43.200	

Appendix 2 Sales Value Method of Joint Cost Allocation - Results

COSTS	JOINT TO ALL PRODUCTS Plasma 11,000,000 Process A 2,100,000 13,100,000	FACTOR VIII Process B $4,700,000	EXCEPT FACTOR VIII Process C $1,900,000	FACTOR II Process D $2,600,000	PLASMA SOLUTIONS Process F $5,300,000
Coagulation Factors					
Factor VIII	4,416,010		309,147		
Factor IX	1,413,490	4,700,000		2,600,000	
Immunoglobulins					
Intramuscular -					
Normal	66,810		14,499		
Normal	66,810		14,499		
Rh (D)	212,220		46,372		
Rh (D)	70,740		15,458		
Tetanus	66,810		14,449		
Hepatitis	463,740		101,439		
Varicella-Zoster	221,390		48,304		
Rubella	35,370		7,729		
Intravenous -					
Normal	882,940		193,217		
Tetanus	132,310		28,982		
CMV	529,240		115,930		
Albumen Products:					
Human Albumin	264,620		57,965		
Human Albumin	2,620		676		
Plasma Solution	4,237,850		927,570		5,278,008
Plasma Solution	17,030		3,864		21,992
	13,100,000	4,700,000	1,900,000	2,600,000	5,300,000

Appendix 2 (cont'd)   Sales Value Method of Joint Cost Allocation - Results

COSTS	ALBUMEN IMMUNOGLOBULINS Process E $1,400,000	INTRAVENOUS IMMUNOGLOBULINS Process G $6,800,000	INTRAMUSCULAR IMMUNOGLOBULINS Process H $6,300,000	HUMAN ALBUMEN Process I $1,100,000	TOTAL $43,200,000	UNIT COST $
Coagulation Factors:						
Factor VIII					9,116,010	182.32
Factor IX					4,322,637	540.33
Immunoglobulins						
Intramuscular -						
Normal	30,760		347,426		459,445	91.89
Normal	30,760		347,426		459,445	30.63
Rh (D)	98,433		1,111,764		1,468,789	244.80
Rh (D)	32,811		370,588		489,597	122.40
Tetanus	30,760		347,426		459,445	153.15
Hepatitis	215,321		2,431,988		3,213,488	2,142.33
Varicella-Zoster	102,534		1,158,088		1,530,316	1,530.32
Rubella	16,405		184,294		243,798	1,218.99
Intravenous -						
Normal	410,137	3,885,715			5,372,009	537.20
Tetanus	61,521	582,857			805,670	3222.68
CMV	246,082	2,331,428			3,22,680	3222.68
Albumen Products:						
Human Albumin	123,041			1,087,315	1,532,941	383.24
Human Albumin	1,435			12,685	17,416	24.88
Plasma Solution					10,443,428	130.54
Plasma Solution					42,886	42.89
	1,400,000	6,800,000	6,300,000	1,100,000	43,200,000	

La Grande Alliance-Restaurant Francaise

Teaching Note

La Grande Alliance case has been used several times to start the second year MBA elective "The Measurement and Management of Product Costs". This is a good case to start an advanced course because it is deceptively simple. The students have a tendency to build exotic allocation procedures that report the cost of each item on the menu. At the end of class, they come to realize that such approaches are inappropriate. The case can be fun to teach, and by using the order forms (See Exhibit TN-1) it creates a good interactive start to a course.

The objectives of this case are to teach students to:

1) think about who is going to use the cost information reported by a cost system and how,

2) consider the use of simple control measures in lieu of sophisticated allocation procedures,

3) be wary of over complex allocation procedures,

4) consider the behavioral implications of cost system design, and

5) understand the difference between <u>pricing</u> and <u>costing</u>.

This teaching note outlines an 80 minute teaching plan.

Suggested Assignments:

This teaching note was written by Professor Robin Cooper as an aid to instructors using La Grande Alliance Restaurant Francais (175-266).

1. Prepare the price list for the dinner menu items in Exhibit 1. For simplification, assume that the luncheon and dinner menus will be similar in terms of food selection. However, total revenues for the week will be estimated as (700 x dinner prices) + (750 x 1/2 dinner prices) and costs as 700 x dinner costs + (750 x 3/4 dinner costs).

2. Be prepared to describe your pricing model in detail.

3. What type of cost accumulation might be appropriate for controlling and for analyzing operations?

Class Discussion

I start by handing out 5 copies of Exhibit TN-1. I pick a mixture of male and female students and ask them to invite one of the people sitting next to them to dinner at La Grande Alliance. I ask them to fill in the form and then determine the cost of their dinner using the prices established during class.

Q1. Please supply me with your price list for the dinner menu.

Prior to class I list out all of the menu items on the board so that I do not have to waste time in class. I get the price lists from three students asking for volunteers with different approaches. I ask each of the students to describe how they determined the selling prices and focus on those students that use cost information to generate prices. I then ask the rest of the students to comment on the various pricing schemes. The students typically demonstrate a strong set of beliefs about what is an appropriate pricing scheme. For example, schemes that have the appetizers being close in cost to the entrees are typically rejected. I point out that the way students think about the pricing schemes illustrates the importance of pricing strategies in the restaurant business. The students' beliefs about what is an acceptable pricing strategy have been developed by their personal experiences.

Q2. If you used costs to help determine prices, how did you determine those costs?

I now document the allocation procedures used by the students who provided price information. If these procedures are neither extremely complex nor simple, I ask for additional procedures from the students, particularly those that are complex or simple. The range of solutions typically varies from simple systems that take food costs and divide by 0.3 to systems that try to allocate labor costs based upon the skill level of the preparer and the time taken. My primary aim at this point in the class is to get the really complex solutions on the board showing how difficult it can be to get "accurate" product costs even in an environment as simple as La Grande Alliance. I do not spend excessive time on these solutions because later in the class we will learn that they are inappropriate. My aim is simply to demonstrate how complex allocation schemes can become if the objective is "accurate" product costs.

Q3. If you allocate labor costs to products based upon preparation time, what type of behavior will this induce?

Here I want to sensitize students to the behavioral consequences of allocation. This issue can be explored in more depth in later cases, in particular Hewlett Packard: Roseville Networks Division (HBS# 9-189-117), Zytec (B & C) (HBS# N9-190-066/7), Tektronix Portable Instruments Division (A-C) (HBS# 9-188-142/3), and Hewlett Packard: Queensferry Telecommunications Division (HBS# 9-191-067).

Students should suggest that allocating labor costs to products based upon preparation time will induce pressure to spend less time on preparing complex meals. I want the students to decide if such pressure is beneficial. The general consensus should be no, weakening arguments in favor of a system that reports "accurate" costs. I close by asking students who is responsible for how the preparation staff spends their time and get the obvious response: the head chef. I ask students what is the best way to control preparation time. Typically, consensus builds around leaving it to the chef. I then ask if the preparation staff becomes too busy should we allow more people to be hired. The student response is typically no. The profitability of the restaurant is determined in large part by keeping head count under control.

Q4. Where did the $15 target come from?

The $15 target sets the price point for the restaurant. It is a signal to the customer about the type of service, and the quality of food they can expect. These characteristics must match the price point if the restaurant is to be successful. Setting the target price and matching the product to the target price is one of the most important decisions that a new restaurant faces. The target price identifies the local competition: For example, a McDonald's is not a competitor to La Grande Alliance.

Q5. What meals did our diners select and how much did they cost?

I get the five students previously selected to identify their dinner choices and the students' pricing of their dinner under each of the three student pricing schemes. This exercise is a good test of how well the schemes achieve the $15 target. Often they are quite far out. Students should favor systems that keep the total cost of the meal relatively closer to $15. A range of $10 to $20 per meal might be considered acceptable, while a range of $10 to $30 might be considered unacceptable. Keeping the range of prices fairly tight is beneficial because it teaches the risk of "cheap" customers and bad surprises.

I ask students to comment on the success of the three pricing schemes and the distribution of orders placed, which quite frequently clump around certain meals. I then show the students Exhibit TN-2 which illustrates the distribution of meals in a typical week at La Grande Alliance. The distribution of actual meals ordered is far from uniform. This makes the pricing decision even more complex. As Exhibit TN-2 shows, using the actual price list for La Grande Alliance, the average meal costs $19 and the modal dinner $17.50. The restaurant is more expensive than planned but still successful.

Q6. What is the product?

I want the students to understand that there are two definitions of the product that we are interested in. One is the market definition, the other is the cost systems definition. This is an important distinction that I visit several times in my course. Students must come to understand that failing to specify the appropriate product for the cost system will create problems. Other cases that illustrate this point in different ways are Mueller Lehmkuhl, and Institutional Furniture.

The market definition of the product is fuzzy and students will spend time trying to understand what is an appropriate definition. Suggestions will include:

- good food
- good experience
- ambiance

I push the students hard to get them to really think about what is the product. Eventually, I get semi-consensus on a <u>chair</u>. La Grande Alliance is really selling the right to sit at a chair and experience the pleasure of dining at a fine restaurant.

This marketing view suggests a simple pricing strategy - a single set price irrespective of order. I let the students discuss this option and discuss a restaurant that I often frequent that allows you to order for multiples of 2 people anything from appetizer, entrees, and desserts for a set price per person. Many students reject this pricing scheme because it risks having too many customers choose the more complex and expensive meals. They want to adjust prices to reflect these factors. This objective leads to another simple pricing strategy, food costs plus a flat fee. However, the prices resulting from such a scheme are considered unacceptable to many because the distribution of prices between high and low cost meals does not match the students' experience. Another alternative is food price divided by some factor. Some students reject the above approaches because they ignore the complexity of preparation. These students want to develop schemes that include allocation procedures based upon the difficulty of preparation.

The next issue discussed is how to distribute the profit between the various courses. The profit margin per course that most students select reflects their personal experience. Appetizers should be less expensive than entrees and soups should be the cheapest of all. I make sure that students recognize their beliefs are drawn by their personal experiences and not some fundamental economic perspective.

The cost systems for the first few alternatives are relatively simple. In the first case you do not need a cost system and in the second only raw material costs need be tracked. However, for more pricing schemes that rely at least partially on costs a more complex allocation scheme will be required. As the suggested pricing schemes become more complex, I get the students to question the validity of cost plus pricing. I bring this issue to the forefront by asking the next question.

Q7. Is cost plus pricing appropriate?

This question causes a lot of discussion and often confusion. Some students want to use market prices established by looking at competitors' menus and then making intuitive adjustments for the skill of the chef and the different price points of the restaurant; others stick to cost plus schemes. I push students to consider where market prices come from and do they represent cost plus pricing, performed by somebody else. Students generally came to accept market based pricing as the appropriate approach. However, many remain confused about the role of cost information in setting market prices. Since this is an early case in the course I do not worry that many students remain confused. Later in the course, the role of market versus cost level pricing should be discussed in more detail.

Q8. What is the cost structure of La Grande Alliance?

I get the students to discuss the cost structure of the restaurant in terms of fixed and variable costs. These concepts are also illustrated in the Bridgeton Industries case (HBS# N9-190-085). A consensus is usually reached that only food costs are variable; all other costs are fixed. There is occasionally some dispute about labor costs being semi-variable but students can be pushed to understand that as long as the restaurant is successful, the labor levels will remain the same, i.e. fixed. I point out that these fixed costs create capacity: effectively, they enable the restaurant to serve the number of meals identified in the budget. Thus, in practice, given a level of success, only food costs vary, all other costs are fixed. Students should be asked to discuss the significance of this observation.

Students that believe in a contribution approach will suggest using raw material as the only cost that matters. The fixed costs can be ignored. I use this observation to discuss briefly the theory of constraints (TOC) that Eli Goldratt has developed. I write the TOC equation on the board:

Profit = {Revenue - Raw Material} - Operating expenses

and suggest that only costs that vary need be considered. This observation suggests a very simple raw material tracking system. However, it does not suggest that prices and food costs be directly proportional. The TOC solution suggests optimizing revenue minus raw material. Operating expenses, i.e., labor and overhead, can be ignored since they are fixed. Many students disagree with this approach. They feel that having individual product costs is critical to managing the restaurant. I want this concern to surface because it shows that students have come to see cost information as a security blanket. I try to shake students loose from this view by asking them to describe the conditions under which they would allow operating expenses at La Grande Alliance to change. Most agree that they would not. This helps them realize how you cannot manage cost at the individual product level in this environment.

Q9. If operating expenses are fixed is it sensible to allocate them to products?

The obvious answer is no. This is a good setup for the Bridgeton Industries Case where the rationale behind the allocation of fixed costs is explored in depth. If already taught, Bridgeton will help the students understand that in some environments allocation makes sense but not in others. The difference in the two cases is the ability to change the level of overhead expenditures. In La Grande Alliance there is little ability to change overhead while in Bridgeton there is a lot.

Q10. For what purpose do we want to use cost information at La Grande Alliance?

This question should provide the three major uses of cost information in firms:

1. Product costing

2. Cost control

3. People control

The students have already looked at product costing and decided that there is little value to the use of cost information at La Grande Alliance. They have not fully considered its use for cost and people control.

Q11. Do we need accurate meal costs for cost control?

Cost control: the only costs that need to be controlled are the variable ones, which in La Grande Alliance are raw material costs. These costs are the province of the chef. If the chef keeps food costs at 30% of revenue then there is no need to worry about expenditures or food. The percentage of food costs to revenue is thus a simple but critical control parameter at La Grande Alliance. If the chef keeps food costs within a tight range centered on 30%, and the quality of the food is high, then as long as the revenues are there, so are the profits.

People control: There is no need to try and control people at La Grande Alliance via a cost system. As noted earlier, the chef is responsible for the kitchen. The decision how many people to hire has already been made. Again, if the chef can deliver food of the appropriate quality and quantity while maintaining the desired 30% ratio, then that is all that matters. No other monitoring is necessary. The same goes for the serving people. The number of servers is set by management; the task of the maitre'd is to ensure that the desired quality of service is met. It is easier and more effective to measure the quality of service by talking to customers and observing how the servers operate than by any cost allocation procedure.   Thus, in this environment, there is little benefit in developing a sophisticated cost system. The restaurant is small and can easily be managed using simple control procedures without worrying about what an individual meal costs.

I point out that the critical decisions that control cost and determines the success of the restaurant have already been made. These decision are:

1. $15 price point

2. its location etc.

3. the appropriate staffing levels

4. the menu

The budget determines the profitability of the restaurant assuming the desired volume is achieved. Pricing should be used to control the mix of meals ordered so that the capacity of the food preparers is used to maximum gain. If a complex meal is ordered too frequently, the capacity of the food preparation staff will be exceeded. The restaurant can control this problem initially by getting the serving staff to recommend different meals or as a last resort by strategically running out of the meal. When a new menu is published, prices for the meal can be modified to reduce demand for the complex meal to acceptable levels.

Summary

The La Grande Alliance case provides a good example of an environment where cost systems play virtually no role in the management of the firm. The three major tasks associated with cost systems--product costing, cost control, and people control--can all be achieved using simple systems that do not require cost allocations. The primary lessons the students should gain from class are:

1. Do not build complex allocation schemes until you know they are appropriate.

2. Think about how cost information will be used before designing a cost system.

3. Think of ways to control costs other than allocation.

4. Consider the behavioral implications of any system you design.

The La Grande Alliance case provides an interesting vehicle to begin a course on product costing by demonstrating that not all firms require exotic cost systems.

EXHIBIT TN-1

LA GRANDE ALLIANCE TEACHING NOTE

ORDER SHEET

	Person 1	$	Person 2	$
APPETIZER:				
SOUP:				
ENTREE:				
DESSERT:				
TOTAL:				
GRAND TOTAL:				

Please order for two.

Assumption of price insensitivity does not warrant unrealistic order patterns: Be reasonable.

The sommelier will choose an appropriate wine –

Exhibit TN-2   La Grande Alliance Distribution of Meals - Typical Week

	ORDERED	PRICE	REVENUE
Appetizers			
Artichoke hearts	123	$ 3.50	$ 430.50
Quiche lorraine	82	3.00	246.00
Escargots	249	5.50	1369.50
Oyster cocktail	123	5.00	615.00
Pate	123	5.00	615.00
	700		6030.00
Soups			
Consomme	62	1.00	62.00
Onion soup	432	2.00	864.00
Vichyssoise	123	1.50	184.50
	617		1110.50
Entrees			
Sole	62	6.50	403.00
Crab	83	10.50	871.50
Coquilles St. Jacques	41	9.50	389.50
Poulet	20	7.50	150.00
Duckling	185	9.50	1738.50
Veal	83	13.50	1120.50
Lamb	62	15.00	930.00
Tournedos	83	14.00	1162.00
Roast beef	83	9.50	788.50
	700		7533.50
Dessert			
Strawberries	206	2.50	515.50
Creme	83	2.00	166.00
Pastry	123	2.00	246.00
Bananas	288	2.50	720.00
	700		1647.00

weeks in month 13,341.00
dinners $57,366.30   x 4.3

Average dinner cost - $19.00

Most frequently served:

Escargots $ 5.50
Duckling   9.50
Bananas   2.50
          $17.50

Ingersoll Milling Machine Company
Teaching Note

The Ingersoll Milling Machine Company provides an opportunity to discuss advanced manufacturing technology and the cost accounting issues that arise with highly automated equipment. In practice, however, the case can be focused more on issues of project or life cycle costing since the accounting for parts machined in the FMS center represents a relatively small fraction of the total manufacturing costs of a machine. If possible, it would be desirable to have the class see a short video of an FMS so that they can have a better sense of what an FMS is and how it works.

Possible Assignment Questions

1. What changes has IMM made in its indirect cost allocation method? Why were the changes made?

2. What alternatives should IMM consider for costing products through the FMS facility?

3. Should IMM change its method for assigning costs to products? What are the pros and cons for such a change?

4. What factors are most critical to controlling the cost of a product at IMM?

Class Discussion

I start the class by asking about the nature of the business IMM is in. The principal points are that only a relatively few machines are produced each year (30-50) and each machine is unique, though there are many commonalities of sub-components and sub-assemblies across

This teaching note was prepared by Professor Robert S. Kaplan as an aid to instructors in the classroom use of the case, Ingersoll Milling Machine Company, 9-186-189.

machines. The machines are quite complex and can achieve some remarkable precision in machining. When we visited the IMM facility, an engineer pressed his thumb firmly on the table and told us that one of the transfer lines being built for a U.S. automobile manufacturer had to achieve tolerances that were finer than the thickness of the oil left on the table by his thumb impression.

The competitive environment consists of 6 other manufacturers, three each in production machines (such as transfer lines) and three in special machines. IMM is the only manufacturer in both of these markets.

At this point, it is good to ask why did IMM implement FMS in its factory? Also, how was the investment justified? As stated in the case, the FMS did not go through a formal financial analysis. While not a necessary feature of this case, the instructor might wish to use this point to initiate a short discussion of whether financial analysis is at all appropriate for deciding about investing in this technology. There are many people who argue that payback, discounted cash flow, and ROI considerations are not appropriate for deciding whether to acquire FMS technology.[2]

IMM decided to invest in the FMS as a commitment to this advanced technology. It could be hard for IMM to sell FMS's to others if it could not demonstrate the value in its own production operations. While seemingly an obvious point, no U.S. machine tool manufacturer used one of its own FMS's until Cincinnati Milacron installed one in 1983. This inattention to its own manufacturing processes stands in sharp contrast to the experience of Japanese machine tool producers who had been experimenting with FMS's since the late 1960s.[3]

In addition, IMM hoped to learn more about the value and procedures of FMS technology by having an in-house production activity. Such learning-by-doing provides an excellent mechanism for feedback to product design, as well as actual experiences to share with existing and potential customers (recall that IMM has a consulting engineering division as well). If one really wants to beat up on declining U.S. competitiveness in the machine tool industry, you can mention that the machines came from IMM's German subsidiary (Bohle) and from a Japanese company.

The class needs to understand the time line for the machine development, manufacturing, and delivery process. This type of manufacturing is very different from turning out hundreds of products each hour.

Marketing and proposal activity:	6 month - 1 year
Engineering design/parts analysis:	3-4 months
Procurement:	2 months
Further engineering:	2 months
(routings, fixtures, orientation, operations, programming)	
Machining	6 months

---

2. Background reading for this discussion could include Robert S. Kaplan, "Must CIM be justified by faith alone?" Harvard Business Review (March-April 1986) plus references in that paper.

3. For one example, see R. Jaikumar's case Hitachi Seiki (A) (#9-686-104). For additional information on the contrast between U.S. and Japanese users of FMS, see R. Jaikumar, "Post-industrial manufacturing," Harvard Business Review (November-December 1986).

Fabrication	3-4 months
Machining	3-4 months
Assembly and Test (A&T)	6 months

During A&T, problems with the machined parts or the design could lead to an ENOC (Engineering Notice of Change) with the part returned back to machining. After A&T, the machine would be dis- assembled, shipped to the customer, and reassembled and tested at the customer's factory.

The importance of the early engineering design stages could be emphasized by showing Exhibit TN-1. Most of the costs of the machine are committed very early in the production cycle. For example, 90 to 95% of the costs could be determined by the time only 3% of the total costs have been incurred.

What is the role of the FMS? The FMS is used for light machining. One should repeat the neat statistic that 25,000 parts are machined in the FMS each year, 70% in batch sizes of one; 50% of the parts will never be produced again. Very few U.S. manufacturers (perhaps no other as of 1987) use their FMS installations this flexibly (see discussion in Jaikumar article referenced in footnote 2). The FMS permits multiple operations to be performed on the same part without having to refixture it. The FMS also achieves virtually instantaneous tool changeover time from one operation to the next (zero set-up time).

Cost System

Having set the stage, we can finally turn to a discussion of the existing cost system. This is truly a job costing system. With only 30 to 50 total products produced per year, it is not difficult to collect accurate product costs. Engineering and Numeric Control programming costs are collected by sub-assembly. The discussion in the case indicates that these should be considered a "joint cost" for the individual parts in a sub-assembly. Overhead costs in the engineering department are assigned based on engineering direct labor dollars.

Machining costs, in contrast, are collected for individual parts. Overhead is assigned based on Direct Labor dollars, with a separate overhead rate for each manufacturing process. It is worth highlighting the history of the overhead allocation process. Prior to 1978, a single burden rate (250% in the 1970s) was used for the entire machining activity. During 1978-80, massive new investment was made but not uniformly throughout the factory. Therefore, IMM went to a system of 40 different overhead rates, one for each cost center. This level of detail, however, proved confusing to cost estimators and also led to peculiar decisions on part routing; for example, avoiding newly installed machines to run parts on "low cost," old technology equipment. By 1985, IMM had 13 different production overhead rates plus 2 additional rates to allocate materials overhead based on direct material $. If students have not seen a materials overhead burden rate before, this feature could be discussed for several minutes.

At this time, the class can turn to the intended focus of the case: how to cost parts that are machined in an FMS environment. The discussion can be initiated by a question such as, "What do you think about continuing to use a direct labor based cost system in the FMS facility?" Try to get the class to suggest what the options are; for example:

Stay with direct labor
Number of operations performed at the FMS
Machine hours
Elapsed time on the FMS.

Direct labor could still be used in the FMS because one operator was still assigned to each of the machines. It is interesting how mundane are the operations that still needed to be performed by the operator; cleaning burrs off the drilling or cutting tool and assuring that the lubricant jet was aimed correctly at the machined surface. It is unlikely that operators will continue to be needed for these tasks several months or a year later. Thus, as IMM gets more experience with its FMS machines, direct labor will cease to correlate well with work being performed.

When students suggest the machine hours or elapsed time measures, you should pin them down to be more specific about how they would measure these times. Some possibilities include:

Start Time	Stop Time
Leave WIP	Re-enter WIP
Leave Set-up Station	Return to Set-up Station
Placed on Input Station	Return to Pick-up Station
Start of machining	End of machining

With the second choice, parts where the AGV makes a long run (say to the last machine) will receive more costs than parts delivered to the closest machine. With the latter two procedures, the cost of the AGV must be spread across all jobs rather than traced directly to each job. With the third option, parts that must wait before the machine grabs them and starts to machine them will cost more than parts which get processed as soon as they arrive at the input station. While one can argue that parts should not be charged for waiting time, they are occupying the input station and hence blocking other jobs from being queued up. The main objective should be to highlight that choosing a machine hours basis does not lead to an obvious choice of how to measure machine hours (after all, the AGV is just as much a machine as the Bohle machines).

At some suitable point, a student (or the instructor) should note that resolving this issue is not critical for IMM. After all, all of light machining represents only $5 million out of annual expenditures of $100 million. Therefore, even the most accurate FMS costing procedure will not lead to major shifts in costs among the 30-50 products produced each year. Offsetting this compelling argument may be two factors: first, the fraction of FMS machining may increase over time; and, second, IMM may wish to work out solutions that its customers can use, for whom FMS machining may be a much higher fraction of total manufacturing costs.

I would close by pointing out that the real cost issue at IMM is life cycle or project costing. It is vitally important for IMM to predict and manage costs over the 18 month design-build-test cycle. IMM engineers must understand the cost consequences of their bidding and design decisions. The move to very detailed cost center burden rates failed because it confused the bidding process- one of the key success factors for the organization.

The analogy can be made to software companies (like Lotus and Microsoft) or to high-tech companies with short product life cycles. In these situations, it is more important to measure profit over the life of the product or the project than to get procedures for allocating costs to stages along the production process.

EXHIBIT TN-1

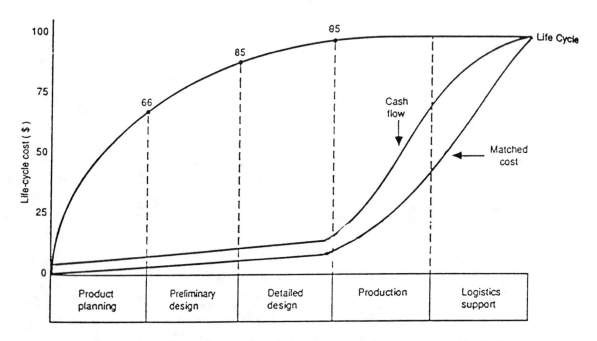

Source: *Adapted from Benjamin S. Blanchard,* Design and Manage to Life-Cycle Cost. *Portland, OR: M/A Press, 1978.*

The Two-Stage Process:
Resources, Cost Centers, and Products

The cases in Chapter 2 present students with a variety of settings that illustrate different aspects of choices in cost systems design. The cases all build on the two-stage framework where support costs are accumulated in support centers, allocated to production cost centers in the first-stage of the process, and then allocated from production cost centers to products in the second-stage. The cases discuss selection of the first-stage cost drivers, the number of production cost centers, and the second-stage cost drivers.

Seligram, Inc.: ETO is an excellent case with which to start this sequence. Seligram can be used to introduce the two-stage process in a simple setting. Its primary focus is to illustrate why multiple cost centers are generally needed in a factory, and the importance of not aggregating dissimilar production processes within the same cost center. It also provides an introduction to why multiple second-stage drivers can be useful, as machine hours replaces labor hours in one newly-defined cost center.

Digital Communications, Inc.: EDD introduces a special topic, the reciprocal allocation of service department costs. This reallocation of costs from one support center to another occurs at the top (resource) level of the two-stage process, before support (or service) department costs are allocated down to production cost centers. Digital Communications also extends the second stage drivers to include machine hours and materials purchases in addition to labor hours.

The *Mayers Tap, Inc.* series covers two important topics. The old cost system in Mayers Tap had only one cost center for two quite different plants. The (A) case provides a description of the company and its old cost system. The (B) case describes a revised cost system for the company in which a separate cost center is defined for each machine class. The task for the students is to choose the appropriate first stage driver for each budgetary line item (support expense category) to allocate resource costs to the 31 machine centers. Students can work individually, or in groups, with a computer program that shows the consequences of their decisions on the burden rates in each machine center. A video tape is also available to give students a guided tour of the two Mayers plants. The (C) case uses the first-stage drivers actually implemented by the company and allows students to explore the consequences on reported product costs of using one, two, or 31 cost centers. The case illustrates how decisions on the number of cost centers can have a significant impact on the reported profitability of products.

Fisher Technologies focuses intensively on the choice of second-stage drivers. The company has recently introduced automated machinery and wants to explore the consequences of shifting from labor to machine hours to assign costs from cost centers to products. This case also uses a computer model to allow students to forecast what the new burden rates and product costs would be if the company shifts from labor to machine hours. The case can be difficult for the students since they must estimate the machine hours from data available in the case. The case illustrates the procedures a company might follow and issues that must be solved when contemplating a switch from labor to machine hour second-stage drivers.

Mueller-Lehmkuhl is a fun case that can be taught in several places in the course. It is a good candidate for the opening case in the course, since it demonstrates vividly the connection between cost systems design and strategy. It could also be used as the opening case in this section, but then more time must be spent to explicate the two-stage procedure, and less time is available to discuss the design problems with the system and their strategic consequences. The main problem with the Mueller system is that not all of the outputs are recognized by the system; in particular the costs of producing attaching machines and supplying service to them are allocated to the fasteners, leading to considerable and systematic distortion of the fastener costs. We placed the case at the end of this section so that students' familiarity with properties of the two-stage process (as developed in Mayers Tap (B)), can be used to unbundle some of the costs that are being allocated to fasteners. We have used this case very successfully in executive programs because it is not too mechanical and illustrates well (particularly with exhibits the instructor can show at the end of the class) the link between cost system design and company strategy.

The first reading at the end of the chapter, "The Two-Stage Procedure in Cost Accounting: Part One," gives an in-depth treatment of the rationale and properties of the two-stage procedure. This reading can be assigned with Seligram ETO or Mayers Tap (B) for students (and instructors) who wish to explore in more depth the issues that arise in choosing the number of cost centers and second-stage cost drivers. "When Should You Use Machine-Hour Costing?" has been included to complement Fisher Technologies and likely should be assigned with that case to help students understand the calculations they are asked to perform.

Seligram, Inc.: Electronic Testing Operations

Teaching Note

The Seligram, Inc.: Electronic Testing Operations case was designed to be taught in the first year control course at the Harvard Business School. It has also been taught successfully in the second year elective "The Measurement and Management of Product Costs."

The case introduces students to three major issues:

1) to demonstrate how cost systems become obsolete over time. In the case of ETO it is technological change that causes the obsolescence.

2) to demonstrate how cost systems can induce subtle and not so subtle shifts in the strategy of the firm. In particular, for ETO how certain types of business are made to look inappropriately attractive or unattractive.

3) to demonstrate the role that the two-stage allocation procedure, and in particular, cost centers and second stage allocation bases play in reporting product costs.

This teaching note outlines an 80-minute teaching plan for an introductory course.

Suggested Assignment Questions

1. What caused the existing system at ETO to fail?
2. Calculate the reported costs of the five components described in

   a. The existing system.
   b. The system proposed by the accounting manager.
   c. The system proposed by the consultant.

This teaching note was written by Professor Robin Cooper and Chris Ittner, Doctoral Student, as an aid to instructors using Seligram, Inc.: Electronic Testing Operations (189-084).

3.   Which system is preferable? Why?

4.   Would you recommend any changes to the system you prefer? Why?

5.   Would you treat the new machine as a separate cost center or as part of the main test room?

Class Discussion

Q1. What is ETO's competitive situation?

The discussion should initially focus on ETO and its competitive environment. ETO tests electronic components. These components are supplied by its customers. ETO therefore has no direct material costs, only direct labor and overhead. Testing processes are becoming more complicated and require increasing more expensive and less labor intensive equipment. In addition, customers are moving to Just-in-Time production which leads to smaller more frequent lots. However, statistical quality control procedures removes the need to test every lot.

Q2. Describe ETO's existing cost system.

The existing cost system is very simple. It contains only one cost center (the entire facility). All overhead is collected into a single cost pool and the total overhead cost is divided by the total number of direct labor dollars consumed to give a single direct labor dollar burden rate. To help the students visualize this system and to set the stage for the more complex systems to come, I would draw the simple two stage allocation procedure diagram for this system (see left hand side of Exhibit TN1).[1]

Q3. How is the 145% burden rate calculated?

I would extend the two stage diagram to show the calculations in case Exhibit 2 (see Exhibit right hand side of TN1). I believe it is important to repeat this calculation of product costing. Students will have to repeat variations of this calculation for each system they design.

Drawing the two-stage allocation procedure diagrams at this time is important. The procedure underlies most modern cost systems. It will help students in latter cases in the course if they develop from the ETO case an in-depth understanding of the two-stage procedure. This understanding and the ability to draw two-stage diagrams will help prepare them for the more advanced cases (such as the Mayers Tap Inc. series, Mueller-Lehmkuhl, and Siemens: Electric Motor Works (A).

Q4. Why does the company use 145% and not the exact number?

---

1. The two-stage procedure is described at length in Robin Cooper's two Journal of Cost Management articles titled **The Two Stage Procedure in Cost Accounting: Parts One and Two**. These articles can be used as student reading to support this case and others in an introductory course.

Once the 145% burden rates has been "proved", a short discussion on the value of rounding is appropriate. Rounding is undertaken to 1) simplify the calculations and 2) acknowledge the softness of the numbers. Rounding make it impossible to "reverse", i.e., take the burden rate and multiply the direct labor hours), the cost system and get the budget exactly.

Q5. What are the reported costs of the 5 products listed in Exhibit 4?

The product costs reported by the existing system for the five components listed in case Exhibit 4 can be computed by simply multiply the direct labor content of the products by 1.45 and adding the result to the labor cost. This gives:

ONE CENTER SYSTEM

PRODUCT	DIRECT LABOR DOLLARS	OVERHEAD @ 145%	TOTAL
ICA	917	1330	2247
ICB	2051	2974	5025
CAPACITOR	1094	1586	2680
AMPLIFIER	525	761	1286
DIODE	519	753	1272

Q6. What is wrong with the existing system?

The case describes several changes to the production economics that are symptoms of obsolescence (direct labor hours per lot declining, smaller lots, more complex technology, and higher support functions). It does not, however, explain why these changes cause obsolescence. It is important that the students be made to identify why the existing cost system is failing and how these changes are aggravating that failure.

The major flaw in the existing system is that **it assumes that all products consume direct labor and overhead in the same proportion**. This assumption is designed into the cost system by the use of only one cost pool and direct labor dollars as the second stage allocation base.

This assumption is flawed. Some products are produced on simple labor intensive equipments while others require very expensive automated equipment. Therefore, it is extremely unlikely that all products consume direct labor and overhead in the same proportion. The symptoms of obsolescence identified in the case all indicate that overhead and labor are consumed not only in differing proportions but also that the difference is increasing.

Q7. Why did they implement the existing system in the first place?

The assumption that all products consume overhead and direct labor in the same proportion was probably quite accurate when the facility was first opened. All of the testing was labor intensive and undertaken on simple machines. While some products probably consumed more overhead per direct labor hours than others the variations probably were not that great.

However, over the years, the introduction of new technologies and testing equipment not only changed the ratio of direct labor to overhead consumption, it has also increased the variation across products of that ratio. For example, a family of parts that requires very expensive automated testing equipment consumes overhead in a very different proportion to a family that is manually tested on very simple machines. The existing cost system cannot capture the economics of this product diversity. The system has slowly become obsolete. Management has become aware of the obsolescence primarily because of customer complaints. While in the classroom it is easy to see what is going on, it is important for students to understand that in practice it can be very difficult to detect gradual changes.

Q8. What types of products will be under and overcosted by the existing system?[2]

The inability of the existing system to capture the relationship between the consumption of labor and overhead for the different types of product can be used to demonstrate the subtle and not so subtle role that cost systems play in the enactment of the chosen strategy of the firm. The following two simple examples, can be used to explain this role:

Example 1

Suppose ETO only tested two types of components, one component required very extensive testing while the other one required very little testing. The overhead consumed by each test irrespective of duration was identical. Which component would the existing cost system favor? The answer is of course the one that required very short testing, because the cost system averages the costs of the two testing procedures. Since the short procedure consumes more overhead per direct labor hour than the labor intensive testing, it is undercosted. In contrast, the long procedure is overcosted.

Now assume a dynamic model. What will happen to the product mix? Assuming ETO's customers shop around, they should begin to send more short duration business to ETO and insource or find someone else to undertake the long duration business. ETO will gradually become a short duration overhead intensive testing facility causing the hours per lot to decrease.

Example 2

Suppose ETO only tested two types of components, one component required very expensive automated testing machinery while the other one required very inexpensive equipment. The time taken for each test is the same. Which component would the existing cost system favor? The answer is of course the one that required very expensive equipment, because the cost system averages the costs of the two testing procedures. Since the capital intensive procedure consumes more overhead per direct labor hour than the labor intensive one, it is undercosted. In contrast, the manual intensive procedure is overcosted.

Now assume a dynamic model. What will happen to the product mix? Assuming ETO's customers shop around, they should begin to send more capital intensive business to ETO and insource or find someone else to undertake the manually intensive business. ETO will gradually become a capital intensive (overhead intensive) testing facility.

---

2. Instructors in introductory courses should consider taking this detour if they are also teaching Mueller Lehmkuhl and\or Siemens Electric Motor Works(A)

To help explain these Examples, the instructor can either develop numerical examples, or use the illustrations shown in Exhibit TN2 and TN3. These two examples are important because the effect of the cost system on product mix (if it is occurring) reinforces changes that are expected in the future (moves to more automated complex testing procedures), management expected such a shift and might have been less sensitive to the distortions in strategy caused by the cost system.

Q9. How did ETO propose redesigning the existing cost system to overcome its failings?

There are two techniques that ETO uses to improve its cost system. The first is to increase the number of cost centers, the other is to change the second stage allocation base. These two techniques are effectively independent (Though in practice the number of cost centers can be used to reduce the number of different types of second stage allocation base required).

Increasing the number of cost centers enable the cost system to capture differences in the way overhead is consumed in different parts of the production process. For example, the three center system differentiates between the electronic and mechanical testing rooms. The cost system still assumes, however, that **all products in each center consume overhead in the same proportion as the allocation base.** Increasing the number of cost centers is like adding terms to a regression equation. It increases the explanatory power.

Changing the second stage allocation base, allows the system to better capture the consumption of overhead by individual products. In the electronic test room, direct labor hours have ceased to be a good estimate of the effort expended on the testing process. The duration of the test, however, according to management, better reflects the consumption of overhead.

Q10. What is the structure of the cost system suggested by the center's accounting manager?

A student should be asked to draw the two-stage diagram for the two center system (see Exhibit TN4a). The next step is to fill in the numbers. These are given in Case Exhibit 3. The two-stage version numbers are shown in TN4b. The burden rate for the two centers, administration and technical and other are 20% per direct labor dollar and $80 per machine hour respectively.

Q11. What are the reported costs of the 5 products listed in Exhibit 4 using this cost system?

The product costs reported by the two center system for the five components listed in case Exhibit 4 can be computed by 1) multiplying the machine hours consumed by each product in the test room by $80.00 per hours, 2) by multiplying the direct labor content of the products by 0.20 and 3) adding the results to the labor cost. This gives:

TWO CENTER SYSTEM

PRODUCT	DIRECT LABOR DOLLARS $	OVERHEAD (M/C HOURS) $	(HRS)	OVERHEAD (DL $) $	TOTAL
ICA	917	1480	(18.5)	183	2580
ICB	2051	3200	(40.0)	410	5661
CAPACITOR	1094	600	(7.5)	219	1913

AMPLIFIER	525	400	(5.0)	105	1030
DIODE	519	960	(12.0)	104	1583

Q12. What insights are provided by the new cost system that were not provided by the one center system?

ICA, ICB and the diode all consume a relatively large number of machine hours per direct labor dollar compared to the capacitor and the amplifier (ratio of direct labor dollars per machine hour for the five products are 50, 51, 146, 105 and 43 respectively). Therefore, switching to machine hours in the test room causes more costs to be allocated to these products. Their reported costs therefore go up. The reports costs of the other two products in contrast decrease, since they consume a relatively low number off direct labor hour machine hour.[3]

Q13. What is the structure of the cost system suggested by the consultant?

A student should be asked to draw the two-stage diagram for the three center system (see Exhibit TN5a). The next step is to fill in the numbers. The machine hour data required to calculate the burden rates are given case Exhibits 3 and 4. The three stage version numbers are shown in Exhibit TN5b. The three burden rates are 20% on direct labor hours, $63.73 per main test room machine hour and $113.29 per mechanical test room machine hour.

Q14. What are the reported costs of the 5 products listed in Exhibit 4 using this cost system?

The product costs reported by the two center system for the five components listed in Case Exhibit 4 can be computed by 1) multiplying the machine hours consumed by each product in the test room by $80.00 per hour, 2) by multiplying the direct labor content of the products 0.21 and 3) adding the results to the labor cost. This gives:

Three Center System

Product	Direct Labor Dollars $	Overhead – (M/C Hours) $	Main (M/C Hours) (HRS)	Overhead – (M/C Hours) $	Mech (M/C Hours) (HRS)	Overhead (DL $) $	Total
ICA	917	535	8.5	1130	10.0	183	2765
ICB	2051	882	14.0	2938	26.0	410	6281
CAPACITOR	1094	184	3.0	509	4.5	219	2011
AMPLIFIER	525	252	4.0	113	1.0	105	995
DIODE	519	441	7.0	565	5.0	104	1629

Q15. What insights are provided by this cost system that were not provided by the other two?

1) The mechanical burden rate is $110 per machine hour compared to $65 for the main test room. Therefore, components that consume relatively more mechanical machine hours compared to main machine hours will have higher reported product costs. These are ICA, ICB, capacitor and the diode.

---

3. Since we are only looking at a subset of the product, the sum of overhead costs for the five products will vary from system to system. If we were working with all products, the total overhead, would of course be constant.

2) For some products, the two corrections reinforce each other while for others they counteract. For example, the reported cost of ICB goes up 13% with the introduction of the second cost center and up an additional 10% with the introduction of the third center. In contrast, the reported cost of the amplifier goes down with the introduction of the second center and up with the introduction of the third one. Some students (hopefully) will have created the following table:

RATIOS OF REPORTED COSTS

PRODUCT	TWO CENTER / ONE CENTER	THREE CENTER / TWO CENTER	THREE CENTER / ONE CENTER
ICA	1.15	1.07	1.23
ICB	1.13	1.10	1.24
CAPACITOR	0.71	1.05	0.75
AMPLIFIER	0.80	0.97	0.78
DIODE	1.24	1.03	1.28
ABSOLUTE CHANGE	.168	.046	.203

3) The magnitude of the overall changes decreases as the number of centers increases. While this decrease is dependent upon the order in which cost centers are introduced. If the system designer understands the economics of production he or she should be able to identify where adding on additional cost centers will have the greatest effect. This trend of reducing effects of each incremental cost center, therefore, shows the designer's skill.

Q16. Are these new reported costs more accurate than the old ones?

The three systems report different costs for each product. It is only natural to question which is the more accurate system. Intuitively, the three center system is the more accurate. However, what does accurate mean in this context?

To give meaning to the term accuracy we have to know the "true" costs and compare them to reported costs. Consequently, this discussion rapidly leads to the question "Are true product costs observable?" Two perspectives typically arise when addressing this question. The first says that given the advent of powerful, low costs information systems, true products can be captured. The second says that true costs can never be determined but that, given a decision context, cost systems can provide reasonably accurate information to aid in decision making.

True product costs are often unobservable for three reasons:

1) There may be no relationship between the consumption of inputs and the products produced.

2) The cost of measurement may be prohibitive. For example, the wear on a cutting tool can be measured using a laser. However, the cost of undertaking this measurement far outweighs the benefit.

3) The relationship between costs and the product may be unobservable For instance, repair and maintenance expenses arise because products are run on a machine. The relationship

between repair and maintenance expenses and particular products cannot be observed, even though it is known that the relationship exists.

Levels or product cost accuracy can be depicted by a target (see Exhibit TN6). "True" product costs are represented by the bull's eye. With most traditional cost systems, the level of accuracy is somewhere on the fringes of the target. As the system is refined to give greater and greater accuracy, it moves closer and closer to the "true" cost. The selection of an optimum cost system is based on tradeoffs between increased accuracy and the cost of system redesign.

Q18. Should the new machine be a separate cost center?

We can use the data provided in case Exhibit 5 to determine the burden rate of the machine. The burden rate for the first year will be much higher than for the Nth year because of start-up costs and depreciation.

	Burden	Variable	Depreciation	Other	Total
1st year	Machine costs	$100,000	$500,000	$225,000	$ 825,000
	Machine hours	400 hours			
	Burden rate\ machine hour	$250	$ 1,250	$562.50	$2,062.50
N^{th}	Machine costs	100,000	120,000[4]	150,000	$ 370,000
	Machine hours	2,400			
	Burden rate\ machine hours	41.67	$ 50	$ 62.50	$ 154.17

If the new machine is not treated as a separate cost center then the new burden rates for the main test room become:

Main Test Room Burden Rates With Machine Included

	Variable	Depreciation	Other	Total
First year				
Existing costs	887,379	88,779	1,126,958	2,103,116
machine costs	100,000	500,000	225,000	825,000
	987,379	588,779	1,351,958	2,928,116
Machine hours		33,000 + 400		
Burden rate\ machine hour	$ 29.56	$ 17.63	$ 40.48	$ 87.67
Nth year	887,379	88,779	1,126,958	2,103,116
Existing costs	100,000	125,000	150,000	375,000
	987,379	203,779	1,276,958	2,478,116
Machine hours		33,000 + 2,400		

---

4. Approximate depreciation charge for year 6.

Burden rate\ machine hour	$ 27.89	$ 8.49	$ 36.07	$ 70.03

As can be seen, failing to treat the new machine as a separate cost center seriously distorts the burden rates.

Q19. How do you know when you have enough cost centers?

Judgment and modelling are two approaches commonly used to determine the "correct" number of cost centers. Judgment may entail performing a periodic "reality" check to determine if the current method of collecting and allocating costs at least makes intuitive sense. Modelling can begin by either moving gradually towards complexity until the optimum is found or by designating as many cost centers as possible and then deleting them. Each method attempts to reach a point where the sum of the cost of errors from product cost distortion, and the cost of measurement is minimized.

The new machine burden rate of $2,062 per hour for the first year is very different for the $65 per hour of the main test center. Students should question the validity of including the start up costs and using the number of low hours for the first year to generate burden rates and hence product costs. They should suggest determining the burden rates for the 2nd or subsequent years.

Using the double declining balance depreciation method on the new machine creates a problem because the depreciation expense varies so dramatically from year to year.

For simplicity, if we use 1/8 of the cost of the machine to give an average picture we get a machine burden rate of $156/machine hour. This is sufficiently different from the main test room rate of $63/machine hour to require the machine being treated as a separate cost center. If students want to think about just variable costs they can compute the variable burden rate these are $27 for the main room under the three center system and without the machine and $30 (29-56) and $250 and $42 for the first and subsequent years for the machine. These rates also suggest that it should be treated as a separate center.

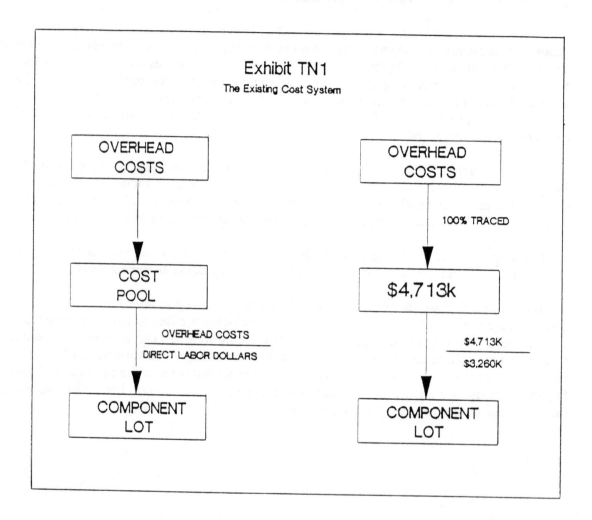

Exhibit TN1

The Existing Cost System

Exhibit TN3

The Impact of Cost System Averaging on the Mix of Business

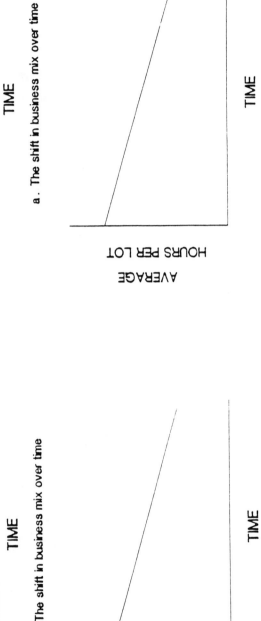

HIGH TECHNOLOGY CONTENT PROCESS

LOW TECHNOLOGY CONTENT PROCESS

% OF BUSINESS

TIME

a. The shift in business mix over time

AVERAGE HOURS PER LOT

TIME

b. The decrease in average hours per lot over time

Exhibit TN2

The Impact of Cost System Averaging on the Mix of Business

LOW LABOR CONTENT PROCESS

HIGH LABOR CONTENT PROCESS

% OF BUSINESS

TIME

a. The shift in business mix over time

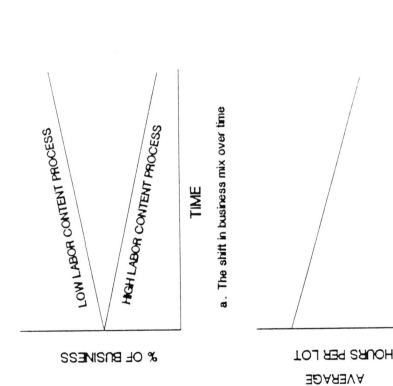

AVERAGE HOURS PER LOT

TIME

b. The decrease in average hours per lot over time

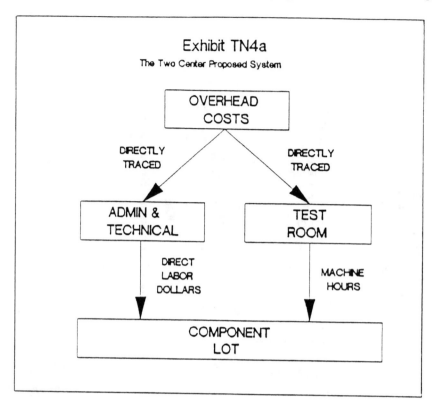

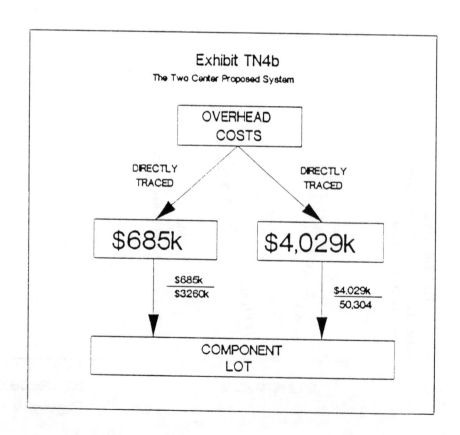

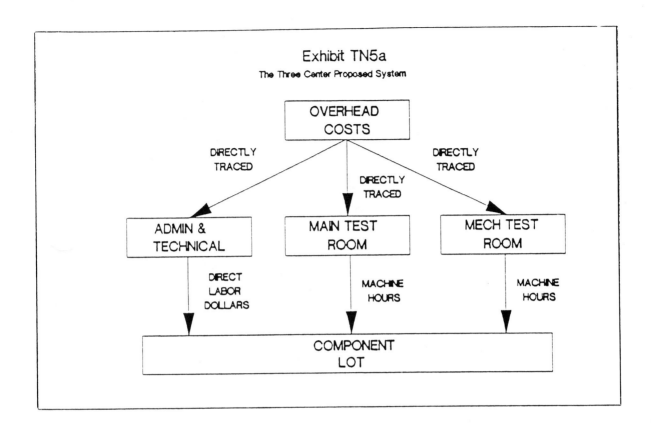

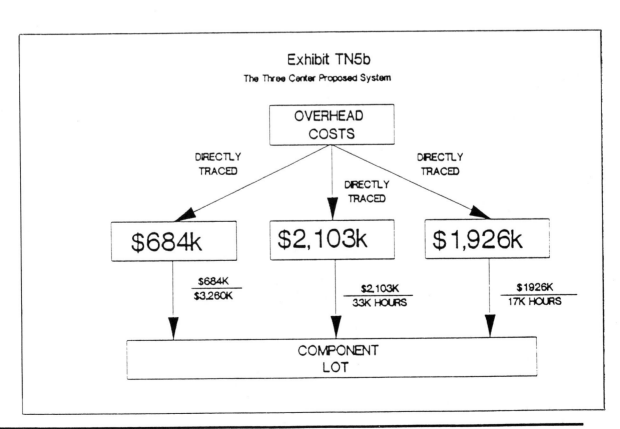

Exhibit TN6

The Accuracy Target

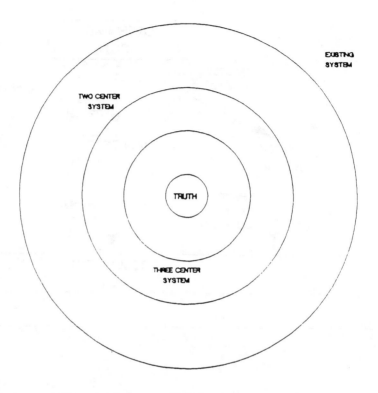

Digital Communications Inc.: Encoder Device Division

Teaching Note

Digital Communications was written to illustrate some design issues in traditional cost systems. It can also be used in an introductory course.

The case introduces students to three major issues:

1) the impact on cost system design of changing the definition of the product,

2) how to increase the number of bases used to assign costs to products in the second stage from one to three,

3) and how to resolve the problem created when service departments service each other.

Most of the calculations required by the EDD case are relatively simple. The only real exception is the reciprocal or matrix method calculations for service department allocations. I choose not to ask the students to perform these calculations, but describe the process in class and then tell them the results. Other instructors might want to add an assignment that requires the students to determine the costs reported by the reciprocal method.

This teaching note outlines an 80-minute teaching plan.

Suggested Assignments:

1. How big a shift in reported product costs for the VRE Board 2 is caused by changing from the direct labor hour system suggested by the financial staff to the direct labor hour, machine hour and material dollar system suggested by the VRE staff? (Use the existing service department allocation).

2. Work through Exhibits 5 and 6. Understand the calculations.

This teaching note was written by Professor Robin Cooper as an aid to instructors using Digital Communications Inc.: Encoder Device Division (189-083). Copyright ® 1991 by the President and Fellows of Harvard College. To order copies, call (617) 495-6117 or write the Publishing Division, Harvard Business School, Boston, MA 02163. No part of this publication may be reproduced, stored in a retrieval system, used in a spreadsheet, or transmitted in any form or by any means—electronic, mechanical, photocopying, recording, or otherwise—without the permission of Harvard Business School.

3. Recalculate the answer to Question 1 using the results of Exhibits 5 and 6. How big is the difference in reported product costs for Board 2?

4. What should Rebecca Wills recommend? Why?

Class Discussion

Q1. What is the competitive environment of EDD?

Students should identify that EDD was in the defense industry and that the products were classified. The facility was configured into a number of factories within a factory to reduce the number of people that came into contact with each of the products. However, several functions were not compartmentalized in this way. These functions were involved in administrative support where contact with sensitive information was not required. These departments were personnel, financial, information services, and plant engineering. The material departments, shipping and receiving, inventory control, and receiving inspection were also not compartmentalized. The production support departments were centrally managed but within each department the employees were compartmentalized.

Q2. What event has caused the design of the existing cost system to be revisited?

The necessity to bid on a subassembly and not a completed device has changed the acceptable definition of products for the cost system. The existing cost system defines the product as a completed device: now it must redefine the product (at least temporarily) as a subassembly.

Q3. What is the structure of the existing cost system?

Using student input to describe the existing system, I draw a diagram on the board that shows all of the interconnections. I purposely draw many first stage lines to show students that a lot is going on in this system (see Figure 1). I ask students how each of the costs are assigned to the cost centers, forcing them to choose between direct charging, attributions (i.e., assignments where causality is captured) and allocations (i.e., where the assignment is arbitrary). If the identification process gets bogged down, I point out that unlike the other cases we have discussed to date, the resources in this system are departments. Therefore, it is quite likely that a mixture of procedures are actually being used. From these discussions, I draw a three-stage version of the cost system to demonstrate how it differs slightly from systems encountered to date (see Figure 2). This treatment of support departments is very common and later on in the course will be revisited.

To simplify the problem, I draw a subset of the system on a second board, focusing on just the four administrative support departments and the VRE department. Students' input can be used to identify the percentages of each department costs that are being assigned to the VRE department. If weaker students are still having trouble with the mechanics of the first stage procedure, I use this opportunity to reinforce the first stage calculations. This case is a good one to use for this purpose because the calculations are simple and the results easily reconciled with case facts (case Exhibit 1).

I ask students if the assignment of costs to the VRE department completes the design of the cost system. This question often leads to confusion until the students understand that there is a second stage in this system, even though it is very simple. The second stage consists of taking the total cost of each department and dividing by the number of devices produced to give a unit cost of the device. This observation allows the drawing of the VRE portion of the cost system to be completed by adding the second stage (see Figure 3). I ask students if the reported costs would change if you used a different second stage bases such as direct labor hours or machine hours. They quickly realize that when only one product is produced, then any bases that captures a characteristic of the product unit will report exactly the same costs as number of units.

Q4. What changes are required to report subassembly costs?

I get a student to describe the new system designs suggested in the case, starting with the simplest--the direct labor approach. I ask a student to indicate the changes required to the VRE diagram. These are: erase the words "device" and "number of units" and replace them with subassembly and direct labor hours respectively. I then ask a student to perform the necessary calculations. These are:

COST ELEMENT	$	BOARD 2	$ ASSIGNED
DIRECT MATERIAL	2,214K	45.00%	997K
DIRECT LABOR	886K	22.04%	195K
PROD'N SUPPORT	3,721K	22.04%	820K
MATERIAL SUPPORT	166K	22.04%	37K
TOTAL			$2,085K

I write this number underneath the subassembly box in the VRE diagram.

Q5. What is wrong with this system?

Students will identify the arguments made by manufacturing in the case. I ask them how the proposed system is different from the direct labor system. Using student input, I draw the second stage of the system on the board next to the VRE diagram (see Figure 4). A student can then be asked to compute the appropriate numbers for both the first stage and the second stage. These are:

Labor Related Costs
Personnel	$ 54,756
Finance	$ 280,984
Pdn Mgmt & Sup	$ 70,603
Prod. Security	$ 121,215
Total	$1,020,275

%	22.04%

Board 2 $ 224,868

Machine Related Costs
    PLT Engineering $1,129,485
    Information Service $1,369,430
    Maintenance $ 54,202
    Prod. Eng. $ 65,603
    Quality Control $ 81,993
    Total $2,700,713

    %   39%

    Board 2 $1,053,271

Material Related %
    Ship and Receive $ 55,373
    Inventory Control $ 27,687
    Receiving Inspection $ 83,060
    Total $ 166,120
    %   45%

    Board 2 $ 74,754

Total Cost
    Direct Materials $ 996,715
    Direct Labor $1,952,675
    Labor Related % $ 224,868
    Machines Related $1,053,271
    Material Related % $ 74,754

    Total Board 2 $2,544,883

I write the reported cost of board 2 under the subassembly box for the three bases system. The two systems clearly report different costs. I ask students if the difference in reported costs is significant in the context of EDD and usually get unanimous agreement.

Q6. Does the proposed three bases system modify the design of the first stage?

This question can cause some confusion. The first stage remains effectively unchanged. The only modification is the way that the assigned costs are aggregated into three separate pools in the cost center. The same amount of each cost element is assigned to the VRE. Some students think this is a significant change to the first stage, others consider it relatively minor. I point out that this treatment would be suspect if the same bases was used for the first stage but different bases for the second stage. The first stage makes assumptions about how costs are consumed in the second stage. While not impossible, it seems unlikely that the same bases would adequately capture the magnitude of the costs consumed in each center when these costs are consumed by the products in different ways. Thus, such a mismatch suggests that the first stage should be reviewed to see if the best bases are being used to assign costs to cost centers.

I ask students to test if this diagnostic is violated in the proposed design at EDD. By drawing the following table on the board, I get them to realize that it is not.

COST ELEMENT	1st STAGE	2nd STAGE
Product Engineering	Usage	Machine Hours
Machine Maintenance Dept.	Usage	Machine Hours
Quality Department	Usage	Machine Hours
Plant Engineering	Usage	Machine Hours
Information Services	Usage	Machine Hours
Product Security	Usage	Direct Labor Hours
Product Management and Supervision	Usage	Direct Labor Hours
Personnel	Headcount	Direct Labor Hours
Financial	Usage	Direct Labor Hours
Shipping and Receiving	Labor Hours	Material Dollars
Inventory Control	Labor Hours	Material Dollars
Receiving Inspection	Labor Hours	Material Dollars

Q7. Have we increased the number of cost centers?

I use this question to introduce the students to some new technology. At this point in the course they have only seen systems that use one bases per cost center in the second stage to assign costs to products. Consequently, the difference between a cost pool and cost center has not been raised. I start by telling students that we need some additional language and introduce the concept of the cost center as a responsibility center and the cost pool as a structure for product costing. I introduce the rule that each cost pool can have only one second stage bases and that this bases must capture the way all of the costs in the pool are consumed by products. That is, the costs in the cost pool must be homogeneous with respect to the products.

Q8. What other changes to the cost system are suggested in the case?

I get a student to briefly describe the service department problem. Using student input, I draw on the board a picture of the four service departments and the production departments, and get a student to identify the linkages (see Figure 5). I ask what is causing the problem and get a student to identify that the core problem is that two or more departments service each other. I point out that we can resolve this problem by selectively breaking the linkages so that all of the costs can be assigned eventually to the production departments.

I ask students why we suddenly have to change the first stage. This question causes a discussion on matching the accuracy levels of the two stages to be initiated. My objective is to ensure that students understand that each stage introduces distortion and that one stage cannot cancel out the distortion caused by the other.

I suggest that the EDD problem is a little too complex to use to illustrate the problem, and draw a simpler, two department problem on the board (see Figure 6). This example can be used for the next 20 minutes to explore different approaches to resolving the service department allocation problem.

Q9. What is the simplest approach to overcoming the service department problem?

I get the first student that suggests ignoring it to work the numbers. For the simple example, these are:

SERVICE DEPARTMENT		PRODUCTION DEPARTMENT			
		PERCENTAGE		DOLLARS	
	Dollars	1	2	1	2
A	1,000	33%	67%	$ 333	$ 667
B	2,000	50%	50%	$1,000	$1,000
				$1,333	$1,667

I ask how this approach compares to the existing system at EDD and get the answer that it is identical. The existing system ignores the service department problem.

Q10. How else can we assign these costs?

As students make alternative suggestions, I get them to explain their approach and work the numbers. There are four common alternatives suggested: highest dollar out, highest dollar department, run both once and then ignore, and repetition (sometimes the reciprocal method is suggested, but I push this back to later in the class). The lowest number of linkages does not arise because both departments intersect with one other department. I discuss the number of linkage approaches when we return to the EDD discussion.

The calculations supporting the various approaches are:

Largest dollars out:

The largest dollars out is from department A to department B. Therefore, in this approach we sever the linkage from B to A. This approach gives the following results:

	B	1	2
A	400	200	400
	2000	1200	1200
	2400	1400	1600

The advantage of this method is that it ignores the smallest number of dollars.

Largest dollar department:

The largest dollar department is B. Therefore, in this approach we sever the linkage from A to B. This approach gives the following results:

	A	1	2
B	200	900	900
	1000	400	800
	1200	1300	1700

Run both linkages and then ignore. This is equivalent to netting out the transfers and then ignoring the problem. This approach gives the following results:

Step 1

	A	B
Original	1,000	2,000
Transfer Out	(400)	(200)
Transfer In	200	400
Net Effect	800	2,200

Step 2

Service Department		Production Department			
		Percentage		Dollars	
	Dollars	1	2	1	2
A	800	33%	67%	$267	$ 533
B	2,200	50%	50%	$1,100	$1,100
				$1,367	$1,633

Repetition:

This is actually the reciprocal method in disguise. I allow students to see how the process works by running three rounds.

		A	B	1	2
Round 1	A		400	200	400
	B	200		900	900
Round 2	A		80	40	80
	B	40		180	180
Round 3	A		32	16	32
	B	8		36	36

Q11. Are any of these solution accurate?

I get the students to accept that each approach other than the last introduces some distortion because linkages are severed. I ask students if they can derive the rule that is likely to minimize the distortion introduced. Hopefully, one of them suggests that breaking in total the smallest dollar value linkages possible is likely to be the most accurate approach short of the reciprocal approach.

Q12. How can we solve the problem exactly?

This allows the students to raise the reciprocal approach. It can be solved in two ways either by matrix inversion or by solving some simultaneous equations. These two ways are different mathematical representations of the same approach. I do not usually bother to go through the mechanics in my class as I am primarily interested in getting the students to understand the range of techniques that are available.

Q13. Who can explain Exhibits 4, 5 and 6 in the case?

I let a student identify case Exhibit 4 as the linkage percentages between the four administration support and production departments. This observation allows me to move onto case Exhibit 5 and get a student to explain the way the ranking of the departments was chosen. I then get him or her to explain the derivation of the step down matrix based on dollars charged out from the matrix of reciprocal usage of support departments. Once everybody is clear where the charge out matrix comes from, I then allow the student to demonstrate how each step assigns costs between the remaining administrative departments.

To help illustrate the process, I draw a step down diagram of the process on the board and use it to follow the calculations. I explain that what we have done is introduced a sophistication into the first stage of the two stage process. It is wise at this point in the class to warn students that sometimes people get confused and think that the step down procedure introduces more than two stages into the two stage procedure. I explain that the first stage is the procedure by which costs are assigned from the resources to the cost centers and that this process can be simple or complex.

I get students to compare the VRE costs reported by the various approaches: ignore service department problem, $ magnitude, number of linkages. If there is time, I give students the matrix inversion solution (see Teaching Note Exhibit 2). These solutions are:

	Ignore Linkages	$ Magnitude	# Linkages	Matrix
VRE COST	$3,327K	$2,602	$3,415	$2,861

Q14. Which of the approaches is the best?

I get the students to discuss the advantages and disadvantages of the various approaches. They should focus primarily on three characteristics of the different approaches: their ease of comprehension, accuracy, and computation complexity. If students indicate that matrix inversion is not a problem, I remind them that some systems have over two thousand departments providing reciprocal service. Inverting a matrix with two thousand columns should not be undertaken lightly.

I close the class by pointing out that any manager "downstream" of this problem cannot be expected to understand the constituents of the costs assigned to his or her department or products. The most appropriate role of the manager under these conditions is to control the demand for services. Downstream managers cannot concern themselves with the price of the services. This is the responsibility of the service department managers.

TN - 1

Digital Communications, Inc.: Encoder Device Division
CURRENT FINANCIAL SYSTEM'S OVERHEAD CHARGING MECHANISM

SUPPORT DEPT.	DOLLARS	CHARGE MECHANISM	VRE % ASSIGNED	VRE $ASSIGNED
GENERAL SUPPORT				
PERSONNEL PLT	$2,190,251	HEADCOUNT	25.00%	$ 547,563
ENG'G/BLD OCC	$3,011,960	SQ FTG	37.50%	$1,128,485
INFO SERVICES	$2,738,860	USAGE	50.00%	$1,369,430
FINANCE & ADMIN	$1,682,000	USAGE	16.70%	$ 280,894
PRODUCTION SUPPORT				
PRDCT MGMT & SUPV	$ 205,009	USAGE	34.44%	$ 70,603
MCHNE MAINTENANCE	$ 153,756	USAGE	35.25%	$ 54,202
PRDCT ENGNEERING	$ 205,009	USAGE	32.00%	$ 65,603
PRODUCT SECURITY	$ 410,017	USAGE	29.56%	$ 121,215
QUALITY CONTROL	$ 256,260	USAGE	32.00%	$ 81,993
MATERIAL SUPPORT				
SHIP AND RECEIVE	$ 221,492	LABOR HOURS	25.00%	$ 55,373
INVENTORY CONTROL	$ 110,746	LABOR HOURS	25.00%	$ 27,687
RECEIVING INSPECTION	$ 332,239	LABOR HOURS	25.00%	$ 83,060

Digital Communications, Inc.: Encoder Device Division

Teaching Note

Figure 1

Allocation of General Support Costs

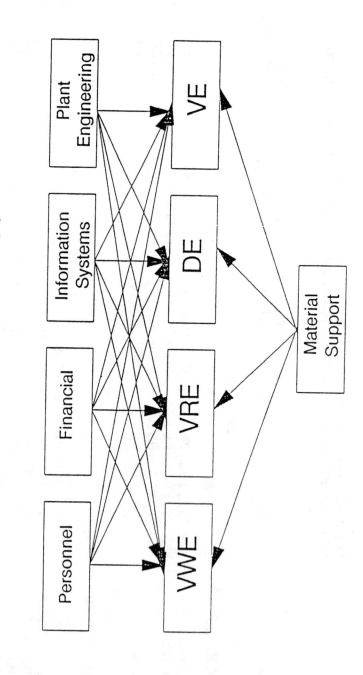

Digital Communications, Inc.: Encoder Device Division

Teaching Note

Figure 2

A Three Stage Picture of the EDD System

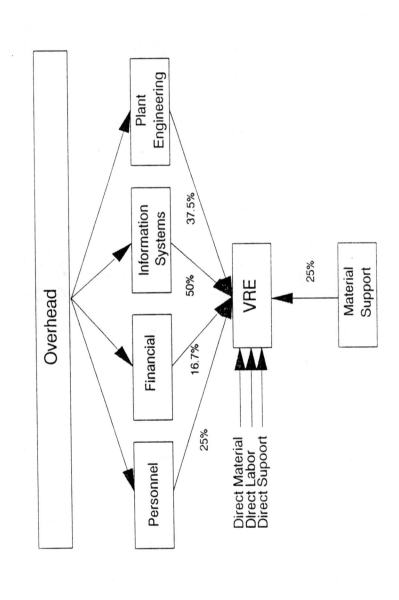

Digital Communications, Inc.: Encoder Device Division

Teaching Note

Figure 3

The Assignment of Costs to the VRE Department

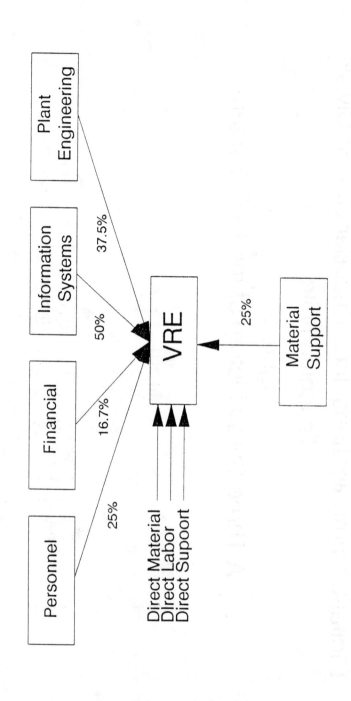

Digital Communications, Inc.: Encoder Device Division

Teaching Note

Figure 4

Manufacturing's Suggestion for the Second Stage

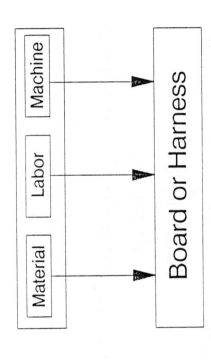

Digital Communications, Inc.: Encoder Device Division

Teaching Note

Figure 5

The Recipical Service Problem

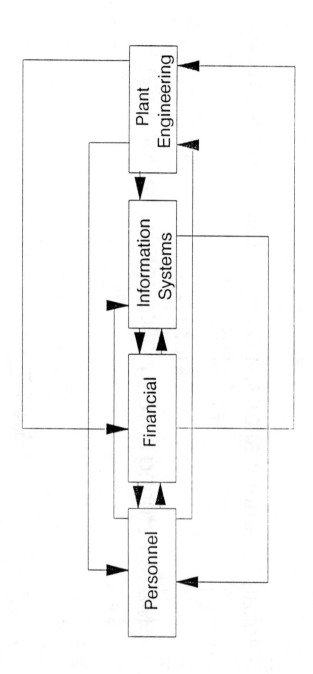

Digital Communications, Inc.: Encoder Device Division

Teaching Note

Figure 6

The Recipical Service Problem

A Simple Example

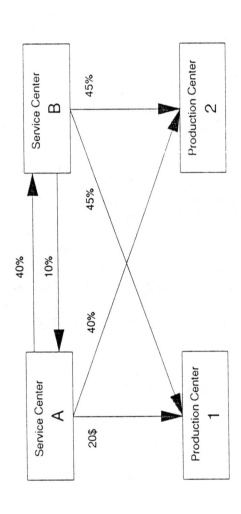

Mayers Tap, Inc. (A-C)

Teaching Note

Introduction

This module is designed to provide a rich contextual set of materials to introduce students to the fundamentals of cost system design.

The material contained in the Mayers Tap, Inc. series cases, coupled with the medium of delivery, is, I believe, unique. The conventional cost accounting cases in the first year are typically armchair exercises; they look at a very limited number of products manufactured in a simplified factory. The lessons learned from such exercises do little to instruct the student in the design of real-world cost accounting systems for even the simplest product. While the basics may have been laid, a true integration exercise that ties together allocation, product costing, contribution analysis, and cost center identification is lacking. The advent of the personal computer provided a mechanism to create such an exercise. More importantly, the PC could support a small but realistic factory. Instructors wishing to use the Mayers Tap Series in their courses will need to order the case software from HBS Publishing (see Introduction to Instructors Manual for instructions). The Mayers Tap video-tape is available from Prentice-Hall for textbook adopters.

Assignment Questions: Mayers Tap (B)

1. Using the Mayers Tap, Inc. (B) computer model, allocate the budgetary expenses using the most appropriate allocation base for each expense. You should be prepared to defend your choice of allocation base. For each budgetary expense, identify whether you think it is predominantly fixed or variable. Print out the burden rates for the machines.

2. For machines J-22 and E-01, replicate the computer calculations by hand.

This teaching note was prepared by Professor Robin Cooper as an aid to instructors in the classroom use of the case, Mayers Tap, Inc. (A-D), (105-111).

3.   Using the Mayers Tap, Inc. (B) computer model, allocate each budgetary expense using direct labor hours as the allocation base. Compare the results to your solution. Is the difference significant?

4.   The case states that under the old system the 1985 direct labor hour burden rate was expected to be $30. Calculate exactly the 1985 burden rate under the old system.

5.   Calculate the burden rates if the company had treated Albany and Denver as separate cost centers but still used the old approach for burden rate calculations.

6.   The two plants have very different production processes. Should this affect the way machine costs are allocated to the products?

Assignment Questions: Mayers Tap (C)

1.   Treating both plants as a single cost center, determine the standard cost of each product using the Mayers Tap, Inc. (C) computer model. Identify the products you feel should be dropped and then investigate the impact on net income of dropping all of these products simultaneously. You should print out the following reports:

      o   Product standard costs
      o   Net income - all products manufactured
      o   Net income - after eliminating the products you feel should no longer be produced (based on their standard cost of manufacture)

      Repeat your analysis, treating each plant as a separate cost center (two cost centers) and also each machine class as a separate cost center (31 cost centers).

2.   Using the 31-cost-center model, investigate the impact on net income of dropping the products you decided were candidates for discontinuance in the single-cost-center scenario. You should print a net income report and compare it to the equivalent singe-cost-center report. Repeat the same analysis for the products you decided were candidates for discontinuance in the two-cost-center scenario. For a given product mix, why do the net income statements differ depending upon the number of cost centers selected?

3.   The Denver plant has three distinct outputs:
      a.   Heat treatment for Albany products
      b.   T-1 for Albany products
      c.   Products 9,10, and 11.

      For the 1-, 2-, and 31-cost-center scenarios, calculate the total cost of running the Denver plant if the company maintains its full line of 11 products. Explain your findings.

Case Background

The Mayers Tap, Inc. series of cases originated in a 1978 consulting contract to design and oversee the implementation of a cost accounting system for a small (revenues $12 million) cutting tool firm that manufactured twist drills, taps, and rotary files. The company produced a catalog containing about 6,000 items, out of which it would manufacture 3,000 in an average year. The productive facilities were split into two, one producing low-volume standard and special tools and the other producing high-volume standard tools. The cost accounting systems were rudimentary, consisting of a single labor and overhead burden rate that was determined by dividing the total nondirect material budgeted costs for the two facilities by the budgeted number of direct labor hours.

In the next 12 months, I designed and oversaw the implementation of a system similar to that portrayed in the Mayers Tap, Inc. series. Once the cost data were produced, it became apparent that the old cost system had seriously distorted the manufacturing costs. In particular, many products in the tap line were being sold either close to or below variable cost; other products were making a substantial contribution. The firm modified its marketing effort to take advantage of the high contribution items, and in the recession that followed, the president identified the new cost system as a major factor in the firm's survival.

I tried writing cases that captured the process of designing cost systems but found it impossible to create the necessary realism to satisfy me. Conventional cases without computer assistance could not portray for students the dynamic situation inherent in systems design.

The real company was too large for a 256K machine using Lotus 1-2-3, and, in any event, I wanted an exercise that was of reasonable size for a three-day series of cases. To reduce the problem to a more appropriate size, two major simplifications were made. First, only the tap line was included in the case series. This reduced the number of machines by two-thirds. Second, the 1,500-odd taps that the firm produced were reduced to 11, chosen as a representative sample of the entire taps line. The resulting productive facilities contained 30 machines (Albany) and 17 machines (Denver) and made eight and three products, respectively. These simplifications do not, in my opinion, dilute the realism of the case setting. Students still must make a number of decisions that require judgment and understanding of the design process.

The budgets are the actual budgets for the tap product line. They have been modified slightly to reflect unavoidable changes due to isolating a single product line and reducing the number of products. The number of budgeting line items and allocation bases is unchanged from the real situation, and the (C) case uses the company's actual allocation scheme.

The greatest deviation from reality is the selling prices and costs for the products. The contraction in the product line was unavoidable and resulted in product costs substantially different from actual. However, all costs are within the range of product costs for the tap line (about $1 to over $100). The average cost of taps for Mayers Tap, Inc. is close to the average for the real company.

The overall burden rates for the two plants and each machine are, on the whole, quite accurate. The less significant machines have burden rates that vary from reality, but the major machines' rates are representative of actual costs.

Considerable attention has been directed to making the numbers in the Mayers Tap series as accurate as possible. While some loss of accuracy and realism was unavoidable, the overall result is a set of four cases that reflect the reality of the site company reasonably well.

This teaching note consists of three additional sections.

1. The (A) case and videotape
2. The (B) case and computer model
3. The (C) case and computer model

The (B) and (C) discussions are each in two parts. In the first part, a teaching strategy is proposed, and the second provides the details of potential solutions to the case assignment.

Mayers Tap, Inc. (A) and Videotape

The (A) case and videotape (9-885-001) provide background for the three decision cases. The (A) case briefly describes the firm's history and the pressures leading to John Mayers's decision to implement a new system.

In reality, two distinct symptoms indicated that the cost system was inadequate. First, the cost accounting system predicted profits much greater than those identified by the firm's financial accounting system. Second, some products were extremely profitable, while others were not. Management was not convinced that the profit figures were real.

The rest of the (A) case describes the product, the terminology used, the manufacturing operation, and, briefly, the production process. The most important item in the (A) case is the description of the production process. This is augmented by the videotape, which goes into considerable detail about the manufacturing process.

After reading the (A) case and viewing the videotape, the students should have a good idea about the Mayers factory and how taps are produced. This part of the experience is important because the average student has never seen a factory, let alone designed a cost system for one. The purpose of the (A) case and videotape is to make the problem real.

Mayers Tap, Inc. (B) and Computer Model (B)

Teaching Strategy

The (B) case requires some pre-class board work to speed up the process. The boards that need to be prepared are:

Board 1   On this board, write down all of the allocation bases and number them the same as the computer model does. These are:

1. Production units	8. Maintenance
2. Raw material ($)	9. Power consumption
3. Direct labor hours	10. Oil system
4. Direct labor ($)	11. Grinding wheels
5. Indirect labor	12. Floor space
6. Overtime	13. Book value
7. Machine hours	

Board 2   On this board, create the following table:

Budgetary Expense	Student			
	1	2	3	4
Nonproductive Labor . . .				

It will have to be in two parts to accommodate all of the budgetary expenses.

Board 3   On this board, create the following table:

		Albany			Denver		
		D-34	N-72	C-86	A-06	D-02	A-41
Student 1	Var						
	Fixed						
2	Var						
	Fixed						
3	Var						
	Fixed						

Board 4

On this board, write the simple two-stage allocation example problem:

Total power costs	$400,000
Total direct labor hours	200,000
Machine XYZ uses	15% power
	5% DL
Product A uses	0.2 DLHrs per part

Q1. Describe the production process.

The (A) case contains a description of the production process and a process diagram. There are three classes of product produced by MTI. These are all-Albany products (except heat treat products), mixed Albany- Denver products, and all-Denver products. The students should be made aware of this split.

The production process can be diagrammed on the front center board as:

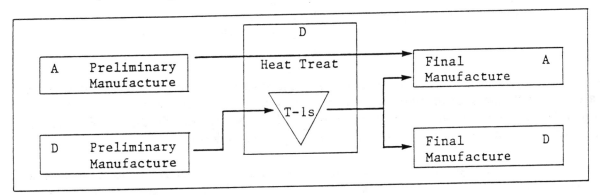

This should be summarized as Denver produces three products: Albany heat treat, Albany T-1s, and Denver products. The point of this is to make the students aware that the two plants are not independent.

Q2. How does the company arrive at product costs in the old system and the new system?

The first board should be raised to show the simple two-stage allocation problem:

Total power costs	$400,000
Total direct labor hours	200,000
Machine XYZ uses	15% power
	5% DLHrs
Product 1 uses	0.2 DLHrs per part

Under the old system, the power costs were allocated using the direct labor hours in one single step, i.e.,

Power component in product 1, machine XYZ

$$= \quad \frac{\$400,000}{200,000} \; x \; 0.2$$

$$= \quad \$0.40$$

In the new system, a two-stage allocation process is used. Ask a student how this two-stage process works in general and draw the following diagram.

```
                  Allocation
                  Base                      DLHrs
Power  ==========================> XYZ ==========================> Product 1
```

The simple example can now be worked:

XYZ power allocation   is $60,000 [$400,000 x 15%]
XYZ direct labor hours   is 10,000 [200,000 x 5%]
XYZ power/hour   = $6/hour
Power component in product 1, machine XYZ
                                 = $6/hr x 0.2 hrs
                                 = $1.20

Using different allocation bases does make a significant difference. Two-stage allocation is at the heart of the (B) case and the students need to understand what it is and why it is used. I would suggest that you work through one or two of the machine hourly rates for J-22 or E-01 at this time to ensure that the students understand what the model is doing.

The advantage of a two-stage process is that we get machine rates and can use these easily to obtain standard costs. If a new product is under consideration, all that is required is the time per part on each machine. The sum of the product of machine burden rates and time per part per machine is the overhead costs for that part. Students may not realize the value of the two-stage process. They should be asked why a two-stage process is useful. The first allocation base deals with changes in costs and the second with changes in product characteristics such as new product introduction and process changes). Separating the two changes allows the firm to calculate the impact of the more frequent process changes easily without having to reallocate.

The process of identifying the allocation bases is described briefly on page 2 of the (B) case but I think it merits elaboration. It is an extremely tough proposition if the company has not kept records. Students lack the knowledge to understand how difficult this is. I would focus on grinding wheels and ask a student how he or she thinks such an item was controlled in the old system. The answer is it was not. Grinding wheels were purchased and released to the floor as received and used as required; no records were kept. It might take some pushing to get there, but I think it is worth it. Our students appear to believe that firms track information for the fun of it. My experience is that if information is not used, it is not kept. The problem then becomes one of estimating costs from invoices and shop floor experience.

be allowed to discuss the significance of switching to machine hours or some other measure. There is no simple answer to this problem. After some discussion, point out that the company has selected direct labor hours and while the problem should be considered, we can continue for the moment with direct labor hours.

Q3. For MTI, what were your choices of allocation base and which did you identify as variable?

This is Assignment 1 of the case, and the company and casewriter solutions are presented later in this note. There will be a wide range of student solutions; one student should be called upon to provide his or her solution. (A handy shorthand is #-V or #-F where # is the allocation base and V or F refers to variable or fixed.)

Once the student's solution is up, the student should fill in the right-hand side board numbers for the variable and fixed components of the six machines. A volunteer is then called to provide a very different solution to the case, and his or her solutions and numbers are recorded. A third student's solutions should also be documented.

The class can then be asked if it makes a difference which allocation bases and cost natures are identified. The consensus should be yes. A general discussion can then follow about what the solution should be. No consensus will be reached, but the complexity of the problem should become apparent.

Q4. What is the machine cost if direct labor is used throughout?

Call on the first student again and document his or her solution and again for the second student to demonstrate that the results depend upon variable and fixed identification. The class can now be asked if the two-stage process is worthwhile. The consensus should again be yes.

Q5. Why do the different machines in each plant have the same burden rate under a direct labor hour first stage allocation process?

Move back to the middle board and demonstrate the following:

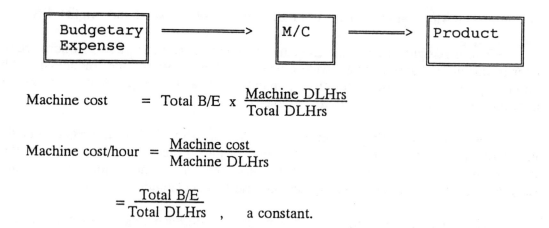

$$\text{Machine cost} \quad = \text{Total B/E} \times \frac{\text{Machine DLHrs}}{\text{Total DLHrs}}$$

$$\text{Machine cost/hour} = \frac{\text{Machine cost}}{\text{Machine DLHrs}}$$

$$= \frac{\text{Total B/E}}{\text{Total DLHrs}} , \quad \text{a constant.}$$

(Each product gets a different charge, depending upon the direct labor hours in the product.)

This is a not an intuitive result, but it demonstrates the problems associated with simple direct labor hour allocation systems. This result turns out to be useful in the final calculations for the Mueller-Lehmkuhl case, which is why we recommend teaching Mayers Tap (B) before Mueller-Lehmkuhl.

Q6. (Assignments 4 and 5 of the case)

The case states that under the old system the 1985 direct labor hour burden rate was expected to be $30. Calculate exactly the 1985 burden rate under the old system. Calculate the burden rates if the company had treated Albany and Denver as separate cost centers but still used the old approach for burden rate calculations.

A student can be asked to calculate the three rates and explain what they mean. The Denver plant has a higher rate because it is a more automated plant, with higher overhead expenses and lower direct labor expenses. But Denver produces more parts per hour, so it ends up cheaper than Albany on a per part basis.

The findings can now be summarized. The significant issues are the two-stage allocation process and the impact of identifying appropriate allocation bases on the machine costs and hence product costs. As a closing issue, the instructor should inform the students that the (C) case will use the company's solution. I would not inform the students of the company's selections.

Assignment Solutions

Assignment Question 1: The budgetary expenses were allocated by the company using the following bases:

Type	Budgeted Expenses		Allocation Base Selected
Variable	Nonproductive labor	3.	Budgeted direct labor hours
Variable	Overtime and night labor	3.	Budgeted direct labor hours
Variable	Power and heat	9.	Power
Variable	Repairs and maintenance	8.	Maintenance
Variable	Grinding wheels and diamonds	11.	Grind wheel
Variable	Other factory supplies	3.	Budgeted direct labor hours
Fixed	Depreciation, machines	13.	Machine book value
Fixed	Depreciation, buildings	12.	Floor space
Fixed	General factory supplies	3.	Budgeted direct labor hours
Fixed	General factory maintenance	3.	Budgeted direct labor hours
Fixed	Factory support expenses	3.	Budgeted direct labor hours
Fixed	General plant costs	12.	Floor space
Variable	Oil filtration expenses	10.	Oil system
Fixed	Inspection cost center	3.	Budgeted direct labor hours
Fixed	Heat treatment costs	3.	Budgeted direct labor hours

The company decided against using a semivariable system in which a budgetary expense could be split into its variable and fixed components. The main argument was that they had selected their budgetary line items so that the total line items were predominantly fixed or variable. There is some truth to their contention, but the split is not that specific. I believe a major consideration was simplicity. The company had come a long way from its original system and felt it had enough to cope with for the moment. Secondly, the company really did not have access to detailed cost behavior data, and the semivariable equation would have been more guesswork than knowledge.

Nonproductive Labor

The company calculated a nonproductive labor allocation basis and yet used the more conventional direct labor hours. I could not obtain a reason why a base was calculated and later abandoned (the same is true for overtime night labor).

Direct labor hours are typically used because the nonproductive time is due to the usual delays in a semicontrolled production process and over time this stabilizes to a set percentage. However, as shown by the ratio, it does vary from machine to machine. In the Denver plant, which is high automated, the firm did not differentiate between direct labor hours and nonproductive time. This is because machine-to-machine differences were not critical. The operators are inherently more flexible and can be moved about more freely. The percentage of nonproductive time is about the same, but the machine differences are much lower.

Given the process by which nonproductive labor occurs, it is clearly a variable cost. The higher the production, the higher labor and hence nonproductive labor. Some students might view it as inversely proportional to production level. The busier the factory, the lower the nonproductive labor. There is some truth to this in Denver but not in Albany; overall the cost is variable.

Overtime and Night Labor

Again, the company calculated an allocation basis and then ignored it. I could not find a clear reason for this decision. The variation in the specific allocation base and the direct labor hour base is much higher for overtime and night labor in the Albany plant (again, they do not differentiate in the Denver plant) than it was for nonproductive labor (differences exceed ± 30% in places).

This is obviously a variable cost. The higher the production, the higher the overtime and night labor. There is some complex behavior when a new shift switches in or one has to be dropped.

Power and Heat; Repairs and Maintenance; Grind Wheels, etc.

These are three straightforward allocations that I would move through quickly. The company has specific allocation bases for all three and the students should use them. These are all variable costs that vary directly with production levels.

Other Factory Supplies

This is the first of the expenses for which there is no special base. The case identifies other factory supplies as including all supplies used by the factory machines (other than grinding and diamond wheels) such as grease, abrasive cutoff wheels, etc. These obviously vary with production, and students might allocate them using machine or direct labor hours. In my opinion, either is acceptable, and it should make little difference, as the two bases are within 10% of each other.

Depreciation, Machines; Depreciation, Building

The depreciation for machines has its own allocation base: machine book value. The students should select this, but hopefully some will observe that many Albany machines have zero entries (J-22 was picked for this reason). This raises the issues of inflation adjustments and whether financial accounting makes an adequate basis for cost accounting data.

Building depreciation is a little trickier because there is no specific allocation base for it. The company uses floor space to allocate the depreciation. No other base appears relevant to me.

Clearly, these are both fixed costs.

General Factory Supplies; General Factory Maintenance; Factory Support Supplies

These three items have no special allocation base. They are all fixed and highlight the difficulty of allocating fixed costs as there is no obvious relationship between the incurrence of the costs and any of the allocation bases. The company uses direct labor hours as a default base (as is common practice in the U.S.), but students might select other bases.

Students might consider some of these costs as variable. This is usually because they use too long a time frame for their fixed versus variable analysis. The appropriate period is 12 months, the interallocation period.

General Factory Supplies

There are several bases that could be used here. The one selected depends upon the students' view of the account. If they view it as non-activity based, they should select an allocation base such as floor space. If they view it as activity driven, then they should select an activity measure base such as direct labor hours or machine hours. The company uses direct labor hours. This line item is very small. It is unlikely that it could ever have a significant effect on product costing. The choice of allocation base is virtually irrelevant.

General factory supplies are a fixed cost. They do not vary with small changes in production.

General Factory Maintenance

I would probably use the floor space for this one. The janitors spend their time cleaning the factory, so floor space seems to be the way to go. This line item is medium to large, and the choice of allocation base might be significant.

General factory maintenance is a fixed cost.

Factory Support Expense

This is a significant cost - nearly 9% of total costs. Its allocation could significantly affect product costs. It is definitely fixed but related to activity - all of the salaried workers are involved in keeping the place going - so some activity measure makes sense. I could see using budgeted production, direct labor hours, or direct labor dollars as the base.

Factory support expense is a fixed cost.

General Plant Costs

The first few in the list are space related (property taxes, general building maintenance, etc.); the others are less clear. The company's solution is to use floor space as the allocation base and not worry about items such as cost of employment ads, etc., which are relatively minor.

The general plant costs that are space related are fixed.

Oil Filtration

This has its own allocation base and students should select it. There is a complex issue. It contains fixed costs and variable costs. A single allocation rate is really insufficient. The company overcomes the problem by including a depreciation charge in the cost of oil filtration and allocating that to the machines, along with running expenses, based upon oil consumption. This cost is a mixture of fixed (oil plant depreciation) and variable (oil filtration costs). The company treats it as variable.

Inspection Costs

These are output related costs, so the students might use budgeted production as the allocation base or, like the company, direct labor hours. This cost is effectively fixed, though substantial increases in production will cause it to alter.

Heat Treatment

This is a messy area! I expect confusion but purposely left the issue of heat treatment highly visible. The different treatment of the two plants' heat treatment costs clearly demonstrates differences between direct cost and overhead. In Denver, heat treatment is viewed as a direct cost and hence has a $0 budgetary expense. The heat treatment costs are reported as line item expenditures such as heat and power, labor, and materials. In Albany it is treated as an overhead item and has to be allocated. The firm uses direct labor hours because it is such a small cost and not worth worrying about. It is viewed as fixed because experience has shown that production levels have little effect on the Albany plant costs.

I ran the model using my best guesses at the appropriate allocation bases:

Type	Budgeted Expenses	Allocation Base Selected	
Variable	Nonproductive labor	6.	Nonproductive labor
Variable	Overtime and night labor	7.	Overtime and night labor
Variable	Power and heat	9.	Power
Variable	Repairs and maintenance	8.	Maintenance
Variable	Grinding wheels and diamonds	11.	Grinding wheel
Variable	Other factory supplies	5.	Budgeted machine hours
Fixed	Depreciation, machines	13.	Machine book value
Fixed	Depreciation, buildings	12.	Floor space
Fixed	General factory supplies	3.	Budgeted direct labor hours
Fixed	General factory maintenance	12.	Floor space
Fixed	Factory support expenses	3.	Budgeted direct labor hours
Fixed	General plant costs	12.	Floor space
Variable	Oil filtration expenses	10.	Oil system
Fixed	Inspection cost center	3.	Budgeted direct labor hours
Fixed	Heat treatment costs	3.	Budgeted direct labor hours

The results are shown in Exhibit TN-1. As can be seen, the resulting differences from those used by the company are small, typically under 7% (see Exhibit TN-2). It is unlikely that the resulting standard costs would be much different from the company's solution.

Assignment Question 2

This is a straightforward, though laborious, task that is required to remove the black box effect from the (B) case. It proves to the students that they know how allocation works. Obviously the exact numbers the students come up with depend upon the allocation bases selected. To illustrate the process, I will use the company's allocations. The resulting burden rates for the two machines are:

Burden Rate	J-22	E-01
Direct labor and benefits	9,556	168,813
Nonproductive labor	822	17,103
Overtime and night labor	617	12,828
Power and heat	3,150	41,520
Repairs and maintenance	1,650	31,675
Grinding wheels and diamonds	4,050	53,600
Other factory supplies	374	10,122
Depreciation, machines	0	123,626
Depreciation, buildings	2,232	32,967
General factory supplies	224	10,061
General factory maintenance	1,121	31,440
Factory support expenses	2,990	88,032
General plant costs	1,093	27,473
Oil filtration expenses	1,200	305,400
Inspection cost center	673	22,637
Heat treatment costs	67	0
Direct labor hours	985	21,102

Direct Labor Hour Burden Rate	J-22	E-10
Direct labor	9.70	8.00
Variable overhead	12.04	22.86
Fixed overhead	9.54	15.93
Total	31.28	46.79

These were calculated using the following allocation bases and overhead allocation bases:

Budgeted Expenses		Allocation Base Selected
Nonproductive labor	3.	Budgeted direct labor hours
Overtime and night labor	3.	Budgeted direct labor hours
Power and heat	9.	Power
Repairs and maintenance	8.	Maintenance
Grinding wheels and diamonds	11.	Grind wheel
Other factory supplies	3.	Budgeted direct labor hours
Depreciation, machines	13.	Machine book value
Depreciation, buildings	12.	Floor space
General factory supplies	3.	Budgeted direct labor hours
General factory maintenance	3.	Budgeted direct labor hours
Factory support expenses	3.	Budgeted direct labor hours
General plant costs	12.	Floor space
Oil filtration expenses	10.	Oil system
Inspection cost center	3.	Budgeted direct labor hours
Heat treatment costs	3.	Budgeted direct labor hours

Allocation Bases	J-22	E-01
Budgeted production (units)	15.457	12.001
Budgeted raw materials ($)	2.546	0.000
Budgeted direct labor hours	0.748	25.152
Budgeted direct labor ($)	0.808	25.152
Budgeted machine hours	0.734	25.339
Nonproductive labor allocation	0.845	25.152
Overtime and night labor	0.463	25.152
Maintenance	1.100	18.100
Power	1.800	17.300
Oil system	0.400	50.900
Grinding wheel	1.800	17.900
Floor space	1.395	21.978
Machine book value	.000	49.451

This, coupled with the budgetary expenses of:

Budgeted Expenses	Albany	Denver
Raw materials	$1,122,536	$705,846
Direct labor	1,132,012	671,172
Nonproductive labor	110,000	68,000
Overtime and night labor	82,500	51,000
Power and heat	175,000	240,000
Repairs and maintenance	150,000	175,000
Grinding wheels and diamonds	225,000	300,000
Other factory supplies	50,000	80,000
Depreciation, machines	120,000	250,000
Depreciation, buildings	160,000	150,000
General factory supplies	30,000	40,000
General factory maintenance	150,000	125,000
Factory support expenses	400,000	350,000
General plant costs	150,000	125,000
Oil filtration expenses	300,000	600,000
Inspection cost center	90,000	90,000
Heat treatment costs	9,000	0

allows us to calculate the burden rates.

Assignment 2 Solution

Budgetary Expense	Allocation Basis	J-22			E-01		
		Budgetary Expense	Allocation Ratio	Burden Rate	Budgetary Expense	Allocation Ratio	Burden Rate
Nonproductive labor	DL hours	110,000	0.748	$ 823	68,000	25.152	17,103
OT and night labor	DL hours	82,500	0.748	617	51,000	25.152	12,828
Power	Power	175,000	1.800	3,150	240,000	17.300	41,520
Repairs and maintenance	Maintenance	150,000	1.100	1,650	175,000	18.100	31,675
Grinding wheels	Grinding wheel	225,000	1.800	4,050	300,000	17.900	53,700
Other factory supplies	DL hours	50,000	0.748	374	80,000	25.152	20,122
Depreciation, machines	Book value	120,000	0	0	250,000	49.451	123,628
Depreciation, buildings	Floor space	160,000	1.395	2232	150,000	21.978	23,967
General factory supplies	DL hours	30,000	0.748	224	40,000	25.152	10,061
General factory maintenance	DL hours	150,000	0.748	1122	125,000	25.152	31,440
General plant costs	Floor space	150,000	1.395	2093	125,000	21.978	27,473
Oil filtration	Oil system	30,000	0.400	1200	600,000	50.900	305,400
Inspection	DL hours	90,000	0.748	673	900,000	25.152	22,637
Heat treat	DL hours	9,000	0.748	67	0	25.152	0

With the exception of a few rounding errors, we get the correct solutions.

Assignment 3

The purpose of this question is to demonstrate that all of the effort was worth it. The two sets of solutions are shown in Exhibit TN-3. As can be seen, the differences are quite large and would obviously seriously affect product costing. There is a demonstrated need for multibase allocation for Mayers Tap, Inc.

In the classroom I would select Machines D-34, N-72, and C-86 from Albany and A-06, D-02, and A-41 from Denver for discussion, as these show the greatest variance.

Many students will notice that all the Albany and Denver machines have the same variable and fixed burden rates per hour (although the two plants are different). This will confuse many students as the results seem counter-intuitive. However, there is nothing wrong with the computer models - the results are correct.

Proof

The model prints out the cost of a single direct labor hour at that machine. However, direct labor hours were used to allocate all costs to the machine, i.e.,

% of each expense item allocated to machine

$$= \frac{\text{budgetary expense}}{\text{total plant direct labor hours}} \times \text{machine direct labor hours}$$

This is then converted to an hourly rate by dividing by the total number of machine direct labor hours, i.e., the machine hourly rate is given by:

$$\frac{\frac{\text{budgetary expense}}{\text{total plant direct labor hours}} \times \text{machine direct labor hours}}{\text{machine direct labor hours}}$$

or

$$\frac{\text{budgetary expense}}{\text{total plant direct labor hours}}$$

which is independent of the machine. That is, all machines cost the same per labor hour. It should be clear that, even so, all products do not cost the same under this scenario. Their raw material and labor costs will be different, and the amount of burden allocated will depend upon total direct labor hours required to produce the product.

Assignments 4 and 5

These are relatively easy calculations if the student understands the old cost system. The calculations are needed to support the (C) case and will be referred to in that discussion. The appropriate calculations are shown below.

	Albany	Denver	Both
Total plant costs	$4,506,048	$4,021,018	$8,527,066
Total nonmaterial costs	$3,383,512	$3,315,172	$6,698,684
Labor hours by plant	131,778	83,897	215,675
Burden rate per plant	$25.676	$39.515	$31.059

As can be seen, the Albany plant costs less per hour than the Denver plant (as expected). The value of the Denver plant lies in its higher throughput.

Assignment 6

This is a thinking exercise for the students. The Denver plant is highly automated and the personnel simply feed the machines often on a multimachine basis. It is clear that direct labor hours are not a good second-stage allocation base. Instead, I would use machine hours. This version of the (B) computer model does not allow this option to be explored. The issue of converting the second-stage allocation basis from direct labor hours to machine hours is explicity covered in the Fisher Technologies case. I would tell students that this issue has been deferred until that case appears. Mayers Tap (B) is a case that explores two critical issues: (1) the effect of splitting a plant into multiple cost centers, and (2) the judgments required in the first stage of the two-stage process; i.e., choosing appropriate drivers to assign different budgetary expenses to each cost center.

MAYERS TAP, INC. (C) AND COMPUTER MODEL (C)

The company has now successfully identified appropriate allocation costs and allocated costs to the machine level. The (C) case and model start from that point. The case and model assume the company's allocation bases.

The main teaching objectives of the (C) case are to (1) demonstrate the significance of selecting cost centers for the accurate determination of product costs and (2) make the student think about the relationship between standard costs and actual costs.

Teaching Strategy

Some board preparation is useful but not necessary for this case.

Board 1

On this board, create the following table:

Price	Product	Number of Cost Centers		
		1	2	31
	2			
	8			
	10			

Board 2

This board should contain the following problem:

Power cost	$400,000
Direct labor hours	200,000
Machine XYZ uses	15% of power
	5% of DLHr
Machine ABC uses	5% of power
	15% of DLHr

XYZ and ABC are the only machines in the Albany plant that use power.

Board 3

On this board, create the following table:

Price	Product	Number of Cost Centers		
		1	2	31
	2			
	8			
	10			
Net Income				

Question 1

What is the cost of Products 2, 8, and 10 under the 1, 2, and 31 cost center scenarios?

A student volunteer should be used to fill in board 1.

Price	Product	Number of Cost Centers		
		1	2	31
$83.80	2	91.66	83.79	79.78
		124.47	112.97	106.64
5.75	8	5.94	5.36	5.33
		8.41	7.49	7.85
1.50	10	1.37	1.63	1.76
		1.87	2.27	2.41

The student should then be asked why there are differences between these three approaches. The discussion should center on averaging effects.

Question 2

What basis do we have for dropping products?

The students should discuss contribution analysis versus full cost or equivalent and mention complementary products. The case situation clearly calls for contribution analysis, and the decision can now be documented on board 3.

Price	Product	Number of Cost Centers		
		1	2	31
$83.50	2	Drop	Drop	Keep
5.75	8	Drop	Keep	Keep
5.75	10	Keep	Drop	Drop

The students should be allowed to discuss these findings. It should be clear that all is not well. Different decisions are being reached under the three scenarios.

This is a good time to ask how accurate these data are. Given the disagreement yesterday on allocation bases and the general acceptance of arbitrariness in allocation, how much can we rely on these numbers? The answer is quite a bit but not to the level of accuracy required to make a decision on Product 2.

The students should be asked if they notice any relationships in the results. The major point is, that under one cost center, Albany products are more expensive and Denver products are cheaper when compared to the 31 cost center numbers. This is to be expected because of the relative costs of the two plants. The averaging effect is showing up.

Question 3

For the one cost center scenario, where do the standard and budgeted cost numbers come from?

(Use board 5)

You want the board to look like this:

	Plan	Standard	Budgeted	(leave blank)
Sales				
COGS, V				
COGS, F				
GM				
SGA				
NIBT				

Put up the layout and ask student to fill in the plan, standard, and budgeted cells. The result will be:

	Plan	Standard	Budgeted	(leave blank)
Sales	9,657	6,864	6,864	
COGS, V	(6,288)	(3,256)	(3,256)	
COGS, F	(2,239)	(1,131)	(2,239)	
GM	1,130	2,477	1,369	
SGA	(500)	(500)	(500)	
NIBT	630	1,977	869	

A student will rapidly point out that the standard is wrong because it does not flex the standard costs. NOTE: Although it is wrong, the standard is exactly what the company was doing before. Some pointed questioning might be required to elicit this fact.

The blank column should be filled in from the equivalent 31 cost center scenario.

	31 Cost Center
Sales	6,864
COGS, V	(3,638)
COGS, F	(2,239)
GM	987
SGA	500
NIBT	487

A student should now be asked to prove the standard and projected numbers (use board 4). The board should have the following layout:

Standard		Units	$/Unit	$000
	Lost sales	28,800 of #2	83.80	(2,413)
		66,000 of #8	5.75	(380)
				(2,783)
	Planned sales			9,657
	Adjusted sales			$6,864
	COGS,			
	variable	28,800	91.66	(2,640)
		66,000	5.94	(392)
				(3,032)
	Planned COGS, variable			6,288
	Adjusted COGS, variable			$3,256
	COGS, fixed	28,800	32.80	(945)
		66,000	2.47	(163)
				(1,108)
	Planned COGS, fixed			2,239
	Adjusted COGS, fixed			$1,131

31 Cost Center		Units	$/Unit	$000
	Lost sales	Same as standard		$6,864
	COGS,			
	variable	28,800	79.78	(2,289)
		66,000	5.33	(352)
				(2,650)
	Planned COGS, variable			6,288
	Adjusted COGS, variable			3,638
	COGS, fixed		Unchanged from budget	

Working this through should make clear to the students the difference between the two net incomes.

Question 4 (a)

In a standard cost system, how is the difference between the standard and budgeted fixed costs reconciled?

The fixed costs difference is called the volume variance, and the students have seen it before.

Question 4 (b)

If you assume that the 31 cost center model is correct (e.e., it will provide accurate cost information), how will the differences between the budgeted variable costs under 1 and 31 cost centers be reconciled?

The variable issue is more complex and needs the simple example.

Power cost	$400,000
Direct labor hours	200,000
Machine XYZ uses	15% of power
	5% of DLHrs
Machine ABC uses	5% of power
	15% of DLHrs

Machines XYZ and ABC are the only machines in the Albany plant that use power.

A student should be asked to complete the problem.

	Power	DLHrs
XYZ	$60,000	10,000
ABC	20,000	30,000
Albany total	$80,000	40,000
		$2/hr

Now drop the product that uses Machine ABC. We get:

Actual power consumed	=	$60,000
Standard power consumed	=	$20,000 ($2/hr x 10,000)
Power spending variance	=	$40,000

[Spending variance defined as Actual Variable Cost
- Standard Variable Cost at Actual Hours]

This spending variance is caused simply by overaggregation of data.

The difference between the 1 cost center and 31 cost center budgeted net incomes of $382K is due solely to this "cost center variance." In a real cost system, this will occur and be untraceable as the 31 cost center numbers are not available.

Question 5

What are the 31 cost center budgeted net incomes given the various decisions?

A student can now fill in the bottom row of Board 3.

Cost Center	Budget	1	2	31
Net Income (31CC)	$630	$481	$582	$698

The choice of cost centers and ensuing decisions obviously makes a big difference. The students should be asked to comment on the sources of these differences.

Question 6

This is Assignment 3 of the case. It is a straightforward calculation and can be found in the assignment solutions.

Once the differences between the one and 31 cost center total costs for Denver have been identified, the instructor can use the (B) case solutions to Assignments 4 and 5 to prove the above results.

In the (B) case we derived the following numbers:

	Albany	Denver	Total
Nonmaterial costs	$3,383,512	$3,315,172	$6,698,684
Labor hours	131,778	83,897	215,675
Burden rate	$ 25.676	$ 39.515	$ 31.059

The error is $709,433 [83,897 x 8.46 (39.515 - 31.059)]. The variation from $709,402 is due to roundings.

This demonstrates how the one cost center system transfers costs between the plants and distorts product costs.

The findings of the (C) case can now be summarized. The significant issue is that improper selection of cost centers can result in very different standard costs and major difficulties in interpreting results.

Assignment Solutions

Assignment 1

The first step is relatively simple. The students simply select the appropriate number of cost centers and let the computer calculate the standard costs. (Instructors should run the computer model for themselves at this preparation point to see the product costs per unit under one cost center.)

With one cost center, Products 2 and 8 are apparently selling below variable cost and would be candidates for elimination. The net income goes from:

Mayers Tap, Inc.
Income Statement
One Cost Center

	Standard	Budgeted
Sales	$9,657,070	$9,657,070
Cost of goods sold, variable	6,288,066	6,288,066
Cost of goods sold, fixed	2,239,000	2,239,000
Gross margin	1,130,004	1,130,004
Selling, general and administrative	500,000	500,000
Net income	$ 630,004	$ 630,004

to:

Mayers Tap, Inc.
Income Statement
One Cost Center

	Standard	Budgeted
Sales	$6,864,130	$6,864,130
Cost of goods sold, variable	3,255,920	3,255,920
Cost of goods sold, fixed	1,131,395	2,239,000
Gross margin	2,476,815	1,369,210
Selling, general and administrative	500,000	500,000
Net income	$1,976,815	$ 869,210

The profit figures can be proved as follows (note the high level of roundings):

	Standard Product 2	Product 8	Total
Sales price	$83.80	$5.75	
Variable cost	$91.66	$5.94	
Fixed cost	$32.80	$2.47	
Volume	28,800	66,000	
Revenue lost	$2,413,440	$379,500	$2,792,940
Variable cost saved	2,639,808	392,040	3,031,848
Contribution increased	226,368	12,540	238,908
Fixed cost "saved"	944,640	163,020	1,107,660
Profit increase	$1,171,008	$175,560	1,346,568

The equivalent analysis using 31 cost centers is:

Mayers Tap, Inc.
Income Statement
31 Cost Centers

	Standard	Budgeted
Sales	$6,864,130	$6,864,130
Cost of goods sold, variable	3,636,807	3,638,807
Cost of goods sold, fixed	1,131,395	2,239,000
Gross margin	2,095,928	986,323
Selling, general and administrative	500,000	500,000
Net income	$1,595,928	$ 486,323

The profit figures can be proved as follows (note the high level of roundings):

	Product 2	Product 8	Total
Sales price	$83.80	$5.75	
Variable cost	79.78	5.33	
Fixed cost	26.85	2.53	
Volume	28,800	66,000	
Revenue lost	$2,413,440	$379,500	$2,792,940
Variable cost saved	2,297,664	351,780	2,649,444
Contribution effect	(115,776)	(27,720)	(143,496)
Fixed cost saved	0	0	0
Profit decrease	$ (115,776)	$(27,720)	$ (143,496)

Instructors should now (for themselves) run the computer model for the 2 cost center scenario. Based on the new reported product costs, students will wish to drop Products 2 and 10. Some may not drop Product 2 because it makes some ($0.01) contribution. The resulting net income numbers after dropping the two products become:

	Standard	Budgeted
Sales	$6,861,130	$6,861,130
Cost of goods sold, variable	3,459,749	3,459,749
Cost of goods sold, fixed	1,261,344	2,239,000
Gross margin	2,140,037	1,162,381
Selling, general and administrative	500,000	500,000
Net income	$1,640,037	$ 662,381

Again, these numbers can be proved (note the high level of roundings).

Standard

	Product 2	Product 10	Total
Selling price	$83.80	$1.50	
Variable cost	$83.79	$1.63	
Fixed cost	$28.28	$0.64	
Volume	28,800	255,000	
Revenue lost	$2,413,440	$362,500	$2,795,940
Variable cost saved	2,413,152	415,650	2,828,802
Contribution increased	288	33,150	33,438
Fixed cost "saved"	814,464	163,200	977,664
Profit increase	$ 814,752	$196,350	$1,011,102

The equivalent analysis using 31 cost centers is:

Mayers Tap, Inc.
Income Statement
31 Cost Centers

	Standard	Budgeted
Sales	$6,861,130	$6,861,130
Cost of goods sold, variable	3,540,312	3,540,312
Cost of goods sold, fixed	1,261,344	2,239,000
Gross margin	2,059,474	1,081,818
Selling, general and administrative	500,000	500,000
Net income	$1,559,474	$ 581,818

Again, these numbers can be proved (note the high level of roundings).

	Product 2	Product 8	Total
Sales price	$83.80	$1.50	
Variable cost	79.78	1.76	
Fixed cost	26.85	0.64	
Volume	28,800	255,000	
Revenue lost	$2,413,440	$382,500	$2,795,940
Variable cost saved	2,297,664	448,800	2,746,464
Contribution effect	(115,776)	66,300	49,476
Fixed costs saved	0	0	0
Profit decrease	$ (115,776)	$(66,350)	$ 49,476

I would drop Product 2 simply because if the standard is even slightly optimistic, the company is losing money. The act of scrapping one above standard scrap rate offsets the effect of making 8,380 good ones!!

Instructors should now run the 31 cost center analysis. The students should want to drop Product 10. The net income numbers become:

	Standard	Budgeted
Sales	$9,274,570	$9,274,570
Cost of goods sold, variable	5,838,052	5,838,052
Cost of goods sold, fixed	2,075,248	2,239,000
Gross margin	1,361,270	1,197,518
Selling, general and administrative	500,000	500,000
Net income	$ 861,270	$ 697,518

Again, the change in profits can be shown to be due to the product being dropped (note the high level of roundings).

	Standard 10
Selling price	$1.50
Variable cost	$1.76
Fixed cost	$0.64
Volume	255,000
Revenue lost	$382,500
Variable cost saved	448,800
Contribution increase	66,300
Fixed cost "saved"	163,200
Profit increase	$229,500

A review of the three product decisions shows that under each cost center scenario, different products are candidates for dropping.

Product	Cost Center		
	1	2	31
2	Drop	Drop	Keep
8	Drop	Keep	Keep
10	Keep	Drop	Drop

While the decision criterion used here is very simple, the three scenarios result in very different decisions. Even if the data are used to focus on products in trouble, the system could still easily produce different results.

Assignment 2

The 31 cost center net income is computed by simulating the actual costs incurred by the factory given the predicted level of production. The simulation is a flexible budget based upon 31 cost center data, the company's selected allocation bases and their identification of fixed and variable costs. It is the best estimate the firm can make of what actual costs will be, given any particular production mix and level.

The purpose of this assignment is to make the students understand how standard cost systems operate and how they adjust for change in production level. The students have five net income figures for both standard and budgeted. There is a distinct pattern to these net income figures.

1. All net incomes, both standard and budgeted, are equal when no products are dropped.

2. All standard net incomes are higher when the identified products are dropped than when they are manufactured.

3. Only the 31 cost center product mix has a budgeted net income that is higher when products are dropped than when they are all manufactured.

4. The standard and budgeted variable costs are the same for a given cost center scenario but are different across scenarios when products are dropped.

5. The budgeted fixed costs are always the same, but standard fixed costs are smaller when products are dropped.

These relationships are key to understanding some of the basics of cost accounting and its limitations.

If no products are dropped, then all net incomes are equal to budget irrespective of allocations used and cost center split because the whole process of cost accounting is a wash. That is, cost accounting takes the budget and assigns it to products in some way. These product costs are then used to accumulate the net income. If budgeted production equals actual, the overall process works irrespective of how good the individual standard costs are.

We have already demonstrated the second relationship in Assignment 1. We only dropped products that apparently had a negative contribution so standard profit must go up.

The cost system will correct itself to the projection as the year progresses. This will occur in two ways.

a. Variable costs - The variable overhead actual will differ from standard as the production mix changes and an untraceable variable overhead spending variances will equal the difference.

b.   Fixed costs - The volume variances will capture unallocated fixed costs.

<u>Note:</u> Material usage and price, labor efficiency and rate, and other
          spending variances will not be predicted by the computer model. However, if standards
          are set accurately, their expected value is zero.

<u>Relationship 3</u>.   In the 31 cost center budgeted net income figures, the actual
production rates are predicted using a 31 cost center flexible budget. Only if the products
dropped really have a net negative contribution under the 31 cost center scenario will the
projected profit go up.

<u>Relationship 4</u>.   The variable costs for the one and two cost center scenarios do not
equal variable costs under 31 cost centers when products are dropped. We have already
described this under Relationship 2.

<u>Relationship 5</u>.   The projected fixed costs are always the same in the budgeted net
income because it is a flexible budget in which fixed costs are held constant.

These relationships are designed to exercise the students' understanding of standard
cost systems and the impact of different cost center designs.

Assignment 3

The Denver plant has three distinct outputs:

o   Heat treatment for Albany products
o   T-1 for Albany products
o   Products 9, 10, and 11

For the 1, 2, and 31 cost center scenarios, calculate the total cost of running the
Denver plant if the company manufactures its full line of 11 products. Explain your
findings.

In the first class, you described the following relationship between the two plants:

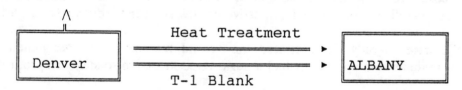

The third assignment is designed to explore the effect of different numbers of cost centers on the apparent total cost of Denver (and hence Albany). The total cost of Denver under the three scenarios can be calculated as follows:

Cost Centers 1	Cost/ Unit	Sales Volume	Total Costs	Albany Costs	Denver Costs
1	$ 17.17	6,000	$ 103,047	$ 103,047	
2	124.47	28,800	3,584,630	3,584,630	
3	24.94	8,000	199,558	199,558	
4	9.04	75,000	677,835	677,835	
5	4.42	46,200	204,032	204,032	
6	3.17	24,000	76,067	76,067	
7	3.40	165,000	516,823	561,823	
8	8.41	66,000	555,121	555,121	
9	1.46	324,000	471,754		$ 471,754
10	1.87	255,000	475,920		475,920
11	4.49	360,000	1,617,280		1,617,280
Shipped to Albany:					
T1 1/4	1.84	112,200		(206,541)	206,541
T1 3/8	0.74	165,000		(122,633)	122,633
T1 5/8	0.53	24,000		($12,685)	$12,685
Heat treat				(404,814)	404,814
Total Costs			$8,527,066	$5,215,439	$3,311,627
Budgeted Costs			$8,527,066	$4,506,038	$4,021,027
Single Cost Center Error		$0	$ 709,401	($709,401)	

Cost Centers 2	Cost/ Unit	Sales Volume	Total Costs	Albany Costs	Denver Costs
1	$ 16.78	6,000	$ 100,670	$ 100,670	
2	112,07	28,800	3,227,563	3,227,563	
3	23.42	8,000	187,393	187,393	
4	3.44	75,000	633,140	633,140	
5	4.19	46,200	193,607	193,607	
6	2.81	24,000	67,489	67,489	
7	3.04	165,000	501,567	501,567	
8	7.49	66,000	494,531	494,531	
9	1.81	324,000	586,071		$ 586,071
10	2.27	255,000	578,410		578,410
11	5.44	360,000	1,956,623		1,956,623

Shipped to Albany:

			Total	Albany	Denver
T1 1/4	2.06	113,200		(231,308)	231,308
T1 3/8	0.84	165,000		($138,500)	138,500
T1 5/8	0.63	24,000		(15,093)	15,093
Heat treat				(515,022)	515,022
			$8,527,066	$4,506,038	$4,021,027

Cost Centers 31	Cost/ Unit	Sales Volume	Total Costs	Albany Costs	Denver Costs
1	$ 16.09	6,000	$ 96,530	$ 96,530	
2	106.64	28,800	3,071,114	3,071,114	
3	23.10	8,000	184,795	184,795	
4	8.34	75,000	625,476	625,476	
5	4.19	46,200	193,409	193,409	
6	2.76	24,000	66,247	66,247	
7	2.90	165,000	477,928	477,928	
8	7.85	66,000	518,179	518,179	
9	1.91	314,000	618,446		681,446
10	2.41	255,000	613,765		613,765
11	5,73	360,000	2,061,176		2,061,176
Shipped to Albany:					
T1 1/4	1.91	112,200		(213,821)	213,821
T1 3/8	0.79	165,000		(130,723)	130,723
T1 5/8	0.58	24,000		(14,034)	14,034
Heat treat				(369,061)	369,061
			$8,527,066	$4,506,089	$4,021,027

The 2 and 31 cost center scenarios both produce budgeted costs of approximately $4,021,000. The 1 cost center produces a total Denver cost of $3,311,676 which is at $709,402 (±) lower than budget. This is because the Denver plant costs more per hour than the Albany plant and the single cost center system averages out the hours. This means that the individual plants will be in error.

Exhibit TN-1 Mayers Tap, Inc. (B) - Direct Labor Hour Overhead Burden Rates

Albany

	K-40	4-10	J-22	G-58	D-34	N-68	C-50	N-72	C-86	N-78
Direct labor	7.88	9.10	9.70	7.18	9.34	9.35	0.00	9.35	9.70	7.18
Variable overhead	11.70	9.20	11.90	5.66	7.24	12.20	0.00	12.13	2.74	11.84
Fixed overhead	8.17	10.35	10.53	5.34	6.07	10.68	0.00	5.28	7.49	7.97
Total	27.74	28.65	32.13	18.19	22.65	32.23	0.00	26.76	19.67	26.99

	A-39	A-40	B-79	C-45	B-86	A-44	A-76	B-81	C-59	F-07
Direct labor	9.70	9.70	9.87	9.70	9.87	9.70	9.70	9.87	9.70	9.10
Variable overhead	5.45	5.44	5.19	2.95	12.03	5.37	5.50	4.96	2.82	9.16
Fixed overhead	19.12	17.44	7.47	6.91	5.84	15.20	16.01	7.91	7.06	11.43
Total	34.27	32.58	22.53	19.56	27.74	30.27	31.21	22.74	19.58	29.69

Denver

	D-43	E-01	F-32	G-05	A-06	B-03	C-03	D-02	A-41	C-31	A-51
Direct labor	8.00	8.00	8.00	8.00	8.00	8.00	8.00	8.00	8.00	8.00	8.00
Variable overhead	26.09	22.87	12.69	26.32	6.60	7.42	20.29	20.38	6.84	20.41	6.76
Fixed overhead	10.63	15.75	9.46	11.40	15.75	13.02	17.96	11.88	15.82	19.62	16.60
Total	44.72	46.61	30.15	45.72	30.35	28.44	46.25	40.26	30.66	48.03	31.36

a. Casewriter's best guess

Exhibit TN-2 Mayers Tap (B) – Direct Labor Hour Overhead Burden Rates Using Company Allocations

Albany

	K-40	F-10	J-22	G-58	D-34	N-68	C-50	N-72	C-86	N-78
Direct labor	7.88	9.10	9.70	7.18	9.34	9.35	0.00	9.35	9.70	7.18
Variable overhead	11.61	8.86	12.04	5.71	8.55	12.10	0.00	12.02	2.47	11.89
Fixed overhead	8.50	10.25	9.54	6.05	6.54	9.65	0.00	6.00	7.49	7.82
Total	27.99	28.21	31.28	18.94	24.43	31.09	0.00	27.38	19.67	26.89

	A-39	A-40	B-79	C-45	B-86	A-44	A-76	B-81	C-59	F-07
Direct labor	9.70	9.70	9.87	9.70	9.87	9.70	9.70	9.87	9.70	9.10
Variable overhead	5.19	5.18	5.20	2.68	12.03	5.11	5.24	5.05	2.55	8.81
Fixed overhead	16.69	17.30	7.48	7.10	6.69	12.69	13.24	7.78	7.21	10.15
Total	31.58	32.17	22.55	19.48	28.59	27.50	28.17	22.70	19.46	28.07

Denver

	D-43	E-01	F-32	G-05	A-06	B-03	C-03	D-02	A-41	C-31	A-51
Direct labor	8.00	8.00	8.00	8.00	8.00	8.00	8.00	8.00	8.00	8.00	8.00
Variable overhead	26.08	22.86	12.69	26.31	6.62	7.41	20.34	20.38	6.88	20.44	6.80
Fixed overhead	11.17	15.93	10.35	11.92	14.58	12.91	17.92	12.04	14.74	17.63	14.97
Total	45.26	46.79	31.04	46.23	29.20	28.32	46.26	40.42	29.61	46.08	29.77

Exhibit TN-3a Mayers Tap, Inc. - Direct Labor Hour Overhead Burden Rates Using Company Allocations

Albany

	K-40	F-10	J-22	G-58	D-34	N-68	C-50	N-72	C-86	N-78
Direct labor	7.88	9.10	9.70	7.18	9.34	9.35	0.00	9.35	9.70	7.18
Variable overhead	11.61	8.86	12.04	5.71	8.55	12.10	0.00	12.02	2.47	11.89
Fixed overhead	8.50	10.25	9.54	6.05	6.54	9.65	0.00	6.00	7.49	7.82
Total	27.99	28.21	31.28	18.94	24.43	31.09	0.00	27.38	19.67	26.89

	A-39	A-40	B-79	C-45	B-86	A-44	A-76	B-81	C-59	F-07
Direct labor	9.70	9.70	9.87	9.70	9.87	9.70	9.70	9.87	9.70	9.10
Variable overhead	5.19	5.18	5.20	2.68	12.03	5.11	5.24	5.05	2.55	8.81
Fixed overhead	16.69	17.30	7.48	7.10	6.69	12.69	13.24	7.78	7.21	10.15
Total	31.58	32.17	22.55	19.48	28.59	27.50	28.17	22.70	19.46	28.07

Denver

	D-43	E-01	F-32	G-05	A-06	B-03	C-03	D-02	A-41	C-31	A-51
Direct labor	8.00	8.00	8.00	8.00	8.00	8.00	8.00	8.00	8.00	8.00	8.00
Variable overhead	26.08	22.86	12.69	26.31	6.62	7.41	20.34	20.38	6.88	20.44	6.80
Fixed overhead	11.17	15.93	10.35	11.92	14.58	12.91	17.92	12.04	14.74	17.63	14.97
Total	45.26	46.79	31.04	46.23	29.20	28.32	46.26	40.42	29.61	46.08	29.77

Exhibit TN-3b Mayers Tap, Inc. - Direct Labor Hour Overhead Burden Rates Using Direct Labor Hours Only

Albany

	K-40	F-10	J-22	G-58	D-34	N-68	C-50	N-72	C-86	N-78
Direct labor	7.88	9.10	9.70	7.18	9.34	9.35	0.00	9.35	9.70	7.18
Variable overhead	8.29	8.29	8.29	8.29	8.29	8.29	0.00	8.29	8.29	8.29
Fixed overhead	8.42	8.42	8.42	8.42	8.42	8.42	0.00	8.42	8.42	8.42
Total	24.59	25.81	26.41	23.89	26.05	26.06	0.00	26.06	26.40	23.89

	A-39	A-40	B-79	C-45	B-86	A-44	A-76	B-81	C-59	F-07	Total
Direct labor	9.70	9.70	9.87	9.70	9.87	9.70	9.70	9.87	9.70	9.10	175.69
Variable overhead	8.29	8.29	8.29	8.29	8.29	8.29	8.29	8.29	8.29	8.29	157.52
Fixed overhead	8.42	8.42	8.42	8.42	8.42	8.42	8.42	8.42	8.42	8.42	159.90
Total	26.41	26.41	26.58	26.41	26.58	26.41	26.41	26.58	26.41	25.81	493.10

Denver

	D-43	E-01	F-32	G-05	A-06	B-03	C-03	D-02	A-41	C-31	A-51	Total
Direct labor	8.00	8.00	8.00	8.00	8.00	8.00	8.00	8.00	8.00	8.00	8.00	88.00
Variable overhead	18.05	18.05	18.05	18.05	18.05	18.05	18.05	18.05	18.05	18.05	18.05	198.51
Fixed overhead	13.47	13.47	13.47	13.47	13.47	13.47	13.47	13.47	13.47	13.47	13.47	148.16
Total	39.52	39.52	39.52	39.52	39.52	39.52	39.52	39.52	39.52	39.52	39.52	434.67

Fisher Technologies

Teaching Note

Fisher Technologies (FT) is designed to follow directly after Mayers Tap, Inc. Unlike MTI, Fisher focuses primarily on the second stage of the two stage process, though some first stage issues are explored. Fisher Technologies illustrates two major issues:

1. In an automated production setting the use of direct labor hours to allocate costs from the cost center to the product can seriously distort reported product costs.

2. It is sometimes necessary to develop allocation ratios from available data rather than measure them directly.

The case provides important insights into when converting from direct labor hour to machine hour costing makes sense. In particular, it introduces the concept of machine-based diversity, where the number of machines running simultaneously differs either by cost center or by product.

The transition from direct labor to machine hour based allocation was, in the 1970's and early 1980's, a major discussion topic in modern cost accounting because the vast majority of existing cost systems relied upon direct labor hours to assign costs from the cost center to the product (in the second stage). As the level of automation increases, the labor content of the product falls and the number of direct labor hours available to allocate costs to the products decreases. This decrease in direct labor hours forces the per hour burden rates to increase, and nowadays it is not uncommon to encounter burden rates of 1,000% or more.

For reported product costs to be accurate, the two-stage process requires that there be a causal relationship between the consumption of resources and the production of output. Furthermore, this relationship must be captured by the allocation base selected to assign costs from the cost center to the product (and from the line items to the cost center). As the quantity of direct labor associated with each product falls, a point is reached where the relationship between number of direct labor hours and resources consumed is no longer sufficiently strong to report adequate product costs.

This teaching note was prepared by Professor Robin Cooper as an aid to instructors using Fisher Technologies (186-188).

When labor hours do not adequately reflect the consumption of resources, it is necessary to select another allocation base. In Fisher Technologies, the alternative explored is machine hours. The selection of other types of second stage allocation bases is explored in the activity-based costing cases in Chapter 5. The emergence of activity-based costing has caused the machine hour costing debate to become less important. Since well designed activity-based costing systems still use machine hours as an important second-stage driver, the debate is not irrelevant.

This teaching note outlines a 80 minute teaching plan

Suggested Assignments:

1. Prepare a presentation to Paul Fisher explaining to him why a shift from direct labor hours to machine hours should be considered for second-stage allocation.

2. Analyze the magnitude of the shift in reported product costs when a machine hour based allocation system is introduced.

3. Critique the existing and your proposed cost systems.

Class Discussion

Q1. What is the competitive environment faced by Fisher Technologies?

FT produces high pressure airfoil blades for experimental jet engines. Production quantities are typically low, and the product has to be manufactured to very high tolerance. Since taking over the company, Fisher has embarked upon an aggressive automation campaign. His stated objective is to have the most modern experimental airfoil manufacturing facility in the business.

The firm competes with five other firms. Three are divisions of larger firms that also produced production airfoils and two other independent companies that like FT are only in the experimental side of the business.

Q2. How would you describe the old production process?

I get a student to briefly describe the old production process ensuring that he or she focuses on the process by which products were produced. In particular, I get the student to describe how each unit has to be clamped into the machine, machined, and then removed, and that all of the pieces in a batch are machined before the batch moves on to the next process. Next, I ask how many such operations a typical product requires to complete and receive the answer about 25. I then focus the discussion on the low quality inherent in this process and point out that Y^x will be a very low number if Y is below one and x is 25. The 2% to tolerance number is thus, not surprising. It is an outcome of the production technology not poor management. My aim is to highlight both the labor intensity of the process and how much setup interferes with the production of parts.

Q3. What is the critical resource to keep busy in this production setting?

The answer to this question is the labor force. I point out that this is appropriate when labor is highly skilled and expensive and the machines are inexpensive. To keep the labor force busy warrants the purchase of extra machines. Thus, FT had a policy of maintaining excess machining capacity at all times.

Q4. Describe the existing multi-cost center system?

If the students have recently completed the Mayers Tap Inc. case series, I do not bother with the single cost center system. The Fisher Technologies case requires careful time control to complete in 80 minutes and extraneous discussions should be avoided.

Using student input, I draw the two stage diagram for the FT direct labor based system (see TN Figure 1). This diagram shows the overhead as consisting of two cost pools, one assigned to cost centers using direct labor hours and the other using direct charging procedures. The costs assigned using direct labor hours in both the first and second stages are not differentiated by the cost system. For these costs there is effectively only one cost center (this lesson was taught in the MTI (B) case when the students were asked to run the 31 cost center system using only direct labor hours in the first stage). Drawing upon this insight the system can now be redrawn as two separate systems. One is a single cost center system that assigns all costs using direct labor hours and the other is a 20 cost center system that uses direct charging in the first stage and direct labor hours in the second (see TN Figure 2). I ask students what percentage of overhead costs are in each system and get an estimate of the actual amount (47%).

Q5. Was this system acceptable under the old production process?

This is a very hard question for students to answer. I push the students to accept the system as relatively well designed for the labor intensive environment that previously existed at FT. I point out that we really do not have enough information in the case to state that the system is acceptable for managerial purposes but there is no evidence to suggest that it was failing. Clearly a shift to machine hours will have no effect since there is always one operator per machine therefore, direct labor hours and machine hours are **directly proportional**. Often in this discussion, students point out that using direct labor hours to drive costs to products focuses attention on direct labor and that given this is the critical resource in the old production process, it is probably the best driver. I agree that the behavioral consequences of choosing the second stage is important and will be explored later in cases contained in Chapter 6. I do not allow any activity-based concepts to enter the room. If a student brings them up, I state that we will discuss activity-based costing later in the course.

Q6. How would you describe the new production process?

Again, I get a student to briefly describe the new production process focusing on the machining process. In particular, the change in nature of the setup personnel and the direct labor force. The change from in-process setup to off-machine setup during the production of parts should be highlighted. The machining process now requires a machine setup followed by almost continuous manufacturing. The direct labor is no longer involved with running the machines but instead in keeping them loaded. There is no guarantee that the direct labor force is working on the same product as the machines they are keeping loaded. Other issues that should be raised include the reduced number of distinct steps in the production process and how this leads to improved quality.

Q7. What is the critical resource to keep busy in this production setting?

The answer to this question is the machines. I point out that this is appropriate. Now the labor is less expensive than the machines. In order to keep the machines busy warrants maintaining an excess capacity of operator time.

Q8. How have these changes made the direct labor based cost system obsolete?

I get students to talk about the problem of multiple machines per operator and introduce the terminology **machine-basis diversity**. I point out that in the new production process, the causal relationship between direct labor and the manufacture of products has been seriously weakened. This leads naturally to the observation that causality is now better captured by machine hours. In addition, it is probably better to focus attention on machine hours.

Q9. In a two stage procedure, what information do we need to develop a machine hour-based costing system?

I draw a simple two-stage picture and get students to discuss what information is required to develop a machine-hour-based system. If necessary, I guide them to focus on the second stage. The information required is the machine hours by product by cost center. Once you have this information, you can sum across products to get the total machine hours in each cost center, thus allowing the machine hour burden rate to be computed and the second stage to be completed by multiplying the machine hours consumed by each product in each cost center by the appropriate machine hour burden rate. The first stage can be completed by summing the machine hours in each center to get the total machine hours in the facility. Dividing the machine hours per cost center by the facility total gives the percentages for a machine hour-based first stage procedure.

In my experience, it is very useful to go through this exercise. The two stage procedures tells exactly the steps we have to undertake to shift to machine-based costing. It provides us with a road map that the software follows to generate the information required to update the FT system.

Q10. What does the machine hour cost system look like at FT?

Using student input, I draw the two-stage procedure for the modified cost system. The new system contains three overhead cost groupings (direct labor based, machine based, and directly changed, 20 cost centers, and a second stage that either uses labor or machine hours to assign costs to products (See TN Figure 3). I ensure that every one is clear that only one base can be used for each cost center. I explain that this constraint was imposed upon the designers by the cost system software that FT was currently using. Such constraints are common, single burden rate centers were the norm until relatively recently and many commercially available packages have to be tricked into accepting more than one base per center. In recent years, this constraint has been removed from many established packages.

To demonstrate that this system is actually simpler than it looks, I observe that if machine hours are used in both stages the cost system collapses to a single burden rate. This observation allows us to redraw the system showing its four constituent parts. A single cost center direct labor based system, a single center machine hour based system, a direct charging first stage with either a labor or machine hour second stage, and a system with either labor or machine hours in the first stage and the other in the second stage.

Q11. How can we tell that a shift to Machine Hours will change reported product costs?

The key lessons of the case can now be explored. I use two simple examples to illustrate the theory. These examples are documented in the article "When Do You Need Machine Hour Costing?". The first example illustrates when converting the first stage to machine hours is appropriate. TN Figure 4 provides the data for the problem. I get students to "solve" the problem for four different cost systems: all direct labor hours, first stage direct labor hours - second stage machine hours, first stage machine hours - second stage direct labor hours, and all machine hours. The four examples demonstrate that if the first stage is direct labor hours the reported costs are always wrong and if it is machine hours the reported costs are always right.

I ask students why the first stage machine hours - second stage labor hours reports accurate product costs and I work towards the answer that direct labor hours and machine hours are strictly proportional. The rule that governs the shift to machine hours in the first stage can now be stated: **when machine-basis diversity is experienced at the cost center level but not the product level, then shifting to machine hours from labor hours in the first stage will cause reported product costs to change. In contrast, shifting to machine hours in the second stage will have no effect.**

Shifting to the second example (see TN Figure 5) demonstrates the second rule: **when machine basis diversity is experienced at the product level then a shift to machine hours from labor hours in the second stage will cause reported product costs to change.**

Q12. We now know the rules, but when in practice should we make the change?

I get the students to identify the three major tests for changing the design of a cost system. These are:

1) Changing reported product costs will influence behavior.
2) Significant dollars are involved.
3) The cost of measurement is acceptable.

Q13. What modifications did you make to the FT system?

The discussion now focuses on the changes students made using the software to the FT cost system.

Not all of the budgetary line items should be allocated using machine hours. The existing system uses a number of different bases although direct labor hours dominates. The students should think through what causes the resource to be consumed and then select the allocation base they think most appropriate. The casewriter's best guess is shown in Exhibit TN-4.

Running the computer model at this stage will provide reported product costs with only the first stage converted to machine hours (see TN Exhibit 5a). Comparison of these product costs to those reported by the existing system shows a maximum shift of 5.25% in standard cost and 9.49% in variable overhead (direct labor and fixed overhead are unaffected by the shift to machine hours) (see TN Exhibit 5b). Product 3 is the only product significantly affected, and this is probably due to the fact that it is manufactured on a brand new machine which does not have an established usage data base yet.

These reported cost differences, with the exception of Product 3, are sufficiently small that in most competitive environments they can be ignored. If it takes a lot of time and energy to maintain a machine hour system for first stage allocation, it is probably not worth the trouble. However, to be on the safe side, if conversion is not a major effort, machine hour base first stage allocation should be implemented.

The next step is to convert the second stage to machine hour based allocation. This is a more complicated undertaking as it requires the manipulation of about 100 numbers (in reality this would be several thousand!). The spreadsheet provides a pre-defined structure that simplifies the calculation of the machine hours associated with each product by cost center.

There are two possible definitions of machine hours that can be supported by the data available in the case.[1] The first defines machine hours as the machine base times the number of direct labor hours. This is an estimate of the run time. The second defines machine hours as run time plus setup time. It is an estimate of the dedicated time, i.e., the amount of time the machine is unavailable to other products because it is dedicated to a given product. The second definition is equivalent to the definition of direct labor hours used in the existing system.[2]

The two-stage process differentiates clearly between these two definitions. The first measures the run time of the machines, it is most appropriate for the assignment of costs that are consumed when the machines are working, for example cutting tool and power consumption. The second measures the time the machine is dedicated to the manufacture of a given product; it is most appropriate for the assignment of costs that are consumed whenever an individual is working on the machine, for example repairs and maintenance (setup was often much harder on the machines than running them) and some factory supplies (Note: this line item also includes the cost of cutting tools).

---

1. There are other definitions of machine hours, that cannot be quantified with the information provided in the case, that the students should be encouraged to consider. These differ from the above definitions by including idle time, repair and maintenance time, and other periods in which the machines are not cutting metal. Students should be forced to decide how they believe the costs that are being assigned behave and which definition of machine hours is most appropriate to allocate those costs to the products.

2. I have never seen students show any concern over the definition of direct labor hours in the original Fisher system. They simply assume that the company has "got it right." Moving to a machine hour basis forces students to reconsider what they are trying to do when selecting an allocation basis. This demonstrates the value of looking at "exotic" production processes as a way of increasing our understanding of more conventional processes.

machines than running them) and some factory supplies (Note: this line item also includes the cost of cutting tools).

A comparison of the two definitions shows minimal variation in the percentage difference at the cost center level with only Product 3 showing any sizeable effects. Large differences at this level do not necessarily signify large differences at the product cost level (however, small differences at the cost center level guarantee small differences in reported product costs). These differences are not large enough to merit further analysis.

Converting the second stage to machine hours does not require that every second stage allocation be based upon machine hours. Given the definition of machine hours, only multiple machine base cost centers need be considered (Exhibit TN-6). The model then requires the entry to the machine hours associated with each product in each cost center (this was calculated earlier (see Exhibit TN-2)). An inspection of the allocation percentages for direct labor and machine hours shows significant differences. This indicates the possibility of major cross-subsidies in the existing cost system.

The cost center burden rates are visibly altered by the shift to second stage dedicated machine hour based allocation as are the reported product costs (Exhibit TN-7). However, note that the cost pools have not changed. The variations in reported product costs range from 6% to 26%, which is significant in most economic settings. Fisher Technologies should seriously consider adopting a machine hour based approach.

Using the run time definition reports product costs that are not significantly different from the dedicated time product costs (Exhibit TN-8). A student might point out that the total machine hours at each center should change with the definition of machine hours. However, the company did not maintain total setup times by cost center; consequently, it is not possible to derive separate total dedicated and run times by cost center. This forces students to use the dedicated times (the dedicated time is used because the definition of direct labor hours in the existing system is equivalent to dedicated labor time). The only way to determine if this approximation has a serious impact on reported product costs is to collect setup times separately from run times for six months and find out.

Using machine hours for the first as well as the second stages has a minor effect on the final reported product costs when compared to just adjusting the second stage (Exhibit TN-9).

The curious student might want to determine the effect of converting the remaining direct labor hours to machine hours. As expected, this has only a minor effect (Exhibit TN-10). First stage allocations appear to have only a minor impact on product costs and the remaining second stage allocations are single machine based so direct labor hours is equivalent to dedicated machine hours.

The two-stage process explains why the conversion to machine hours makes a difference to the reported costs in the FT setting.

1.   In the first stage, it is because the relationship between machine hours and direct labor hours varies by the cost center. Consequently, the size (not the number) of the cost pools is changed. This, in turn, changes the burden rates for each cost pool (irrespective of the

second stage allocation basis selected). In the FT environment, these differences are relatively small and the resulting change in reported product costs is also small.

2.   In the second stage conversion, the effect is more subtle. The firm's products demonstrate machine base diversity, i.e., the number of machines that an operator runs simultaneously is dependent upon the product being manufactured. If all products were manufactured using the average machine base for each cost center, then the conversion to machine hours would have no effect on reported product costs.[3]

3.   In Fisher Technologies, the products demonstrate machine base diversity, and converting to a machine base approach for the second stage allocation basis substantially affects the reported product costs. Machine base diversity is a good example of the subtlety of the forms that product diversity can take. It is not sufficient to look at the product itself; it is necessary to look at the way it is manufactured.[4]

Summary

The two-stage process explains when there is a need to move to a machine hour based approach as the level of automation increases. The Fisher Technologies case allows students to wrestle with some of the implications of this move.

The case focuses predominantly on the second stage of the two-stage process. It should extend students' knowledge of how to use the analytical framework provided by the two-stage process to select allocation bases for the second stage.

At the end of this case, students should have developed an enhanced understanding of the two-stage process, in particular the second stage, and how allocation bases are selected, along with some insights into the use of machine hours instead of direct labor hours for costing purposes.

---

3. This is because the number of machine hours associated by each product would be the product of direct labor hours and machine base and the total number of cost center machine hours would be the total direct labor hours times the same machine base. In other words, the machine base would cancel out.

4. I have visited several firms whose products do not display machine base diversity and who were talking about converting to machine hours using a Fisher Technologies approach. This would have been a futile endeavor. If they managed to "keep everything straight," reported product costs would not have changed. Without the two-stage process framework, it is difficult to see a priori what will happen ahead of time.

Exhibit TN-1 Reported Product Costs (Company Solution)

	Budgeted Production	Direct Labor	Variable Overhead	Fixed Overhead	Standard Cost
Product 1	425	43.37	86.51	31.39	161.27
Product 2	500	49.39	108.75	43.73	201.86
Product 3	12	73.89	106.53	11.96	192.38
Product 4	300	52.91	107.65	43.09	203.66
Product 5	850	43.37	80.70	12.40	136.47

Exhibit TN-2 Comparison of Direct Labor Hour and Machine Hour Intensity by Cost Center

Cost Center	Average Machine Basis	Direct Labor Hours	Direct Labor Hours (%)	Machine Hours	Machine Hours (%)	Difference (%)
1	2.00	2,796	2.33%	5,592	2.89%	-.56%
2	3.00	336	.28	1,008	.52	-.24
3	3.00	2,004	1.67	6,012	3.11	1.44
4	1.00	1,128	.94	1,128	.58	.36
5	2.00	5,088	4.24	10,176	5.26	-1.02
6	1.25	7,980	6.65	9,975	5.15	1.50
7	1.25	4,260	3.55	5,325	2.75	.80
8	1.00	2,496	2.08	2,496	1.29	.79
9	2.00	25,284	21.07	50,568	26.13	-5.06
10	1.00	1,440	1.20	1,440	.74	.46
11	1.50	2,748	2.29	4,122	2.13	.16
12	1.00	9,408	7.84	9,408	4.86	2.98
13	2.00	1,404	1.17	2,808	1.45	-.28
14	2.50	7,056	5.88	17,640	9.11	-3.23
15	3.00	8,748	7.29	26,244	13.56	-6.27
16	1.00	48	.04	48	.02	.02
17	2.00	1,788	1.49	3,576	1.85	-.36
18	1.00	13,008	10.84	13,008	6.72	4.12
19	1.00	22,308	18.59	22,308	11.53	7.06
20	1.00	672	.56	674	.35	.21
Total		120,000	100.00%	193,554	100.00%	

Exhibit TN-3   Machine Hour Percentages-First Stage Allocation

CC1	2.89%	CC11	2.13%
CC2	0.52	CC12	4.86
CC3	3.11	CC13	1.45
CC4	0.58	CC14	9.11
CC5	5.26	CC15	13.56
CC6	5.15	CC16	0.02
CC7	2.75	CC17	1.85
CC8	1.29	CC18	6.72
CC9	26.13	CC19	11.53
CC10	0.74	CC20	0.35

Exhibit TN-4   First Stage Allocation Selections (Casewriter Solution)

Base	Variable Overhead		Base	Variable Overhead (continued)	
2	Indirect Labor-Variable	20%	1	Taxes and Miscellaneous	100%
8		80%	8	Heat, Light, and power	100
3	Overtime and Night		6	Nonproductive Labor	30
	Premium	50	1		70
1		50			
1	Holiday-Vacation Wages	100		**Fixed Overhead**	
1	Payroll Taxes	100			
1	Employee Benefits-		7	Depreciation	90%
	Insurance	100	1		10
1	Workmen's Compensation-		1		10
	Insurance	100	1	Property Taxes	100
4	Repairs and Maintenance-				
	Equipment	60			
8		40			
5	Factory Supplies	80			
8		20			

Available Allocation Bases

1	Direct Labor Houses	5	Factory Supplies
2	Indirect Labor Hours	6	Nonproductive Labor
3	Overtime and Night Premium	7	Depreciation-Equipment
4	Repair & Maintenance-Equipment	8	Machine Hours

Exhibit TN-5   Reported Product Costs and Percentage Differences

a) First Stage Machine Hours

	Budgeted Production	Direct Labor	Variable Overhead	Fixed Overhead	Standard Cost
Product 1	425	43.37	86.37	31.39	161.13
Product 2	500	49.39	109.65	43.73	202.77
Product 3	12	73.89	96.42	11.96	182.28
Product 4	300	52.91	112.25	43.09	208.26
Product 5	850	43.37	81.47	12.40	137.24

b) Company Solution

	Budgeted Production	Direct Labor	Variable Overhead	Fixed Overhead	Standard Cost
Product 1	425	43.37	86.51	31.39	161.27
Product 2	500	49.39	108.75	43.73	201.86
Product 3	12	73.89	106.53	11.96	192.38
Product 4	300	52.91	107.65	43.09	203.66
Product 5	850	43.37	80.70	12.40	136.37

c) Percentage Difference in Reported Costs

	Budgeted Production	Direct Labor	Variable Overhead	Fixed Overhead	Standard Cost
Product 1		0.00%	0.16%	0.00%	0.09%
Product 2		0.00	-0.83	0.00	-0.45
Product 3		0.00	9.49	0.00	5.25
Product 4		0.00	-4.27	0.00	-2.26
Product 5		0.00	-0.95	0.00	0.56

Exhibit TN-6   Second Stage Allocation Selection (Casewriter Solution)

Select		Allocation Base		Select		Allocation Base
1	CC1	Machine Hours	: :	1	CC11	Machine Hours
1	CC2	Machine Hours	: :	0	CC12	Direct Labor Hours
1	CC3	Machine Hours	: :	1	CC13	Machine Hours
0	CC4	Direct Labor Hours	: :	1	CC14	Machine Hours
1	CC5	Machine Hours	: :	1	CC15	Machine Hours
1	CC6	Machine Hours	: :	0	CC16	Direct Labor Hours
1	CC7	Machine Hours	: :	0	CC17	Machine Hours
0	CC8	Direct Labor Hours	: :	0	CC18	Direct Labor Hours
1	CC9	Machine Hours	: :	0	CC19	Direct Labor Hours
0	CC10	Direct Labor Hours	: :	0	CC20	Direct Labor Hours

Exhibit TN-7   Reported Product Costs and Percentage Difference

a) Second Stage Machine Hours

	Budgeted Production	Direct Labor	Variable Overhead	Fixed Overhead	Standard Cost
Product 1	425	43.37	102.64	38.39	184.39
Product 2	500	49.39	140.88	63.72	254.00
Product 3	12	73.89	93.99	8.55	176.43
Product 4	300	52.91	120.91	50.24	224.06
Product 5	850	43.37	73.32	11.95	128.64

b) Company Solution

	Budgeted Production	Direct Labor	Variable Overhead	Fixed Overhead	Standard Cost
Product 1	425	43.37	86.51	31.39	161.27
Product 2	500	49.39	108.75	43.73	201.86
Product 3	12	73.89	106.53	11.96	192.38
Product 4	300	52.91	107.65	43.09	203.66
Product 5	850	43.37	80.70	12.40	136.47

c) Percentage Difference

	Direct Labor	Variable Overhead	Fixed Overhead	Standard Cost
Product 1	-22.30%	-18.65%	-22.30%	-14.34%
Product 2	-45.71	-29.54	-45.71	-25.83
Product 3	28.51	11.77	28.51	8.29
Product 4	-16.59	-12.32	-16.59	-10.02
Product 5	3.63	9.14	3.63	5.74

Exhibit TN-8   Reported Product Costs (Second Stage—Run Time)

	Budgeted Production	Direct Labor	Variable Overhead	Fixed Overhead	Standard Cost
Product 1	425	43.37	102.62	38.38	184.37
Product 2	500	49.39	140.88	63.72	254.00
Product 3	12	73.89	94.39	8.59	176.87
Product 4	300	52.91	120.93	50.25	225.09
Product 5	850	43.37	73.33	11.96	128.66

Exhibit TN-9 Comparison of Reported Product Costs

a) Both Stages Direct Labor Hours

	Budgeted Production	Direct Labor	Variable Overhead	Fixed Overhead	Standard Cost
Product 1	425	43.37	86.51	31.39	161.27
Product 2	500	49.39	108.75	43.73	201.86
Product 3	12	73.89	106.53	11.96	192.38
Product 4	300	52.91	107.65	43.09	203.66
Product 5	850	43.37	80.70	12.40	136.47

b) First Stage Machine Hours

	Budgeted Production	Direct Labor	Variable Overhead	Fixed Overhead	Standard Cost
Product 1	425	43.37	86.37	31.39	161.13
Product 2	500	49.39	109.65	43.73	202.77
Product 3	12	73.89	96.42	11.96	182.28
Product 4	300	52.91	112.25	43.09	208.26
Product 5	850	43.37	81.47	12.40	137.24

c) Second Stage Machine Hours

	Budgeted Production	Direct Labor	Variable Overhead	Fixed Overhead	Standard Cost
Product 1	425	43.37	102.64	38.39	184.39
Product 2	500	49.39	140.88	63.72	254.00
Product 3	12	73.89	93.99	8.55	176.43
Product 4	300	52.91	120.91	50.24	224.06
Product 5	850	43.37	73.32	11.95	128.64

c) Both Stages Machine Hours

	Budgeted Production	Direct Labor	Variable Overhead	Fixed Overhead	Standard Cost
Product 1	425	43.37	102.87	38.39	184.62
Product 2	500	49.39	143.42	63.72	256.53
Product 3	12	73.89	83.26	8.55	165.71
Product 4	300	52.91	126.68	50.24	229.83
Product 5	850	43.37	72.73	11.95	128.05

Exhibit TN-10 Comparison of Different Hours of Adoption of Machine Hours-Based Allocation

a) Both Stages Machine Hours
(Casewriter Solution)

	Budgeted Production	Direct Labor	Variable Overhead	Fixed Overhead	Standard Cost
Product 1	425	43.37	102.87	38.39	184.62
Product 2	500	49.39	143.42	63.72	256.53
Product 3	12	73.89	83.26	8.55	165.71
Product 4	300	52.91	126.68	50.24	229.83
Product 5	850	43.37	72.73	11.95	128.05

a) Both Stages Machine Hours
(All Allocations Machine Hours-Based)

	Budgeted Production	Direct Labor	Variable Overhead	Fixed Overhead	Standard Cost
Product 1	425	43.37	102.59	38.39	184.35
Product 2	500	49.39	146.87	64.22	260.48
Product 3	12	73.89	68.40	6.43	148.72
Product 4	300	52.91	134.52	51.37	238.81
Product 5	850	43.37	71.92	11.83	127.12

Fisher Technologies
Teaching Note
Figure 1
The Existing Cost System

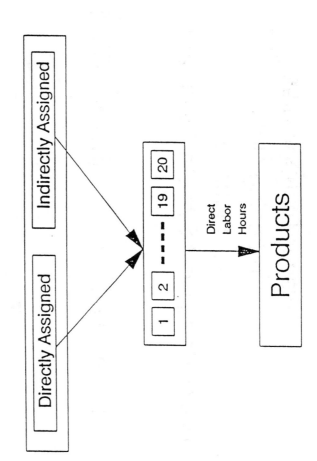

Fisher Technologies
Teaching Note
Figure 2

The Existing Cost System (Alternate View)

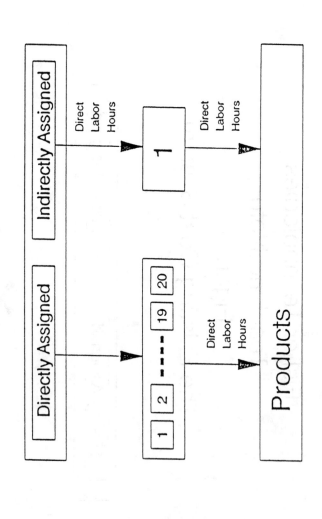

Fisher Technologies
Teaching Note
Figure 3
Machine Hour Cost System

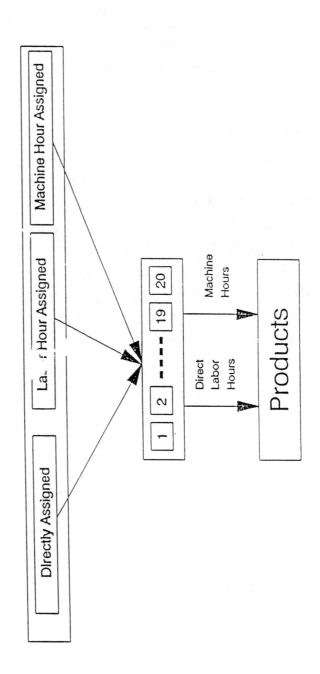

Fisher Technologies
Teaching Note
Figure 4
Simple Example 1

A company manufactures product P1, which takes
one hour of machine time to produce. The Production
facility conconsists of two cost centers. Center A
contains 3 identical machines (M) and center B contains
one of these machines. Each center requires one operator.
The entire facility is budgeted to consumed $40,000 of
power and 20,000 direct labor hours (10,000 per center).
The machines consume all of the power. P1 can be produced
simultaneously on all three machines in center A and on the
single machine in center B.

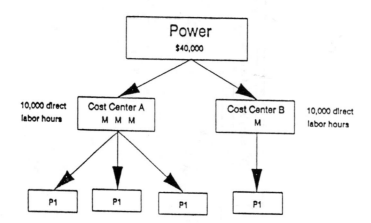

Fisher Technologies
Teaching Note
Figure 5
Simple Example 2

A company manufactures equal numbers of products P1, P2, and P3.
each take one hour of machine time to produce. The production
facility conconsists of two cost centers. Center A
contains 4 identical machines (M) and center B contains
one of these machines. Each center requires one operator.
The entire facility is budgeted to consumed $40,000 of
power and 20,000 direct labor hours (10,000 per center).
The machines consume all of the power. P1 can be produced
simultaneously on three machines in center A and on the
machine in center B. P2 can be produced simultaneously on all four
machines in center A and on the machine in center B. P3 can
be produced on two of the machines in center A and on
machine in center B.

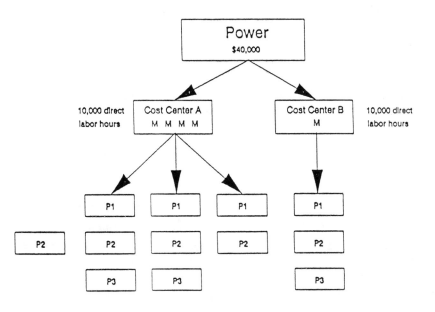

Mueller-Lehmkuhl GmbH

Teaching Note

The Mueller-Lehmkuhl GmbH (ML) case is designed to expose students to several important issues:

1. How a poorly designed cost system can affect the strategy of a firm by misreporting product costs.

2. How more accurate product costs can be estimated by identifying the sources of errors in reported product costs and adjusting for them.

3. How changing market conditions can cause a cost system to become obsolete.

4. How inaccurate cost systems create openings that can be exploited by focused competitors.

ML is a sophisticated case. Students must undertake a strategic analysis of the firm and the market it operates in; identify what is wrong (the bundling of the attaching machines and the fasteners); correct the error using case facts; recompute product costs; and decide how to compete with the Japanese given the existing market conditions.

ML can be taught without prior exposure to the two stage procedure but this requires modifying the teaching strategy described in the note either by:

1. Giving students a more structured version of Assignment Question 2 to explain how to correct for the attaching machine costs.

This note was prepared by Professor Robin Cooper as an aid to instructors using Mueller-Lehmkuhl GmbH (187-048).

2. Allowing the students to discuss the case up through the point where the new product costs are calculated. Taking the students through the calculations and then allowing the discussion to center on the graphs in this teaching note.

Alternatively, particularly in executive programs, you can hand out Exhibit TN-1 in advance as part of the assignment questions, to save students the exercise of ferreting out the relevant numbers for attaching machine costs from the case text.

This teaching note outlines an 80-minute teaching plan.

Suggested Assignments:

1. How much profit does Mueller-Lehmkuhl make on the sale of fasteners? On the sale and rental of attaching machines?

2. Exhibit 6 shows the reported product costs for five representative products. How accurate do you think these numbers are? If you think they are inaccurate, what is your best estimate of the product cost?

Note: Total budgeted direct labor dollars (including setup) for 1986 were $1.61 million (Exhibit 1). The direct labor dollar content (including setup) of the five representative products is:

	S-spring	Ring	Prong (B)	Prong (SS)	Tack
Direct labor $	$1.32	$1.32	$0.14	$0.27	$0.70

These numbers include direct labor dollars in the finishing department.

3. What additional information would you like before giving a definitive answer to Question 2?

4. How would you change the firm's pricing strategy to compete better with the Japanese? Would you implement this change?

5. Should Richard Welkers be worried about the Japanese?

Class Discussion

Q1. What Is the Competitive Environment?

Historically the competitive environment has been relatively pleasant. It consists of a stable oligopoly of four major firms and numerous small firms. The major players leave each other's customers alone and do not engage in price wars. Aggressive price competition would lead to a state of disequilibrium and would backfire on the initiating company, since all customers use multiple sources and competitiors could easily retaliate.

This can be illustrated by using the following simple example:

	Customer A	Customer B
PILONI	Primary Source	Secondary Source
ML	Secondary Source	Primary Source

If PILONI tries to convert customer B to a primary source, ML can retaliate by trying to convert Customer A. These interlocking customer-supplier relationships make direct competition very difficult to initiate successfully.

Other forces that dampen competition are:

1. long-standing personal relationships
2. the rental policy
3. pricing complexity -- no published prices, every deal separately negotiated.
4. high customer satisfaction
5. high switching costs due to customized machines and fasteners.

The dimensions on which the major players traditionally compete are:

1. quality of fasteners
2. attaching speed (machine technology)
3. service
4. new products
5. new markets

The economics of the product are not overwhelming (9% operating margin, i.e., before corporate charges). The peaceful coexistence among competitors guarantees at least this modest return.

Unlike the USA, which can frequently be viewed as a homogeneous market, Europe is a complex market. ML competes in 20 different countries and has to deal with different languages, business codes and tariffs. ML ameliorates many of these complexities by hiring locals as agents or distributors. There are three distribution channels. The differences among the channels are:

	Commission	Other Lines	Inventories
Agents	6 - 10%	Yes	No
Distributors	Not Specified	No	Yes
Regional Sales Offices	No	No	Yes

ML sees itself as a company "designing solutions for a customer's fastener problems." It develops attaching machines and customizes them to a customer's specifications. The machines are rented out cheaply, since future revenues from fastener sales are expected to yield the long-term gains from such a deal. Very often, not only machines, but also the product is customized, i.e., no other company's product could be run on a machine, and, if returned, the machine could not be rented to another customer without significant rework.

Since the market is mature, most sales are made to long-standing customers. It seems that everything in this market is negotiable. Prices differ from customer to customer and even agents' commissions can be individually negotiated. Even though ML tries to find new applications for its products in the fashion industry, the product is not marketing driven. The most important task of marketing and sales is to maintain old customer relationships.

Recently, a Japanese company has been trying to gain market share by price cutting. This issue will be addressed later.

Q2. What is the product?

ML sells two distinct types of product: snap fasteners and attaching machines. They view and sell these products as a single package which links fastener sales to machine rentals.

Q3. What is the production process?

The case provides very little insight into the production process. Students should be able to draw simple block diagrams of the flow:

Fasteners

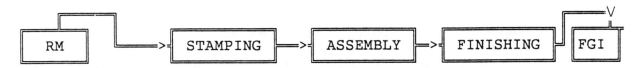

Attaching Machines

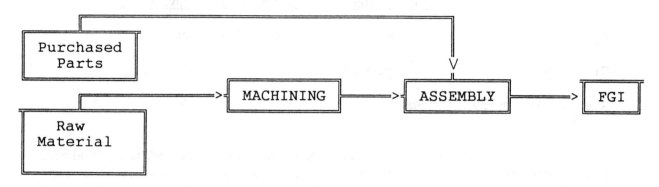

The fastener diagram is important because it will form the basis of the diagram of the cost system.

Q4. What is the company's cost system?

Materials and direct labor are directly traced to the products in the two major departments (stamping and assembly). Overhead costs are charged to the products based on direct labor dollars content in each product. The costs of producing the attaching machines are contained almost exclusively in the general overhead account. They are not traced or broken out separately. Therefore the fasteners absorb a huge burden charge which includes the costs of producing the attaching machines. The cost system therefore "overcosts" the fasteners while not providing any information on the cost of attaching machines. Furthermore, the cost system distorts product costs. Overhead (including attaching machine costs) is allocated based on direct labor dollars. Labor, however, is only a small part of total product costs and most likely not the major cost driver. The cost system therefore penalizes products with a relatively high labor content by allocating to them costs that are not driven by direct labor dollars.

If the students have completed Mayer Tap (B), their attention should be drawn to the treatment of general overhead. It is traced to the product using the same first and second stage allocation bases. This means that each product is charged the same general overhead cost per direct labor hour irrespective of where the direct labor is consumed. In effect, there is only one rate for general overhead while there are many for machine overhead.

The finishing department does not use direct labor dollars to trace costs to products; instead, equivalent units are used. Later it will be necessary to assume that equivalent units and direct labor dollars are substitutable.

Q5. What is the product according to the cost system?

From a marketing perspective, the product is a complex bundle of attributes that include the fasteners, the rental of the attaching machines and any service provided. To the cost system, it is the fastener: the only cost element recognized. The product according to the cost system thus often differs from the product that the market perceives. Students should be sensitized to this fact and ML provides a good example of the difference.

Q6. Where are the costs of the attaching machines?

Since the only cost element is the fastener, the cost of the attaching machines must either be allocated to the fasteners or treated as a period cost. Exhibits 1 and 5, and especially the footnote to Exhibit 5, show that the cost of the attaching machines is allocated to the fasteners.

Q7. What is the effect of reported fastener costs on the treatment of the cost of attaching machines?

There are two effects that should be highlighted:

1. All fasteners will be overcosted.
2. Labor intensive fasteners will bear more of the cost of the attaching machines than fasteners that consume little labor.

The first point while obvious should be drawn to the students' attention. It raises an important question about product costing that will be explored later--namely, does overcosting all products have strategic significance? The second point is more subtle and of critical importance to the ending discussion.

Students who have been exposed to activity-based cost systems might raise more subtle biases:

> Customers that use higher than average volumes of fasteners per attaching machine will be allocated more than their fair share of attaching machine costs. Since these are likely to be some of ML's best customers, unless pricing is adjusted appropriately, there is a risk of overcharging high volume customers.

This is an interesting point that cannot be resolved from case facts. It highlights the need to do customer profitability analysis as well as product profitability. The significance of this difference in the analytic perspective is illustrated in the Winchell Lighting cases in Chapter 7.

Q8. How much profit does Mueller-Lehmkuhl make on the sale of fasteners? On the sale and rental of attaching machines?

Revenues

Attaching machine and fastener revenues can be found in two ways:

1. By deducting the $96 million from fastener sales (see Exhibit 3) from the $103 million total revenues (Exhibit 1), i.e., attaching machine revenue is $7 million,   OR

2. From Exhibit 2, taking the number of machines sold or rented in a year and multiplying by the sale price or annual rental fee and deducting this number from the $103 million total revenues (Exhibit 1), i.e., fastener revenue is $96.15 million.

	CURRENT PRODUCTION RATE AND RENTAL BASE			ASSUMING STEADY STATE AT PRODUCTION LEVEL[5]		
M1	35	$ 200	$ 7,000	35	200	7,000
M2	70	250	17,500	70	250	17,500
M3	105	500	52,500	105	500	52,500
A1	1,350	300	405,000	3,500	300	1,050,000
A2	2,250	500	1,125,000	2,800	500	1,400,000
A3	3,500	1,500	5,250,000	4,200	1,500	6,300,000
			$6,857,000			$8,827,000

One route students might consider (erroneously) is to use the sales data in Exhibit 3 and the cost data in Exhibit 6. The sales data can be used to derive unit volumes from the average sales prices in Exhibit 6 and these can be used to factor up the individual fastener costs. Unfortunately (for the students), this simply recreates approximately the 1986 budget (case Exhibit 2).

The machine and general overhead numbers requires correction because they exclude finishing machine general overhead. The overhead in the finishing department can be estimated by backing out the labor dollars (which have been double counted) and apportioning the remainder (i.e., the overhead) in the percentage of machine to general overhead for the other two departments:

Split of Finishing Labor and Machine and General Overhead

Total Finishing Costs	$9341	
Labor Content	$ 460	Total Labor Less Stamping And Assembly Direct and Setup Labor
Overhead Content	$8881	Total Cost - Labor Cost
Estimated Machine Overhead	$1068	Overhead Content * 4,500/(4,500+ 32,890)
Estimated General Overhead	$7812	Overhead Content * 32,890/(4,500+ 32,890)

Thus an estimated budget very similar to the 1986 budget is derived:

	1986 Budget	1986 Calculated
Material	$31,000.00	$31,123.32
Direct Labor	1,610.00	1,584.02
Machine Overhead	4,500.00	4,394.71
General Overhead	32,890.00	31,285.04
TOTAL	$70,000.00	$68,386.70

This entire exercise simply proves that the cost system "works" in aggregate and that the products are truly representative. The missing $1.5 thousand is due to the products not being perfectly representative.

---

5. These numbers are calculated to show how many machines would be outstanding if current production level had been held constant over 10 year useful life.

	S-SPRING	RING	PRONG (B)	PRONG (S)	TACK	TOTAL
SALES $000	$12,000.00	$9,000.00	$30,000.00	$30,000.00	$15,000.00	
AVERAGE SELLING PRICE	$ 46.75	$ 39.83	$ 15.28	$ 20.32	$ 38.40	
VOLUME	$ 256.68	$ 225.96	$ 1,963.35	$ 1,476.38	$ 390.63	
MATERIAL PER 000 UNITS	$ 10.24	$ 9.38	$ 6.38	$ 6.06	$ 12.55	
VOLUME * MATERIAL/000 UNITS	$ 2,628.45	$2,119.51	$12,526.18	$ 8,946.85	$ 4,902.34	$31,123.23
LABOR PER 000 UNITS	$ 1.32	$ 1.32	$ 0.14	$ .27	$ 0.70	
VOLUME * LABOR/000 UNITS	$ 338.82	$ 298.27	$ 274.87	$ 398.62	$ 273.44	$ 1,584.02
MACHINE O/H PER --- UNITS	$ 1.56	$ 1.72	$ 0.17	$ 1.13	$ 1.37	
VOLUME * M/C O/H/000 UNITS	$ 400.43	$ 388.65	$ 333.77	$ 1,668.31	$ 535.16	$ 3,326.31
GENERAL O/H PER 000 UNITS	$ 21.03	$ 17.40	1.16	$ 5.55	$ 9.40	
VOLUME * GNL O/H/000 UNITS	$ 5,398.07	$3,972.38	$ 2,277.49	$ 8,193.90	$ 3,671.88	$ 2 3 , 4 7 3 . 0 4
FINISHING PER 000 UNITS	$ 5.66	$ 8.28	$ 1.88	$ 0.56	$ 3.84	
VOLUME * FINISHING/000 UNITS	$ 1,452.83	$1,870.95	$ 3,691.10	$ 826.77	$ 1,500.00	$ 9,341.65

Q9. What do the attaching machines cost?

Since the cost system lumps fastener and attaching machine (AM) costs together, the costs for the production of the attaching machines have to be isolated. Obviously, some assumptions have to be made. Since the attaching machine costs are contained in the general overhead accounts, the best approach is to analyze these accounts line by line to identify AM related costs (see TN Exhibit 1).

Total Cost By Product Type ($ million)

	Total Costs	Total AM Costs	Total Fastener Costs
COGS	70.0	$16.7	$53.5
SG&A	23.5	2.9	20.6
	$93.5	$19.6 = 21% of total	$73.9

Profit Calculations ($ millions)

	Total	Fastener	Attaching Machine
Revenue	$103.0	$96.1	$ 6.9
Cost			
- COGS	70.0	53.3	16.7
- SG&A	23.5	20.6	2.9
Profit	$ 9.5	$22.2	($12.7)

The firm is following a razor blade strategy by "giving away" the machines and pricing high on the fasteners. This strategy introduces two major risks.

1. If competitors can unbundle the fasteners from the attaching machines, they will be able to compete on price with the fastener. ML, not knowing the impact of the attaching machine cost on the fastener cost, might be unwilling to compete aggressively enough. This is the risk of overcosting all products.

2. The end-user does not pay a realistic economic rent for the attaching machine and therefore might accept or demand machines that have higher throughput and more features than are economically justified. This assumes that the customer does not understand the relationship between fastener price and attaching machine cost. Even if the customer perceived this relationship, the cost system charges each fastener with an average attaching machine cost not a specific machine cost. Therefore, the very expensive machines are subsidized.

There is some evidence that this is occurring since the companies that only manufacture attaching machines produce much simpler machines.

The firm is following a razor blade strategy by "giving away" the machines and pricing high on the fasteners. This strategy introduces two major risks.

1. If competitors can unbundle the fasteners from the attaching machines, they will be able to compete on price with the fastener. ML, not knowing the impact of the attaching machine cost on the fastener cost, might be unwilling to compete aggressively enough. This is the risk of overcosting all products.

2. The end-user does not pay a realistic economic rent for the attaching machine and therefore might accept or demand machines that have higher throughput and more features than are economically justified. This assumes that the customer does not understand the relationship between fastener price and attaching machine cost. Even if the customer perceived this relationship, the cost system charges each fastener with an average attaching machine cost not a specific machine cost. Therefore, the very expensive machines are subsidized.

There is some evidence that this is occurring since the companies that only manufacture attaching machines produce much simpler machines.

Q10. What is HI's strategy?

HI is trying to unbundle the sale of attaching machines from fasteners. If it can achieve this, it will be able to disrupt the stable European market. The 20% "discount" the Japanese are offering is about equivalent to the average correction factor for attaching machine cost (16.7/70.0). The management of ML appears to be correct in believing that ML is cost competitive. However, their strategy of bundling fasteners and AMs coupled to the design of their cost system hides this fact.

Q11. Exhibit 6 shows the reported product costs for five representative products. How accurate do you think these numbers are? If you think they are inaccurate, what would you estimate they cost?

Note: Total budgeted direct labor dollars (including setup) for 1986 were $1.61 million (Exhibit 1). The direct labor dollar content (including setup) of the five representative products is:

	S-spring	Ring	Prong (B)	Prong (SS)	Tack
Direct labor $	$1.32	$1.32	$0.14	$0.27	$0.70

These numbers include direct labor dollars in the finishing department.

Since AM costs are included in overhead, it is obvious that all fastener products are currently being overcharged.

$16.7 million of general overhead was identified as being attaching machine related. Since total labor dollars in all departments were $1.610 million, $10.37 per direct labor dollar

	S-Spring	Ring	Prong (B)	Prong (S)	Tack
DL$	$ 1.32	$ 1.32	$ 0.14	$ 0.27	$ 0.70
Correction DL$*$10.37	13.69	13.69	1.45	2.80	7.26
Price	46.75	39.83	15.28	20.32	38.40
Old Cost	39.53	37.69	9.64	13.54	27.67
Old Profit	7.22	2.14	5.64	6.78	10.73
Old Margin	15.4%	5.4%	36.91%	33.37%	27.94%
Price	46.75	39.83	15.28	20.32	38.40
New Cost	26.12	24.41	8.28	10.77	20.60
New Profit	20.63	15.42	7.00	9.55	17.80
New Margin	44.12%	38.71%	45.82%	47.00%	46.35%

The change in reported product cost and margin are quite dramatic. Not only do all fastener become more profitable (as expected) but S-Spring and Ring fasteners become almost as profitable as the other lines. This is best illustrated using Graph 1 (Permission is hereby granted to create transparencies from the graphs and Exhibits in this Teaching Note.) Again as expected, the products that benefit the most are those that consume the most direct labor. This illustrate that it is often easy to estimate the direction of a bias in reported product costs. It is much more difficult to estimate the magnitude.

Two major points can now be reiterated:

1. Fasteners are overcosted and it is easily understandable how the Japanese can come in and underprice by such a margin without a competitive advantage. For ML a price drop of 20% should have rendered many products unprofitable. In light of the new cost breakdown, this would not be the case.

2. ML's strategy of subsidizing attaching machine costs through future fastener sales works as long as the two products are bundled together. Since, however, they are not inseparable and the bundling is not entirely enforceable, the Japanese entry tears a hole into ML's strategy.

Q12. What additional information would you like before giving a definitive answer to Assignment 2?

1. The adjustment procedure ignores the use of equivalent units in the finishing department as the second stage allocation basis. This is an approximation that should be investigated before any strategic actions are taken.

2. A more detailed analysis of the costs is required. Simply asking managers for estimates will get you in the ball park but these changes are sufficiently great that a more detailed analysis is called for.

3.   The entire cost system is oversimplistic: An activity-based system might be required.

Q13. Did the firm react to the apparent profitability of the products?

Figure 2 shows the perceived profit margin versus market share for ML and its 5 major product lines. This graph tells a powerful (though untested) story. The firm has high market share in the products it perceives as highly profitable and low market share in those that it perceives as having low profitability.

After the students have finished discussing Figure 2, show Figure 3. This shows fastener sales by competitor. It is interesting to note that ML & Yost appear to be following similar strategies while Poloni and Berghauser are following a second strategy. Students should speculate on whether the various cost systems of these firms are causing the two different strategies to evolve.

Q14. How would you change the firm's pricing strategy to compete better with the Japanese? Would you implement this change?

In order to compete successfully with the Japanese, the company should price attaching machines at higher levels (at least to cover costs) and drop the price of the products to match the Japanese. This should send a signal to the Japanese to back off. Dropping prices in Germany would disrupt the long-term traditional competitive equilibrium. Significant Price drops could be interpreted as initiating a price war.

It seems that adjusting prices is not the right answer to the "Japanese" problem because the company is constrained by the prevailing market conditions. Is it worth shaking up the current equilibrium to fight off the (so far) small Japanese threat? It seems that a better way to deal with the Japanese is to make clear to customers that ML machines will be pulled if customers do not conform to their contractual obligation of buying ML products only. Maybe pulling a machine from a "not so great" customer can communicate that contracts will be enforced. Of course, here the question is whether you would go as far as pulling machines from a Levi Strauss.

Exhibit TN-1   Analysis of Attaching Machine Costs

<u>Attaching Machine Costs in Factory Expenses</u>

<u>Line Item</u>	<u>($ million)</u>	<u>Basis</u>
Factory support	$0	Case facts
Factory supplies	0	Case facts
Technical admin.	$4.5 + .3 x (6.5-4.5) = $5	$4.5M attaching machine service costs; AMs cause 30% of rest
Support department	0	Case facts suggest that few if any of these costs should be allocated to AMs
Machining dept.	$1.4 + $9.7 = $11.1	$1.4M (10% of 7,000 machines * $2,000 per machine) for rework of attaching machines $9.7 M ($13.5M total - $1.4 as explained above = $12.1M. Of that 80% dedicated to AMs
Tooling department	$0.5	Tooling for AM is inexpensive. This is a best guess estimate!
TOTAL	$16.7	

This means that of the $70 million in COGS, $16.7 million or 24% is directly related to attaching machine production.

<u>Attaching Machine Costs in SG&A</u>

<u>Line Item</u>	<u>($ million)</u>	<u>Basis</u>
R&D	$1.9	$5.8*1/3
Administration	$0.3	10% of total based on % revenues
Marketing	0.7	10% of total revenue. Most marketing is for fastener sales.
Shipping	0	Negligible
Commission	0	
	$2.9	

This means that of the $23.5 million SGA, about $2.9 million is due to attaching machine sales.

Figure 1
Mueller-Lehmkuhl GmbH
Comparison of Reported Product Margins

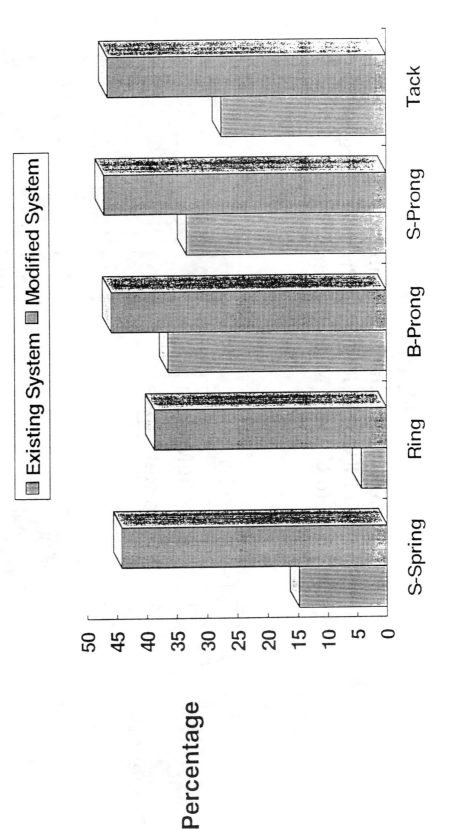

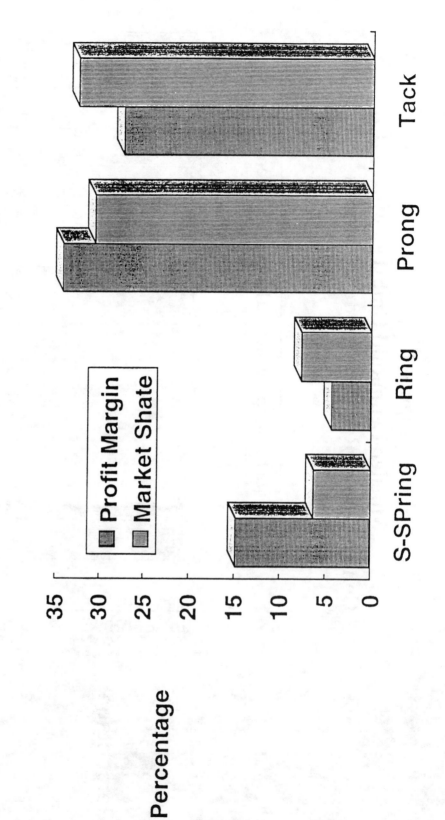

Figure 2
Mueller-Lehmkuhl GmbH
Comparison of Existing Reported Product Margins
to Current Market Share

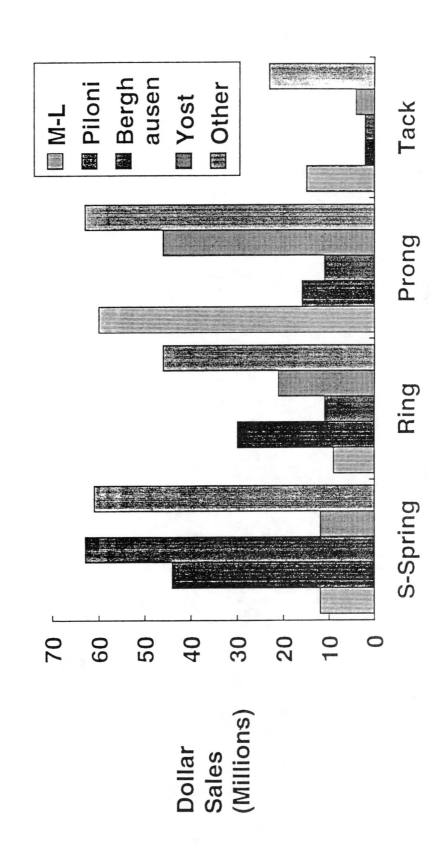

Figure 3
Mueller-Lehmkuhl GmbH
Competitive Ananlysis

Assigning The Expenses of Capacity Resources

The cases in Chapter 3 enable students to focus on accounting issues that arise when assigning the expenses of capacity resources to managers and products. The precursor case for this chapter is Bridgeton Industries in Chapter 1. If this case was not taught at the beginning of the course, it could be inserted with the cases in Chapter 3. Understanding the issues surrounding capacity costing is essential when the course moves on to activity-based cost systems in Chapters 5-7. Unless the costs of excess capacity in support departments are identified and treated separately, the estimates of activity costs will be biased upwards. Rather than deal with this added complexity when discussing ABC systems, we feel it preferable to discuss excess capacity costing issues within the context of traditional cost systems. The conclusions can then be easily extended to the ABC setting when needed.

Polysar describes the problems of performance evaluation when managers of comparable plants must coordinate production but are evaluated separately. It is a simple example that illustrates the dysfunctionality of assigning a manager responsibility for a volume variance over which he has limited influence. The numbers have been simplified but still require students to understand the calculations of cost of goods sold, inventory values, and spending and volume variances when products flow between two plants and selling volumes differ from production volumes. The case provides a wonderful opportunity for students to role play the two plant managers in class, though the best results occur when the selected students are given at least several hours of advance warning to prepare their positions.

Micro Devices Division addresses capacity costing issues for an integrated circuit manufacturer. The case enables students to discuss the alternative definitions of capacity, presented in the chapter text, when assigning capacity expenses to products. In addition to discussion of theoretical, practical, normal, and actual capacity utilization, the discussion can be extended to encompass the role of protective and surge capacity.

Schulze Waxed Containers continues the discussion of the impact of alternative definitions of capacity by focusing on the appropriate treatment of seasonal capacity. In a highly seasonal business, how should the excess capacity cost in the slack season be assigned? The resolution of this issue is of considerable interest for telecommunications and utility industries where the seasonality occurs daily. Full capacity is needed to handle peak-load demands during the day. In the slack (or non-peak) periods, considerable excess capacity exists. Thus, the discussion in Schulze can range well beyond the paper cup manufacturer in the case to the problems faced by many manufacturing and service organizations that have non-uniform demands for their output.

No readings were selected for this chapter. We tried to summarize the relevant issues in the chapter's textual material.

Polysar Limited
Teaching Note

Case History

In November, 1985, I met Pierre Choquette at a cocktail reception for AMP students. When he learned that I was teaching the first-year Control course in the MBA program, he shared with me problems that he had encountered repeatedly in his company due to managers not understanding the concept of volume variance and the problems this caused him in explaining the relative performance of his operating division. This case focuses on these issues and is motivated by the relevance of accounting variances to Polysar managers.

During 1986, the material for the case was collected. Interestingly, this was a time of some change at Polysar as the top layer of management prepared succession plans in anticipation of senior level retirements within the next 3 to 4 years. It was anticipated that Dudley, President, and Ambridge, Group Vice-President of Rubber (the largest Division), would retire in the near future since both men were approaching 65 years of age.

From my conversation with managers at Polysar, Bentley, Henderson, and Choquette were in contention to succeed Dudley. All were considered high potential and the company had sent all three to AMP on consecutive years.

Choquette was interviewed at Harvard in 1985 and at Sarnia in 1986; Henderson was interviewed at Harvard in 1986 while in attendance at AMP.

On September 1, 1986 a series of promotions and moves were announced:

· Ambridge was moved laterally to the newly created position of Group Vice-President -Corporate Development;

· Choquette was promoted to Group Vice-President - Rubber;

This teaching note was prepared by Professor Robert Simons as an aid to instructors teaching Polysar Limited, HBS case 2-187-098.

- The top job in Diversified Products was upgraded from a Vice-President to a Group Vice President; Henderson was promoted to this position and returned to Sarnia from Europe;

- Beaton moved laterally to Europe to take over the position of Vice-President EROW vacated by Henderson;

- Bentley remained in his position as Group Vice-President - Basic Petrochemicals.

Teaching Objectives

1. Provide a strong understanding of the relationship between capacity utilization and the absorption of fixed costs. Illustrate why accountants have developed the volume variance. Through assignment questions, motivate students to formulate a presentation to explain volume variances to others.

2. Reinforce student abilities to use budgets, pre-set standards, and ex post income statements to evaluate performance. Reinforce understanding of flowthrough relationship between production, inventory, and sales.

3. Explore the interaction between performance measurement of divisions and performance measurement of managers.

4. Provide an opportunity for students to propose improvements to a functioning information and control system based on their knowledge of the structure and functioning of the business.

Assignment Questions

1. Prepare a presentation for the Polysar Board of Directors to review the performance of the NASA Rubber Division. Pay particular attention to questions that may be raised concerning the accuracy and meaning of the volume variance.

2. What is the best sales and production strategy for EROW Division? NASA Division? Rubber Group in total?

3. What changes, if any, would you recommend be made in the management accounting performance system to improve the reporting and evaluation of Rubber Group performance?

Teaching Strategy

The case can be taught by covering three broad topic categories: (1) mechanics of calculating volume variance, (2) evaluation of NASA Division, and (3) consideration of system improvements. The inclusion and time spent on each of these segments will depend on the students' previous exposure to volume variances and the placement of the case in the course.

If this case represents the first exposure of volume variances in class, the bulk of class time should be spent on the mechanics, perhaps using simple graphs to illustrate the procedure. However, enough time should be left in the class to discuss the evaluation of NASA Division since the case demonstrates that an understanding of accounting techniques is necessary for general managers to discharge their operating responsibilities. At the end of the class, instead of leading a discussion of possible system improvements, the instructor can reveal the changes made in the system by Pierre Choquette (to be discussed at the end of this note).

If the mechanics of volume variances has already been covered by students, the class time can be split between an evaluation of NASA performance and a discussion of possible system improvements. Since much of this discussion will focus on the volume variance and capacity issues, it is a good idea to spend 10 minutes at the beginning of class to review the calculation of the volume variance (by asking a student to review his calculation?) to ensure that all students enter into the discussion on the same footing. During the student discussion, the instructor may wish to push students to show that they understand the mechanics that underlie the accounting statements.

I. Mechanics[1]

This segment can be structured by the instructor by asking a series of questions:

Starting with Exhibit 1, Statistics and Analyses,

(a) What is the purpose of this statement?

The top half of the statement shows volume statistics and the bottom half reveals fixed costs of production?

(b) Why is this important?

Volume statistics are important in any business because they are simple indicators of the physical throughput of the business and do not become clouded with accounting allocations and approximations.

Fixed costs are important in this business because it is a capital intensive, continuous process industry. As suggested in the case, even direct labor is treated as fixed since the labor component of the plant does not vary significantly with the level of production. Just as eskimos have 11 different words to describe different types of snow, Polysar uses three different descriptors for fixed costs - direct, allocated cash, and allocated non-cash.

(c) How are fixed costs accumulated in the company's accounting records?

---

1. Note that the company has structured the statements so that positive figures increase profit and negative figures decrease profits. Note also that Canada uses the metric system of weights and measures and that 'tonne' signifies a metric or long ton = 1,000 kilograms (2,204 lbs). The American 'ton' refers to a short ton of 2,000 lbs.

Each of the Fixed Cost lines (Direct, Allocated Cash, and Allocated Noncash) represents the <u>debit</u> side of accounts which have been accumulating charges throughout the year. For example, the Allocated Noncash line reports the depreciation expense account which has been built up during the year by a series of entries which sum to:

Dr. Depreciation expense	$15,625
Cr. Accumulated Depreciation	$15,625

Other examples include payroll costs in direct labor and allocation of service center costs in Allocated Cash; these can be illustrated by T-accounts if necessary.

(d) What does the line, "Fixed Cost to Production," represent?

In the budget column, this is the amount of <u>total</u> fixed costs that were budgeted for the first 9 months of the year. If we assume level spending[2], the <u>annual</u> budgeted amount of total fixed costs is

$$\$44,625 \,/\, (9/12) = \$59,500$$

In the actual column, $44,127 represents the amount actually spent to date. Subtraction indicates that the Division has spent $498 less than budget (is this good? - it depends on what has been cut back).

(e) Can someone explain why the "Fixed Cost of Sales" on Exhibit 1 agrees exactly with "Total Fixed Costs" on Exhibit 2? Doesn't the "Fixed Cost to Production" line of Exhibit 1 represent <u>total</u> fixed costs?

Exhibit 1, Statistics and Analyses, presents total fixed costs, both budgeted and actual, that were spent to support a certain level of <u>production</u> (in this case 55,000 tonnes budget and 47,500 tonnes actual). However, not all of these fixed costs go to the income statement since not all of this production was sold by NASA. Some products (and costs) go to/from inventory on the Balance Sheet and some products (and costs) are transferred to/from EROW. The remaining fixed costs represent the production that was sold by NASA and this cost is properly <u>matched against sales</u> on the income statement.

(f) What are the mechanics by which fixed costs are transferred to the income statement?

Polysar, like many other companies, uses a standard cost system to allocate fixed costs to its products. The formula is described in the case as,

$$\frac{\text{Standard Fixed Cost}}{\text{per tonne}} = \frac{\text{Estimated Annual Total Fixed Costs}}{\text{Annual Demonstrated Plant Capacity}}$$

$$= \frac{\$59,500}{85,000 \text{ tonnes}} \qquad = \$700/\text{tonne}$$

---

2. The analysis in this note assumes that spending and production for the last 3 months of the year will equal 1/3 of that recorded for the first 9 months. This assumption is not unrealistic for this business.

We can trace these costs through the statements quite easily,

Statement of Net Contribution:

Sales: actual = 35,800 tonnes x $700 = $25,060
                budget = 33,000 x $700 = $23,100

Statistics and Analyses:

Transfers[3]
        - inventory
                actual = 1,600 tonnes x $700 = $1,120
                budget = 3,500 x $700 = $2,450

        47.5 (prod) - 35.8 (sales) - 12.2 (to EROW)
        + 2.1 (from EROW) = 1.6 addition to inventory.

        - to EROW = 12,200 x $700 = $8,540

The transfer from EROW has a different costs allocation per tonne based on the unique fixed costs and capacity of the Antwerp plant. It is,

2,100 tonnes x Y   = $1,302
        Y   = $620/tonne

(g) What is the denominator of the allocation equation, "Demonstrated Capacity"?

Demonstrated capacity, as used by Polysar, is described in Exhibit 3, an excerpt from the Controller's manual. Companies must choose a production base over which to spread fixed costs. Choices may range from actual past production (which may include correctable inefficiencies) and theoretical capacity (which may never be met due to design constraints, shutdowns, maintenance, etc). Polysar has chosen "demonstrated capacity" which they define as the annualized extrapolation of what the plant has achieved in short periods of high, but unsustained, throughput. Clearly, the choice of the denominator will affect the magnitude of the volume variance.

Let's now look at the Fixed Cost section of the Statement of Net Contribution:

(h) We have identified the origin of the Standard Fixed Costs, what could be included in Cost Adjustments?

The origin and calculation of this amount is not obvious from the statements and need not be pursued in class. The adjustment represents the difference in fixed cost per unit for EROW sourced butyl sold by NASA (all units sold have been costed at NASA standard cost of $700/tonne; the EROW units, however, have only $620/tonne allocated fixed cost).

---

3. Note that transfers to/from EROW are effected through the inventory accounts of the respective Divisions and are therefore not reflected on the income statements.

2,100 tonnes x [$700 - $620] = $168,000

(i) What does the spending variance represent?

The spending variance is the difference between the amount of total fixed costs which were budgeted to date and the actual spending. We have seen this number before on the statement of Statistics and Analyses, Fixed Cost to Production.

(j) What is the volume variance and how is it computed?

The volume variance represents over(under) absorption of fixed cost due to actual production not coinciding with the denominator (in this case, demonstrated capacity) used to allocate fixed cost. It is calculated,

	Actual	Budget
Demonstrated capacity		
annual	85.0	85.0
9 months (9/12)	63.75	63.75
Production	47.5	55.0
Shortfall	16.25	8.75
Fixed cost / tonne	x $700	x $700
Underabsorbed F.C	$11,375	$6,125

Using demonstrated capacity instead of budgeted production to allocate fixed costs is somewhat unusual. This method results in two volume variances being rolled into one,

Variance due to excess capacity (budgeted in advance)		$6,125
Variance due to production less than budget:		
Shortfall due to EROW (7.3 * 700)	$5,110	
due to other (0.2 * 700)	140	$ 5,250
Total Volume Variance as reported		$11,375

II. Evaluation

This segment can be opened either by leading a general discussion on the performance of NASA or by asking (calling upon?) one or more volunteers to act as Choquette and Devereux, NASA Controller, in making a presentation of Division performance.

Points to be raised include the following:

Analysis Of NASA Performance

Sales revenue is up due to increased volume with slightly lower prices.

Volume	[35.8 - 33.0] x $1850	=	$5,180
Price	[$1840 - $1850] x 35.8	=	- 358
Net increase			$4,822

Variable cost efficiency variance is favorable (241) indicating that the plant operated more efficiently than expected (we cannot, however, tell from the case if the Sarnia plant is more efficient than Antwerp - to do this we need input utilization factors).

Fixed cost spending variance is favorable (498) which suggests overhead costs have been carefully managed (although this would require more information to ensure that timing differences or cut backs on maintenance, etc. were not the cause).

Volume variance is highly unfavorable ($11,375). This is due to expected excess capacity of the plant and underproduction of 7,500 tonnes. Underproduction is due to EROW taking 7,300 tonnes less than budget. This shortfall seems large both in an absolute sense and compared to past years. Perhaps EROW makes up its butyl production shortfall at year end and transfers during the last three months will be correspondingly larger.

NASA's budgeted profit was $2 million; it has recorded a loss of $.9 million. Eliminating the volume variance would yield an adjusted budgeted profit of $8 million and an adjusted actual profit of $10.5 million.

Comparison of NASA and EROW[4]

The EROW operation is more profitable than NASA. Revenue per tonne is higher due to reduced competition. Variable costs are lower due to lower European feedstock prices. Fixed costs per tonne are lower (as per analysis in Section I).

	NASA	EROW
Net Revenue/tonne	$1,766 (63,239/35.8)	$1,879 (89,920/47.85)
Variable cost/tonne	623 (22,294/35.8)	599 (28,662/47.85)
Contribution/tonne	$1,143	$1,280
Gross margin	64.7%	68.3%
Fixed costs/tonne	700	620
Gross profit margin	8.2%	35.7%

The fixed cost per tonne of Sarnia 2 is not $700, but really much higher if fixed costs are spread across budgeted production. The $700 figure is based on a "demonstrated capacity" of 85,000 tonnes. Based on budgeted production of 73,000 tonnes (55 x [12/9]), fixed costs per ton are approximately $815 ($59,500 / 73,000).

The capital cost structure of the two plants is very different. The Antwerp plant has charged only $4,900 of depreciation against its butyl sales. This is because the plant, built in 1964, is probably close to fully depreciated; current depreciation charges probably represent amortization of the 1979/80 refit (remember also that depreciation charges in Antwerp are split

---

4. Foreign currency accounting may change the results of the analysis. We have no information on this.

between butyl production and halobutyl production; the case, and Exhibit 5, show only butyl production. A depreciation charge of a like amount was probably charged against the halobutyl statement).

The Sarnia plant has $15,600 of depreciation charged against operations. If depreciated on a straight line basis, the plant (original cost $550 million) is probably being depreciated over approximately 25 years (550 / [15.6 x (12/9)]).

Given the cost structures of the two regions, it is preferable to produce in Europe rather than in Canada. Contribution per tonne is higher in Europe. It should be noted that evaluation of respective Divisional performance is even more critical when the Corporation overall is hovering around the breakeven point. Managers may be considering divestitures.

Incentives For Managers

Henderson and Choquette have moved up together quickly to senior positions. They are both ambitious and capable individuals. Their sequenced attendance at AMP suggests they are being considered for more senior responsibilities in the near future (of which there are only 2 levels - Group VP and President. With similar backgrounds, Henderson and Choquette are rivals for these promotion slots.

Bonuses (and presumably advancement) for Henderson and Choquette depend significantly (50%) on how much profit they deliver as compared to budget. Employees at all levels also have an interest in Divisional profits and any accounting allocation that may affect profits and, hence, bonuses.

What do you think Henderson's strategy was? As he told me with a chuckle, he tells his people to "sell more at higher prices and produce more in Europe." For every extra tonne that Henderson produces, his profit increases in two ways: his fixed costs are already covered so that the contribution goes right to net profit; and, he avoids having to receive a tonne from Sarnia with high variable and fixed costs. Sarnia's fixed cost are variable costs to Henderson and he will be willing to spend up to $700/tonne to boost Antwerp yield and avoid having to take product from Sarnia. In the longer term, there is incentive for Henderson to add capacity in Europe when the Rubber Group has considerable excess capacity.

For every tonne that Henderson does not take from NASA, Choquette's profit falls by $700 as the volume variance increases. NASA is also charged for any excess inventory (working capital charge from corporate) due to EROW not taking budgeted volume.

Since Henderson arrived at EROW in 1982, EROW has taken less butyl than budgeted each year [Exhibit 4]. What are Henderson's incentives to work to beat accurate budgets (or, more cynically, to overstate budgeted transfer estimates)?

Other

Is NASA really a profit center? The significant transfers (1/3 of production) to EROW are not acknowledged in NASA's income statement and Choquette has only partial control over the effects of the volume variance on profits. Although selling almost a third of NASA's output, EROW is not paying a proportionate share of the capital investment in NASA.

Note: transfers at cost between inventory accounts of NASA and EROW are for internal management reporting only. For legal entity reporting, profits on shipments are split between the two countries.

III. System Improvements

Pierre Choquette, in his new role of Group Vice-President, says that he is unwilling to talk in presentations and reviews of NASA and EROW as separate businesses. He now talks in global product terms. As he claims, "it is meaningless to separate the two Divisions when assets are in one place and revenues are in another." The amount of cross shipment of product between Divisions and directly to customers suggests that this approach has merit.

Choquette still maintains that the Divisions be treated as profit centers due to their size. This being the case, consideration can be given to having transfers at a price which splits the profit between the two Divisions rather than having the profit rest with EROW and the unabsorbed fixed costs with NASA.

Choquette also believes that NASA should continue to show the volume variance on their books, "I won't hold them accountable in the same way as things they can control, but I want them to know and worry about it."

The bonus plan is problematic and has been changed for employees in 1986 to reflect overall corporate performance only. Division managers are still rewarded based on division performance. It seems that more thought can be given to developing a bonus scheme for managers. Options include factoring in global product line performance, Group performance, and correcting the results for items such as the portion of the volume variance due to actions of other Divisions.

However, it is important to recognize that the Company is not rewarding based on absolute results, but rather based on budgeted results. Bonuses are based solely on the increment over budget. Thus, to the extent that excess capacity is budgeted through the volume variance, the manager is not being held responsible for it. The issue becomes how much stretch to build into the budget. Perhaps it makes sense to hold NASA responsible for underabsorbed fixed costs if so doing will cause actions to boost production to compensate for the unexpected efficiencies of EROW.

As for the volume variance, the company has chosen to divide fixed cost by demonstrated capacity (85,000 tonnes) and charge the volume variance to the plant P&L. Another possibility would be to divide fixed costs by budgeted production (which would increase per unit fixed cost). A preferred solution, in my opinion, is to charge off the fixed costs due to overcapacity as a period cost at the Group level. Using this method, Divisions would be charged only with fixed costs used in production.

Wrap - Up (announce September 1, 1986 promotions)

It is up to Choquette to explain the above information, to the extent it is not obvious, to those who must evaluate his performance and that of NASA Division. Can we assume that managers, the recipients of accounting reports, understand the calculations that lead to accounting numbers such as the volume variance? Choquette and Henderson have made it their business to understand. In fact, in the interviews, Choquette stated that he believed that he and Henderson were the only senior managers who truly understood the volume variance and its effect on performance measurement.

Micro Devices Division

Teaching Note

The Micro Devices Division case illustrates three aspects of capacity costing:

1. Several potential definitions of capacity utilization that can be used for product costing and transfer pricing purposes.

2. Several ways excess capacity can arise.

3. The appropriate treatment of excess capacity costs in a cost system.

This teaching note outlines an 80-minute teaching plan.

Suggested Assignments:

1A. The "excess" capacity of the facility is associated with four causes:

   a. Long-term yield variation
   b. Short-term yield fluctuation
   c. Changes in product mix
   d. Lumpy capacity acquisition

Should the cost associated with any of these causes of excess capacities be included in product costs or transfer prices?

1B. If excess capacity costs are excluded from product costs, how should these excess capacity costs be accounted for and made visible to management?

This teaching note was written by Professor Robin Cooper as an aid to instructors using Micro Devices Division (191-073).

2.   What definition of capacity should be used for product costing and transfer pricing purposes--theoretical, practical, normal, actual?

3.   Should all fixed costs be ignored for product costing and transfer pricing purposes?

Class Discussion

Q1. What is the competitive environment of the MDD?

Students should identify several factors that are critical to the way MDD competes. These include:

-   captive supplier
-   provides 40% of parents chip requirements
-   only produces propriety chips
-   not a low cost producer
-   when chip becomes a commodity, it is outsourced to other competitors
-   dependent on technology transfer from competitors in exchange for commodity chip business
-   excess capacity caused by unexpectedly high yields
-   strategy of parent forbids using excess capacity for commodity chips

Q2. What are the uses of cost information at MDD?

-   transfer pricing
-   outsourcing
-   make versus buy analysis
-   investment analysis
-   performance evaluation

Q3. What is the cost structure of this firm?

Case Exhibits 6 and 7 allow the calculation of the firm's cost structure:

Direct Material	8%
Direct Labor	15%
Overhead	77%

Exhibit 7 allows the overhead to be split into different categories. Fixed overhead of $52.791 million is much larger than variable overhead which amounts to $30.781 million. Thus, this firm has very high fixed overhead compared to other costs. The way this overhead is assigned to products is going to make a big difference in reported product costs.

Q4. What design element of the two stage procedure are we exploring in this case?

Students should rapidly identify the definition of resources as the issue that is being explored in the case. For a cost system to be able to report accurate product costs, the definition of resources must match the definition of products. That is, only resources consumed by the products whose costs are being reported must be included in the definition of resources and that all of the resources consumed by those products must be included (recall the discussion in the Mueller-Lehmkuhl and Institutional Furniture cases).

Q5. What is the structure of the existing cost system?

With student input, I draw the two stage diagram for the system on the board (see TN-Exhibit 1) and then discuss the minor variation caused by splitting the wafers into dies. I point out that this is a variation on what happens when two subassemblies are combined in conventional manufacturing and then further work is performed upon them. The existing system is relatively simple, it reports actual costs not standard costs. The actual yields are used to determine both the number of dies in the die lot and the number of finished products.

Q6. What are the options identified for the treatment of excess capacity?

I get a student to list the four alternatives in the case. These are:

      Theoretical
      Practical
      Normal
      Actual

I introduce the following simple example and get students to "work the numbers". The example, with solutions, is:

Total capacity costs $12,000,000

Capacity Definition	Units	$/Unit
Theoretical capacity	120,000	$100
Practical capacity	100,000	120
Normal utilization or volume	80,000	150
Actual utilization or volume	75,000	160

I suggest that we use the practical capacity definition as an example and run the system to see what happens. I get a student to work the numbers. Actual production of 75k units at $120 units equals $9,000,000. I ask students what happened to the other $3,000,000 and get them to understand it is the cost of excess capacity. I ask students how we would handle these costs in a two stage system and draw the appropriate diagrams on the board (see TN-Exhibit 1). With the excess capacity costs being identified separately from reported product costs.

Q7. What are the benefits of treating the $3,000,000 as excess capacity costs?

Students should be able to identify several benefits. These include reporting more accurate product costs (reported product costs now only reflect the cost of the resources consumed), and higher visibility to the excess capacity costs. These excess capacity costs can be "reduced" by increasing throughput, finding some way to reduce spending on the excess capacity (see Bridgeton Industries Teaching Note for a discussion on this point), or writing-off the assets that are considered excess capacity.

Q8. What is the best choice for the definition of capacity?

Having demonstrated the benefits of not assigning the costs of excess capacity to products, I focus the students on what is the best definition for MDD. Practical capacity is usually the modal choice. Theoretical is rejected because the firm can never assign all of the capacity costs to products because it can never manufacture at the theoretical capacity. Normal and actual are usually rejected, especially if the students have been exposed to the Bridgeton Industries case, because they risk inducing the death spiral. I usually draw up a table of the four approaches and get students to identify the strengths and weaknesses of the various approaches. This discussion is typically very general and the students have not developed a good theoretical model of how to choose between the various alternatives.

Often when I teach the case, the students keep raising the causes of excess capacity that are identified in the case (long and short term yield, change in product mix, and lumpy acquisitions). I try to get the students to put this discussion off until the theory of how to identify excess capacity has been established. Most of the time, I am successful but occasionally the students won't let go. I then have to interrupt the confusing discussion that follows and state the central rule for identifying excess capacity. Otherwise, I ask the following question:

Q9. What rule can I develop to identify excess capacity?

I never expect any answer to this question. I develop a simple example to focus student attention on the problem faced. This example consists of a firm that competes in an industry that has a stable cycle that oscillates $\pm 20\%$ around the average. I ask students what is the practical capacity of the firm under these conditions. I draw a simple diagram that shows the theoretical and practical capacity of the plant. I set the practical capacity (current definition) at the top of the cycle and identify 80% as the average utilization, and 60% as the bottom of the cycle. I ask the students whether we want to use our current definition of practical capacity for product costing purposes. Students rapidly focus on the 80% as the appropriate definition of practical capacity for product costing purposes. I label the difference between 80% and 100% as SURGE capacity. I ask students if we should exclude surge capacity from our definition of practical capacity. I then return to my original simple numerical example and ask students to calculate the cost per unit given the 80% average utilization. The cost per unit is now equivalent to the normal capacity previously calculated. Thus the cost is $150 per unit. I then try three different actual outputs. 60, 80, and 100. I show that the average excess capacity figure is 0. It starts at the bottom of the cycle at $3,000,000, is zero at 80,000 units, and (3,000,000) at 100,000 units.

I try to get the students to develop the "rule" from this example and generally fail. I then turn to another example where the rule is more obvious. This time, the customers demand the ability to meet sudden increases in demand. I suggest that keeping 20% reserve capacity is optimum for the firm. The incremental business due to being able to satisfy customer demand is matched by the incremental cost of maintaining additional capacity. I ask students to identify what is the appropriate practical capacity for product costing purposes in this setting. I work for consensus on 80%. I now tell students that the rule should be apparent. I let them struggle until they realize that the way the customer orders products defines the surge capacity that must be maintained. In other words, for product costing purposes, the product should be assigned the costs of the capacity that the customer demands.

Students rapidly realize that the same physical product if ordered in different ways by customers will require different surge capacity. If I am teaching the Schulze Waxed Containers case later in the course, I postpone this discussion. Otherwise, I agree that is the case, and suggest that some manufacturing costs are really customer driven and should be assigned to the customer not the product. This issue is dealt with in more detail in the Kanthal case (Chapter 7).

Having established the "rule" I now turn to the various causes of excess capacity at MDD. I start with long-term yield. I let the students discuss the situation for a while. They normally realize that the use to which the capacity is put defines how it should be treated. I let the discussion continue and then if they have not reached a clear solution, I pose the following dichotomy. The capacity can be used to manufacture other chips but usually the firm cannot find any to manufacture or the parent refuses to let them bring in additional business because it would have a negative effect upon the transfer of technology. I ensure that students understand that the treatment of the two cases is different. The first case creates excess capacity which is the responsibility of the division. The reported product costs should reflect the capacity that has been created by the higher yields. In the second case, the parent should "pay" for the unutilized capacity. I ask if the products should be assigned the costs. If the student consensus is yes I set up a simple example where the product would cost $50 if the excess capacity costs are not assigned to the products, and $75 if it is assigned to the products. I point out that further downstream a manager has to choose between our product and a competitors' that costs $60. I ask if we really want that manager to outsource the product. I get a student to suggest that charging the parent for the strategically unused capacity in a single lump sum is the best solution. Reported product costs reflect the higher yields and the strategic planners are aware of the costs of not utilizing the capacity thereby created.

I draw a simple two stage diagram that has two types of excess capacity costs recognized: strategically unutilized and excess capacity. I explain that reporting each of these excess capacity costs separately allows the parent to both put pressure on the division to maintain capacity utilization and to stop the division from destroying the strategic balance between the corporation and the commodity chip manufacturers.

Q10. What about short-term capacity?

This is the capacity required to buffer the bottleneck machines from statistical fluctuations in yield. This capacity is also known as protective capacity. It is different from surge capacity because it is required even if demand is constant. In principle, these capacity costs should be assigned to products because they are an unavoidable part of the production process required to satisfy customer demand. The costs of excess capacity, i.e., some capacity could be removed without any loss of productivity, should be assigned to period costs. The appropriate level of protective capacity is a judgement call. Therefore, it is very difficult to differentiate between excess and protective capacity.

Q11. What about the capacity created by product mix changes?

The short product life compared to the production machine life expectancies often creates excess capacity. This capacity once created should not be associated with existing products. The costs of this capacity are clearly not product costs. This capacity is excess and its costs should be treated as a period cost. An alternative view, is that the costs of this excess capacity should be assigned to the products that used the machines when they were produced. This would require estimating the life cycle of the products that use the machines and then amortising the machine costs over that expected life. Then, if the estimates were accurate, when the "excess" capacity appeared, its costs would have already been assigned to the appropriate products. For example, "excess" capacity costs can be assigned equally to all production units using the basis "units of production" and a forecast of total production volume over the life of the equipment.

Q12. What about the capacity caused by lumpy acquisitions?

The appropriate treatment of these costs depends upon the reason for the lumpiness. If the lumpiness is due to management decision to buy extra capacity because it is cheaper if purchased in one as opposed to multiple "lumps", then the extra capacity is excess and its associated costs should be treated as a period cost and management held responsible. If however, there is no choice about how much capacity is acquired, then the extra capacity is unavoidable and should be treated as a product cost. For example, equipment is sometimes acquired that will only be used at 60% of its rated capacity across its life.

Summary

The MDD case provides a rich example of the issues surrounding capacity costing. The main lessons include:

1. The definition of capacity that is appropriate for product costing purposes should not depend upon actual usage but upon the available capacity.

2. Using an available capacity removes the risk of a death spiral commencing.

3. The appropriate definition of capacity centers on both the ability of the production process to produce products and the way the customer demands products. Capacity that is reserved for a particular customers use is unavailable and should not be treated as excess capacity. Instead, it is an appropriate cost to charge to the customer either as a product cost or as a strategic cost.

I summarize the case to students by drawing a capacity costing diagram that illustrates the difference between technical, practical, surge, excess and actual capacity (see TN-Exhibit 3).

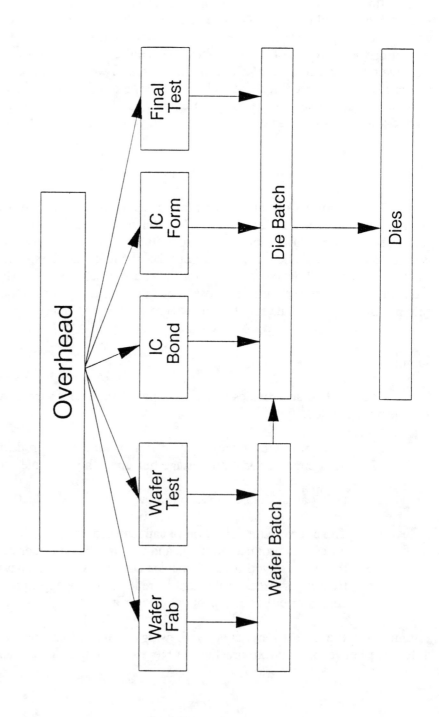

Micro Devices Division

Teaching Note

Exhibit 1

The Existing Cost System

Micro Devices Division

Teaching Note

Exhibit 2

The Exclusion of Excess Capacity Costs

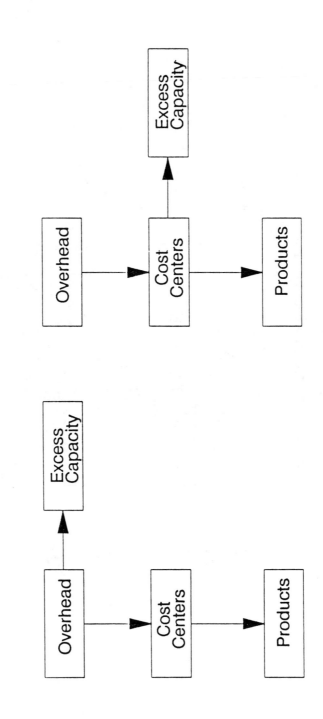

a) Excess capacity costs excluded at overhead level

b) Excess capacity costs excluded at cost center level

Micro Devices Division

Teaching Note

Exhibit 3

Capacity Chart for Product Costing Purposes

Theoretical
Capacity

Practical
Capacity

| Unavailable | Protective | Surge | Excess | Actual |

Volume →

Legend:

Production volume for product costing purposes

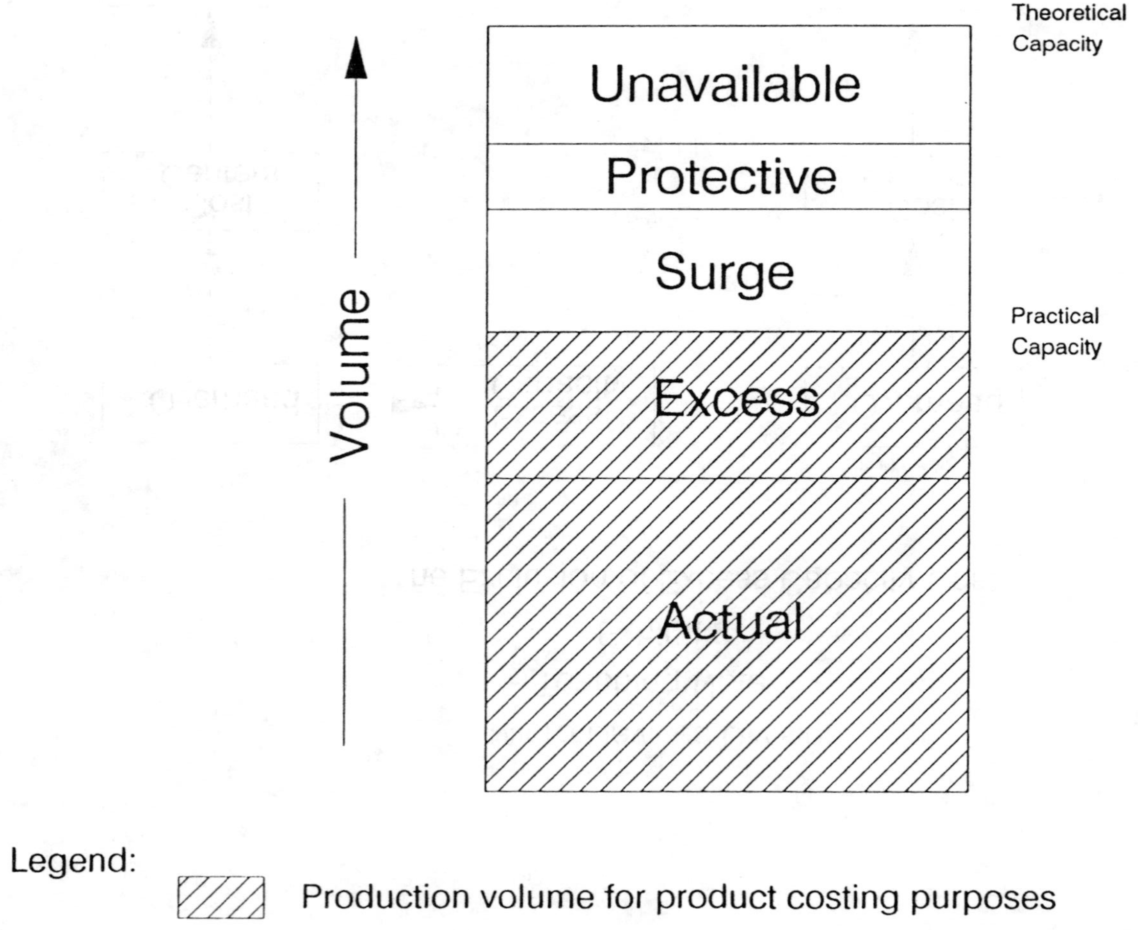

Schulze Waxed Containers, Inc.

Teaching Note

The objectives of this case are to teach students to become familiar with:

1. The death spiral caused by allocating capacity-related costs to products when production capacity is under-utilized.

2. The use of average production volumes to overcome the death spiral.

3. The appropriate definition of capacity for product costing purposes in a seasonal business.

4. How to cost products in a seasonal environment.

This case outlines an 80 minute teaching plan.

Suggested Assignments:

1. Evaluate the firm's existing strategy.

2. Evaluate the existing cost system. How does it determine product costs?

3. Evaluate the new cost system. How does it determine product costs?

4. Evaluate the firm's new strategy.

    a. Does emphasizing the low volume custom segment make sense?
    b. Does the 25% minimum margin rule make sense?

This teaching note was written by Professor Robin Cooper as an aid to instructors using Schulze Waxed Containers, Inc. (188-134).

5.   Which of the three segments is the most profitable?

6.   What changes would you make to the firm's cost system and strategy?

Class Discussion

Q1. What is the competitive environment that SWC faces?

1.   SWC is a small private firm competing in a market dominated by large vertically integrated firms--the largest competitor is about 10 times larger than SWC. There are six national competitors and 3 regional ones.

2.   SWC is a secondary supplier to most of its high volume accounts.

3.   SWC competes in three market segments:

High volume - custom print In this segment jobs are manufactured in very high volumes. The high volume segment has a very focused customer base--there are only 5 customers. It is a very cut-throat segment with prices set by the market (i.e., large competition). The large players are very active in this segment. Sales are direct to the customer.

Low volume - custom print jobs In this segment jobs are manufactured in small volumes. Customers are numerous and change from year to year (they both go out of business and shop around). The large players are less active in this segment than they are in the high volume segment. Sales are via distributors.

Stock - standard print jobs In this segment jobs are manufactured in relatively high volumes. Customers are numerous and change frequently, but since the patterns are not customized, this is less significant than in the low volume custom segment. Sales are typically via distributors.

4.   SWC cannot be the low cost producer due to its lack of vertical integration, older machinery, and inability to get bulk discounts. To be profitable, it must find a niche where it can differentiate itself and charge premium prices.

Q2. What are the products that SWC produces?

SWC manufactures a range of waxed paper products. The most important difference among products is size.

Q3. What is the production process?

SWC has a relatively simple production process. It consists of four stages: printing, cutting, waxing and packaging. An important point to bring out is that each machine can make only one size though it can make products for any segment. Thus, capacity is shared across segments not sizes.

Q4. What was the firm's previous strategy?

SWC's strategy is to sell a mixture of high and low volume products. The high volume products fill the plant, but generate little, if any, profits. The low volume custom products generate the majority of the profits. In order to sustain this strategy, the firm places a heavy reliance upon distributors and maintains good relations with them by granting local geographical monopolies. In addition, SWC differentiates itself from its larger competitors by providing superior service to smaller customers. This differentiation requires SWC to accept all orders from existing customers even if they require overtime and are not profitable.

Q5. How does the existing cost system function?

The existing cost system is extremely simple, it contains only one cost center and allocates overhead to products using the basis "# of units." The existing cost system ignores all product variations when allocating overhead. It assumes that high and low volume product costs are the same per unit; that there are no differences across the three segments in terms of printing costs, obsolescence or any other factor; and that indirect costs are the same regardless of the size of the product. The cost system's treatment of printing and cutting costs as overhead is somewhat surprising. A more sensible approach would treat them as separate cost centers. Selling, general, and administrative costs are treated as period costs despite the fact that there are undoubtedly differences across segments.

The existing system reports product costs according to the following equation:

Unit Product cost =   Direct Material + Direct Labor + constant

where the constant is equal to the overhead of the facility divided by the total number of units budgeted. Since the direct labor content of products hardly varies, variations in reported product costs are primarily driven by material cost.

Q6. Why is this system so simple?

The existing cost system is so simple because, prior to the adoption of the new strategy, product cost information played a relatively minor role in the firm. Three factors caused product cost to be of relatively little importance at SWC. First, prices were set predominately by the market so there was no cost-based pricing. Second, the strategy of accepting all business meant that cost-based product mix decisions were not important. Third, since overhead is only about 25% of manufacturing costs the distortion introduced by such a simple system is probably small.

Since individual product costs were not important, the cost system's only significant function was to value inventory. A very simple system was more than adequate for this task.

Q7. What is the new strategy?

The new strategy consists of two major modifications to the existing strategy, 1) increased sales to the low volume custom segment and 2) minimum selling prices based upon reported product costs.

a) Low Volume Custom Segment

This segment looked like a sensible choice to emphasize because it is primarily handled by distributors and the larger competitors are not well positioned to serve it. Also reflecting the difficulty of servicing (low volume, short lead time) it is the highest margin segment with selling prices about 17% higher than the high volume segment.

b) Minimum Selling Prices

The rationale behind the second element of the new strategy, the 25% minimum acceptable gross margin, is easy to explain but difficult to justify. The firm was unprofitable in the prior year and one of the causes identified by top management was marketing selling products at too low a price. To keep prices up, a minimum margin was established.

The 25% minimum is an _internally_ set number. It is designed to ensure a reasonable profit margin at expected volumes. Using an internally set minimum margin ignores the realities of the market place. One unfortunate outcome of this rule was the loss of two major high volume customers amounting to 20% of SWC sales volume.

To be fair to SWC management, they expected to lose some high volume business under their new strategy. However, they did not expect to lose so much so quickly. While one customer was lost by sticking to too high a price, the other one was due to competitive actions that were only partially price related.

Q8. What was the impact of the new strategy on the importance of the cost system at SWC?

The adoption of the new strategy with its 25% rule forced the cost system to begin to play a critical role in the marketing strategy of the firm. Unfortunately, it was inadequately designed for this role.

The loss of 20% of sales volume highlighted a major flaw in the existing cost system. As production volume dropped, the reported fixed overhead cost per unit increased. Therefore, reported product costs also increased and with them minimum acceptable prices. These increased minimum prices meant that the firm risked losing even more business, which would cause reported product costs and hence prices to increase. Adopting a minimum cost plus price rule coupled to the existing system caused SWC to embark upon a death spiral. The VP of marketing, recognizing that the firm had entered such a spiral, reverted to 1986 reported costs, and hence kept minimum prices constant.

Q9. How does the capacity-based cost system function?

The flaw in the existing cost system was its failure to identify capacity costs and treat them as period costs (TN-Fig. 1). The new cost system was designed to correct this flaw (TN-Fig. 2).

The new capacity-based cost system defines capacity for a given product size as follows:

a)   Capacity Definition:

Total available Production time	=	Total Labor Hours	-	Planned Labor Idle Time	-	Planned Machine Idle Time	-	Unplanned Machine Idle Time

Maximum Available Capacity	=	Total Available Production Time	x	Machine Output Per Unit Of Time	x	Number of Machines

This calculation generates a capacity much greater than both current and 1986 production (1.74 billion compared to 0.91 billion and 1.06 billion respectively). The capacity-based cost system therefore reduces the reported costs of all products by about 4% (using 1986 volumes as a reference). Marketing, reacting to these lower costs and hence minimum selling prices began implementing its new strategy by selling aggressively to customers in the low-volume segment. Unfortunately, the definition of capacity imbedded in the new system ignored seasonality. Another potential problem is that the 25% minimum margin was calculated using the old cost system's definition of capacity. With excess capacity costs being treated as period costs, the 25% rule may no longer be appropriate. If management wants to keep a minimum margin rule they need to update it to match the new cost system's definition of capacity.

Q10. How does seasonality effect the appropriate definition of capacity?

To understand the effect of seasonality on the appropriate definition of capacity for product costing purposes a simplified example can be used:

Assume a firm sells a product with the seasonal pattern shown in TN-Figure 3. The higher volume sold in the high season exactly fills the capacity of the plant. The lower volume sold in the low season only half fills the plant. Like SWC, the firm has no ability to move to a level production strategy.

The new SWC cost system assumes that the shaded area is available capacity. However, unless there is a way to remove demand seasonality or go to level production, there is no way to sell this capacity, it is seasonally unavailable.

This seasonally unavailable capacity is not excess capacity. It is capacity required to service customer demands. Therefore, it is a valid product cost and should be assigned to the products accordingly. Consequently, product costs should be computed using not the maximum available practical capacity, but the seasonally adjusted maximum available capacity. This is the maximum available capacity minus the seasonally unavailable capacity.

A simple approach to seasonal capacity is to assume it is unavailable and reduce the capacity of the plant accordingly. In the simple example, the seasonally unavailable capacity is 25% of maximum available capacity. The seasonally adjusted maximum available capacity is therefore 75% of total capacity.

This approach will report the same costs for a product irrespective of the season in which it is manufactured, which is counter-intuitive because economic conditions in the high and low seasons are different: in the high season all machines are busy while in the low season half are idle.

Q11. Can we design a system that reports different costs for the same product manufactured in different seasons?

If we want to design a cost system that indicates that a product manufactured in the high season has a different cost from one manufactured in the low season then we must adopt a shorter time period than a year. We cannot use an annual perspective because, as already demonstrated, this will report the same product costs for both seasons.

Using the simple example, two different approaches to seasonal costing can be explored. One approach yields product costs that are higher in the low season than the high season and the other higher costs in the high season. The first approach, as illustrated in TN-Figure 4, allocates the costs of the seasonally unavailable capacity to the products produced in the low season. In the low season, seasonally unavailable capacity is high and therefore the reported product costs are high. In the high season, seasonally unavailable capacity is low (in the simple example it is zero) and therefore reported costs are low. The problem with this approach is it leads to counter intuitive results. In the high season, marketing should want to charge higher prices and in the low season, lower prices. However, this cost system when coupled to the 25% minimum margin rule tells them to do exactly the opposite.

The second approach, as illustrated in TN-Figure 5, allocates the costs of the seasonally unavailable capacity to the products produced in the high season. This system views the seasonally unavailable capacity as being caused by the products produced in the high season. This perspective is sensible because the seasonally unavailable capacity is maintained to support high season not low season production. This approach reports higher costs for products produced in the high season then those produced in the low season. When coupled to the 25% minimum margin rule, the cost system at least sends marketing more intuitively satisfying pricing signals. A much better solution is to run a linear program of the production problem and determine the shadow costs of production for each season. This will also report high costs in the high season. However, these costs will reflect opportunity costs not just historical costs.

Q12. How seasonal are the three segments?

The seasonal capacity utilization patterns for SWC are more complex than in the simple example. TN-Figures 6, 7, 8, and 9 show the capacity utilization profiles for the high volume custom, low volume custom, stock segments and for the firm as a whole, respectively. The seasonality of the business in all three segments is clear.

A very simple way of estimating the percentage of total available capacity that is seasonally unavailable is to multiply the highest volume month's unit output by 12 and divide this figure into the annual production volume. For SWC the resulting percentages are:

H-V	65%
L-V	59%
Stock	70%
Total	66%

Note the lower percentage of the low volume segment. The seasonality of the low-volume segment is much higher than the other two segments. A more complex and accurate approach would be to compute the unavailable percentage by season, quarter or month and then generate an average annual figure.

TN-Figure 10 shows the profiles of the high and low volume custom business on the same graph. This graph identifies two important issues. First, the two segments peak at the same time so there is no complementary and, second, as indicated above, the low volume segment is more seasonal than the high one.

The high seasonality of the low volume custom business coupled to this business and peaking at the same time as the other segment identifies a potential flaw with the new strategy. As the percentage of low volume custom business increases, the seasonally adjusted maximum availability capacity drops. While the low volume custom earns higher margins, it is not obvious that it is more profitable.

Q13. Which is the most profitable segment?

There is not enough information in the case to tell which of the three segments is the most profitable. To actually determine long-term segment profitability is very complicated; it requires considering seasonality, product mix variations, segment stability, etc. However, using available data from the case, it is possible to show that the low-volume segment appears to be the most profitable, despite its higher seasonality.

To identify the most profitable segment, the contribution generated by each segment at full seasonally adjusted available capacity if it were the only segment serviced is determined. The segment with the highest contribution is assumed to be the most profitable. The magnitude of the approximations introduced by not adjusting for product mix differences by segment and not looking for ways to better fill the plant by a using a mix of segments are unknown. However, the calculations show students how to think about determining the relative profitability of the segments.

Taking the highest month for each segment multiplying by 12 and dividing the total into the maximum available capacity of 1,740,720,000 gives the multiplier for each segment to convert actual segment sales to segment sales at full capacity. The full capacity for each segment is:

SEGMENT	MULTIPLIER	ANNUAL SALES	FULL CAPACITY SALES
HIGH	3.19	381,953	1,218,560
LOW	3.28	313,868	1,028,950
STOCK	5.87	211,139	1,239,679

Multiplying the total sales for each size in each segment by the unit sales price given in case Exhibit 5 gives the total revenue per segment by size. Summing these revenues gives the total revenue for each segment. Dividing total segment revenues by the total number of units sold in that segment gives the average unit selling price by segment. These prices are:

SEGMENT	TOTAL REVENUE	UNIT SALES	AVERAGE PRICE
HIGH	$9,127,908	381,953,000	$0.0240
LOW	$9,671,728	313,868,000	$0.0308
STOCK	$4,612,855	211,139,000	$0.0219

Multiplying the full capacity sales by the average unit price gives the full capacity revenues for each segment. If the somewhat heroic assumption is made that the average variable cost of a unit in each segment is the same we can calculate the contribution generated by each segment at full capacity.

The average variable cost of each unit is obtained by dividing the total variable cost by the number of units produced. From Case Exhibit 8, we get the breakdown of variable ($15,243) and fixed ($2,788) manufacturing costs. Therefore, dividing the total variable cost by the total number of units produced gives a variable cost per unit of $.0168. Subtracting the average unit cost from the average selling price gives the average unit contribution. Multiplying the average unit contribution by the full capacity sales volume gives the total contribution for each segment if it were the only segment and at full capacity.

SEGMENT	FULL CAPACITY	UNIT CONTRIBUTION	TOTAL CONTRIBUTION
HIGH	1,218,560	0.0071	8,638,000
LOW	1,028,950	0.0140	14,428,000
STOCK	1,239,679	0.0050	6,245,000

According to this approach, the low volume segment is by far the most profitable segment. The contribution generated by each segment at full capacity identifies the impact on profits of switching sales between segments when the firm is at full capacity.

Summary

If SWC wants to use the cost system as a vehicle for identifying which business to go after it will have to make four major changes to its new capacity costing system.

1. Account for the costs of seasonally unavailable capacity.
2. Set a different minimum acceptable margin for each segment.
3. Use the minimum prices as a guideline, not an inviolate rule.
4. Include S,G, & A costs in product costs.

The acceptable minimum margin for each segment might have to vary by the period because in the high season the cost of accepting an incremental order is much higher than in the low season. There is no guarantee that any cost system will reflect the appropriate opportunity cost. Setting different minimum acceptable margins for each season is one way to include opportunity costs in the price setting mechanism.

How would you modify SWC's new strategy?

Students suggesting modifications to the new strategy should consider:

1. Setting limits on the acceptable mix of business by segments. This will avoid accepting too much business in the more profitable but seasonal low volume segment.

2. Relax the minimum acceptable margin rule. This modification will allow fine tuning of the pricing strategy by segment and season.

3. Create incentives for customers to shift production from peak to other months.[1]

---

[1]Incentive to shift production to the low season by reducing seasonally unavailable capacity increases the maximum available capacity of (seasonally adjusted) the plant because every unit of production that can be moved to the non-peak months increases the effective capacity of the plant by one unit.

FIGURE 1
EXISTING COST SYSTEM

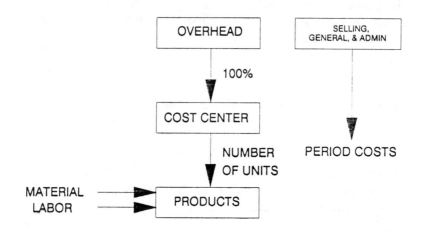

FIGURE 2
NEW COST SYSTEM

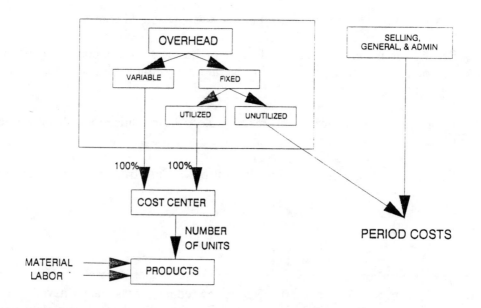

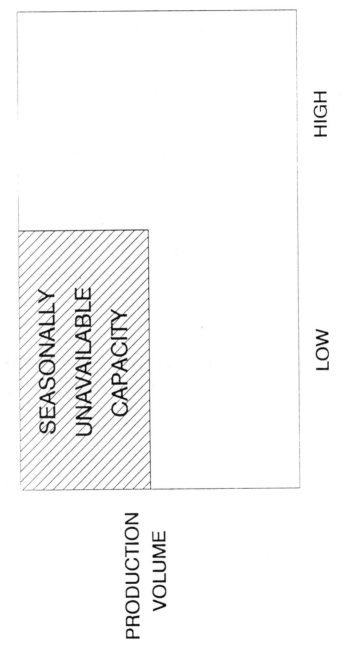

FIGURE 3

A SIMPLE EXAMPLE

FIGURE 4
TRADITIONAL TREATMENT OF SEASONALLY
UNAVAILABLE CAPACITY COSTS

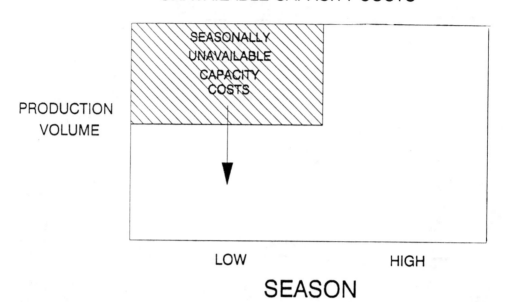

FIGURE 5
A CAUSAL TREATMENT OF SEASONALLY
UNAVAILABLE CAPACITY COSTS

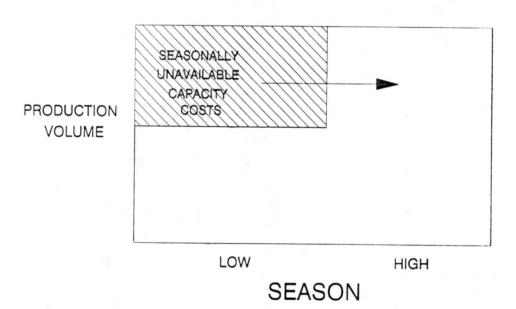

Figure 6

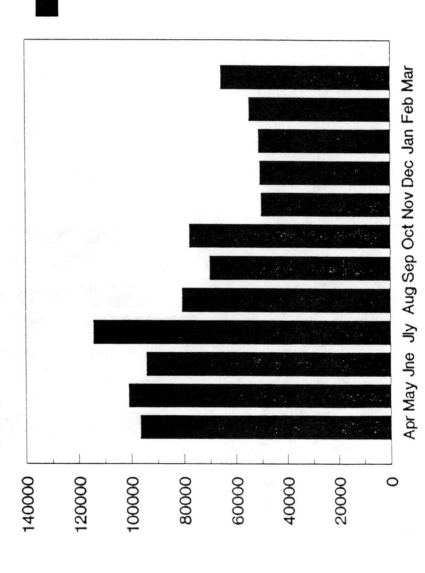

Schulze Waxed Containers
1987 Sales All Segments

Figure 7

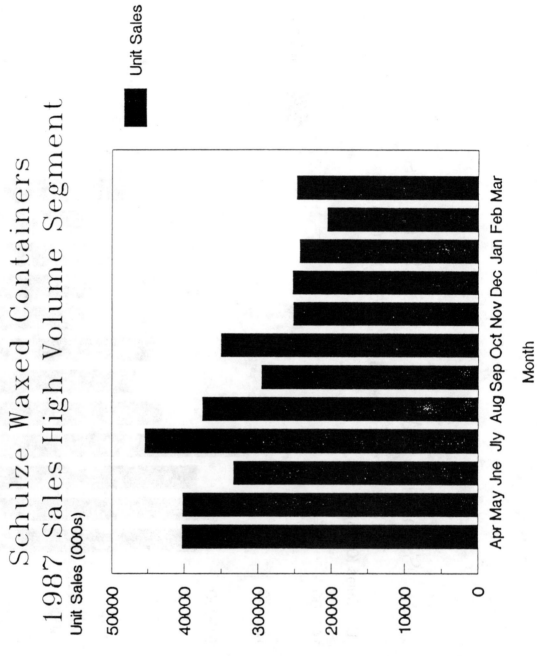

Schulze Waxed Containers
1987 Sales High Volume Segment

Figure 8

Schulze Waxed Containers
1987 Sales Low Volume Segment

Unit Sales (000s)

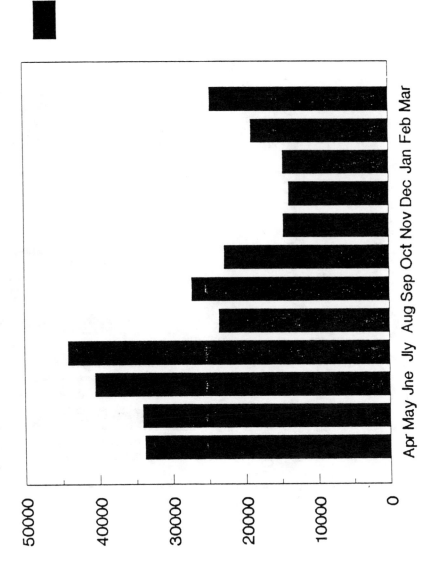

Unit Sales

Figure 9

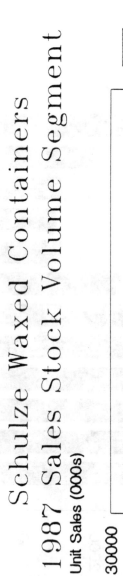

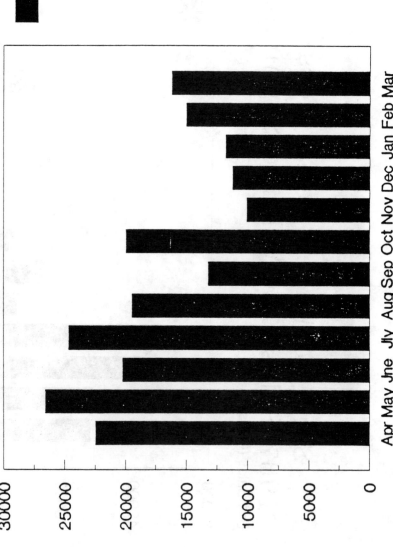

Figure 10

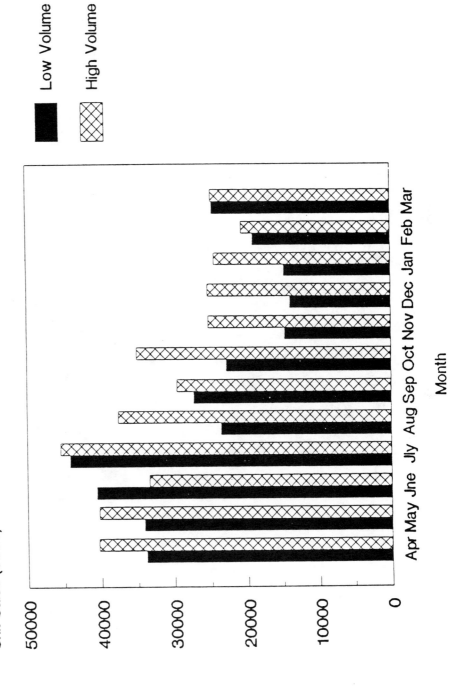

Schulze Waxed Containers
1987 Sales High and Low Volume Segments

Systems For Operational Control And Performance Measurement

The cases in Chapter 4 emphasize the operational control/ performance measurement function of management accounting systems. In our courses, we initially placed these cases at the end of the course, after covering the new material on activity-based cost systems. This led to two problems. First, the material seemed tacked on, almost as an after thought, and the students couldn't get motivated to focus on the central issues. Second, in deferring this discussion until after the ABC material, questions on how ABC would be used for performance measurement and monthly reporting would occasionally arise, leading to a digression, at that point, on the multiple roles for cost systems. By placing the performance measurement material in the middle of the course (as we have done in the book), we highlight the importance of the topic and also deal with it before moving on to the strategic profitability measurement systems that will be encountered in Chapters 5 and 6.

The *Union Pacific* cases (presented in Chapter 7 of the book, with other service industry cases) could very effectively be taught in this module as well, especially as a bridge between Chapter 4 and Chapter 5. Union Pacific (A) describes the monthly reporting system, used for operational and spending control, but demonstrates the complete absence of relevant information for product and customer profitability. The Union Pacific (B) case shows the new systems, essentially ABC systems, developed for product costing and profitability analysis, and provides a smooth transition to the manufacturing ABC cases in Chapters 5 and 6.

The *Metabo* case contains several good messages. First, it provides an international dimension to the course with its description of a typical, highly detailed (and expensive) German cost accounting system. Second, the new system installed at Metabo is virtually a textbook example of a well-functioning cost accounting system, complete with marginal costs and flexible budgeting. With its daily reporting and extensive number of cost centers, it shows a considerable advance over a typical U.S. system, as described in the Paramount Cycle case at the beginning of Chapter 1 of the book. Third, it enables students to confront why a company would be willing to invest in such an elaborate system. What managerial purpose is really served by it? The main limitations of the system are the lack of accurate product costs (only marginal costs are accurately measured at the product level) and the lack of operational or physical information for operational control. This latter topic leads to the next series of cases.

Texas Eastman describes a company with an extensive array of operational and physical measures; more than 30,000 observations are taken every few hours. In such an information-rich environment, we can properly question the value and role for a monthly financial summary of performance. The surprising innovation in the Texas Eastman case is that a department manager has independently produced a daily income statement to support operators' quality and productivity improvement efforts. The case provides an excellent opportunity to discuss the interplay between operational and financial measures. The case also helps to expose students to an organization with a complete and effective commitment to total quality management. The initial discussion of the case could focus on the quality program, even before delving into the measurement aspects.

Analog Devices continues the themes introduced in Texas Eastman. We encounter a company with a strong commitment to quality improvement, time-based competition, and innovation and improvement. Unlike Texas Eastman, an innovative operational measurement system -- the half-life method -- is functioning effectively to motivate the quality, time-compression, and improvement activities, with the financial reports playing a clearly subsidiary role. In fact, Analog can be used to describe the dysfunctional aspects of several cost accounting and financial measures. Analog also introduces the Balanced Scorecard for performance measurement, in which monthly and quarterly financial summary measures are "balanced" with measures on customer satisfaction, effectiveness of internal manufacturing processes, and rates of learning and innovation.

The module closes with the *Texas Instrument Cost of Quality* cases which again features the interplay between financial and non-financial performance measures. The Cost of Quality measurement is being tried by many companies today, and continues to be advocated by quality gurus so the TI cases provide a good context to discuss this measurement. In the TI cases, the divisions are experimenting with the Cost of Quality metric to motivate and evaluate their quality improvement efforts. After initial acceptance, the Cost of Quality measure has become less valuable to many operating managers than more direct measures (defect rates, yields, etc.) of their quality programs. One might contrast the TI Cost of Quality measure with the daily financial report developed by Steve Briley in the Texas Eastman case, which also quantified financially the cost of bad quality but in a way quite different from the Cost of Quality approach.

These cases, perhaps concluding with Union Pacific, will introduce students to contemporary ideas on operational control and performance measurement. Much work remains to be done so the number of cases available more reflects our limited knowledge base in this area that a conscious effort to downplay its importance. As companies learn that the traditional monthly variance analysis from their standard cost systems is an inappropriate tool for performance measurement in the 1990s, new methods need to be developed and tested. The cases in this chapter provide some early glimpses of where the field might be going.

The reading with this chapter, by Tom Johnson, describes the opportunities for new measurements in the competitive environment of quality management and time-based competition. It can be used in conjunction with the Analog Devices case and also provides a bridge to the activity-based cost systems to be encountered in Chapter 5. Other readings on the inadequacies of traditional cost accounting systems for operational control and performance measurement can be found in Measures for Manufacturing Excellence (Robert S. Kaplan (ed.) (HBS Press, 1990). For example,

Chapter 1: Kaplan, "Limitations of Cost Accounting in Advanced Manufacturing Environments"

Chapter 3: H. Thomas Johnson, "Performance Measurement for Competitive Excellence" and

Chapter 4: Howard M. Armitage and Anthony A. Atkinson, "The Choice of Productivity Measures in Organizations."

Books describing the new opportunities for performance measurement include:

Richard L. Lynch and Kelvin F. Cross, Measure Up! Yardsticks for Continuous Improvement, (Basil Blackwell: Cambridge MA, 1991)

Callie Berliner and James A. Brimson (eds.), Cost Management for Today's Advanced Manufacturing: The CAM-I Conceptual Design (HBS Press: Boston MA, 1988)

METABO GmbH & Co. KG
Teaching Note

The Metabo case provides an excellent example of a well-functioning traditional cost system. One can use Metabo to illustrate the application of many principles articulated in popular cost and managerial accounting textbooks, but which are frequently lacking in the systems found in actual companies. Metabo also illustrates the commitment of many German companies to have accurate cost systems for cost control and reporting. At the same time, however, Metabo can be used to show how even extremely well designed traditional cost systems may fail to provide accurate information on the differential demands that products make on organizational resources; i.e., product costs. It provides a natural bridge between the cases illustrating inadequate traditional cost systems (e.g., Mayers Tap, Fisher Technologies, and Mueller-Lehmkuhl) and the new, activity-based cost systems of Siemens (another German company), John Deere, and Schrader Bellows. Even by fixing all the problems revealed by inadequate traditional systems, an additional conceptual breakthrough is required to understand the total demands made by products for support resources. Thus, instructors can use Metabo to highlight the distinction between a cost system designed to facilitate operational control and the systems designed to provide accurate product costs. As a side benefit, the case description reveals several aspects of employee training and company practices in German companies that differ from the practices of companies in several other Western nations.

Suggested Assignment Questions

1. How did Metabo's old cost system differ from those of the U.S. companies we have examined earlier in the course?

2. What factors contributed to the dissatisfaction with the old cost system? Think about broad general trends in Metabo's competitive environment as well as the specific complaints identified in the case.

3. Why is Häussler so enthusiastic about the new system? What functions does the new system do particularly well?

This teaching note was prepared by Professor Robert S. Kaplan as an aid to instructors in the classroom use of the case, Metabo, GmbH & Co. KG, 9-189-146.

4.   What limitations remain in the new system, if any? Is the new Metabo system a prototype for the cost management systems that contemporary manufacturing companies should install?

Class Discussion Outline

Q.   Describe Metabo's competitive environment. Has it changed in recent years?

Metabo views itself as the "Rolls Royce" of the hand power tool market. Metabo appeals to professionals and sophisticated do-it-yourselfers, who wish a high-quality, high-performance product. This view is manifested in its complete vertical integration strategy ("You get quality only if you do it yourself,") and its commitment to offer a full product line (2,000 different end products) so that customers are not tempted to purchase a competitive brand for a particular application.

Metabo believes that it can command premium prices for its products, but that prices are still determined by market conditions, not cost considerations. The case suggests, however, that Metabo does not want a big price gap to open up relative to Bosch or emerging Japanese competitors (e.g., Makita) who also offer good quality products. Thus, we can expect Metabo to be increasingly concerned with cost control issues.

Q.   How would you characterize Metabo's old cost system?

Metabo's old cost system is a job order cost system in which actual labor, machine processing and materials costs were calculated for individual jobs. Budgeted overhead expenses were determined, in the annual budgeting process. for each of 1,500 machine classes and 250 cost centers. Overhead expenses were applied to production lots passing through each machine and cost center based on actual labor, materials, or machine times. Total expenses applied to each production lot were divided by the actual volume of good parts released from the cost center to calculate an "actual" unit cost for the lot. This actual unit cost was then passed on to the next stage of production. Materials overhead was applied based on direct materials cost, and was not included in the production overhead rates of machines and production cost centers.

Estimated actual production volumes were used to divide budgeted overhead expenses at machines and cost centers. These volumes were typically obtained from the previous year's actual volumes, adjusted informally (by Häussler) for known unusual conditions in the prior year. At the end of the year, actual overhead expenses were calculated and allocated back to production departments based on actual production volumes.

The allocation of cost center accumulated expenses to individual machines was accomplished by the 50-50 method (50% based on machine hours, and 50% based on machine-traceable costs). Such a seemingly arbitrary method is almost surely the consequence of a political battle. In this case, the initial method (based on traceable costs only) made newly purchased machines (authorized and actively encouraged by the owner to maintain technological leadership) appeared unusually expensive. The owner objected to this outcome so the company shifted to machine hours (unburdening the new machines that had high operating speeds) but this approach must have made certain products or perhaps the manually operated machines seem too expensive. So the 50-50 compromise was agreed to. An alternative procedure would have kept common cost-center expenses at the cost center level (not allocated to machines) and assigned them to products based on time spent in the cost center. This procedure would have averaged departmental costs across all machines rather than making individual types of machines seem more or less expensive. All such procedures, however, are ad hoc, and not reflective of the demands of products for cost center or secondary support center resources.

Q.   **What aspects of the old Metabo system differed from those we studied in U.S. companies such as Mayers Tap, Fisher Technologies, and Ingersoll Milling?**

Even the old Metabo cost center contained some interesting features worthy of note. First, Metabo had 1,500 different machine hour rates and 250 cost centers. Contrast this level of detail with the one cost center for **two** plants in Mayers Tap (A) and the maximum of 20-30 cost centers found in most U.S. factories. Managers in German companies do not like aggregate rates that mask underlying differences in machine productivities and efficiencies, and seem willing to invest in detailed recording and reporting to reveal differences among machines and processes.

Metabo was also willing to use accounting conventions for internal costing and control that differed from those used for external reporting. Replacement costs were used to calculate machine depreciation charges, so that machine rates would not be distorted by the age of the machines. Also, interest was charged on inventory and an approximation of a machine's market value (50% of replacement cost). At the end of the year, an accountant had to reconcile from the product costs calculated for internal purposes to the methods acceptable for external reporting. This procedure is in stark contrast to Western European and North American companies where external accounting conventions tend to be primary, and management accounting conventions are forced to be consistent with those used for external reporting. Unlike other companies in other Western countries, the cost accounting (or cost-engineering) departments of companies in German-speaking countries (which includes also Austria and eastern Switzerland) report to manufacturing not finance. These companies have separate staffs for internal cost calculations and for preparing statements to tax authorities and external suppliers of capital.

As long as the instructor is launched on a discussion of differences between German and other Western companies, he/she can inquire about other management practices noted in the case that depart from Western European and North American practices. The career path of Mr. Häussler was deliberately inserted to allow mention of the German apprenticeship program, where high school graduates are given extensive practical, technical training in German industrial companies. German workers may spend several years in companies learning about machinery and how to operate complex machines before being allowed to produce parts. Western companies, perhaps because of their more mobile work force, tend to tell new employees about their fringe benefit packages on the morning of their first day of work and turn them loose in the factory that afternoon. Also, German companies can depend on the high school graduates they hire to be able to read and do quantitative analysis, skills that are notably lacking in many employees currently being hired by U.S. companies. These educational and training differences help to explain the flexibility of workers in the Metabo plant ("German workers could perform a variety of skilled tasks and were rotated frequently among cost centers").

Note also that Häussler, the controller came from a technical, manufacturing background, not from public accounting. He was familiar and comfortable with manufacturing processes and shop floor workers, enabling him to understand well the limitations of Metabo's existing cost system and what features he wanted in the new system. Again, Häussler's training illustrates that German companies take manufacturing and manufacturing control seriously; cost reports are primary, not derivative from a system constrained to produce GAAP financial reports.

Q.   What problems existed with Metabo's old cost system?

The case is reasonably explicit about the sources of Häussler's dissatisfaction with the previous cost system.

1.   Costs were strongly influenced by the volume assumption used to calculate machine and cost center burden rates.

2.   Only fully allocated costs were reported so that the effects of fluctuations in production volumes could not be reflected in the reported numbers. No split was made between costs expected to be fixed and those expected to vary with volume fluctuations.

3.   The actual costs (materials, labor, and machine-time) incurred in the processing of a production lot in a cost center were passed on to the next cost center. This full cost rollup made it impossible to trace cost variances back to individual departments. Also, the actual reported unit costs would be significantly affected by the loss of units due to sub-standard quality in a department, and the addition of re-worked items into the production lot released by the department.

4.   The system was manual, leading to extensive delays and much manual processing to calculate cost reports and prepare financial statements from the operating data.

5.   Even the 250 different machine centers was too coarse to capture operating differences among different models of machines of the same type (e.g., injection molding machines).

6.   The treatment of fringe benefits distorted the costs of workers temporarily re-assigned to other cost centers.

7.   No budgets were prepared for operating cost centers. Therefore, Häussler had little basis for assessing the cost control performance of departmental supervisors and managers.

8.   The case describes the long and variable setup times required for the turning machines. Also, extensive preparation was required for the setups. The costs of setups, especially the wide differences among jobs, were not assigned to the actual production runs.

9.   If the students have previously been exposed to the reciprocal service department costing issue, they may mention the failure of the old Metabo system to reflect the interactions among support departments before allocating their costs to production cost centers and machines.

Q.   Well this is a pretty long and indicting list of problems? Were there any virtues to Metabo's previous cost system? Did the company get any benefit from a system that assigned 200 different cost codes to 250 cost centers and 1,500 machine classes?

The old Metabo cost system was designed to capture full product costs, not promote production efficiencies. By having an "actual" product cost system,[1] Metabo could adjust selling prices to reflect shifts in the costs of materials and labor and changes in machine efficiencies. In the current environment, cost increases probably could not easily be passed on to customers because of competition from Bosch and Makita. The company wanted to shift from a product cost accumulation system to one that promoted responsibility accounting so that cost control and production efficiency considerations could be actively encouraged and monitored. In effect, Metabo was making a transition from a customized producer of unique products to a competitive producer of high-quality but increasingly standard products in which prices were determined by the marketplace and cost control needed to be emphasized.

Q.   What changes were introduced by the new cost system?

The Plaut/Kilger/SAP cost system installed at Metabo is a textbook example of a well-designed responsibility accounting system. It incorporates virtually all the features recommended in many cost accounting textbooks, but rarely-implemented by actual companies.

First, the number of cost centers has expanded from 250 to 600 to eliminate heterogeneity of machines within a cost center. Second, the Appendix illustrates the operation of an integrated flexible budgeting scheme. Flexible budgets are prepared for both production and support departments. Activity levels in support departments are calculated based on anticipated demand from the production departments. The support department fixed costs are allocated to production departments proportional to their forecasted annual demands, and held at the calculated level throughout the year. Similarly, support department budgeted variable cost rates are calculated by dividing budgeted variable operating support department expenses by anticipated demand. Each period, the actual production department demands for support resources are multiplied by the standard variable rate to charge out support department costs to production departments. This leaves spending and efficiency variances in both variable and fixed costs in the support department. These variances are closed to production cost centers monthly in a separate calculation, that relieves the production cost center manager from responsibility for their origin. Presumably this latter calculation is performed to allow major, non-controllable variances to be reflected in updated inventory valuation/cost of goods sold calculations for financial reporting. The instructor may wish to work through parts of the numerical example in the Appendix to illustrate the operation of the flexible budgeting system. The effect of the integrated flexible budgeting system is to eliminate all volume variances in both support and operating departments. Reported results are unaffected by fluctuations in capacity utilization (assuming the linear cost structure and identification of variable costs and their drivers are accurate).

The system was installed on a main-frame computer and integrated with the production control system. Therefore, it provided an accurate and timely summary of operations. The computerized system also provided a simulation capability that enabled Metabo to explore different scenarios about product volumes and mix, and changes in input prices and operating efficiencies. A file on current (not standard) input prices was readily accessible in the system to permit updates on standard product costs. While not stated in the case, Metabo intended to run its system daily to produce daily operating reports to cost center managers. Häussler wanted a system in which responsibility managers could not alibi out of an unfavorable variance by claiming

1. I put "actual" in quotes, because only actual labor, materials, and machine times were accumulated; overhead was assigned based on predetermined rates [budgeted overhead and forecasted production volumes].

defects in the cost center design (such as too few cost centers, support department allocations were arbitrary, or the information came too late for me to act).

Detailed examination was made of the activity drivers in each cost center. Therefore, a wide variety of cost drivers were used. In addition to the usual suspects --labor hours, machine time, and materials purchases--Metabo used kilowatt hours, area of materials processed, units processed, and --anticipating activity-based systems-- setup hours. Also, multiple cost pools (with different second-stage drivers) could be defined in a single cost center.

Q.   **Well is this it? Is this as good as we can get in designing cost systems? Should we stop here, close down the course, and use our remaining time to study marketing, production and human resource management [instructors are encouraged to substitute their own favorite courses in this question]?**

The Metabo system is an excellent system for Häussler who wants department managers to watch and control costs closely. I have not taught the case enough times to get extensive comments from students and executives, but based on my visit to the company, discussions with the designers at Plaut and SAP, and the actual writing of the case, I can not think of any improvement I could make to the system's design to improve its functionality for cost control. Some students may properly remark that the system provides feedback only on costs and does not reflect operational variables such as quality (defect rates), yields, cycle times, and on-time delivery. If this issue arises, I would note it as important and an excellent observation, but defer more detailed discussion until the class studies cases such as Texas Eastman, Analog Devices: Half-Life System, and Texas Instruments: Cost of Quality.

What the system does not do is implied at the end of the case. In its emphasis on responsibility accounting and short-run cost control, many operating expenses must be considered fixed costs, unaffected by the volume and mix of products produced. In calculating product costs, either these fixed costs must be ignored (the direct cost philosophy) or allocated arbitrarily to products (fully-absorbed product costs), probably using the same activity drivers used to assign variable overhead and operating expenses from cost centers to products. The flexible budgeting, short-run marginal costing approach developed and implemented by Plaut is an excellent management control tool for short-run cost control and for predicting short-run spending based on actual product volumes and mix. But it provides little insight about the magnitude and source of the "fixed cost" component of operating expenses.

Many expenses such as tooling, programming of CIM machines and NC machine tools for individual products, scheduling, purchasing, information systems, process engineering, engineering change notices, and product engineering will likely be lumped into the fixed cost pools and not be traced causally to the products creating the demands for these resources. This issue will be explored extensively in the cases developing the rationale for activity-based costing so the instructor need not spend much time on this point. As stated at the end of the case, Häussler is not prepared to make decisions based on individual product costs. Metabo is committed to offering a complete product line (a position that many Japanese companies also advocate).

I would attempt to get the class to understand the limitation of the Metabo system for product costing without getting into too much of the details. In future sessions, as the class discusses the activity-based cost systems, the issues of cost control and responsibility accounting will inevitably arise again. At that time, I would remind them of the Metabo system as one they might wish to install for cost control, and recall with them its limitations for measuring accurately all the demands made by products on the factory resources. Thus they can develop in their mind a picture of two cost systems operating simultaneously: (1) the Metabo system for daily, weekly, and monthly cost control that compares current actual expenses with the expenses authorized in the annual budgeting process; and (2) a separate activity-based system, perhaps running on a micro computer, but downloading information from the integrated mainframe SAP-like system with its general ledger financial information, and extensive, accurate data on operating expenses, products, processes, and production.

Another analogy can be made if the class has discussed the Union Pacific case series (or will discuss it in the future). The Metabo system can be viewed as comparable to, although more integrated and powerful than, UP's Management Control of Costs (MCC) system. Yet UP still needed separate and new NCS and CPMS systems to obtain product costs for pricing and product mix decisions. If Metabo's fixed costs continue to grow, it too may find it necessary to develop a supplementary system that helps it understand how demands for many support and service resources can be traced back to decisions made about product designs, product mix, and operating methods.

Texas Eastman Company

Teaching Note

The Texas Eastman case provides an excellent opportunity to discuss how financial measurements can support a company's Total Quality Management program. Occasionally, industrial engineering and operations management types denigrate financial measurements and encourage companies to cut all ties between their direct physical and operational measurements and their company's financial system. In effect, they are saying that quality improvement efforts can only be inhibited by financial measurements. The Texas Eastman case provides a vivid counter-example to such claims. First, the financial measurement system is devised by a chemical engineer department manager, not a finance or accounting person. Second, and more important, the financial system he develops plays a vital role in the success of the quality program. The case always generates a highly active and interesting discussion in class. In order to avoid over-selling the approach demonstrated in the case, the instructor needs to understand well the conditions in Texas Eastman that enabled the 3B Daily Income Statement to become an effective tool for enhancing quality and productivity.

I found the Texas Eastman (TEX) situation after making a specific inquiry to a major computer manufacturer. I was interested in learning how the much greater flow of information about production processes in computer-readable form would affect performance measurement in general and financial performance measurement in particular. I had noted the trend towards greater use of computer-integrated-manufacturing (CIM) processes in which continual data are available about products and processes. Rather than start with a CIM installation, I decided to look in a process industry, that had a long history of continual data collection and analysis. The TEX site was found by the computer company as one of its leading-edge and innovative customers in capturing information on production processes, and processing this information in sophisticated and intelligent ways. I view the TEX case as being relevant not just for continuous process industries but also for the future of discrete-part manufacturing as more emphasis is

---

This teaching note was prepared by Professor Robert S. Kaplan as an aid to instructors in the classroom use of the case, Texas Eastman Company, 9-190-039.

placed on shortening cycle time (with JIT efforts) and introducing more digitally controlled production processes.

Background reading on the situation in this case can be found in, R. Jaikumar, "An Architecture for a Process Control Costing System," Chapter 7 in R. S. Kaplan (ed.) Measures for Manufacturing Excellence (HBS Press: Boston, 1990), 193-222.

Assignment Questions

The introduction to the case can be taught from several viewpoints. The instructor can (and should) choose assignment questions to evoke the emphasis he or she wishes the class to focus on initially. One set of questions is:

1. Describe the Quality Management program initiated at Texas Eastman. What role did the new information systems play in the quality program?

2. Identify the strengths and weaknesses in the existing financial reporting system? What was the value of the period Departmental Cost Sheets (see Exhibit 4) in the information-rich operating environment of Texas Eastman?

3. How have the operators in Briley's 3B Cracking Plant been using the new Daily Income Report? Why is this report useful to them?

4. What were the information requirements for the new report? Which factors change daily, and which data stay the same from day-to-day? Why?

5. What should Pat Kinsey, the Chief Accountant do next? How should the reporting environment in the Texas Eastman plant be modified in light of the experience in the 3B Cracking Plant? What role should be played by the central accounting and finance group?

Discussion

The case discussion can start from different viewpoints. Sometimes, I describe the existing monthly financial reporting system and then ask about its limitations in the Texas Eastman (TEX) operating environment or why this system needed to be supplemented. Other times, if I know the class has not had much prior exposure to Total Quality Management programs, I start from the TEX quality initiative.

Q. **Why did the management of the chemicals division adopt a strong Total Quality Management program? What were the key features of the TEX program?**

The motivation for the quality improvement program (foreign competition in chemicals, demands from sophisticated customers (e.g., Ford)) is described in the case. Instructors can also mention that the Chemicals Division was surely aware of how Fuji Film came to challenge Kodak's supremacy by developing lower-priced products that rivaled Kodak's historic quality. Clearly, the senior management of Eastman Chemicals was strongly committed to significant quality improvements. The quality triangle, of Teamwork, Performance Measurement, and

Statistical Process Control, also deserves mention. It shows how TEX drew ideas from a variety of sources and integrated them into a comprehensive program.

Q.   Why was a new and extensive computer system needed by the manufacturing organization?

TEX, like other chemicals companies, had collected extensive data on its operations for years. But the data, manually collected, processed, and stored, were not available for analyzing quality problems. First, the data could not easily be processed in real time for SPC analysis of the many operating parameters in the plant. And, if a customer called in with a complaint [e.g., the polyethylene film tore apart in my machine; it must have been produced out of spec], it might take an engineer several days or longer to find the papers on which the operating conditions of the defective batch were recorded. In the meantime, the off-spec operating conditions might still be occurring.

The manufacturing computer system enabled the data to be entered soon after it was collected with the computer performing automatic SPC analysis, noting exceptions on operators' display screens. Not all of TEX's plant had direct digital readout into the computer system. Most of the data still came from reading dials and meters as operators made their plant tours. The case is not explicit about how these data were entered into the system but some type of remote digital entry system was probably used. It would seem wasteful for operators to write operating statistics down on paper, and then have to record the data a second time at a computer terminal.

The new computer system could also incorporate fault diagnosis routines and suggest courses of action should an out-of-control situation be detected. One can speculate with the class about whether operators, with only a high school education, can be trained to write small expert system routines to encapsulate their knowledge about recommended actions when certain interruptions or deviations occur in the process.

Q.   OK, I think I understand how TEX is currently operating. What kind of financial reporting system is being used to provide feedback on operations?

To save time, and avoid getting bogged down in detailed discussion and analysis of the Departmental Period Cost Report, I usually provide my own summary of this report. Also, I tend to be more generous about the system than the students in this situation. The Period Report is actually a well-designed system. Building from projections and commitments made in the budgeting process, as encapsulated in the Annual Operating Plan, the report is a sensible summary of period operations. It is flexed with respect to the volume and mix of actual output. The five variances help to identify the principal sources of variation of actual from budget, such as volume, mix, and external price changes. I particularly like how promised improvements from capital expenditures are linked into the standards. Some students complain about incorporating only 50% of realized operating improvements into next year's standards. This is a reasonable objection, but fails to consider the disincentive to innovate if any short-term gains are ratcheted up into tougher standards. In an environment, such as TEX, where department managers took pride in meeting their efficiency standards, the 50% sharing probably represents a good compromise between incentive effects and sustaining improvements on a permanent basis.

The thoughtful treatment of volume variances also deserves mention. In most companies, production managers receive favorable volume variances for producing in excess of budgeted amounts. Also, they are penalized with an unfavorable volume variance during a period when production falls short of budgeted amounts. This practice usually makes it impossible for an organization to achieve just-in-time operations. Though told by JIT not to produce unless the next stage is ready for the product, department managers are penalized for following this discipline, and rewarded for over-producing even when the production could be of the wrong products or in excess amounts. At TEX, most volume variances are treated as non-controllable at the departmental level. Favorable, controllable volume variances are earned only when demand exceeds rated capacity and the manager squeezes out extra yield and output to meet this demand. Conversely, a controllable unfavorable volume variance occurs only when production falls short of budgeted amounts and fails to satisfy existing demand.

In summary, the TEX Departmental Period reporting system is a thoughtful, well-designed standard cost system, whose specifications are updated to reflect current operating conditions. Many companies have a lot worse.

Q.   **How useful is the Departmental Period Reports in the information-rich environment of TEX, where 30,000 observations are being produced about the processes every 2-4 hours?**

It doesn't take very long to get consensus from the class that the Period Report comes out much too late and at too aggregate an activity level to be useful for operators or department heads. I usually draw a timeline on the board, labeling days 1 and 2 on the LHS of the line and day 28 on the RHS. I continue the line until about day 45 when the report would actually appear. I then ask, "What do the managers and operators say to the finance group when this report is issued?" The typical (and expected) response is "Too late, it's history; doesn't tell us about the future." I then describe how the finance and accounting people go to continuing education seminars to learn how to do faster closings so that the report can be released by day 35 or even 33. "What do the operators and managers tell us now?" The answer, "Still too late!" I then comment on the ingratitude of operating people who don't appreciate the tremendous learning and effort required to reduce closings from 15 days to less than a week. The point, of course, is that even were the information available at the end of day 28, it is still too late for effective action. I then repeat the wonderful analogy in the case about trying to teach someone to bowl but only letting him (or her) see how many pins were knocked down after 28 days of bowling. The class usually recognizes that the periodic reports are probably helpful for senior management, to get a sense of the long-run trends in operating performance, but are next to useless for improving actual operations.

Q.   **I can see that the information comes too late for action. Would a daily version of the same report be helpful to managers and operators?**

This is a tougher question. The format of the report with its emphasis on historical standards and variances would likely be difficult for an operator to understand and link back to operations that occurred yesterday. Operators can relate to quantities of inputs and outputs, not variances.

Q.   **Well then, is there any need for a financial report? Maybe we should just have the operators monitor the tens of thousands of observations each day and use these to make the continuous improvements. Why did Briley need to invent the Daily Income Statement for the Three B Company?**

The answer to this question is the main focus of the class discussion. I have identified at least five key benefits from the Daily Income Statement.

1.   At a behavioral level, Briley's actions are a wonderful example of "worker empowerment." Many organizations talk about empowering workers but few deliver. What better symbol of telling workers that they "own" the production process than to issue them shares of stock in their department (see the stock certificate in Exhibit 5). If workers are shareholders in the department, I say, then aren't they entitled to a periodic statement of performance? The income statement helps operators to understand the economics of their department; the assets invested and the magnitude of materials, energy, and supply expenses that get used each day to produce output. This economic awareness provides the basis of encouraging them to take actions in the best interests of the enterprise.

A vivid example of this appears in the case, when the midnight shift supervisor, on his own, ordered immediate and emergency repairs to the hydrogen compressor when it failed. Normally, he would have reported the failure on the shift report and Briley would have authorized the repair when he arrived the next morning. The shift supervisor, however, knew from the daily income statement that the value of the lost output was measured in thousands of dollars whereas the expedited repair was measured in the hundreds of dollars. He was empowered to act, had the information on which to act, and he acted.

2.   The daily statement gives a timely summary report of the operating conditions of the preceding day. It lets the operators know when they had a good day (so that they can recall what they did right) but, more important, provides an early signal when operating conditions had deteriorated. This feedback is especially important in a complex production environment where the conversion process is not completely understood. Even though catalytic cracking is an easy process to diagram (inputs of feedstock and energy, outputs of ethylene, propylene and by-products like hydrogen and oxygen), the conversion process is one of the most complex chemical processes with thousands of control points (as described briefly in the case).

Briley gave a good example of this during the case-writing process. He remembered that a heat exchanger had become dirty and was not functioning well. The operators took the exchanger off-line, repaired it, and put it back into the process. The next day, the daily income for the plant dropped. After investigation, the operators determined that the temperature change across the heat exchanger was now too high; they de-tuned the exchanger so that a smaller temperature drop occurred and output turned upwards. Perhaps the operators would have seen the decline in output without the daily income statement. But perhaps not; the unexpected signal from the statement prompted immediate action.

The daily signal kept the operators focused on quality and provided a clear signal on the returns that were being earned from improvements in quality. Over time, as described in the case, the operators learned about the key parameters to focus on to keep quality and income up.

3.   The financial summary gave operators a signal about trade-offs among various factors. Everyone knows that we should improve quality, increase yield, and use less energy. The

non-financial production types would give operators signals on quality, yield, and energy consumption and tell them to get better along all three dimensions. But, as the case notes, these parameters can be in conflict. By using more energy and running the plant at a higher temperature, more output can be produced but the quality may become less certain. Where is the optimal point among these three dimensions? Only a financial model can allow trade-offs to be made. Other trade-offs occur when the production mix shifts from ethylene to propylene; output and yield decreases but more of the higher value product (propylene) is produced.

Additional trade-offs are mentioned in the case such as the decision to take a normal 7 day shutdown for maintenance, or shut down for only 4 or 5 days, using overtime and 3rd shifts for maintenance to get the plant back on-line sooner. When demand is below capacity, is it more efficient to operate at capacity for 5 days and shut down for 2 days, or do we do better to operate at lower capacity utilization continuously over 7 days. A financial model of the plant enables these decisions to be evaluated.

4.   The financial report also helps to set priorities for operator attention. It guides them to areas where improvements will be most beneficial, and not have them make improvements to save $80 here and $100 there in a system consuming $200,000 worth of inputs every day. For engineers, the financial model helps them decide which projects or investments will likely have the highest payoffs.

5.   The financial model's treatment of quality enables the department to internalize costs that typically are measured elsewhere. For example, when quality is not high, implying a high level of contaminants in the transferred product, subsequent departments incur higher costs to purge the impurities and change their catalysts more frequently. With the new report, the costs of impurities get recorded in the 3B plant where they are created. The penalty for producing off-spec material is the central issue in the Daily Income Statement. It enables an "intangible", the quality of output, to be priced out just like any other output. Generalizing from this example, if timeliness (such as on-time-delivery) is important for a department, the manager could estimate the penalty in $/day for delivering the product late or early. Through this mechanism, the cost of bad quality or late deliveries is internalized in the department where the problem is created not in the department that bears the consequences from the off-standard production.

I usually tell about another unexpected incident that the quality improvement in 3B produced. The operators got so good in eliminating impurities that a subsequent process got fouled up. It turns out that trace elements were carried by the impurities. When all impurities were eliminated, so were the trace elements that turned out to be important for the chemical process at a subsequent stage. The 3B plant was encouraged to allow a little bit of impurity to remain so as to allow subsequent processes to continue to operate efficiently. Prior to the tremendous drive to improve quality instilled by the Daily Income Report, this phenomenon had never been noted because the quality had never reached such pure levels.

Now that the benefits from the Daily Income Statement have been identified, I turn to a discussion of the structure of the report.

Q.   **What information did Briley need in order to produce the Daily Income Statement?**

This question enables the class to explore the critical design issues in the Daily Income Statement.

1.   Most important is that the statement requires accurate measurements of the **quantities** of inputs consumed and outputs produced each day. Also it requires an accurate assessment of the **quality** of the outputs produced. Fortunately, these data were already being produced as part of the extensive investment in information technology made by TEX, so no additional measurements were required for this report. This is an important point. It would be unusual for it to be worthwhile to make new measurements just to produce a financial report. But with the tremendous expansion of information collected about production processes, financial reports can be much more timely and comprehensive by building on to the new information freely available in production and production control systems.

2.   In contrast to the accurate measurement of quantities and quality, Briley could rely on ballpark estimates of the **prices** of outputs and inputs. This is most clear in the case of the 50% discount for off-spec material. I ask, "How did Briley know whether it was 50% or 52% or 49%?" Of course, he didn't. For the purposes he wanted, getting the quality discount approximately correct was fine. Similarly the prices of the intermediate products and the inputs to the production process need only be roughly estimated. This is an important point for organizations thinking about applying the Briley Daily Statement to their departmental operations. Accurate prices for the intermediate products, such as stuffed printed circuit boards or etched wafers, need to be roughly estimated to value the output, but detailed studies need not be performed.

Building on this concept, I ask, "Should Briley change the prices of the output products and input factors daily in response to changes in market prices?" I believe the answer to this question is "No." Changing the prices daily would focus operators' attention on changing the mix of inputs consumed and outputs produced based on daily fluctuations. This is not the mission of the 3B Department. Production targets and mix are determined centrally. The goal of the operators is to learn how to produce the desired mix most efficiently while maintaining quality. Changing prices daily can only confuse the operators and distract them from their fundamental task. Only if the company wanted operators to change the mix of inputs used, or outputs produced, in response to external price changes [as occurs in some paper companies using a combination of expensive input chemicals] would it be helpful for them to see daily price changes. Should there be major changes in relative prices, such as a dramatic increase in the price of energy or feedstock, or decrease in prices of outputs (ethylene and propylene) then these changes should be incorporated to signal the new economics of the cracking process.

3.   It is also worth noting the treatment of capital cost. I ask, "How would an accountant record capital cost in an income statement?" The answer, "Depreciation." I mention the difficulty of explaining depreciation to MBAs and executives, much less to the high school graduates operating the 3B Department. In order to make this concept real to the operators, the capital cost is treated as a mortgage payment to repay the company for use of the equipment. Most of the operators would be familiar with the mortgage concept, from incurring loans for their house, farm, automobile or truck. The mortgage analogy is even better than depreciation since it can include a return on capital (the interest rate) in addition to the return of capital. The equivalent daily mortgage payment for equipment

employed was calculated by the TEX finance staff for Briley, and the amount held constant each day. Operators were not to take action based on this figure, but needed to see it to understand that much of the apparent profits from daily operation were needed to repay the heavy capital investment in the plant.

4.   The report also allowed for loan repayments for special projects that were implemented to increase yield or quality. This allowed operators to formulate new investment proposals and see the cost of the investment in these proposals. The instructor can also note Briley's "manipulation" of the facts to place a 50% premium on the use of cooling water. As with the discount for bad quality, Briley is internalizing his estimate of the long run cost of using an input resource beyond that currently reflected in the standard cost of that resource.

Q.   Was the Daily Income Report accepted? How do we know?

The operators welcomed the report each day; as evidence, note the incident in the case when Briley would return from a business trip, the operators asked him to calculate the daily income for the days he was away. I remark in class, how often does the finance staff get a call from operating departments asking where the monthly variance report is and when would it be delivered?

Initially, the motivation for the Daily Income Report came from attempting to achieve the targeted period profit that would earn the operators a new kitchen. But even after the kitchen was earned, the operators continued to want to see the daily statement, without any explicit incentive now tied to achieving income goals.

At this point, I shift the tone of the discussion away from the details of the report to a more conceptual plane by the following transition question:

Q.   I'm a little confused at this point. We all seem to be accepting the usefulness of the daily income statement in the 3B plant. But I have been hearing a lot of criticism of American management being too short-term oriented, of paying too much attention to achieving quarterly income goals. Why are we happy with a daily income statement for 3B yet critical of a quarterly income statement for U.S. corporations? Should we give a daily income statement to the President of Eastman Chemicals or the CEO of Eastman Kodak?

(The last question is more than apocryphal. When Tom Wilson, Controller at TEX was showing the Chairman of Kodak the 3B Daily Income Statement, the Chairman asked why he couldn't get some version of that statement each day for himself.)

Students find it difficult to describe their intuitive feelings about why they like the 3B daily income statement yet believe that quarterly income statements are less representative of a company's operations. I generally just call on several people and let them struggle a bit until they get to what I believe to be the essential difference. In the 3B Cracking Plant, all inputs are converted to outputs in almost a continual stream. Certainly, a day is a long enough period to match the output and revenues produced with all the inputs consumed in the 3B plant. In companies, however, especially for the types of decisions taken at the highest levels of the corporation, many inputs are not fully converted into outputs for several years. Thus expenditures on R&D, new technology, advertising, promotion and distribution, and employee training and skill enhancement yields benefits for many periods and years into the future. A quarterly income statement measures expenditures on these categories well but most of these expenditures have yet to be converted into outputs. The 3B income statement works because virtually all expenditures are converted into output each day.

Alternatively, you can characterize this situation by indicating that Briley has estimated the price (value) of all outputs produced each day, including a penalty for off-spec production. If companies could price out the value created by expenditures on R&D, new technology, advertising, and employee training, then short-term, quarterly income statements would be much more meaningful.

This point enables us to generalize from the 3B situation to other companies. For production processes that take one week or longer for inputs to be converted into outputs, a daily income statement would not be helpful. We would have too much trouble valuing the status of work-in-process inventory. This suggests that an income statement be created for a time period commensurate with the duration of the production process, at a time when we can get a full accounting for inputs consumed and outputs produced.

Q.   **What should Pat Kinsey, as Chief Accountant, do next? What role should the central finance staff play in disseminating the 3B innovation?**

The answer to this question leads to an active discussion about the role for the finance group versus decentralized initiatives. Some argue that the finance group should just stay out of the way and let local initiatives flourish without encumbrance or formality. Others raise the conflict that will occur if department managers think they are doing well, but the periodic TEX financial reports show unfavorable trends. It would be confusing to have local income signals pointing in one direction, when the centralized, more official system points in the opposite direction. In general, the class comes to conclude that the central finance staff can play a useful integration and support role in extending the 3B report:

1.   Provide hardware and software support to reduce the burden on other department managers who wish to develop the new report. Briley prepared his department's report by hand for several months. Not everyone will be as committed as he in taking on all the extra work this involved. In fact, the TEX finance staff did work to find a user-friendly programming system, a download system from the main-frame computers, and a standard user-interface for department managers to use to prepare their customized statements. This process, however, took longer than expected and, to date, has slowed down the dissemination of daily income reporting.

2.   Establish standards for internal pricing. Ideally, the output prices established by 3B should be used as the input prices for departments that take 3B's output. Otherwise, the finance staff will have to strip out inter-departmental profits and losses in attempting to get a global picture of the plant's operations. Attempting to have the output priced from one department be the value of inputs transferred to the next department will encourage a dialogue about the value of intangibles such as quality, on-time-delivery, and adherence to budgeted product-mix.

3.   Monitor external prices to determine when prices should change in local departmental models. Also monitor inventory levels between departments (if any) to reconcile between profits reported locally and profits reported at the plant.

4.   In an ideal world, the finance staff might be able to produce its 4 Week Report by aggregating and reconciling the daily income reports from each department. In this way, the financial results would be prepared from managerial reports. This would be in sharp contrast to the situation in companies today where financial reports are prepared first and then mailed to managers who then try to extract useful information from them.

Analog Devices: The Half-Life System
Teaching Note

The Analog Devices: Half-Life case illustrates innovative approaches to performance measurement in a continuous improvement environment. While the case is set in a high-tech, semiconductor manufacturing company, the concepts should be applicable in all organizations attempting to improve quality, reduce the time to accomplish tasks, and provide better customer service. Thus the principal subjects of attention -- the half-life method, and the balanced scorecard -- should be of interest not only to people interested in manufacturing, but also to managers in service, retailing, utility, and not-for-profit and governmental organizations.

I usually teach this case in conjunction with the Texas Eastman case. Texas Eastman also describes an organization committed to Total Quality Management, and illustrates an innovative financial summary of daily operations to motivate and evaluate its quality program. In Analog, the appropriate role for financial summaries is much less apparent. The company's array of performance indicators seems to provide sufficient short-run indications of quality improvement. It is only at the end of the case that the instructor can drop a bombshell to demonstrate that operational, non-financial numbers are not sufficient by themselves for organizational performance measurement.

Potential Assignment Questions

Not all of the questions below should be assigned. Instructors should choose among them to get students focused on the issues they wish to discuss in class.

What is the role of Schneiderman's "Half-Life" target-setting system in Analog Devices' Quality Improvement Program?

What assumptions does the Half-Life System make? What could limit the applicability of the method?

This teaching note was prepared by Professor Robert S. Kaplan, with assistance from Arthur Schneiderman of Analog Devices as an aid to instructors in the classroom use of the case, Analog Devices: The Half-Life System, 190-061.

How would a company get started implementing such a procedure? Where would the estimates of half-lives come from?

Why do conflicts arise between the operational QIP measures and the measures reported by the financial summaries, such as in Exhibit 7?

Compare the presentation of information of On-Time Delivery percentages in Exhibit 6 with the financial summaries in Exhibit 7.

Evaluate the Corporate Scorecard in Exhibit 5? What role does each set of measures in this exhibit play?

How much emphasis should be placed on the financial versus the operating (physical) measures in Exhibit 5? Is there a difference in the appropriate mix of measures for local operating people plant managers, division managers, or senior company managers?

Classroom Discussion

Sample questions and the range of responses are presented below:

Q: What is the purpose of the Half-Life method?

This question can be answered at different levels. At the most obvious level, the half-life method measures the rate of progress in a Quality Improvement Process (QIP). It identifies the rate of improvement in measures that the organization is attempting to reduce (defects, % of missed deliveries, absenteeism, customer complaints, etc.).

At a different level, Analog Devices Inc. (ADI) is implementing a total quality improvement process, that stresses continual problem solving. The company managers describe the process as the PDCA cycle: Plan, Do, Check, Act; (see TN Exhibits 1 and 2). TN Exhibit 1 shows the PDCA cycle as different points around a circle. This formulation emphasizes that a quality program is not something an organization does once or twice, to correct some problems, and then moves on to something else. Rather, the QIP must embody a continual problem-solving commitment. Viewed in this way, the half-life method serves as the <u>speedometer</u> for measuring how fast the organization is traveling around the PDCA cycle (see also TN Exhibit 3).

Q: Why should an organization be concerned with the rate of improvement?

Given the quotes in the case, the answer to the question is obvious but it serves to allow Ray Stata's quote to be put in front of the class early:

"the rate at which individuals and organizations learn may become the only sustainable competitive advantage .. "

Note, this quote says it is not new product designs, or effective marketing programs, or advanced process technologies that create sustainable competitive advantage. It is the ability of the organization to continually improve and learn that is critical.

The wisdom or truth of this statement is not obvious. Basically it implies that competitors can copy or catch up to a company's products and the equipment it uses, but they cannot capture the learning environment or culture for continuous improvement that has been created in an organization. The interpretation and truth of this statement can be the basis of a brief discussion with the class, which is unlikely to be conclusive or decisive, but should clarify what Ray Stata meant by his provocative statement.

The instructor can bring out examples of other companies that are explicitly attempting to measure improvement. For example, in 1989, the (privately held) Milliken Co. won one of the first Malcolm Baldridge Quality Awards. The Chairman and major shareholder, Roger Milliken, was concerned that the organization might become complacent after winning the award. He instituted the 10-4 program, requiring that organizational units achieve a ten fold improvement (in reducing defects, eliminating waste, ...) during the next four years. (The ten fold improvement implies about 3.3 "half-life" cycles or a half-life of between 10 and 11 months; that is, to meet Mr. Milliken's goals, the organization would have to reduce defects by 50% every 10-11 months over the next four years.) Motorola, IBM, and Hewlett-Packard are known for their 6σ goals, to reduce defects from their current levels to less than 10 parts per million.

In terms of the organization, the continual improvement occurs through making problems visible, identifying the sources of the problems, and solving them (though some Japanese believe that problems are never "solved"; they are just made better). If students are familiar with management approaches such as just-in-time, employee involvement, design-for-manufacturability, concurrent engineering, and computer-integrated-manufacturing (CIM), the instructor can point out that these are all manifestations of the underlying philosophy of <u>kaizen</u> or continuous improvement; activities that organizations engage in to learn more about their environment so that they can improve and get better. This is a different philosophy from what many believe to have come from the scientific management approach, where engineers study processes, break complex processes into simpler steps, and develop standards for performing each step. Employees are to follow, without discretion or individual initiative, the procedures established by the industrial engineers. The employees are held accountable for meeting the engineered or pre-determined standards through a reporting system of efficiencies and standard costs. The <u>kaizen</u> philosophy does not develop static standards for processes; it attempts to have employees continually improve the standards by eliminating waste and defects, thereby making processes more efficient.

Q: **What things are we trying to improve with the half-life method?**

Again, this is a simple question but important in making it explicit that the approach is not limited to reducing the incidence of defective parts. As Schneiderman's statement in the case makes clear:

> I used the word "defect" in its most general sense: any measurable quantity that is in need of improvement.

Q: **What assumptions does the half-life method make?**

Mathematically, the method assumes a constant rate-of-reduction in defects. A simple numerical example, perhaps put on a side board, can help to clarify the method. Suppose we have a process with a half-life of six months. The reduction in defects is shown below:

Month	Defects (PPM)
0	1,000
6	500
12	250
18	125
24	62
36	31

In 36 months, we have gone through five "half-life" cycles, reducing the incidence of defects to only 3% of the initial value (a direct consequence of the mathematics since $2^5 = 32$, and 1/32 is about 0.03). The same process with a half-life of 12 months would have gone through 3 "half-life" cycles in 3 years so that the PPM defect rate at the end of 36 months would be 250. The eight-fold difference between the two processes reveals the power of shorter half-lives in reducing the incidence of problems.

The mathematics of the method is straightforward. What is more mysterious is the process that leads to the empirical regularity noted by Art Schneiderman in Exhibits 2 and 3 of the case. Near as I can understand it, the phenomenon reflects the problem-solving methodology of the PDCA cycle in which there is a constant rate of problem solving. It implies the Pareto distribution of root causes; that 80% of the problems are caused by only a few problems. By systematically studying errors or defects and identifying their causes, a few problems emerge that, if solved, will eliminate a large percentage of the errors. Once these problems are solved, the remaining errors will again have only a few root causes and these become the focus of the next round of problem-solving activities. The half-life method assumes that problems can be solved at about a constant rate (more on this later).

The data in Exhibit 2 on Yokogawa Hewlett-Packard provides a valuable summary of the half-life method. The graph shows a half-life of 3.6 months. Over a 28 month period, the company made 8 "half-life" cycles, allowing a more than 100 fold improvement in defects ($2^8 = 256$), reducing defect rates from about 0.3% to around .001%. The process stabilized at that defect rate for 10-12 months before starting down another improvement curve. Schneiderman reported that to make further improvements (below the failure rate experienced after 28 months of effort) involved redesigning the printed circuit boards, requiring a cross-functional development effort that had a longer half-life. Thus a process may go through several half-life cycles and eventually hit a barrier preventing further improvement without an inter-organizational effort that requires more time to be successful.

Occasionally, students will contrast the half-life method of learning with the more familiar **experience** or **learning curve** that they have encountered in their operations management or corporate strategy classes. The experience curve assumes that learning occurs through cumulative production (learning by doing), whereas the half-life method assumes that learning occurs through time. While there are some similarities between these two approaches, I think that they differ in fundamental ways. With the experience curve philosophy, one can catch up to a competitor only by finding ways to increase production so that you match the competitor's cumulated experience. The half-life method assumes that you can catch up to a more experienced competitor by being a faster learner, by having a shorter half-life for solving problems; in effect, by moving around the PDCA cycle at a faster clip. I also think that the experience curve tends to measure the consumption of resources (materials, labor, capital) to produce a given amount of output, whereas the half-life method focuses on defects or waste explicitly. Perhaps the focus of the two approaches is identical, but it is not obvious to me. I have only rarely had a good discussion in class contrasting the experience curve with the half-life method, so I would not push the issue too hard if the class is not energized by it.

Q: How does an organization get started with the half-life method?

This issue seems to bother many in the class, particularly the executives to whom I have taught this case. They are intrigued with the method but concerned about how to implement it in their organization. There are two approaches that can be considered:

1.   "Just do it!" The "just do it" approach says that organizational units should embark on a problem-solving process and measure the rate of improvement in defects and waste. The early rate of defect reduction can then be used to establish the half-life of improvement for the unit. This approach is simple and action-oriented but has the problem of allowing an ineffective problem-solving process to produce a too slack standard for improvement rates. This limitation can be ameliorated by comparing the half-lives for similar organizational units, working on similar types of problems.

2.   The more analytic approach attempts to use Schneiderman's insight in Exhibit 4 of the case. This exhibit shows how half-lives can be estimated based on the complexity of the problem and the number of different organizational units (both internal and external to the firm) that need to be involved to solve the problem. Schneiderman has some specific examples of the use of his model:

Project Type	Examples	Model Half-Life	Expected Range
Single Dept.	Operator Errors Work-in-Process	3 months	0 - 6 months
Cross-functional	New Product Cycle Time Outgoing PPM	9 months	6 - 12 months
Multi-entity	Vendor Quality Warranty Costs	18 months	12 - 24 months

An example of a issue with both high technical and organizational complexity is the production of Application Specific Integrated Circuits (ASICs). The design and production of ASICs involves people from the customer, product design, manufacturing, and marketing. Simple problems within a single department tend to be the focus of tasks worked on by Quality Circles. Schneiderman claims that Analog is now willing to reorganize to reduce organizational complexity; to eliminate functional barriers that slow down the rate at which problems can be solved.

Having given all this guidance, Schneiderman (and I) concur that determining half-lives for processes is a "subject that is ripe for considerable research." In practice at ADI, Schneiderman estimates half-lives from his model and recent experience, and then negotiates the actual targets with department managers.

Q: What are the strengths and weaknesses of the Half-Life concept?

The following list comes from responses of managers within ADI.

Strengths

Brings measurement focus to the <u>kaizen</u> (continuous improvement) efforts
Easy to understand [I suppose they mean the graphical presentation.]
Makes sense
Performance targets are data based
Accepted by line organization
Focuses on results, not the process
It works!

Weaknesses

Not benchmarking; may not reflect where ADI needs to be
Logarithmic scale is difficult to understand
Assumes instant start-up of QIP
Assumes only a constant rate of learning   (Japanese competitors are not happy with only
                                                       a <u>constant</u> rate of learning)

Focuses on results, and not the process

This list indicates that one person's strength is another person's weakness (e.g., ease of understanding, emphasis on results versus process).

The benchmarking issue also arises in the half-lives estimated to achieve the 1992 goals. Not stated in the case is the process by which the half-lives were determined. The 1992 goals started from asking key customers what kind of performance they expected from their #1 supplier. The customer's Purchasing people specified only modest improvements from 1987 performance. The customers' Operations people were much more demanding since they compared ADI to all their suppliers, not just to linear IC manufacturers. If ADI could not reasonably expect to meet the goals specified from their toughest customers, it then looked to see what its best competitor was currently doing, and could be expected to be doing in 1992; and this became the target. Only if ADI could not meet its toughest competitor with its currently projected half-life improvement rate was the target specified by extrapolating from current half-lives. Some in ADI felt that if it could not meet the performance of its best competitor, then perhaps ADI should consider exiting that line of business.

Q: **If improvement and the QIP measures are such a good thing, why do conflicts arise with the measures reported by the financial system? Which numbers should we believe when conflicts occur between them?**

This case provides some excellent examples of how, in the short-run, operational and financial indicators come into conflict.

1.   As yield (a QIP measure) improves, fewer wafer starts are required in order to meet final demands for good die. But overhead rates are based on the number of wafer starts, so as wafer starts are reduced, unfavorable volume variances arise. Note that since "fixed" overhead is not applied to products, the volume variance is caused only by the "variable" overhead, primarily direct labor (which is considered a variable cost, but which does not vary with short-run fluctuations in activity levels).

2.   On Time Delivery (OTD) performance can conflict with the need to realize income at the end of a fiscal quarter. As described in the case, if the company wants to recognize additional income, it might ship high margin products at the end of a quarter and delay the shipment of low-margin products. The change in product scheduling at the end of a quarter would adversely affect the OTD performance of the last month in the quarter and the first month in the subsequent quarter.

3.   Meeting customer requested delivery requests (CRD) can conflict with income recognition when wafers are started into production near the end of a quarter to pass through several inventory vouchering points, permitting some period overhead to be absorbed into inventory. But by starting more wafers into production, the lead-time quotes for the next set of orders are lengthened because more wafers are sitting between the new starts and finished production. Also, requests for small orders may get delayed until sufficient orders arrive to make an economic batch size worthwhile to produce.

4.   An interesting conflict between two important operational indicators occurs when engineers design a new circuit and want several wafers fabricated so that they can evaluate their designs. These engineered or "hot" lots take priority over regularly scheduled production lots because until they are fabricated, the engineers can not test or improve their designs. Thus expediting the hot lots reduces the time for introducing new products but adversely affects the on-time delivery performance of existing orders.

5.   The example on yield trends at the end of the case illustrates that financial measures are not always the culprit when financial and operational indicators conflict. In that example, overall chute yields increased but the yield variances were unfavorable. Subsequent study revealed that chute yields had increased because the mix had shifted towards easier-to-produce products. The yield variance signaled that the chute yield had not increased as much as it should have, given the mix shift that had occurred in the last quarter.

6.   Another conflict occurs between the OTD and Quoted Lead Time QIP operational indicators. Initially, the different performance measures were linked by slack ropes so that it was possible to reduce all indicators simultaneously. As obvious forms of waste were managed out of the system, the slack between measures disappeared and the measures became more tightly linked. Currently, attempts to reduce quoted lead times even further would result in much worse performance for OTD, because of the uncertainty of process flows still in the system. Alternatively, attempts to increase the OTD % further could only be accomplished by quoting longer lead times or producing and carrying more inventory. Neither alternative is desirable. Further simultaneous improvements in both Quoted Lead Times and OTD will require substantial improvements in manufacturing cycle time, a task that sounds easy but is in fact quite difficult to accomplish at present (or, more accurately, a process that has a long half-life of improvement).

Q: **If the QIP measures are relevant for improving operations, what function is served by the financial measures (in Exhibit 7)?**

The financial measures in Exhibit 7 are aggregate summary measures for departmental and senior managers. They probably are not useful for employees and shift supervisors in their present form. The financial measures report the financial consequences from operating performance. The income statement (Exhibit 7) combines both revenue effects (volume and mix) with production efficiencies and volume. This can be a valuable statement but its content and presentation could likely be improved. As Lou Fiore states in the case, he monitors spending, particularly on discretionary items on a monthly basis, but doesn't feel that the variances are meaningful to him. The challenge for the finance staff is to distinguish its financial reporting role (which leads to the clutter of variances in Exhibit 7) from its role to provide useful financial summaries to managers.

Q: **Apart from content, what differences do you notice between Exhibit 6 and the financial exhibit (7)?**

The contrast between the graphical presentations in Exhibit 6 and the numerical presentations in Exhibit 7 illustrates that data presented graphically conveys information in a much more accessible and powerful form. The messages in Exhibit 6 can be grasped in a matter of seconds; we can quickly identify divisions whose beginning of year performance was superior but whose rate of learning has been disappointing. We also quickly notice divisions whose beginning of year on-time delivery performance was poor but who are experiencing rapid rates of improvement. The data in Exhibit 7 would likely take several minutes of study before one can discern trends, outliers, and significant problem areas. The differences in presentation have nothing to do with the content of the exhibits. Financial data can be displayed graphically, and with trends. The apparent six digit precision reported in Exhibit 7 is illusory; The essential message can be obtained by knowing how many zeroes are in the number and the first two significant digits, information that can be communicated graphically. Accountants and controllers should reflect on how modern graphics packages greatly facilitate the graphical reporting of results to busy operating managers.

Q: **What purpose is served by the scorecard shown as Exhibit 5?**

Exhibit 5 is a summary information sheet, reviewed quarterly by the senior executive group of ADI. This exhibit is part of an Executive Information System at ADI. If a senior manager wants to understand the sources of a poor on-time delivery statistic, for example, he can query the system and get the more detailed monthly data on OTD for each operating division. If one division seems to be causing the problem, the executive can probe more deeply about that division, until reaching a screen enabling him to see information on all items shipped from that division yesterday to individual customers.

Exhibit 5 is organized by information concerning various company stakeholders. The top panel, Financial, presents information to the company's suppliers of capital: Sales, Sales Growth, Contribution Margin, and Return on Assets. The second panel reports on other stakeholders: Customers and Employees. On Time Delivery reports the percentage of orders shipped on the factory commit date for delivery (on time delivery represents a window of x days early [as specified by the customer] up to 0 days late). The "CRDs Not Matched" reports on the difference between the Factory Commit Date and the Date Requested by the Customer (CRD). It is a measure of how close ADI has come to meeting the customer's requests. (OTD measures how well ADI performs relative to its commitments to those requests.) Excess Lead Time measures the deviation between the Factory Commit Date and the Customer Request Date, again a measure of ADI's inability to meet customers' requests. Labor Turnover is a weak attempt to measure employee satisfaction. Schneiderman asked the Human Resources Department for an appropriate employee measure. HRM, while not happy with the "turnover" measure, did not supply an alternative metric.

The third and fourth panels of Exhibit 5 are measures of internal business processes. These measures are considered more under the control of operating managers than the customer-based metrics in the second panel, and are also considered the underlying drivers of the customer metrics. That is, if cycle time and defects can be reduced, and yields increased, then it should be easier to meet customer delivery requests and to ship orders when promised. The fifth panel gives information on new product developments. These measures are used by the Chairman, Ray Stata, and the Executive Vice President, Jerry Fishman, as leading indicators of long-term success. Schneiderman reports that looking at average measures for all new products is not very meaningful, so that ADI now tracks every new product (more than 1,000) separately with product-specific performance measurements. Executives can access these data by clicking on the appropriate cell in the fifth panel and working their way through the executive information system.

The variances between the benchmarks in the Quarterly Scorecard, as determined by the five year plan and the half-life method, are color coded on the screen and on the paper reports prepared from this data. "Red" gaps are used to identify areas where additional action apparently needs to be taken, and "green" (favorable) gaps represent instances where the reasons for success should be communicated and shared more widely in the organization.

Exhibit 5 contains a powerful message that the instructor should make sure arises in the class discussion. It communicates the need for a **balanced scorecard**. No one measure or type of measures is sufficient to evaluate recent performance. The balanced scorecard -- displaying financial, customer, internal, and new product measures, all compared with benchmarked rates of improvement -- gives a more comprehensive picture than can be obtained by looking too narrowly at only one set of measures, whether financial or QIP operating measures. The customer-based metrics are clearly very important for predicting future changes in market share and product margins. But improvements in the manufacturing metrics will indicate how much future improvement in the customer-based metrics will be possible. And the new product metrics indicate whether future customer demands will likely be met. Finally the financial metrics indicate whether improvement in customer, employee, internal processes, and new product introductions have been converted into benefits to shareholders.

The balanced scorecard also reveals when good or excellent performance in one metric may have been achieved in an inappropriate way. For example, meeting a quarterly sales goal by accelerating high margin shipments and delaying low margin shipments will be indicated by a deteriorating OTD percentage. And using excess production to produce large amounts of finished goods inventory for meeting OTD or CRD requests could be revealed by increasing cycle times and deteriorating ROA. Also, harvesting existing products and cutting back on R&D might show good short-term financial performance but should soon lead to deteriorating performance on the bookings for recently released and future products. Thus, the balanced scorecard with its financial, customer, internal, and future based measures may be the appropriate focus of attention for senior management reviews of current operating performance. The EIS structure enables the senior managers to probe more deeply into the operations of individual divisions and departments when exceptional problems or unusually good performance is revealed on the scorecard.

At this point in the class, I would say, "Let me describe ADI's progress in its QIP program over the three year period, ending about when the case was prepared," and present the following table:

	July 1, 1987	July 1, 1990
On Time Delivery	70%	96%
Outgoing Defects	500 PPM	50 PPM
Average Yields	26%	51%

"This represent pretty good progress, doesn't it? A seven-fold improvement in reducing missed delivery times, a 10 fold improvement in defects, and a doubling in yields. There's only one statistic that has not shown improvement. The stock price on July 1, 1990 was one-third the level on July 1, 1987!"

After an entire class spent on how to improve OTD, reduce defects, and increase yield, the idea that ADI has not been rewarded for its achievements generally comes as a surprise to the class. The reasons for the lower stock price need to be explored. Many quality and just-in-time gurus argue either that financial performance is irrelevant, or, more intelligently, that good financial results are the result of improving operations in a fundamental way, as ADI has done. The experience of ADI, however, indicates that financial results are not directly tied to operating improvements. The reasons for the disconnect are worth reserving 5-10 minutes of discussion time at the end of the class.

Basically, I believe that the improvements in OTD, PPM, yields, and most other QIP measures do eliminate waste and give the organization greater capability and capacity. But how the organization utilizes its greater capabilities and capacities becomes critical, and is not trivial. Overall, industry growth slowed in the late 1980s so that ADI, if it wanted to increase revenues, either had to charge higher selling prices or expand market share as a consequence of its better customer service. In ADI's case, its customers did not permit higher prices to be charged; and since ADI was already the leading supplier of analog/digital and digital/analog devices to many of its largest customers, they were reluctant to have ADI's share increase even further, for fear of becoming over-dependent on a single supplier. In any case, ADI had yet to translate its performance improvements into either higher unit prices or faster growth in unit sales. Perhaps, the QIP improvements just enabled ADI to stay abreast of its competitors. That is the operating gains were captured entirely by customers. If ADI had not made the dramatic improvements over the past three years, it might have suffered financial reversals that would have made its stock price performance even worse.

Another alternative to raising prices or increasing unit sales is to use the QIP improvements to lower operating expenses. For ADI, operating expenses could only have been lowered by laying off people. But employees were the primary sources for the impressive productivity and QIP improvements ADI had enjoyed during the past three years. Slowdowns in the Massachusetts economy during 1988-1990 made turnover and attrition rates very low, and senior company managers knew that layoffs would almost surely cause the QIP program to stop. Thus ADI had a dilemma. The quality and productivity improvements it had made were real, but unless it could increase sales volume to take advantage of its newly-created extra capacity and capabilities, the company would not enjoy the benefits from its improvements. In effect, the QIP gains of the past three years had produced just excess capacity and not improved financial performance.

Of course, this insight puts the pressure on to the engineering department to increase the flow of new products that can be produced with the currently excess capacity, and on to the marketing department to reach new customers through aggressive low-margin pricing and highly competitive delivery terms. Such a new marketing policy, however, directly contradicted ADI's marketing culture of selling high performance products in low volumes and high margins for specialized applications. As Art Schneiderman remarked, during a discussion of the present dilemma, "We need to extend the QIP philosophy outside the production areas, to new product design and to marketing and sales."

This situation indicates that a new model is needed to forecast how improvements in quality and timeliness will translate into higher revenues (increased unit volume and/or increased prices). Without this model (in effect a general demand curve - with quality and timeliness supplementing the economist's usual price variable to explain changes in quantity sold; that is, a model of revenue creation), the company can not forecast how QIP improvements can produce higher contribution margins for the organization. Revenue models, however, will be much harder to build than expense models (such as activity-based cost models).

Thus at the end of the case discussion, the class has seen a new measurement tool to reinforce continuous improvement activities. The half-life method provides a timely benchmark for the rate of improvement of processes throughout the organization. The balanced scorecard shows how no single measure or set of measures can motivate or evaluate the short-term (monthly, annual) performance of complex organizations, facing highly competitive and demanding market conditions. And the discussion at the end of the class reveals that improvements in quality and timeliness give companies the opportunity to improve financial performance, but only a financial measure can reveal whether the company has seized that opportunity. Additional actions either to increase throughput (higher volumes and/or higher prices) or to decrease operating expense are required for the company to capture the gains from its operating improvements.

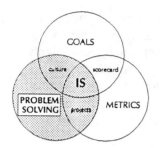

TN-Exhibit 1   The Deming Cycle

THE DEMING CYCLE

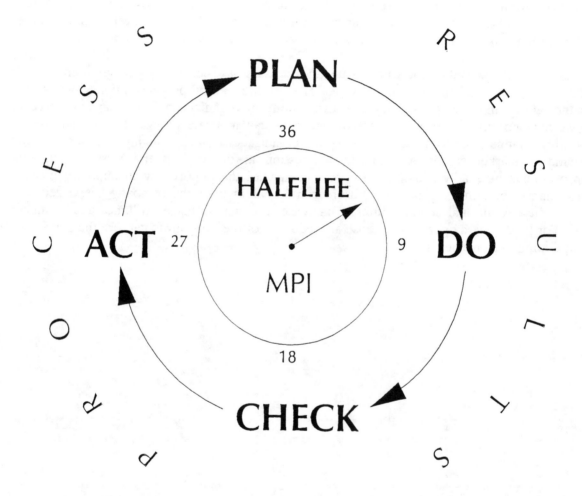

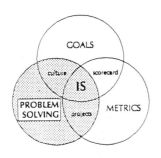

TN-Exhibit 2   Problem Solving

PROBLEM SOLVING
The Deming Cycle (PDCA)

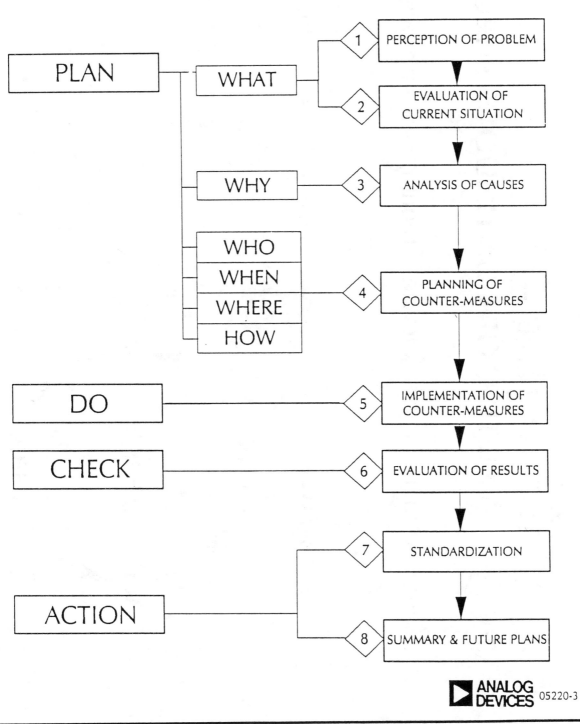

TN-Exhibit 3   The "Half-Life" — A Metric of Continuous Improvement

THE "HALFLIFE" --
A METRIC OF CONTINUOUS IMPROVEMENT

(% improvement / cycle) X (cycles / month) = % improvement / month

40% / cycle   X   1 cycle / 4 months   =   10% / month

or

≈ 50% / 5 months

5 month halflife

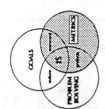

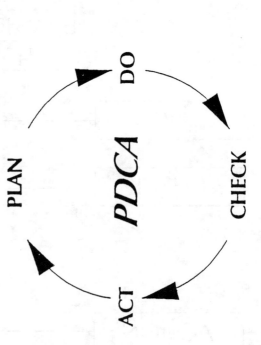

ANALOG
DEVICES 10170-2

Texas Instruments: Cost of Quality (A) and (B)

Teaching Note

The Texas Instruments case series provides an introduction to measurement and managerial issues that arise when implementing the Cost of Quality (COQ) approach. While much has been written about COQ, little has been written about the data companies are actually collecting for COQ calculations or about the organizational issues that emerge as the COQ system matures. This case series describes the application of the concept and the evolving quality measurement issues in two divisions within an actual company. In particular, this series can be used to:

1. Illustrate a successful management led cultural change and system implementation.

2. Discuss the COQ concept and analyze the concept's strengths and weaknesses.

3. Examine and critique the COQ mechanics adopted by a particular company, including the factors selected for measurement and the methods for calculating the data.

4. Compare Cost of Quality measurement to direct measures of quality (DMOQ) such as yields, defect rates and statistical process controls.

Assignment or Discussion Questions for the (A) Case

1. What factors led to the adoption of the COQ system? Why do you think the company chose to adopt a financial measure of quality?

This teaching note was prepared by Doctoral Student, Christopher Ittner, under the supervision of Professor Robert S. Kaplan, as the basis for class discussion rather than to illustrate either effective or ineffective handling of an administrative situation.

2.   What are the strengths and weaknesses of the COQ concept? Compare COQ measurement to direct measures of quality such as yields, defect rates and statistical process controls.

3.   Evaluate the COQ variables adopted by the Materials & Controls Division. Should they be changed? Why?

4.   What value are the four quality cost categories (prevention, appraisal, internal and external failure)? How can this information be used?

5.   What changes to the COQ system should Werner Schuele, the Vice President of People & Asset Effectiveness, recommend?

Discussion

The case discussion should begin with an analysis of Texas Instruments' competitive environment and the company's "Total Quality Thrust". During the 1970s, Texas Instruments operated with a strong financial focus and a quality orientation that one manager summed up as follows, "If we didn't get some defective product back from the customer, we were doing too good a job." As foreign competition intensified in the late 1970s and early 1980s, TI management realized that a greatly expanded commitment to quality was necessary.

Several factors contributed to the success of the resulting "Total Quality Thrust." First, senior management took a lead in quality training. Over 450 TI managers were sent to quality training courses conducted by Philip Crosby to "get quality religion." The managers then proceeded to teach quality training courses to all exempt employees. Along with the employees, managers were trained in quality tools such as control charts and statistical process control.

Next, a quality reporting system that was consistent with the strong financial orientation within the company was implemented. By designing the "Quality Blue Book" in the same format as the existing financial "Blue Book," a strong message was sent that quality performance was to be considered equal in importance to financial performance. Finally, a COQ system was implemented to integrate quality with the strong financial culture at TI.

COQ Strengths and Weaknesses

Several passages in the case identify benefits from COQ measurement. These include:

- Quantifying the financial significance and profit impact of quality.
- Helping to set priorities for quality improvement projects.
- Evaluating the performance of quality improvement activities.
- Helping to determine optimal relationships among various quality improvement alternatives.
- Focusing attention on major sources of quality costs.

Of all the above reasons, the first is perhaps the most important. Senior managers with a financial bottom-line mentality may pay lip service to improving quality but if all the control and performance measures emphasize financial performance and variances from standards, it will be hard to sustain a strong commitment to quality throughout the organization. The Cost of Quality measure provides a single number that can relate directly to bottom-line financial performance. It indicates what fraction of an organization's sales dollars, or manufacturing costs, is consumed either in producing defects, testing for defects, correcting defects, or preventing defects from occurring. Only when senior managers see what a high fraction of their costs are generated by bad quality production may they launch and sustain an effort to reduce the incidence of defects.

We can see this impact in the (A) case. One manager at M&C described why the group implemented COQ measurement rather than relying on direct measures of quality (DMOQ) as many Japanese manufacturers do.

> The Japanese weren't trying to dismantle the misguided management system we had before. We had to dramatically change the quality attitude. This couldn't be a completely cold change. We had to show that quality improved profitability. Japan didn't have to overcome this obstacle.

Limitations to the COQ approach include the following:

- Cost of Quality measurement does not solve quality problems.
- COQ reports do not suggest specific actions.
- COQ measures may not provide accurate short-term feedback on current operations.
- COQ measures are susceptible to short-term mismanagement or measurement error and bias.
- It may be difficult to match effort and accomplishment in a single time period.
- Important costs may be omitted from COQ reports.
- Inappropriate costs may be included in COQ reports.

With so many limitations, why did TI adopt COQ reporting rather than relying on direct measures of quality? Before attacking this question, it may be useful to digress a moment to discuss the attributes of direct measures of quality. Direct measures of quality (DMOQ) include such things as defect rates, machine uptime, product throughput, adherence to production and delivery schedules, first pass yields, and statistical process controls. DMOQ have certain advantages relative to Cost of Quality measures. Direct measures are easily quantified and understood by factory workers as well as managers. Direct measures can also provide immediately useful information for quality improvement activities because they direct attention to some physical process that needs improvement rather than merely recording the magnitude of the quality problem in some category. On the down side, DMOQ measures are disaggregate and cannot provide a single measure of quality performance (such as can be provided by a dollar-denominated measure). This makes the analysis of tradeoffs among DMOQ measures difficult.

M&C's Existing COQ System

Attention can now be focused on M&C's existing COQ system. The class can be asked to evaluate the variables and methods currently employed by the group. Attention can be directed to Exhibit 2 and the so-called "soft" estimated numbers. Carl Sheffer, one of the group's PCC General Managers, says in the case that he primarily focuses on the "hard" numbers. Should "soft" numbers be eliminated from the COQ calculation? Should more accurate data be gathered for these variables? Basically, a distinction exists between a measure (COQ) primarily intended as attention-getting and attention-directing, and measures, such as DMOQ, which serve a score-keeping feedback control purpose. Soft measures are sufficient to get and direct attention, but hard measures are needed to monitor and measure actual performance. The discussion should consider the measure's purpose as well as the trade-offs between more accurate information and the additional costs involved in increasing information accuracy. Other potential areas for discussion include the definition of a quality cost (i.e. is engineered scrap a quality cost) and the trend distortion issue.

Quality Cost Categories

During the discussion of the current system, the question can be asked, "What purpose is served by measuring the Cost of Quality in the four categories of prevention, appraisal, internal failure, and external failure costs?" These four categories appear in almost all COQ systems.

The basic concept behind the four category quality cost reporting scheme is that the most costly condition exists when a customer finds a defect. Had the manufacturer, through inspection or testing, found the defect, it would have saved money through reduced warranty costs, liability claims, or lost customers. And if the quality program had been geared towards preventing defects rather than inspecting them out (the "do it right the first time" approach), quality costs would be reduced even further. Studies of electronic components, for example, have found that a defective resistor caught before use in the manufacturing process costs two cents. If the defective resistor is not caught until the end product is in the field, however, the cost of repair can run into the thousands of dollars. Accordingly, an increase in the cost of prevention should result in a larger decrease in the cost of failure, thereby reducing total quality costs (i.e. an ounce of prevention is worth a pound of cure). The four categories can thus be used to manage quality costs.

Again, we can see the role of the COQ measure for attention getting. Most companies when initially adopting a COQ system found that they were spending most of their costs in the internal and external failure categories. As explicit quality programs got implemented, more money was spent in prevention and perhaps appraisal, but sharp reductions in internal and external failure were realized. Overall, the Cost of Quality falls as more resources are devoted to prevention, and fewer to repairing internal and external failures. As the commercial says, you can pay me now (in prevention) or you can pay me later (in correcting defects in the field, or attempting to placate unhappy customers). Now is cheaper. Unfortunately, we do not have much empirical evidence on the optimal or even desirable proportion of spending across the four categories, though the zero defect philosophy suggests the goal of spending 100% of quality costs in the prevention and appraisal categories.

Attention can be turned to Exhibit 7. Looking at the trend in COQ costs as a percent of net sales billed, we see that internal and external failure costs as a percent of total quality costs have been falling while the prevention and appraisal costs as a percent of total quality costs have been rising. This is consistent with the intended usage of the quality cost categories.

COQ in the Future

In the (A) case, the dilemma faced by Werner Schuele is whether indirect quality costs, initially omitted from the system, should be incorporated into the COQ system. Considerations include not only the costs vs. the benefits, but also the ability to define and measure quality in indirect areas at all. The problem of losing comparison with trends of past COQ measures, because of an expansion in categories being included, also arises. On a broader level, the question is: what role should a Cost of Quality system play in an organization that has institutionalized a quality culture? Carl Sheffer, the PCC General Manager, noted:

> COQ still motivates; it is still a large number. But it is losing its value. We need to do other things. This includes placing more emphasis on direct diagnostic measures.

Mac McDonnell, Vice President and General Manager of Texas Instrument's Industrial Systems Division (the locus of the (B) case), observed a similar evolution in quality measurement within his organization (see quote on page 253 of the text).

In effect, these managers are claiming that once the attention-getting function of the COQ measurement has been achieved, they can focus day-to-day on DMOQ measures. Thus, measuring COQ monthly may be redundant, costly, and even confusing once more direct measures have become institutionalized and accepted.

This is not to say that Cost of Quality systems should be abandoned as soon as the company achieves quality awareness. In general, companies have taken one of two approaches as the COQ system begins to lose some of its original effectiveness. One approach entails the expansion of the system to cover untapped areas for quality cost measurement. This is the approach being advocated by Werner Schuele in the (A) case. The second approach is to abandon monthly or quarterly COQ reporting in favor of less frequent, perhaps annual, measurement, using COQ measures as periodic scorecards over longer periods of time. The information can then be used to answer questions such as: Am I doing better than last year? Are the quality improvement projects really making an impact? Are costs shifting away from the internal and external failure categories? While neither approach is superior to the other, each represents a significantly different approach to quality measurement.

Assignment or Discussion Questions for the (B) Case

1. Why did ISD's first attempt to implement a COQ system fail?

2. Compare ISD's COQ system to M&C's system. Why do you think they are so different?

3. Why was COQ measurement becoming less useful to ISD management?

4. What is the relationship between COQ and the direct measures of quality now being used?

5. Should ISD reinstate COQ measurement? If so, what form should it take?

Discussion

Before diving into the specifics of ISD's Cost of Quality system, we should compare the differing business environments of ISD and the Materials & Controls Group. M&C operates several relatively stable and mature businesses that are facing increased price competition from foreign competitors. Consequently, the group has been forced to reduce costs while maintaining superior quality in order to retain its position in the market place. ISD, on the other hand, operates an emerging business faced with constant demands for product innovation and customization. While this distinction may seem unrelated to the selection of COQ system characteristics, it has had a major impact on the approach taken by each organization.

Failed COQ System Implementation

It is interesting to contrast the successful COQ system implementation at M&C with the unsuccessful initial effort at ISD. In each case, management was sent to Crosby's Quality College where the principles of Cost of Quality measurement were introduced. Why then did the outcomes differ so dramatically? Three reasons seem to explain the results.

First,and probably most important, while the M&C system was actively supported by top level group management, the ISD system development was relegated to a low level quality engineer who had little active support of upper management.

Second, M&C recognized that the integrity of the data would have a major impact on the system's acceptance. It was clear that the Control & Finance organization, as the principal source of financial information in the group, was in the best position to provide credible, consistent numbers. Although Control & Finance (C&F) initially resisted the added of responsibility (and workload) of COQ reporting, a compromise was soon worked out in which C&F supplied the COQ data to the Quality department. Quality then took responsibility for publishing the results in the Quality Blue Book. ISD, on the other hand, relied on the individual managers to calculate their own quality cost numbers based on unclear guidelines. Not surprisingly, the numbers lacked consistency and credibility.

Finally, M&C avoided using the COQ data to "hammer" the group's managers. Rather, the quality measures were used to focus on long-term trends of quality improvements and to highlight potential sources of quality problems. This stands in sharp contrast to the information's use at ISD, where managers were held responsible for monthly performance and progress was compared across organizations.

ISD's Existing COQ System

After discussing the failings of the initial system, students can be asked to evaluate ISD's existing system. It is readily apparent that the variables selected for measurement are considerably different than the variables tracked at M&C. In fact, if one looked at the quality cost components discussed in the literature, ISD's choices may not look like quality costs at all. Why were these variables selected for measurement? As discussed in the case, ISD's management team sought to focus on major management issues and major sources of cost. The team recognized the value of the COQ concept for attention-getting. But rather than accepting the traditional definition of quality costs, the team molded the COQ concept to meet its particular and pressing needs. Noted Don Schenck, Manager of Quality and Reliability:

We applied the 80/20 rule that says 80% of your costs are caused by 20% of your problems. By trying to focus on the variables that account for 80% of our costs, we tried to set up motivation for improving a few things that can have a major impact. We had a consensus that these were important items.

But are these quality costs? Students can debate the value of the variables ISD selected for measurement relative to more traditional quality cost variables such as those tracked by M&C. ISD management believes that the focus of their system is more consistent with their competitive situation than a traditional COQ system would be. Explained Mac McDonnell, ISD's General Manager:

We are an emerging business, so we need to be strategically oriented. Attleboro (headquarters for M&C) made the right strategic decision years ago. They can afford to have a more operational focus. Because they are a stable business with an operational focus, they can set up systems that try to remove every unnecessary penny from the cost of their products. This is what their Cost of Quality system does. We have to concentrate on product innovation and meeting ever-changing customer needs. As a result, our system must focus on broader areas than theirs does.

Reduction In COQ Usefulness

The (B) case states that the Cost of Quality system was receiving less attention as the division's management began to focus on other measures of quality such as cycle time and on-time delivery. Students can be asked to examine the reasons behind this shift in emphasis. Again, the distinction is between the COQ measure, which is primarily intended as an attention-getting device, and feedback control devices such as DMOQ. COQ measures are limited in their ability to pinpoint specific problems or suggest corrective action. The division's General Manager clearly feels that an overemphasis on any financial measure, including COQ, may obscure the underlying drivers that actually determine manufacturing performance.

ISD management views the shift in emphasis away from COQ measurement as a natural outgrowth of cultural maturity. Based on their experiences in institutionalizing a "quality culture," the management team has developed a model of the manifestations of cultural maturity (see Exhibit TN-1 of this note). Within this framework, tools and metrics change as the culture matures. In the case of quality measurement, the COQ system was most useful in the Awareness phase of maturity. As the division institutionalizes a quality culture, the use of more refined tools, such as DMOQ, is warranted. This framework is now being used to measure the cultural maturity of other areas.

Although some of the members of ISD's management team claim that DMOQ are now the appropriate measures of quality, it is curious that improvements in the other measures have not produced significant reductions in quality costs. Substantial improvement had been made in cycle time, one of the primary direct measures of quality used by the division. Similar achievements were being realized in on-time delivery, another prime quality indicator within the division. Exhibit 2, however, shows little reduction in quality costs as a percent of net sales billed (note that within the division, little or no attention is paid to the distribution of costs among the four quality cost categories). Discussions with division management shed little light on this contradiction, other than their concern with "micro-managing" if they focused too much on reducing quality costs.

The Future of ISD's Cost of Quality System

After much discussion, ISD's management team decided in 1988 to retain the COQ system in its existing format. The decision was based on the ability of the COQ system to serve as a useful periodic score card of the division's quality progress. Rather than reporting monthly, however, the team decided to report on a quarterly basis.

Sil Pena, the division's Controller, continued to lobby for increased emphasis on quality cost reduction programs. He felt that the limited improvement currently shown in quality cost is a clear indication that the concept should not be relegated to a minor role in the division's quality management practices. Interestingly, Pena was a recent addition to the ISD management team, having transferred from a division that utilized a more traditional COQ system.

Summary of the COQ Concept

Several minutes should be left at the end of class to summarize the Cost of Quality concept. In general, the concept provides a valuable tool for increasing an organization's awareness of quality's impact, and serves as a useful score card for measuring quality progress. Cost of Quality measurement, however, does not pinpoint or solve quality problems. After the attention-getting function of the COQ measurement has been achieved, the use of DMOQ for measuring quality may be more valuable for many organizations.

As seen in the (B) case, the basic COQ concept is not limited to traditional definitions of quality. Hewlett-Packard, for example, has adapted the concept to productivity measurement in its Direct Marketing Division. The "productivity loss index" measures the costs of process flaws

that affect either H-P or customer productivity. A partial list of variables includes the costs associated with orders returned by the customer, late deliveries, customers who are placed on hold for longer than one minute, computer
system downtime, days lost to industrial accidents, and late customer payments.

Similarly, Northrop Aircraft has developed a "Supplier Performance Rating System" that measures the added administrative costs associated with supplier quality and delivery nonconformances. The resulting cost measures help to pinpoint supplier problems that require corrective action and provide a basis for evaluating future bids.

As these examples illustrate, the measurement of unnecessary costs in a COQ-type system can be a valuable tool for focusing attention on problem areas, guiding the selection of improvement projects, allocating resources, and measuring subsequent results.

Exhibit TN-1   Stages of Cultural Maturity

STAGES OF CULTURAL MATURITY

STAGES OF MATURITY / CULTURAL MANIFESTATIONS	CHAOS AND CONFUSION	AWARE OF NEED	SIGNIFICANT REPETITION	RECOGNIZED DISCIPLINE	INSTITUTIONALIZED
PROCEDURES	NON EXISTENT TO RANDOM	• A FEW EXIST, BUT NOT FOLLOWED	• RAPID DEVELOPMENT • BROAD SCOPE • EMERGING ENFORCE-MENT	• WELL DOCUMENTED • COMMONLY ENFORCED • REGULARLY UPDATED	• THOROUGH, COMPLETE • VOLUNTARY COMPLIANCE THROUGH TRAINING • CROSS MANY BOUNDARIES
TOOLS	NON EXISTENT TO RANDOM	DEVELOP AFTER THE PROCEDURE EMERGES	• BUILD AS YOU GO • SHARED BY PEERS	• COMMON, USEFUL • POORLY DOCUMENTED • SPORADIC TRAINING	• REFINFD, EASY TO USE • WELL DOCUMENTED FOR EASY TRAINING
METRICS	NON EXISTENT TO RANDOM	NON EXISTENT TO RANDOM	• EMERGE AFTER TOOLS • SIMPLE, CRUDE, UNCERTAIN VALUE • BOTTOM LINE	• FAMILIES OF METRICS • USED BY MANAGERS AS REFERENCE	• REFINED AND INTER-RELATED • MANAGERS USE WITH CONFIDENCE
ORGANIZATION STRUCTURE	NON EXISTENT OR INEFFECTIVE	• LOOSE FUNC-TIONAL • FEW EXPERTS, IF ANY • UNABLE TO FOCUS	• STRONG FUNCTIONAL • EMERGING EXPERTS	• STRONG FUNCTIONAL • MANY EXPERTS • CALL EXPERT FOR HELP	• ANY FORM WILL DO • EVERYONE IS AN EXPERT • AVOID PROBLEMS

Activity-Based Cost Systems
for Manufacturing Expenses

The Chapter 5 cases introduce students to the rationale and design principles for activity-based cost (ABC) systems. The cases focus on analyzing manufacturing support expenses in traditional discrete-part manufacturing settings. The application of ABC to high-tech electronics companies is covered in the Chapter 6 cases; the extensions to service companies and to selling and administrative expenses occur in Chapter 7.

The text for Chapter 5 is the most extensive for any chapter in the book. It integrates ideas that we had published in separate articles as the concepts behind ABC emerged during the late 1980s. These articles included:

"How Cost Accounting Distorts Product Costs," Management Accounting (April 1988), 20-27.

"Measure Costs Right: Make the Right Decisions," Harvard Business Review (September-October 1988), 96-103.

"Cost Classification in Unit-Based and Activity-Based Manufacturing Cost Systems," Journal of Cost Management (Fall 1990), 4-14 [Robin Cooper sole author].

"Profit Priorities from Activity-Based Costing," Harvard Business Review (May-June 1991).

Rather than reprint these articles at the end of the chapter, we decided to combine the ideas in them into a complete introduction to activity-based cost systems for the book. Because the text was written after we had written and taught the cases in this chapter many times, some of the ideas -- such as the hierarchical model, the spending versus consumption distinction, and the different types of cost drivers that can be used -- go beyond how managers described in the cases thought about their ABC systems. The cases, however, should provide an excellent context for discussing these concepts.

The cases in the chapter are sequenced so that the early cases (Destin and Siemens) show the development of simple ABC systems to remedy the failings of traditional cost systems for companies offering a diverse product line. John Deere shows a complete ABC system for a limited part of a factory (the machining shop). Sentry enables students to see the impact of revised product costs on the company's product line and pricing strategy. And Schrader Bellows is a comprehensive case taking students through actual design, interpretation, and implementation issues for ABC systems.

Destin Brass Products Co. is a simple case that introduces students to the difference between unit, or volume, based cost drivers and the transaction-based cost drivers that reflect better the demands different products make on factory support resources. It was originally written to serve as a final examination question for the first year MBA accounting course and continues to be successfully used to expose students to the difference between traditional and ABC product cost calculations.

Siemens Electric Motor Works (A) describes an early and simple implementation of ABC. This case has been used consistently in the first year MBA course and in many executive programs to show how a company's new strategy -- to offer customized products for individual customers -- would likely have failed without the development of a new cost system. Siemens is an excellent case for this purpose since its existing traditional system is probably as good as any in the world today. It uses 600 production cost centers, with either direct labor or machine hours used as the cost driver for each cost center. It also uses a materials overhead pool to assign materials purchasing and handling expenses to products. The company determined, however, that two new cost pools were needed to accumulate and assign the expenses of handling individual customer orders and to design customize motors. Even though only 9% of manufacturing expenses ended up in these two new cost pools, they had a dramatic impact on calculated product costs. The case discussion can close with a discussion of the actions that Siemens might take based on this new information.

John Deere Component Works (A) and (B) is a good follow-up case to Siemens allowing students to see a more complete ABC system. (Incidentally, students may be interested to learn that we took the name "activity-based cost systems" from the John Deere case, where the term was coined by the system's developer, Keith Williams.) John Deere (A) enables students to identify the symptoms of when a traditional cost system has failed. It also describes the addition of five new cost pools and associated activity drivers to more accurately assign indirect expenses to products. The John Deere system provides an excellent opportunity to introduce the hierarchical model since the new system has all four types of factory support drivers: unit, batch, product-sustaining, and facility-sustaining. The (A) case focuses on motivation for the new system, the design of the system, and calculations of product costs with the new system. The (B) case permits a discussion on the action implications that flowed from the new ABC system including decisions on pricing, product mix, process enhancements, and design. The (B) case also enables the consumption versus spending distinction to be highlighted as management contemplates various action alternatives.

The *Sentry Group* case has been used several times as a final examination question for the course. It describes the types of information used and decisions confronted by the ABC system's designer. Students will see a greater variety of cost drivers that were used and their implications on product costs, pricing, and product introduction decisions.

Schrader Bellows provides a complete ABC design experience for the students. Complete with interviews, and computer modules and videotapes (that instructors must order separately and directly from Harvard Business School Publishing), Schrader Bellows is a unique classroom experience. Having learned the theory of ABC in earlier cases, students are now asked to design a limited portion of an ABC system themselves. After the design experience, students then must interpret the results from their system and provide an analysis for management. The case series closes with an entire session on developing an action plan and monitoring the implementation of the new system (which, as they learn midway through the final session, was ultimately rejected by the company).

The readings at the end of the chapter provide more background and detail about activity-based cost systems. The Miller-Vollman "Hidden Factory" article introduces students to the concept of how transactions, not unit volume, create the demands for many factory support activities. This reading should be assigned with the first ABC case taught from this chapter. The three articles on "The Rise of Activity-Based Costing" can be assigned as optional reading with any of the cases. They provide additional examples of activity-based cost systems, describe the motivation for developing them, and guidance on the number and type of cost drivers that can be used in an ABC system. The final reading, "Implementing an Activity-Based Cost System," can be assigned with the final case taught from this chapter. It describes the steps taken to implement successfully (as contrasted with the Schrader Bellows experience) ABC systems in several large companies. This reading can also be used by itself (rather than accompanying a case) to discuss how to implement change in an organization. Attempting to change a company's measurement system is a major task, quite separate from the technical issues that arise in designing a new system. It is worth sensitizing students to the types of resistance that will be encountered and the steps that might be encountered to overcome organizational resistance and inertia.

Destin Brass Products Co.
Teaching Note

Substantive Issues Raised

The managers of Destin Brass Products are struggling to understand the relationship between their costs and prices for each of the three products produced and sold by Destin. One of the products, pumps, is coming under increasingly competitive price pressure. As a result, Destin has been unable to maintain its desired profit margin. At the same time, Destin has been able to raise prices on another product, flow controllers, apparently with no effect on demand and no increase in competition from other manufacturers. As a result of these situations, management is increasingly questioning whether they know the true manufacturing costs of their products.

At the time of the case, Destin was using a conventional cost accounting system in which all overhead was allocated to product based on direct labor dollars. The controller had already recommended to the company president that they might consider a more modern cost accounting system with a somewhat more refined allocation system, using material cost and machine hours to allocate overhead related to material receiving and handling. A third possible system in which overhead would be allocated based on transactions (an activity-based costing system, or ABC system) is described in the case by the manufacturing manager in such a way that the costs of products under that system can be estimated and compared to the costs under the other two alternative systems.

With three sets of product costs to compare, managers are in a position to ask questions about what is causing costs, which system gives the best information for possible decisions they might make, and for understanding the competitive responses they are observing in their product

---

Professor William J. Bruns, Jr. prepared this teaching note as an aid to instructors in the classroom use of the case Destin

markets. Finally, the importance of linking information collected by the cost system to strategic choices in product design, manufacturing technology and process, and product line decision making is clearly illustrated.

Assignment Questions

1.   Use the Overhead Cost Activity Analysis in Exhibit 5 and other data on manufacturing costs to estimate product costs for valves, pumps, and flow controllers.

2.   Compare the estimated costs you calculate to existing standard unit costs (Exhibit 3) and the revised unit costs (Exhibit 4). What causes the different product costing methods to produce such different results?

3.   What are the strategic implications of your analysis? What actions would you recommend to the managers at Destin Brass?

4.   Assume that interest in a new basis for cost accounting at Destin Brass remains high. In the following month, quantities produced and sold, activities, and costs were all at standard. How much higher or lower would the <u>net income</u> reported under the activity-transaction based system be than the <u>net income</u> that will be reported under the present, more traditional system? Why?

Question 3 can be enhanced to stimulate student thought about the way in which flow controller design, production process, and schedule affect costs. A revised question might be:

3.   What are the strategic implications of your analysis? Could the production process for flow controllers be changed in such a way to allow Destin Brass Products to reduce the unit cost of flow controllers? How would the change in the lot size for flow controller production affect unit costs? Has Destin Brass Products adopted the most profitable distribution system in the flow controller market? What actions would you recommend to managers at Destin Brass Products Company?

Pedagogical Objectives

The essence of choice between cost accounting systems frequently involves selecting the proper means to assign overhead costs to products. By illustrating two systems and enabling students to calculate costs under a third, the Destin Brass Products case quickly destroys the idea that product costs can be uniquely determined for any product. From a technical standpoint, each of the three systems illustrated or described in the case is satisfactory. Determining which of the three systems provides the most useful information for one or more of the many purposes that we maintain cost accounting systems is more difficult.

The case requires students to estimate product costs using an ABC system based on information provided in a case exhibit about the number of transactions that affect each product. Students are required to assign each cost category to a cost pool and then to allocate it to units of product. When costs are summed, the picture provided by the ABC system is quite different from that provided by the conventional or modified system for which calculations have already been included in the case.

By the time students understand that costs are a product of the cost system that measures them, they are prepared to grapple with the relationship between the way the activities have been organized and the costs they have identified. If the level of costs is truly dependent upon the number of transactions that relate to a particular product, then questions must be raised about whether the number of transactions can be changed by producing more or less product with more or less parts and more or less production runs or fewer or more customers and purchases and customer deliveries. The circular reasoning involved in this process proves to be revealing to many students. They see that costs result from how we have been doing business and that different costs might result if we did business a different way. The use of a cost accounting system to stimulate production process improvements is clearly illustrated and is something most students have not thought about.

The final objective which this case serves is to illustrate that the amount of profit a firm reports, assuming inventories do not change, is not dependent directly upon the cost system. Only if the cost system generates different decisions or causes actions to be taken which change the level of expenditure will the level of profit change. A cost system is about allocation of the costs that are being incurred to provide information about products. If all the overhead is absorbed in the products and all the products are delivered, the profits reported in any accounting period will be the same regardless of the cost system--provided investment in inventory remains the same.

Opportunities for Student Analysis

Questions included with the case encourage students to start their analysis by developing activity-based costs for each of the three products using the description of such a system by John Scott in the case and the information provided in Exhibit 5. For most students this is not a difficult task once they understand the nature of the process by which an activity-based system allocates overhead to products. The result of their analysis is likely to resemble the summary of costs as shown in Exhibit TN-1.

In estimating these costs, students will discover that material, costs, set-up labor, and direct labor are identical with those produced in the modified system illustrated in Exhibit 4. The difference between the activity-based system and the modified system in Exhibit 4 is the greater detail provided by assigning each class of overhead expense to a different cost pool and using activities to assign those costs to product. While the exercise of doing this requires some clear thinking, it is not difficult because of the way information in the case has been structured.

Machine depreciation is assigned a cost pool and then to products based on the annual depreciation charge for machines, the number of hours they are operated during a period, and the amount of time to produce each unit ($270,000.00 ÷ 10,800 hours = $25.00/hour x machine usage per unit as shown in Exhibit 2.) For all other categories of cost, the total cost is first assigned to a cost pool using the percentages shown in Exhibit 5 and then is assigned to units using the units of each product produced during an operating month. The total cost per unit is simply the sum of the direct cost and the activity based assignments of each category of overhead cost.

Having unit costs for each of the three products, students are then invited to compare those costs to the cost by each of the other systems. The most effective student comparisons will be those that produce a matrix that shows the total cost per unit for each product produced by each of the systems in a way that they can be compared. Such a matrix is shown in Exhibit TN-2 along with the apparent profit margin percentages at current prices for each of the three products under each system. In preparing this matrix, students should wonder what is causing the difference in product cost under each of the three systems. Hopefully, in most cases, they will see that the assumptions about the way in which overhead costs are attached to products can cause large and significant differences in our judgements about which products are more profitable than others.

As they continue their analysis, students will begin to see some possible reasons for the actions of competitors. The price pressure in the pump market is possibly caused by competitors using cost systems more similar to the activity-based costing system; such competitors could be thinking margins in that product are more generous than does Destin Brass Products. If that is true, then we also may have a clue or evidence as to why we can raise the price of flow controllers without inviting competition. The activity-based costing system makes flow controllers look much more costly to produce than other costing systems, even to the extent of giving them an apparently negative gross profit margin. To clarify their understanding of industry conditions and the possible effects of cost systems, students must consider what causes the different methods to produce different costs and what possible actions Destin Brass Products might take in order to take advantage of its competitors beliefs about costs or to exploit their own superior knowledge of what true costs really are.

In considering the strategic implications of this analysis for Destin Brass Products, some students will begin to see what is different about activity-based systems from other kinds of systems. ABC systems assume that costs are caused by activities or transactions. The dramatic increase in apparent cost of flow controllers under the activity-based system occurs because there are more parts, more production runs, more material received, and more shipments to customers for flow controllers. If those actions and events are what cause costs to happen, and the costs that are measured by the ABC system are closer to the true product costs, then several options are available to the managers of Destin Brass Products.

The first and most obvious action to consider might be to reduce the number of production runs. The case does not give us any clue as to why the flow controllers are being produced in 10 separate production runs instead of fewer runs; an inventory could have been used to hold product between the time it was manufactured and shipped to customers. Maintaining an inventory is one way of reducing the number of activities represented by production runs.

A second step that might be taken would be to reduce the number of shipments to customers. This could be done by offering incentives to customers to accept flow controller shipments in larger lots and in effect, to maintain the inventory of flow controllers for Destin. Alternatively, Destin could contract with a distributor to accept fewer shipments each month and to break those shipments into the order size that may be demanded by customers of flow controllers. There would be some cost to doing this in terms of the price that could be charged since the distributor would need to make a profit, but it might be that the benefits of making fewer shipments and the savings that could be incurred in overhead cost would outweigh the margin that would now have to be provided for the distributor to provide this service.

Finally, Destin may want to consider the flow controller design. One of the reasons the number of activities causing costs in the manufacture of flow controllers is so large is that there are 10 parts. Could the product be redesigned to have fewer parts? Could sub-assemblies be purchased that would reduce the handling and transactions in receiving components for flow controllers? This, and each of the preceding strategic questions, will be obvious to students after they have done their analysis and thought about why costs are different, but they would not have been so obvious if they had not done the activity-based cost analysis.

The final case assignment question asks whether or not the profits that will be reported monthly by Destin Brass Products will be different under the activity-based costing system than under the present, more traditional system. The answer is, of course, that the profits will be exactly the same assuming there are no inventories or inventory levels do not change. All overhead will be absorbed into products and all products will be delivered to customers at presumably the same selling prices and, therefore, profits will not be affected. This often comes as a revelation to students who think that cost accounting systems cause profits when, in fact, all they are doing is allocating a proportion of the net income for the period to each product line.

One final opportunity for student analysis is to consider whether the costs that have been allocated products under these systems are fixed or variable. Most students will conclude that material, direct labor, and set-up time are clearly variable costs. Analysis of the modified cost accounting system may encourage some to think that certain handling costs, for example, receiving and materials handling overhead and, possibly, packing and shipping, may also be variable costs. By using information in case exhibits or constructed during the ABC analysis, students can determine that all of these products are very attractive from the standpoint of Destin Brass Products since all produce fairly substantial contribution to profits when the selling price and variable costs are compared. Analysis will cause them to conclude that none of these products should be dropped from the product line and what is necessary is to strategically price products so that capacity can be used most effectively and profits enhanced through strategic pricing, product design, and production decisions.

Suggestions For Classroom Use

The temptation to jump immediately to the first assigned question included with the case is great. Students will have spent most of their time in preparation trying to perfect their estimates of product costs using the activity-based costing system. Nevertheless, experience in teaching this case has proven that it is more valuable to start by asking students to analyze how costs have been estimated in each of the alternative systems which are described in the case. The existing cost accounting system at Destin Brass Products simply takes all overhead costs and sums them and divides them by the total labor cost. The result is the overhead absorption rate of 439% of direct labor dollars. In most respects this is an extremely simple system that will meet all the requirements for inventory valuation and for federal income tax reporting, and it appears to fairly (if arbitrarily) assign a portion of the total overhead cost to each product line and each unit of product.

The proposed modified system which Peggy Alford discussed with Roland Guidry recognized that direct labor dollars may not be an appropriate basis for allocating overhead to products. In this system, two new overhead absorption rates were established. This clearly illustrated the two-stage process of assigning overhead costs to products. Overhead costs were first accumulated in pools of similar costs and then allocated using an overhead absorption rate appropriate to those products. This is clearly illustrated in Exhibit 4, but it is useful to direct student attention to the fact that we now will have a different overhead absorption rate using a different basis for each of the two classes of overhead which have been established. In addition, removing the set-up labor and assigning it as a direct cost in the system makes a minor change in the total size of the overhead pool but illustrates the principle that a cost that can be directly related to a product line and units of product should probably be assigned in that way.

It is at this point that students are prepared to discuss the procedures they used in implementing the activity-based costing idea based on the transaction data Exhibit 5. A full development of the new product costs should be accomplished, the new unit costs determined, and then those costs compared much as they are shown in Exhibit TN-2. Student confusion about how to assign each category of cost to products is easily eliminated by focusing on the two-step process by which each of the overhead costs is first assigned to a cost pool and then converted to the unit cost basis.

At this point, students are prepared to discuss why each of these systems gives a different cost. Some discussion about which one gives the more correct cost is appropriate, even though the idea of correctness may have little relevance here. The point to be made is that every cost system produces unit costs that are different from every other cost system. To say one is more right than another presumes the purpose for which the cost system was designed. Recognizing this sets the stage for the discussion for the way in which cost systems may modify the strategies which Destin Brass Products may choose in the face of its pump price cutting competitors and apparent monopoly position in the flow controller market.

In the strategy discussion, it is useful to stimulate student thinking about whether the company would be better off dropping the now apparently unprofitable flow controllers. The answer is clearly not, as under almost any set of assumptions, the flow controllers show a positive contribution to profit. There are ample strategic possibilities for reducing the number of activities and transactions that relate to flow controllers and to reduce the costs assigned to them.

Two final questions provide ample grist for student discussion in the waning minutes of a class period. The question of whether the cost system affects income can generate a discussion that has two parts. The cost system per se does not affect income. The cost system may, however, stimulate managers to take actions which change prices or change product mix and hence may change total income. It is not the cost system that affects income, but rather the actions which are a result of the knowledge gained by managers looking at alternative information about product costs. Finally, there is the inevitable question of how accurate do costs need to be. If no system produces costs which are necessarily correct, students may conclude that accuracy is not very important. To some extent this is a valid conclusion. On the other hand, careful tracing of cost to products gives managers confidence that they can use the information from a cost system to make better judgements about the strategic dimensions of product management and pricing.

Exhibit TN-1

DESTIN BRASS PRODUCTS CO.

Activity Based Costs

	Valves	Pumps	Flow Controllers
Material	$16.00	$20.00	$22.00
Set-up Labor	.02	.05	.48
Direct Labor	4.00	8.00	6.40
Machine Depreciation	12.50	12.50	5.00
Receiving and Materials Handling	.88	3.34	42.90
Engineering	2.67	2.40	12.50
Packing and Shipping	.24	1.10	10.95
Maintenance	1.40	1.39	.53
Total Cost per Unit	$37.71	$48.78	$100.76
Margin % at Actual Selling Price	35%	40%	(4%)

Exhibit TN-2

DESTIN BRASS PRODUCTS CO.

Product Costs

	Valves	Pumps	Flow Controllers
Direct Labor Cost Based Allocations (DLC)	$37.56	$63.12	$56.50
Material and Machine Hour Based Allocation (MMH)	49.00	58.95	47.96
Activity Based Costs (ABC)	37.71	48.78	100.76

Profit Margins at Current Prices

DLC	35%	22%	42%
MMH	15%	27%	51%
ABC	35%	40%	(4%)

Siemens Electric Motor Works (A)
Process Oriented Costing
Teaching Note

Purpose

This case illustrates how managers at Siemens Electric Motor Works used their product costing system to support their decision to change strategies. The case exposes students to a simple activity-based cost system and is, therefore, ideal for introducing the concepts of activity-based costing. The (B) case of the series (not included in the book) builds on the student's knowledge of the cost system to examine Siemens' organizational structure and transfer pricing system.

Overview

In the late 1970's, Siemens Electric Motor Works (EMW) found itself facing an environment in which it was becoming increasingly difficult to compete. Managers began to understand that continued survival in the A/C motor market required changing strategies. As a result, they made a decision to de-emphasize the production of standard motors and to specialize in the production of small lots of custom motors.

The custom motor business required the evaluation of many motor designs and a way of accurately estimating the production cost of literally thousands of potential products. Early on, the only tool managers had to assist them in their estimation was their product costing system. This system was a "traditional system" that, though it had been extended and updated over time, had essentially the same structure in 1970 as it did in 1926. EMW managers found this system totally inadequate to the job they faced, and so set out to develop a new cost system.

This teaching note was written by Professor Karen Hopper Wruck with Professor Robin Cooper as an aid to instructors using Siemens (A) (9-189-089).

The system they came up with was an activity-based cost system, which by design accounted for the costs of order processing and the handling of special components in a way that the traditional system could not. Costs that varied with the number of orders processed, and costs that varied with the number of special components required in a motor design had become an important part of the total cost of production. By isolating these costs and allocating them appropriately, managers were able to get more "accurate" estimates of the cost of producing a custom motor. Therefore, the task of evaluating orders and deciding which ones to accept for production could be done more profitably.

Assignment Questions:

1.   Calculate the cost of the five orders in Exhibit 3 under the traditional and new cost system. Hint: first calculate the revised cost of processing an order and handling a special component.

2.   Calculate traditional and revised costs for each order if 1 unit, 10 units, 20 units, or 100 units are ordered. Graph the product costs against volume ordered.

3.   Does the new cost system support the strategy of the firm in ways that the traditional system cannot? Is Mr. Karl-Heinz Lottes overestimating the value of the new cost system?

Teaching Strategy

Q.   What were the competitive conditions facing EMW in the late 1970's?

The important points to be raised in this discussion are summarized below:

- The Eastern bloc has an insurmountable advantage over EMW due to their lower labor rates.
- EMW will be forced out of business unless it changes its strategy.
- EMW chooses strategy of becoming a custom motor firm.

Q.   What changed at EMW because of the new strategy to produce more custom motors?

- Production process becomes more complex.
- Production technology changes to high technology.
- Volume and number of products produced increased dramatically.

Note: The Eastern bloc cannot follow this strategy because they do not have access to high technology manufacturing.

Q.   How did EMW's new strategy change the way products were manufactured?

- In the 1970's EMW manufactured about 200 different types of motors, by 1987 they were manufacturing 10,000 unique products.

- 1970's manufacturing was nearly all large batch production for inventory. Only 20% of motors produced were custom motors, and the authors suspect that "customizations" were fairly trivial.
- 1980's manufacturing is dominated by low volume custom orders. However, a significant number of the motors produced are still to fill large orders of standard motors.

Note: The EMW facility was well run with manufacturing technology ranging from hand-manufacture of "low" technology small volume motors through flexible machining systems for high volume custom components. The diversity of production technologies in one facility makes it a very difficult environment in which to calculate product costs.

Q.   Was the strategy successful?

While it is not possible from case facts to determine unambiguously if the strategy was successful (largely because we cannot observe what would have happened had EMW stuck to its old course) certain points can be made:

- EMW is still in business.
- EMW's product mix has shifted considerably.
- Siemens Corporation has invested heavily in EMW; so senior management clearly believes in the new strategy.

Q.   What is EMW's product mix? or To what extent has EMW adopted the new strategy?

Exhibit 1 provides the data to look at the mix of business at EMW.

- Low volume orders: 74% of orders are for under 5 motors and account for 12% of total volume, and 88% of orders are for under 20 motors and account for 25% of total volume.
- High volume orders: 2.3% of orders are for over 100 motors and account for 44% of total volume, and 12% of orders are for over 20 motors and account for 75% of total volume.
- Siemens has maintained its standard motor business and added 25% in low volume custom motors. A simple and productive way to think about EMW's production facility is to view it as two factories within a factory (with two different production processes). One factory produces high volume standard motors, and the other low volume custom motors.

Q.   Describe the 1970's cost system at EMW.

A diagram of the cost system can be drawn, relying upon the concept of a product costing system as a 2-stage process (see Exhibit TN1). The important points to be brought out are:

- there are 600 machine- based cost centers
- three allocation bases are used
    DM direct materials to trace material costs
    direct labor hours or machine hours to trace manufacturing overhead

cost to date to allocate support overhead.

Students should be made aware that this is a sophisticated "traditional" system and probably better designed than most traditional systems.

Q.   Why such a complex cost system?

- Technological complexity of factory
- Cost Control

Q.   Describe the 1980's cost system at EMW.

Again, a simple diagram of the cost system can be drawn, relying upon the concept of a product costing system as a 2-stage process (see Exhibit TN-2).

The important points to be brought out are:

- Existing system has been retained; the two new activity pools have been added on to the traditional system.
- Simple system structure; only two additional allocation bases.

Q.   If you split EMW into two facilities one producing only standard motors the other producing only custom motors how would you tell which factory you were in?

Put these two categories on the board and let the students identify the differences.

| Custom | Standard |
| Factory | Factory |

After the students have completed their list, you can organize many of the differences into costs that are driven by the increased number of orders processed and the increased number of special components handled in the production of the custom motors. These costs are behind the structure and design of the Process Oriented Cost System. For example,

# Orders	# Special Components
# customers	# engineering change orders
# shipment	# engineers
# production lot	# purchase orders
# inspection	# incoming receipts
# schedules	# schedules
# expedites	# inspection-incoming
	# expedite
	# production lots

Q.   How did the "traditional" cost system trace the overhead costs of order processing and special components handling to the products?

These costs were treated as support overhead and allocated to the products based upon the cost to date.

Q.   How does the new cost system trace the overhead costs of order processing and special components handling to the products?

These costs form the two new activity pools and are traced using number of shop order and special components. You may want to do these calculations here:

Per order: 13,800,000 DM/65,625 orders = 210

Per special component: 19,500,000 DM/325,000 special components = 60

Q.   Why did the "traditional" cost system prove useless to managers?

The "traditional" cost system traced the overhead costs of order processing and special components handling to the products based upon cost to date. Consequently, large volume orders of 100 motors received approximately 100 times as much of these overhead costs as an order of one. Yet the analysis of these costs show that each order consumes about the same amount of the overhead regardless of the number of units (but not the number of special components).

The new system overcomes this bias by tracing an equal amount of order processing overhead to each order and an equal amount of special components handling overhead to each type of special component required by an order's design. This might be a good place to introduce the cost hierarchy described in the text for the chapter. Both the order cost and the cost of handling special components are examples of **batch-related** costs. The order processing and component handling activities are triggered by performing a batch of work, but are independent of the number of motors in the batch. The traditional cost system failed because even with three different allocation bases (materials, labor, and machine time), all costs were assigned to products based on the number of units produced, independent of the batch size. Note that there are no **product-sustaining** activities in the new Siemens system. Apparently the system's designers felt that the amount of activities triggered by the number of different motors was not significant to warrant the additional complexity in the system.

Q.   What are the reported costs of the five orders in Exhibit 3 with the new cost system? [Answer to Assignment Question 1]

	A	B	C	D	E
Base					
Motor	295.0	295.0	295.0	295.0	295.0
Components	29.5	59.0	88.5	147.5	295.0
Order					
Processing	210.0	210.0	210.0	210.0	210.0
Component					
Handling	60.0	120.0	180.0	300.0	600.0
Total	594.5	684.0	773.5	952.5	1400.0

Q. What are the reported costs of the five orders in Exhibit 3 under the traditional system?

From Exhibit 3, the costs for the two new activity pools come from the support related overhead categories: 6,300,000 from engineering costs, and 27,000,000 from administrative costs. In order to calculate the traditional cost system costs, the support related overhead reported in Exhibit 3, based on cost to date, must be grossed up to reflect these costs: 94,500,000 total support/61,200,000 (applied under the new cost system) = 1.54.

	A	B	C	D	E
Pre-Support Related Overhead Cost					
Base Motor	240.0	240.0	240.0	240.0	240.0
Components	24.0	48.0	72.0	120.0	240.0
Support Overhead	60.5	66.0	71.5	82.5	11.0
	x 1.54	x 1.54	x 1.54	x 1.54	x 1.54
	93.4	101.6	110.1	127.0	169.4
Total**	357.4	389.6	422.1	487.0	649.4

OR Alternatively, one can use the 35% support related overhead burden rate (presented in the table at the top of page 289) and apply it to the pre-support related overhead numbers presented in Exhibit 3.

	A	B	C	D	E
Pre-Support Related Overhead Cost					
Base Motor	240.0	240.0	240.0	240.0	240.0
Components	24.0	48.0	72.0	120.0	240.0
Total	264.0	288.0	312.0	360.0	480.0
	x 1.35	x 1.35	x 1.35	x 1.35	x 1.35
Total**	356.4	388.8	421.2	486.0	648.0
New Cost System/ Traditional	1.67	1.76	1.84	1.96	2.16

** Minor differences in the two sets of product costs are to be expected. They represent rounding errors.

Answer to Assignment Question 2

Revised Product Cost per Unit

	A	B	C	D	E
1 unit	594.5	684.0	773.5	952.5	1400.0
10 units	351.5	387.0	422.5	493.5	671.0
20 units	338.0	370.5	403.0*	468.0	630.5
100 units	327.2	357.3	387.4	447.6	598.1

* For example,	Per Unit		Total
Base Motor	295.0	295.0 x 20=	5900.0
Components	88.5	88.5 x 20=	1770.0
Order Processing 210/20=	10.5		210.0
Component Handling 180/20=	9.0		180.0
Total	403.0		8060.0

At this point Exhibits TN-3 and TN-4 can be handed out or shown on an overhead projector. Exhibit TN-3 shows the relation between the revised product costs and the number of motors ordered. Exhibit TN-4 shows how the revised product cost as a percent of traditional cost falls as the number of motors ordered increases. To the left of the point where each curve crosses 1.00, the traditional system cost underestimates the cost of production by a significant amount. To the right of this point, the traditional system overestimates the cost of production.

Q. Did changing to the new cost system make a significant difference in reported product costs? In the way managers made decisions?

Managers at EMW felt the system helped support their new strategy and did make a difference in the way they made decisions, especially in deciding which orders to accept and which to reject. Even though the costs being reassigned with the two new activity pools comprised only 9% of total costs, the new system produced major differences in reported product costs.

Summary

If time remains at the end of the class, instructors can ask students what impact the revised product costs would have on Siemens' operations. Pricing decisions are obvious, as are decisions on whether or not to accept new orders, especially when the plant is receiving more requests than it can accept. We generally suggest the following strategy: "Accept the orders on which you make money." Of course whether you make money on a given order can only be determined by having a reasonable estimate of the cost of fulfilling the order. Salesmen may encourage customers to order motors with fewer customized components in order to lower the cost (and price) of the order, or if a highly customized motor is desired, to order it in sufficiently large quantities to offset the setup cost of soliciting and handling the order, and processing all the specialized components.

Attempting to get customers to pay a lot more for customized motors, ordered in small batches, or to demand less customization, however, may ultimately undermine Siemens EMW's strategy to focus on the custom motor business. Sharp students may notice this apparent conflict between the actions implied by the new cost system and the competitive analysis that led to the change in Siemens' strategy. If this point is not raised by a student, it is a good question to ask back to the class (e.g., "Isn't Siemens, as a result of the new cost numbers, going to discourage just the new types of customers it wants?")

There are at least two responses that can be made to this point. One is that a differentiated strategy (in Mike Porter's terms) is only successful if the value from differentiation (i.e., the price premium for a custom motor or a small lot of motors) exceeds the incremental cost to differentiate the product or service. The new cost system better informs management about the cost of differentiation (ordering customized motors in small batches) and hence enables the company to see whether its strategy is succeeding. Retaining the old cost system with the new strategy will force the company out of the standard motor business entirely and encourage it to think that it is making money on small lots of customized orders with 15-20% price premiums, thereby encouraging acceptance of such orders, but ultimately leading to much larger demands for support resources.

The second response sets the stage for material in the John Deere case that follows. Siemens EMW now knows the cost of following its new strategy. It costs DM210 for each order it handles and DM60 for designing in each special component. To be successful as a custom motor producer, Siemens must work to reduce the order cost and the component handling cost so that the additional cost for small orders and for customizing orders keeps decreasing. The DM210 order cost is now visible and becomes a target for improvement activities so that the company becomes much more efficient, perhaps by deploying additional information technology, in handling customer orders. Previously, the cost of order handling was buried in the general support costs, and improvement activities were directed at reducing labor and machine times since only those factors affected product costs. Thus the new cost system directs management's attention to the business processes that must be improved in order to implement the new strategy successfully.

Exhibit TN-1   Process Oriented Costing

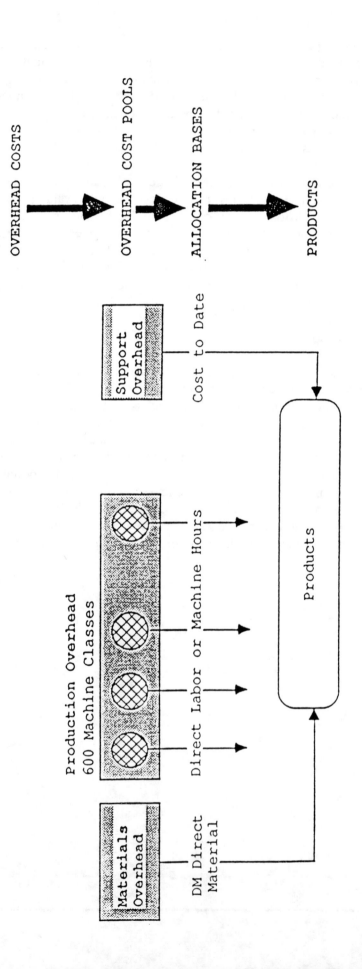

Exhibit TN-2   Process Oriented Costing

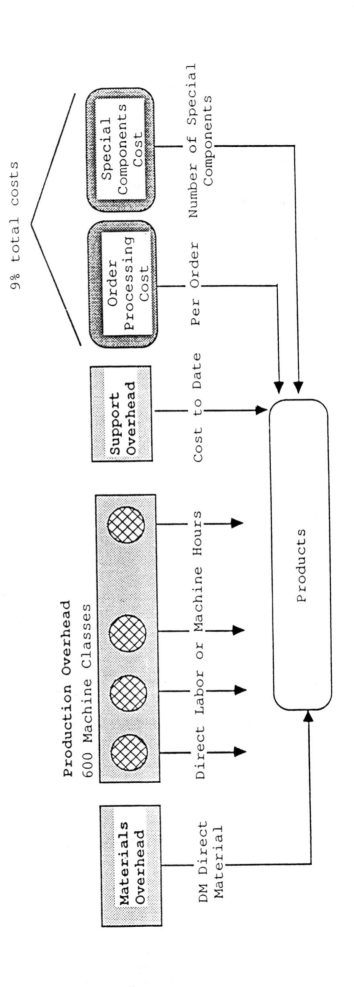

Exhibit TN-3   Process Oriented Costing   PROKASTA Cost for Orders

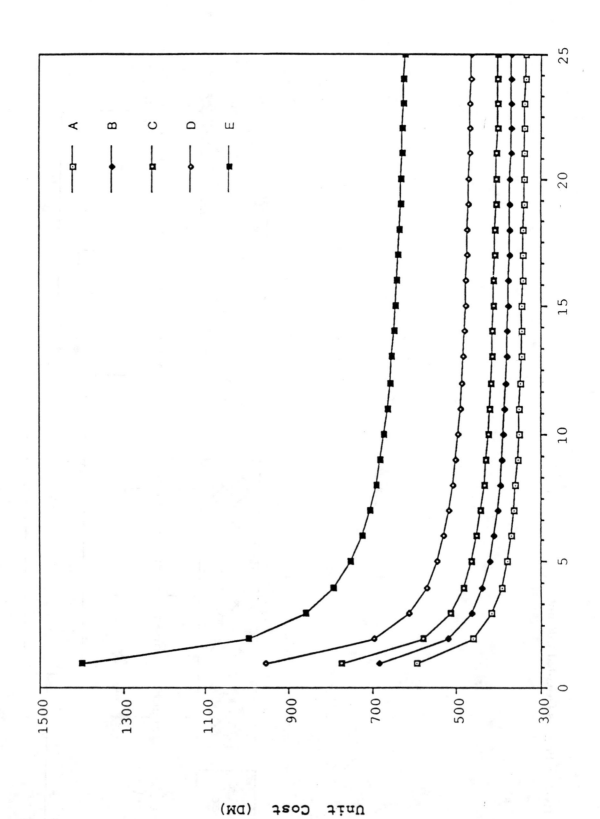

Number of Motors Ordered

Unit Cost (DM)

Exhibit TN-4
Process Oriented Costing

PROKASTA Cost/Traditional Cost
for EMW Orders

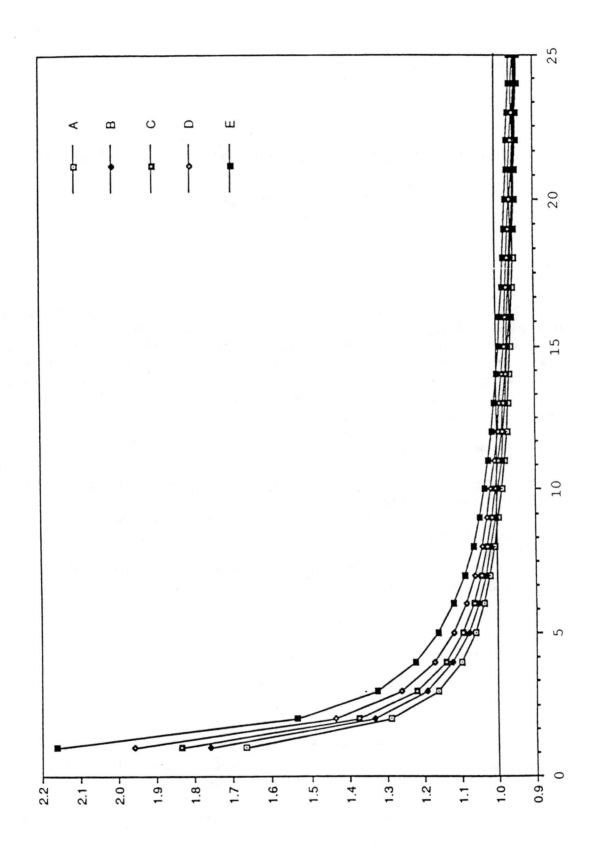

Number of Motors Ordered

Ratio of PROKASTA Cost
to Traditional Cost

John Deere Component Works (A) and (B)

Teaching Note (Modified)

Introduction

The John Deere Components Works (JDCW) case provides an excellent introduction to Activity-Based Costing. The company's existing product costing system was considerably better than most systems found in contemporary (mid-1980s) practice since it used three separate bases for allocating overhead costs to products (direct labor $, machine hours, and material $). Yet even this well-designed traditional system failed as JDCW attempted to bid for outside business. In order to capture the underlying economics of its production processes, JDCW had to develop a completely new system for tracing overhead costs to products.

The case can be used to:

1.   Demonstrate how traditional product cost systems fail to capture the costs of product diversity and complexity;
2.   Indicate the design and implications of activity-based cost systems;
3.   Illustrate a well-conceived procedure for designing and gaining acceptance for a new system for measuring product costs; and
4.   Discuss the implications of the new product cost system for product pricing, design, and mix decisions and process improvement decisions.

This teaching note was prepared by Professor Robert S. Kaplan as an aid to instructors in the classroom use of cases John Deere Component Works (A) 9-187-107 and John Deere Component Works (B) 9-187-108.

JDCW(A)

Assignment Questions

We have used the following assignment questions for the JDCW (A) case:

1. How did the competitive environment change for the John Deere Component Works between the 1970s and the 1980s?

2. What caused the existing cost system to fail in the 1980s? What are the symptoms of cost system failure?

3. How were the limitations of the existing cost system overcome by the ABC system?

4. Compare the cost of product A103 (see Exhibit 5) under the existing cost system and under the ABC approach.

Discussion

Competitive Environment:

I start by asking students to contrast the competitive environment for JDCW pre- and post- 1980 . Prior to 1980, the company experienced high growth. The main challenge was to add capacity fast enough to keep up with demand. JDCW was a captive supplier providing highly machined components to the tractor and other equipment divisions. Key success factors would be reliable delivery and high quality production of a wide variety of parts. Cost performance would be a secondary concern to throughput and on-time delivery since the machined parts were likely a small fraction of the total cost of building a tractor, and the booming agricultural market and inflationary period of the 1970s permitted cost increases to be recovered in higher prices. The full cost transfer pricing policy reinforced the emphasis on production and delivery performance, but not necessarily cost savings. Individual product costs could be distorted but this was not likely a problem since all component parts eventually found their way into John Deere final products. Thus, being right on average across all component parts was sufficient for the company to get roughly correct costs of their final products.

The 1980s brought a completely new competitive environment as demand collapsed for virtually all John Deere final products. The divisions now found themselves with large amounts of excess capacity. As a consequence, the assembly divisions were much more aggressive in searching for low cost suppliers leading to much more outsourcing. The components divisions were thus subject to a double whammy. Even if they retained all the internal supply business, production volumes would be well below capacity. But their former internal business was no longer assured as the purchasing divisions looked for lower price outside competitive bids. Therefore, the components divisions now had to compete to retain their internal business plus look for new outside business if they were to use their human and capital resources efficiently.

Process:

Turning machines are useful for high volume, precision machining of complex metal parts. The machines can take several hours to setup for a production run, perhaps 4-6 hours for a complex new part. Process engineers specify the sequence of operations to be performed at each spindle of the machine. After completing one such sequence, the spindles rotate, the part moves to the next sequence of operations and the next part starts the machining process. Once set-up and adjusted properly, the machines turn out finished parts at a rapid rate.

Is The Existing Cost System Broken?

Once the discussion of the competitive environment, products, and process has been completed (perhaps allow 10-15 minutes for this material), I ask, "What's broken? How do we know we have a problem with the cost system?" The case has enough discussion on this point that the class quickly points out the classical symptoms of cost system failure. The division is winning orders for parts that it is least well configured to produce (the low volume, simple parts) and losing bids on parts where it should have a competitive advantage (high volume, complex machined parts). I specifically included in Exhibit 2 a summary of the characteristics of parts won and lost to have this point be quite obvious without much analysis required by students. While the relationship is not perfect, JDCW tended to win bids on parts that had low direct labor and ACTS hours, and to lose bids on high volume parts requiring relatively more direct labor and ACTS hours.

How do we know that the cost system is causing this problem? What other explanations exist for this occurrence? Winning the wrong bids and losing bids for products it wants to produce is not prima facie evidence of cost system failure. Perhaps the division's technology is inferior or substantially different from its competitors. This point needs to be resolved by operating and general managers of the division. They have to make a judgment as to whether their process technology is similar to or substantially different from competitors, and which products they feel are best suited for their production environment. In this case, the call from division to headquarters for help in computing product costs provides evidence that the cost system was felt to be the culprit, not the production processes. I generally get a good response from the class by asking, rhetorically, "Do you know how desperate a plant has to be before it calls corporate staff for help?"

While on the subject of the competing bids, instructors may wish to diverge to a brief look at Exhibit 1 which contains detailed information on a sample of 44 parts. Many academics (and some managers as well) are skeptical that cost systems are used for pricing purposes. They believe that markets set prices, not cost systems. Even a casual look at Exhibit 1, however, reveals that markets for highly specialized, perhaps unique, products may not exist. There is an enormous variation from the lowest to the highest bidder for each of the 44 products. For many parts, the ratio of highest to lowest bid is 3 to 1 or higher. For this type of product, the company has virtually no choice but to rely on its cost system to generate bid prices. (I am not saying that this is true in general, but it certainly seems to be true here.) Without the information on competitive prices - obtained because the purchaser was a division in the same company - JDCW may not even have known the extent of its pricing (cost?) disadvantage.

Existing Cost System:

Once we decide the cost system has a problem, we need to understand and analyze the existing cost system.

Standard Product Costs

At present, JDCW uses three allocation bases to allocate overhead costs to products (see Exhibit TN-1). Originally, only direct labor was used to allocate overhead costs to products. In the late 1960s, however, cost analysts noted that much of the overhead had little to do with the conversion of raw material into new shapes and forms. They segregated overhead costs associated with handling materials into a separate overhead pool and applied these costs to products based on material dollars. Since that time, the materials overhead pool was split even finer to reflect costs that could be traced to specific types of materials. Only in the mid-1980s did many other discrete part manufacturing companies separating materials-related costs from those involved in direct conversion and assembly of products.

The instructor can pursue, with the class, the question of what the consequences would be if a separate materials overhead pool were not used. Obviously, the expenses of activities like purchasing, receiving, incoming inspection, scheduling deliveries, vendor negotiation, and materials handling would be in the general overhead pool, and applied to products based on direct labor (or machine) hours. Those parts or components with the most conversion activity in the factory would therefore bear the bulk of the materials overhead costs. Eventually, suppliers would offer to supply these heavily burdened parts and components at a lower price. The company, in a make versus buy analysis, could conclude that its high overhead structure made it an inefficient producer of these items and decide to outsource them. As the high labor and machine time parts and components get outsourced, more materials support activities would need to occur, leading to higher expenses in these categories. But the allocation bases (direct labor and machine hours) would decrease, causing even higher burden rates on the items still fabricated in the plant. Following this cycle several times would lead to a "hollow factory," as fabrication activity was diminished. One way to stop the distortions leading to hollowing-out factories is to establish a materials overhead pool, as John Deere did in the 1960s, and apply the expenses of materials-related activities to the materials directly, rather than through a conversion base like labor or machine hours.

In 1984, a further innovation was accomplished by splitting the conversion overhead pool into two components: one that related to direct labor hours and one that related better to machine run time. Again, at the instructor's discretion, one can get into a discussion of the circumstances as to when it is desirable to switch from direct labor to machine hours for allocating overhead. An increasingly automated production process is not, by itself, sufficient justification for such a switch. If direct labor is, to a first approximation, proportional to machine hours (such as if workers always operate an identical number of machine), then product costs will not be affected by a switch from labor to machine hours.[1]

The product cost system also distinguished between variable and non-variable (called period) overhead (see Exhibit 3). It is interesting that costs which did not vary with short-run fluctuations in volume were not called "fixed costs." I think this was a deliberate decision to emphasize that period costs were not "fixed" in that they could not be cut. They were

---

1.   See Robin Cooper, "When is Machine Hour Costing Appropriate," in Chapter 2, for an excellent discussion of when a machine hours basis provides more accurate product costs than direct labor hours. This point is also the main issue in the Fisher Technologies case.

discretionary costs that were authorized through the budgeting process each year; hence the term "period costs." General Electric now refers to these as "readiness-to-serve" costs.

One additional feature of the product cost system worth mentioning is the use of "normal" volume for determining overhead cost rates. The normal volume equaled "through the business cycle" volume and therefore was higher than the forecast volume for JDCW in 1985 and 1986 when depressed economic conditions continued to keep demand well below capacity. The use of a somewhat artificially high forecast of volume is, I believe, an excellent idea. Companies that allocate excess capacity costs to existing volume will assign high overhead costs to today's products. When such costs are used for pricing purposes, by having potential customers pay for the company's excess capacity, even higher excess capacity costs will exist in subsequent years. One mechanism for halting the death spiral of allocating existing capacity costs to a shrinking volume of products is the use of "normal" volumes to smooth over economic cycle fluctuations.[2]

At this point, I would discuss (or demonstrate) how the existing system computes the cost of a typical product (A103). Particularly with executive groups, I just hand out a copy of Exhibit Exhibit TN-2 and discuss it briefly. Note that while direct labor for this part equals $2.36, the three overhead allocations (material, labor, and ACTS hours) total $13.39. Thus, the overhead costs are 567% of direct labor costs. This ratio is close to the ratio of 593 % for total overhead ($ 10,171) to direct labor dollars ($ 1,714) in the machining department (see Exhibit 3 in the case), though this latter calculation does not include any materials related overhead. Product A103 appears to have a typical amount of overhead allocated to it.

In general, I find the JDCW cost system to be quite good. The product costing system uses multiple measures to allocate overhead costs to products. It separates short-run variable from period expenses, and has made a thoughtful innovation by introducing the normal volume concept. If limitations have to be noted, I might point to the single aggregate overhead rate that fails to recognize process diversity within each department. Given the overall excellence of the JDCW system, its failure in the new competitive environment tells an even more dramatic story than otherwise. Clearly, just going to more extensive materials and machine hour costing bases will not solve the problems that have been revealed by the bidding process for the John Deere purchased parts.

Activity-Based Costing

At this point, I ask the class to describe why they think the existing cost system has failed. Given all the information in the case, I don't need rocket scientists in the class for them to figure out that the existing cost system does not properly reflect the cost of set-ups, material movements, process engineering, parts administration and other overhead resources. If this is the first time that the students have seen this issue arise, I announce that we will briefly study a related but different "caselet."

The "caselet" uses an example of two physically identical factories, one of which produces 1,000,000 units of a single product (vanilla ice cream or blue pens) and the other produces 1,000,000 units of 2,000 different but related products (e.g., vanilla, chocolate, strawberry, maple fudge swirl, mud pie, .. ice cream; or blue, black, red, green, purple, fuschia,.. pens). I ask the class what would they see in the second plant that they wouldn't see in the first plant. It doesn't

---

2.   Issues on costing for capacity resources arise more directly in the Bridgeton, Micro-Devices Division and Schulze Waxed Container cases.

take long to get the following list of what there would be more of in the second than in the first plant:

Inventory
Purchasing People
Materials handlers
Set-ups and set-up people
Production control people
Inspectors (especially for first item inspection)
Cost accountants
Expediters (to find and "hotwire" the delayed order for purple pens)
Process engineers (writing and correcting routines for new parts)
etc.

I point out that if blue pens and purple pens have the same amount of direct labor hours, material quantities, and machine hours, they would have the same costs by any traditional (read "volume-related") product cost system, even when the ratio of blue to purple pens produced each year is 1,000 to 1 (or higher). This example serves to motivate the demand for a more accurate attribution of resource costs to products than any system can accomplish which relies solely on the "usual suspects" (labor, materials, machine hours) for allocating costs to products.

To illustrate the newly designed ABC system at JDCW, I would draw (or show) the diagram in Exhibit TN-3. This exhibit shows the four new transactions bases devised by Vintilla and Williams after a careful study of the turning machine department's overhead resources:

Set-up hours
Number of orders (equal to number of set-ups)
Number of materials loads
Number of parts
Value added (direct labor + all other overhead expenses)

Unit, Batch, Product- and Facility-Sustaining Activities[3]

The John Deere activity-based cost system provides an excellent opportunity to illustrate the hierarchical ABC cost model. The three drivers used by the existing system (direct labor $, machine hours, and materials $) are all unit-level drivers that assign overhead expenses proportional to the number of units produced. The existing system failed because a growing proportion of overhead expenses, which was a very large cost category (more than 5 times direct labor expense), were not proportional to the number of units produced.

Many expenses were associated with batch-level activities. Three of the new drivers — setup hours, number of production orders, and material movements — are batch drivers, that will assign overhead expenses proportional to the number of batches made. The demands on the batch-level resources vary with the number of batches made, but are independent of the number

---

3.   The unit, batch, and product-sustaining classification of product support expenses was developed in Robin Cooper, "Cost Classification in Unit-Based and Activity-Based Manufacturing Cost Systems," Journal of Cost Management (Fall 1990), pp. 4-14.

of units produced within each batch (with the exception of some materials movements caused by transporting additional materials for a very large batch of work).

The expenses associated with the fourth of the new drivers, Number of Parts, are product-sustaining. They are caused by the activity, "Parts Administration;" that is, maintaining the ability to produce more than 2,000 different products. The demands on resources performing parts administration vary with the number of different products produced but are fixed with respect to the production volumes (either number of units or batches) of individual products. Product-sustaining expenses can be traced to individual parts and products, but the resources consumed by product-sustaining activities are independent of how many units or batches of products are produced. Examples of resources used for product-sustaining activities include the information system and engineering resources devoted to maintaining an accurate bill-of-materials, process standards, and routing for each product. Other examples are the resources to prepare and implement engineering changes, to perform the process engineering, tooling, and test routines for individual products, to expedite orders, and to perform product enhancements. These product-sustaining activities are done more often or with greater intensity as the number of products in the plant increases.

The fifth new activity pool, General and Administrative, is an example of a facility-sustaining activity. Expenses that might fall into the facility-sustaining category include building depreciation and insurance, general heating and lighting, general support functions (bookkeeping security, housekeeping, landscaping), and the expenses of senior plant management, including the plant manager. The General & Administrative category created difficulty for the JDCW systems designers because the expenses of this activity could not be linked causally to resource demands by individual products. This led to the compromise solution of allocating these expenses using the value-added driver, a driver that spread these expenses across all products in proportion to their conversion expenses (direct labor, machine time and the four batch and product-sustaining expense categories). Based on the insights from the hierarchical model, we might now recommend that the G&A expense pool not be driven down to individual products; that it be kept at the plant level, with the contribution margins earned from sales and production of individual products being sufficiently high to cover the facility-sustaining expenses.

Based on the numbers in Exhibit 4 of the case, we can see that 41% of the overhead costs were shifted on to the five new activity bases (or overhead pools). Exhibit TN-4 shows the shifts in overhead costs from direct labor and ACTS hours under the old system to the five new bases. Of course, some of the costs traced via the fifth new driver (value-added) will flow back to the direct labor and ACTS hour bases. Exhibit TN-5 contrasts the difference in the cost structure of the plant revealed by the traditional and the ABC systems.

At this point, I would discuss how product A103 is costed with the new system (see Exhibit TN-6). This allows the class to be sure it understands how costs become a function of the new set of transactions drivers. Note how the cost of product A103 increases by 44% because of the transactions-driven overhead: 8.4 set-up hours per year, 2 production orders, 4 material movements (2, back and forth, for each set-up), and 1 parts administration fee. The cost is reported in $ per 100 units. Since the total annual volume is 8,000 units, the cost of each transactions driver is divided by 80 to get the cost per 100 units.

Some instructors may wish to reduce the amount of time spent getting to this point so that they have more time to discuss the implications of the revised product cost shown in Exhibit TN-6 and illustrated in Exhibit TN-7. In the traditional cost system (see calculations in Exhibit TN-2 and diagram on the left-hand side of Exhibit TN-7), product costs are "caused" by direct materials expense, direct labor dollars, and machine hours. Managers, attempting to reduce the cost of this product, get signals from this product cost buildup, to undertake the following actions:

Lower Materials Costs

Outsource, perhaps in low labor rate countries, far away from the plant. (This leads to higher coordination costs, higher inventory levels, and erratic deliveries but the cost accounting system recognizes only materials purchase prices and not all the indirect cost effects.)

Get bids from alternative suppliers, perhaps lowering purchase costs. (This could lead to purchasing lower quality parts in higher volumes, again leading to higher indirect expenses.)

Reduce Direct Labor Expense

Do extensive industrial engineering studies to design out tenths of an hour of direct labor.

Automate production processes.

Encourage employees to work faster, harder, and longer.

Reduce Machine Hour Expense

Attempt to run machines faster (perhaps leading to less preventive maintenance, more erratic quality being produced, and higher frequency of machine breakdowns).

Add Volume to Spread Overhead Over More Items

Proliferate the product line, to "absorb overhead," leading to product complexity, congestion, and confusion in the factory; again creating expenses that will not be directly traced to the products creating demands for higher levels of support activities.

Under the activity-based system, managers see new opportunities to reduce costs. They can:

Reduce setup times (from hours to minutes).

Find ways to handle production run activity more efficiently; e.g., improve quality to reduce resources devoted to first-item inspection, rework and scrap.

Improve factory layout to reduce materials handling expenses.

Improve product design, using fewer and more common parts, to reduce parts administration expenses.

The actions stimulated by the ABC product costs are all "continuous improvement activities," attempting to reduce or eliminate waste (or non-value added activities). The ABC analysis is therefore highly compatible and integrated with the total quality management, just-in-time, and design-for-manufacturability activities being advocated by manufacturing people. The traditional product cost system focuses industrial engineers on running machines faster and designing tenths of direct labor hours out of processes. The ABC cost buildup directs industrial and manufacturing engineers to reduce setup times, improve materials flows, improve quality, and improve product design; quite a different set of activities.

One final point can be made about the product cost calculation for item A103. The analysis shown in Exhibit TN-2, Exhibit TN-6, and Exhibit TN-7 results in calculating a "unit-cost" for A103 under a traditional and activity-based system. Based on the discussion of the hierarchical model, it is misleading to assign all the factory costs to individual units of A103, implying that spending will go up or down by that amount based on how many units are produced. It would be preferable to aggregate expenses at the product level as shown in Exhibit TN-8, showing the total amount of expenses associated with maintaining and producing product A103, but not implying that this calculation leads to a more accurate "unit cost." In aggregating product-specific (unit, batch, and product-sustaining) expenses to A103, we would preferably exclude any allocation of facility-sustaining expenses since these can not be causally related to producing or maintaining A103 as an individual product.

This discussion should put you at or beyond the end of available time (assuming an 80-90 minute session for the case). I would wrap up quickly, pointing out that we have seen how a traditional cost system fails and how very different product costs can be generated by a system that better reflects the different demands that products make on the organization's resources. Parts of the discussion that could not all be delivered in one class could be deferred until the discussion of the (B) case.

JDCW (B)

Questions:

1. What were the characteristics of products that were both helped and hurt by the ABC system?

2. What insights does ABC provide about the types of products to manufacture and the appropriate production processes to use? Why did the existing system fail to provide these insights?

3. What actions are being stimulated by the ABC analysis?

4. Comment on the development, implementation, and acceptance of the ABC approach.

Introduction:

The (B) case seems short and much less dense than the (A) case, but the issues raised generate ample opportunities for discussion so that the instructor should have little trouble filling the available time with substantive material.

Exhibit 1:

What did the ABC cost study reveal? Clearly there are major shifts in costs among the 44 sample products. Exhibit TN-9 provides a summary of the characteristics of the 10 parts most helped and most hurt by ABC. (Incidentally, this is a very nice mechanism for presenting the results of the study to plant managers; rather than a complete list of all the products studied, one learns a lot by looking at the extremes of the distribution.) Despite statements made in the (A) case, volume does not seem to be the explanation between most helped and most hurt products. Direct labor and weight show an average 2:1 differential but the range of direct labor $ and weight for the two groups is quite close. Machine hours per part shows a greater separation between the two groups (1.9: 0.4) but again there is a fair overlap in the range of ACTS hours between the two groups. Total ACTS hours - the product of unit volume and ACTS hours per unit and total DL$ provide the best separation.

The main message is that there may not be a single explanation for cost differences between the two systems. Intuitively, parts that had high amounts of the allocation bases used exclusively under the old system (direct labor $ and ACTS hours) are most likely to have lower costs under ABC since the opportunity exists for overhead costs to shift off these two bases. Conversely, parts that had few labor and ACTS hours are most likely the ones to have higher costs under ABC since there is more opportunity for overhead costs to be reallocated to them with the five new activity-costing bases.

What factors cause major cost shifts to occur with activity-based costing? We identify two causes. First, the overhead costs we are reallocating should be large relative to costs that are already being directly traced to the product. If we apply ABC to small cost categories, there will not be enough dollars to spread around to make much of a difference. Second, look for product diversity. The diversity could come in a variety of ways: large differences in annual production volumes, set-up times, batch sizes, machine hours, weight, etc. Without significant diversity along one or more dimensions, going to a finer partition of overhead and support costs may not produce major shifts in product costs. Thus the two rules:

1. Big dollars at stake, and
2. Significant diversity among products.

What do we learn from the ABC costs? There is good news and there is bad news. The good news is that ABC clearly shows that small, simple parts are much more expensive to produce than had been previously indicated. Costs increase by 200% or more. These results match the intuition of the JDCW operating managers. The bad news, however, is that the cost reductions on the "good" parts are likely not enough to win lots more bids. Only two parts showed decreases in costs of more than 10%.

What does JDCW do now? Hoist a white flag over the factory and start to shut down the turning machine operation?

Exhibits 2 and 3

Exhibits 2 and 3 simulate the impact of shifting production from low to high ACTS hour jobs. Exhibit 2 shows the present distribution of parts on the screw machines Note that 64% of the parts have fewer than 50 annual ACTS hours. These parts account for less than 15% of the labor and machine hours but 44% of the setup hours and 49% of the production orders (or set-ups). Thus these jobs generate a disproportionate share of demand for support resources. Exhibit 3 simulates the impact of eliminating all jobs (parts) with fewer than 100 annual ACTS hours and using the freed up labor and machine orders to take on new parts equally split between the 500-1000 and >1000 ACTS hour categories. Thus the machine shop would have the same volume of activity for the jobs described in Exhibit 3 as in Exhibit 2. Note, however, that there are 77% fewer parts, 59% fewer setup hours, and 62% fewer production orders.

The bottom portion of Exhibit 3 projects that overhead costs should decline by 21% because of the shift in product mix. Would savings of this magnitude be realized in practice (remember, the department has been loaded to accomplish the same physical quantity of work)? You can turn to Keith William's quote on pages 304-305 to get his beliefs about the realizability of the savings.

The analysis in Exhibits 2 and 3 provides a superb opportunity to illustrate the resource consumption basis of activity-based costing. By reducing the diversity in the product line, and using the same number of machine hours and direct labor hours to produce just high volume parts, the demands on support resources will be reduced by more than 20%. Whether the company can reduce **spending** on these resources by 20% is a function of management, and not of the costs themselves. The What-If ABC analysis in Exhibit 3 shows management where the opportunities for overhead expense reduction lie, should they implement the indicated action. Unlike traditional overhead reduction activities, the reduction can not be uniform, across-the-board cuts (which are rarely sustainable since the drivers leading to the higher overhead support resources have not changed). The ABC analysis reveals that based on a decision on product-mix, how much and where overhead resources can be reduced. For example, the same demands will be made on overhead resources related to direct labor and machine hours. But consumption of product-sustaining resources should be reduced by 77%. Should the product-mix shift be implemented, it becomes management's responsibility to redeploy or eliminate the soon-to-be-surplus resources. This example shows that costs are only fixed if managers do not take the requisite actions to make them variable. The ABC analysis can therefore be used as a "zero-based budgeting" routine, identifying all support resources (other than facility-sustaining) as variable with decisions and actions related to product volume and mix, manufacturing processes, and product design.

Additional Issues

The class can now be encouraged to mention the other changes stimulated by the ABC approach. The cost of inefficient processes (long setup times, extensive materials movements, high cost of maintaining parts in the system) was now highlighted and provided further stimulus to the continuous improvements in processes underway at JDCW. Specific actions being taken included focusing the factory by outsourcing some LVA jobs and producing the remaineder on general purpose machines in a designated LVA job-shop area. Processes were being rearranged to improve materials flow, and (not mentioned in the case) designers were increasing the commonality of parts used in different tractors. The division now had more confidence about its bids and hence was now willing to accept orders that covered ABC costs but were below the full costs calculated under the old system.

If not covered in previous cases on capacity costing, a discussion could occur on the desirability of costing on the basis of par volume. My current belief is to recommend that all capacity costs be spread based on a measure of "par" volume, perhaps defined as some long run efficient capacity utilization such as 80 to 85%. In this way, product costs will not be affected by the current utilization of capacity resources. (Should the firm be at or over capacity, I would relax this assumption and raise the cost of using the constraining resources.) This recommendation runs exactly counter to current practice where capacity costs are high when demand is low, and capacity costs are low when the plant is filled.

The rationale for costing at "par" volume is to recognize that excess capacity costs are not costs attributable to current production. They are costs of the period caused by unexpected downturns in demand, or to capacity that was installed in anticipation of future demand. In either case, the firm will get a better estimate of its long run variable production costs by using par volume as the denominator rather than projected volume for next period. This practice will conflict with financial accounting practice since not all overhead will be "absorbed" into production during low demand periods. But a separate and visible classification of "excess capacity costs" will provide a signal to management that a capacity utilization problem exists, and will also not distort product costs due to fluctuations in capacity utilization. The instructor may or not buy into this position but it should provide the basis for an active discussion in class.

The issue of whether ABC should be incorporated into the "official" system is also controversial. Many companies, with a strong financial culture, want to have one system for measuring performance. My preference would be to allow experimental cost systems like ABC to be developed "off-line," especially as more powerful personal computers become increasingly available, and not require that the general accounting system be modified to accept dramatic new product costing concepts. After a period of experimentation and acceptance, the company can begin to think about transferring the successful and surviving product cost systems into the main financial reporting system.

If time remains, a final point of discussion could be stimulated by asking, "How would you evaluate the process of developing and implementing ABC at John Deere Component Works? Leaving aside the intellectual contribution of Keith Williams in devising the ABC approach, would you give him high marks as a 'change-master' (to use a Rosabeth Kanter term)?"

My personal evaluation awards a high grade to both Williams and Vintilla along this dimension. First, Williams must have been thinking about the ABC approach for some time as a remedy to traditional volume-based measures for allocating overhead. But he waited until an operating division called him for help. He did not try to push his new approach on to a division that did not think it needed help. Second, he assigned Nick Vintilla to do the development. Vintilla had previously worked in an operating position at JDCW and therefore was familiar with the people at the plant.

Vintilla worked effectively with the operating and financial managers at JDCW. He interviewed them to find out what was going on and had them respond to early formulations of the model. Thus, he obtained their buy-in and approval to the quite radical new approach he was taking.

Williams and Vintilla chose not to tackle an entire new cost system for JDCW. They focused on one key area, the screw machine department, where big dollars were being spent and where the old cost system likely distorted product costs the most. They also chose to analyze a relatively few products, not the thousands that potentially could be produced in the screw machine area. This enabled them to build the ABC model on a Lotus 1-2-3 spread-sheet that could run on an IBM PC. With this focused, rifle-like approach, they could obtain near-term results quickly and inexpensively. With the approach validated, based on the insights shown in the (B) case, it should be easy to get approval for a full scale project for the entire division.

Having the ABC model on a Lotus spreadsheet permitted sensitivity analyses and simulations as shown in the (B) case. Thus the system could be seen as a useful management tool rather than as a system that merely supplied a new set of product costs. The approach taken by Williams and Vintilla could be contrasted with the much more elaborate approach taken in Schrader-Bellows where, ultimately, the division managers completely rejected the new product costs reported by the transactions-based system developed by the corporate planning group.

Exhibit TN - 1   John Deere Component Works Existing Cost System

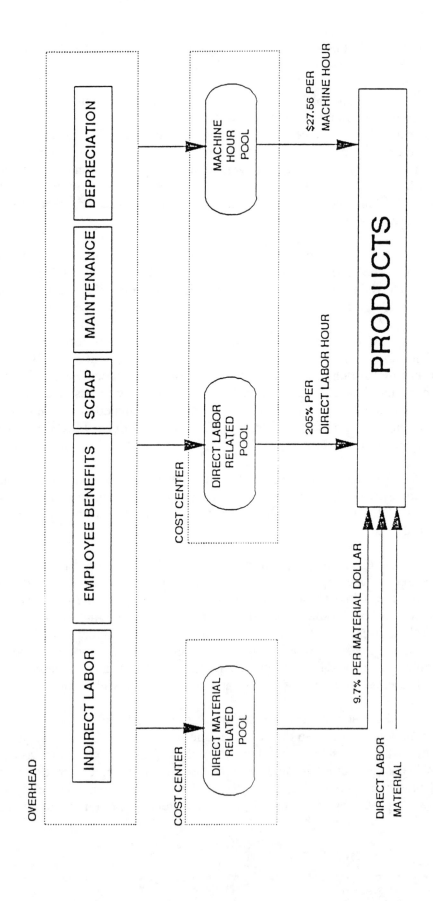

Exhibit TN - 2   Part A 103 Cost Under Old System

MATERIALS	$ 6.44
Direct Materials O/H @ 2.1%	0.14
Period Materials O/H @ 7.6%	0.49
TOTAL MATERIALS COST	$ 7.07
DIRECT LABOR (0.185 DLH* $12.76)	$ 2.36
DL O/H @ 117%	2.76
Period DL O/H @ 88%	2.08
DIRECT LABOR COSTS	$ 7.20
MACHINE HOUR O/H	
DIRECT (.310* $9.83)	$ 3.05
PERIOD (.310* 17.73)	5.50
MACHINE HOUR COSTS	$ 8.55
TOTAL PART COST	$22.82

188-049

Exhibit TN - 3   John Deere Component Works — An Activity-Based Cost System

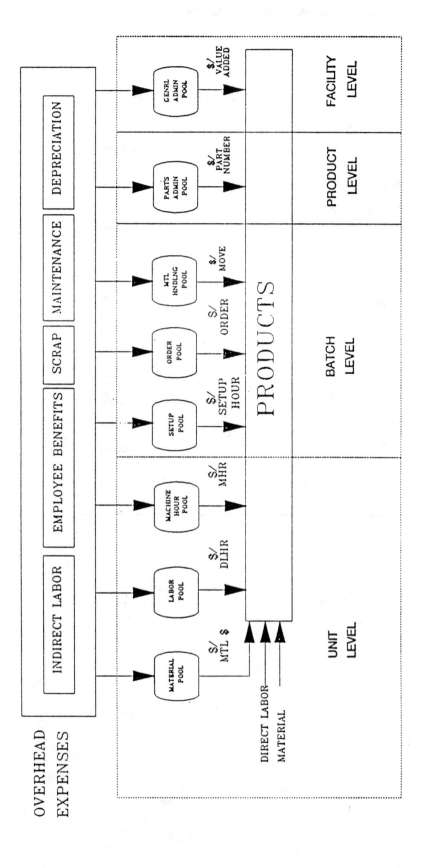

SOURCE: HBS CASE #9–187–107

Exhibit TN - 4   John Deere Component Works How Overhead is Traced to the Products

SYSTEM	VOLUME RELATED		TRANSACTION
	DL$	MHRS	
OLD	35%	65%	0%
NEW	19%	40%	41%

Exhibit TN - 5   Total Factory Overhead Expenses: Traditional Versus ABC Perspective

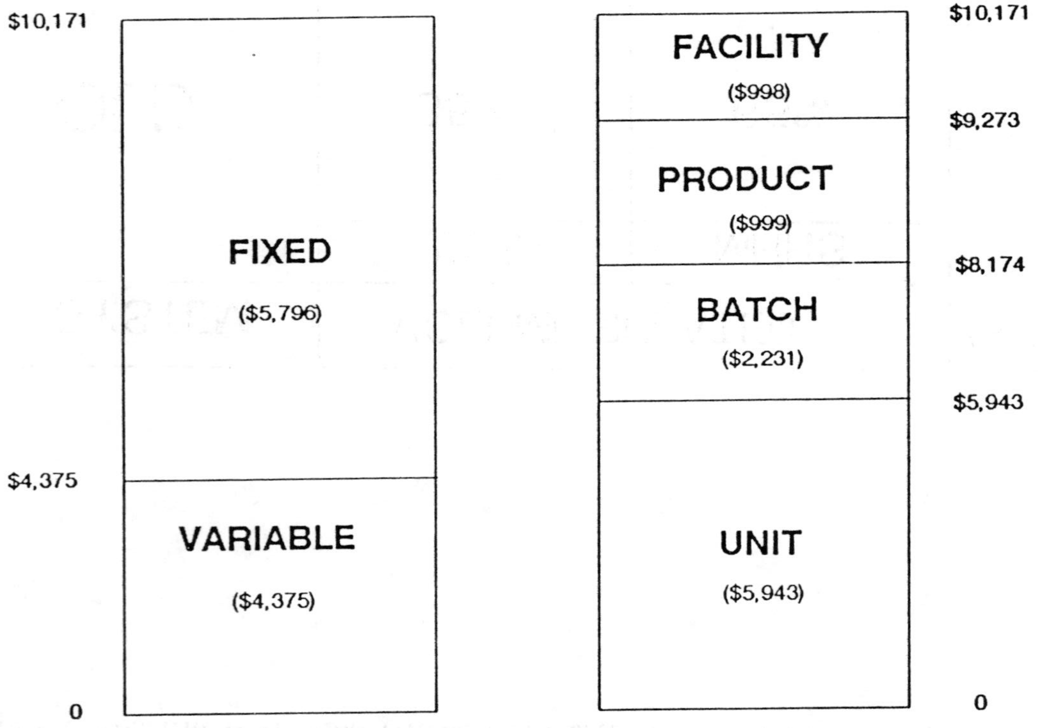

$10,171

$4,375

0

FIXED

($5,796)

VARIABLE

($4,375)

$10,171

$9,273

$8,174

$5,943

0

FACILITY

($998)

PRODUCT

($999)

BATCH

($2,231)

UNIT

($5,943)

Exhibit TN - 6   Part A 103 Cost Under ABC

TOTAL MATERIAL COST $ 7.07

DIRECT LABOR (.185* 12.76)   2.36

OVERHEAD:

    1. DIRECT LABOR @ 111%   2.62

    2. MACHINE HOURS (.31* $16.60: 6 SPINDLE RATE)   5.15

    3. SET UP (2* 4.2* 33.76/80)   3.55

    4. PRODUCTION ORDER (2* 114.27/80)   2.86

    5. MATERIAL HANDLING (19.42/80 *4   0.97

    6. PARTS ADMIN. ($487/80)   6.09

    7. G & A (.091*   2.15

       [2.36 + 2.62 + 5.15 + 3.55 + 2.86
       + 0.97 + 6.09])   _____

TOTAL COST $32.82

PREVIOUS COST $22.82

DIFFERENCE $10.00 (44%)

DEPARTMENTAL OVERHEAD

ABC COSTING $23.39

EXISTING SYSTEM   13.39

DIFFERENCE $10.00 (75%)

Exhibit TN - 7   The Cost Structures of a Typical Part Highlight the Sources and Magnitude of Inaccuracies of the Old Cost System

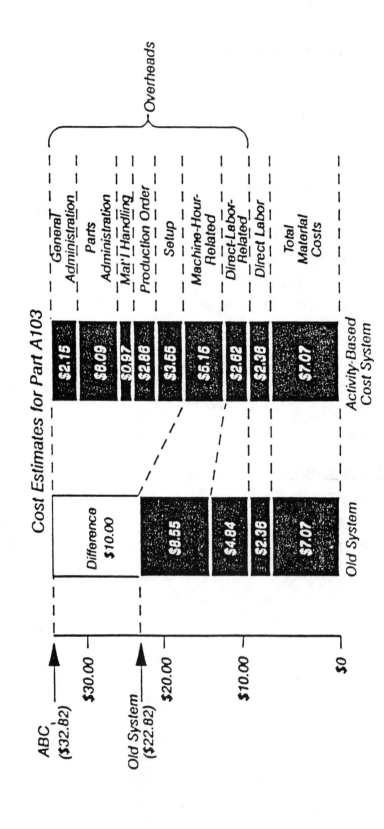

Exhibit TN - 8   Activity - Based Total Product Expenses, A 103

Unit-Level Expenses (per 100 units)

Materials	$ 7.07
Direct Labor	2.36
Direct Labor Overhead @ 111% per DL$	2.62
Machine Hour Overhead @ $16.71 per MHr.	5.15
Total per unit	$17.20

Unit-Level Expenses for 8,000 parts @ $17.20 per 100 $1,376

Batch-Level Expenses:

2 setups @ 4.2 hours each	@ $33.76/setup hour	284
2 production runs	@ $114.27/prodn. run	228
4 material moves	@ $19.42/move	78
Total Batch-Level Expenses		590

Product-Sustaining Expenses

1 part	@ $487	487

Total Product Expenses $2,453

Facility-Sustaining Expenses (allocated by company to product)
                        9.1% of Value Added   172

Total Expenses Allocated to Product $2,625
                                                                                     =====

Exhibit TN - 9   John Deere Component Works Summary of Outcomes From ABC Study

	TEN PARTS MOST HELPED	TEN PARTS MOST HURT
VOLUME	4,660* [1,155-71,200]**	2,800 [692-11,092]
DIRECT LABOR $	0.13 [0.04-0.57]	0.06 [0.02-0.42]
ACTS HOURS/100	1.9 [0.4-3.4]	0.4 [0.2-1.0]
ANNUAL ACTS HOURS	109 [26-266]	13 [2-24]
WEIGHT	1.2 [0.17-3.70]	0.7 [0.04-2.8]

*MEDIAN

**RANGE

Sentry Group

Teaching Note

The Sentry Group case has been used on several occasions as a final examination for the second year MBA elective "The Measurement and Management of Product Costs." The case works well as an examination because of the balance between numerical calculations (30%) and interpretative responses (70%).

The Sentry Group case illustrates the following five issues:

1) The calculation of product costs in an activity based cost system,

2) Some of the issues faced in the design of an ABC system,

3) The application of ABC principles to a small firm,

4) The use of ABC reported product costs in helping set prices, and

5) Equivalent factor or number of units-based cost assignments.

This teaching note outlines an 80 minute teaching plan.

Suggested Assignment Questions:

1. What is the reported product cost of Product C300 under:

    a. The existing single burden rate system.
    b. A multi-rate system where each production department has its own overhead rate and all other overhead is allocated using direct labor dollars.
    c. The activity-based system designed by Anne Abbot.

This teaching note was written by Professor Robin Cooper as an aid to instructors using Sentry Group (191-027).

2. Critique the activity-based system designed by Anne Abbot.

    a.   What are its strengths and weaknesses?
    b.   What changes would you make to it and why?

3. Would you recommend that Sentry Group implement the activity-based cost system (after making any modifications you recommended in Question 2?)

4. What is the <u>approximate</u> profit differential between pricing the C300 at $90 and $80 (assume that the marketing sales estimates are correct, i.e., the firm will sell 50,000 units at $90 and 70,000 units at $80):

    a.   using a fully absorbed traditional approach,
    b.   using a variable cost traditional approach,
    c.   using an ABC approach?

5. What price would you recommend for the C300? Why?

If using these questions for a final exam, a recommended allocation of grading points is:

1.	20%
2.	40
3.	10
4.	20
5.	<u>10</u>
	100%

Class Discussion

Q1. What is the competitive environment?

Sentry has established a reputation for high quality and innovations in the industry. Its patent protected plastic production process gives it a strong advantage in the low end of the market. The plastic products have been very successful, but since they have a different cost structure from the traditional metal safes, the validity of the reported product costs is critical for having a successful strategy in this niche.

Q2. What is the structure of the existing cost system?

The existing system was extremely simple and typical of systems encountered in small firms. The system directly assigns the costs of direct labor and materials to the products. Overhead is assigned to products using a single burden rate based upon direct labor dollars. (Similar single burden center systems were encountered in Bridgeton Industries, Mayers Tap, Inc., and Seligram Inc.: Electrical Testing Operations.)

The treatment of indirect labor costs is interesting. The firm lacks the ability to differentiate between direct labor and indirect labor in the production departments. The calculation to back out the indirect labor costs allows the direct labor portion to be directly assigned, and the indirect portion indirectly assigned. Such adjustments are common in small companies, and are indicative that the cost system is, in Bob Kaplan's terms, somewhere between stage 1 and 2 (see "The Four-Stage Model of Cost Systems Design," Management Accounting, February 1990, pp. 22-26).

The system can not differentiate between the overhead consumption patterns for the metal and plastic products. The managers, while aware of this limitation of their system, can not estimate the magnitude of the distortion introduced by the single burden center system. Management discomfort with the system suggests that the distortion is sufficiently large to warrant developing a more accurate system.

Q3. What is the structure of the new activity-based system?

The ABC contains three major sections. The first contains a redesigned traditional system for the seven direct manufacturing cost centers, (press, spot welding, MIG welding, insulation, clean and paint, final assembly, and plastics assembly). The second assigns factory costs to the production cost centers and the products, and the third assigns support department costs to products using a number of non-unit level drivers.

Each of the manufacturing cost centers has its own cost pool. Expenses accumulated in these cost pools are assigned to the product lines based upon direct labor hours, and then to the products within the line using number of units produced. This product line costing approach is common when products within a product line are relatively homogeneous and the difference in the way they consume overhead can be captured with a single attribute. This attribute is commonly called an equivalent factor. It can be a physical characteristic of the product such as area or volume, or a complexity factor. In the Sentry Group environment, the equivalent factor for all products within the product lines is units and therefore, the number of units can be used to assign the costs to products. The structure of the traditional segment of the new ABC system is shown in Teaching Note Figure 1.

In the second section of the new system, factory overhead expenses are assigned to products via the manufacturing cost centers. These expenses were first assigned to the production cost centers using five different allocation bases, then to the product line via direct labor hours, and finally to the individual products using the number of units produced. This segment of the cost system is illustrated in Teaching Note Figure 2.

The cost of the next four departments are assigned using activity-based principles. These departments are shipping and receiving, quality control, materials management, and engineering.

The cost drivers used for these costs and their level in the manufacturing cost hierarchy are:

Activity	Cost Driver	Hierarchy
Shipping	Bill of lading	Batch
Receiving	Invoices	Batch
Materials		
Requisition	Requisition	Batch
Maintenance	Work Orders	Facility
Quality Control	Production run	Batch
Purchasing	Purchase orders	Batch
Inventory Storage	Sales Dollars	Product
Engineering	ECO's	Product
Corporate	Square feet	Facility

The Sentry Group system provides an example of a full implementation of activity-based costing.

Q4. What are the strengths and weaknesses of the design?

Strengths:

1.   The shift of some SG&A costs to product: The recognition that some of the S,G&A costs are assignable to products illustrates an important part of a good cost system design. The SG&A costs have typically grown over time and often contain costs that can be meaningfully assigned to products. At Sentry Group, $3.5 million (20% [$3.5 million/ $17.5 million] of total manufacturing overhead) of costs could be transferred out of SG&A into product costs.

2.   Increased accuracy: The new system, with an increase in the number of production cost centers, and with an explicit assignment of quality control, purchasing, and other support expenses, better captures the economics of production.

3.   Complexity: The new ABC system is not excessively complex. The seven production centers and nine cost drivers only required 16 cost pools which lie within the 10-20 cost driver/pools heuristic that has recently been identified by ABC practitioners.

4.   Product line costing: The decision to cost the product lines and not the products, reduces dramatically the number of cost driver quantities that have to be measured. It assumes that all products within each line are equivalent, but this assumption appears to be valid. The equivalence assumption, while reasonable within the production center, is inappropriate for the support activities. Consequently, the cost driver quantities for support resources must be collected at the product, not the product line, level.

Weaknesses:

1.   The system still relies upon the 22% split between direct and indirect labor.

2.   Treatment of capacity utilization: The system simply takes all of the costs of the resources consumed and divides by the total driver quantity. The cost of any unutilized capacity is assigned to the products.

3.   Short development time: The short time frame in which the system was designed should be viewed as a weakness. The designer did not have enough time to really check the stability of the estimates or their accuracy. The product costs reported by the system should be used cautiously until the data underlying the design can be tested, across a longer time frame.

4.   Treatment of SG&A: The remaining SG&A costs are still treated as period costs and effectively ignored. The case suggests that distribution costs are the same in both channels but this assumption should be tested; also, do customers differ? The Kanthal and Winchell Lighting cases in Chapter 7 cover these topics in more depth.

5.   Inventory cost assignment: The costs of holding inventory are assigned using sales dollars. Sales dollars is a proxy for actual inventory levels. It is not obvious that inventory levels change according to the actual sales. Budgeted sales might be a better choice as they do not vary with the actual sales.

Q5. What changes would you make to the design of the ABC?

1.   Treatment of indirect labor: The treatment of indirect labor costs is clearly suspect. The correction, at a minimum, should be made at the production cost center level.

2. $18 per direct labor hour: The assumption that an average direct labor rate is sufficient for product costing purposes should be explored in more depth. Actual or standard labor rates by class of employee might be more appropriate.

3.   How does the introduction of the new product change the driver rates? The introduction of a new product is preceded by a lot of activities that are required before production of a new product can commence. Were these activities recognized in the interviews; how should these pre-production expenses for new products be assigned in the ABC system?

4.   Identify cost behavior in the production cost centers: The system as currently designed assumes that all production costs are unit based. The nature of these costs should be analyzed in more depth.

5.   Treatment of cooperative advertising and freight charges: These costs should be assigned to the appropriate channel (mass merchandising) so that channel profitability can be better determined.

Q6.   What are the reported costs of the C300 product under the existing single burden center?

The reported cost of the C300 product under the single burden rate system is the sum of the material, direct labor and overhead costs assigned to the product. These are:

Material		$40
Direct Labor		
Insulation	0.2 hrs.	
Assembly	0.3 hrs.	
Total ($18/hour)	0.5 hrs	$ 9
Overhead at 1.74		$16
		$65

Q7. What is the reported product cost of Product C300 if each production department has its own overhead rate and all other overhead is allocated using direct labor hours?

Students that have studied the Mayers Tap Inc. case series will recognize that this system is equivalent to a seven cost center system where direct labor dollars are used to assign the indirect costs in the first stage, and all costs in the second stage. The use of the same driver in both stages causes the cost system to collapse to a single burden rate for the indirect costs. The reported cost of C300 is given by the cost of material, labor, production departmental overhead, and general overhead. These are:

Material		$40
Direct Labor		
Insulation	0.2 hrs.	
Assembly	0.3 hrs.	
Total ($18/hour)	0.5 hrs.	9
Production Overhead		
Insulation		
($34/hour)	$6.80	
Assembly		
($14/hour)	5.20	
Total		12
General Overhead		10
		$71

The general overhead rate is calculated by first determining the size of the general overhead cost part and then dividing by the total direct labor dollars expedited in the plant:

Total overhead is	$13,840 (Case Exhibit 1)
Total Production Department	
Overhead is	$ 4,924 (Case Exhibit 5)*
General Overhead	$ 8,916
Direct Labor Dollars	$ 7,960
Rate	1.12

* Total cost - total direct labor cost
 $12,884   - $7,960

Q8. What is the reported cost of product C300 under the new ABC system?

The first three elements of the reported costs are the same as the previous calculation: The only difference is the treatment of the general overhead. In addition, the ABC is the only one of the three systems that is sensitive to the volume of production. Therefore, it is necessary to report the cost of C300 at the two different potential sales and production volumes. The general overhead costs for C300 at a production volume of 50,000 units are:

Per Unit	Volume 50,000 Units		
	Driver Quantities	**Cost Driver Rates**	**$**
Supervision	0.15	20	$3
Building	0.5	7	3.50
Total Unit level cost/unit			$6.50

Total Produced

Work orders	6	3216	$19,296
Bills of Lading	500	80	40,000
Invoices	35	736	25,760
Requisitions	2000	56	112,000
Purchase Orders	70	1216	85,120
Inventory	$415 mil	0.0112	504,000
Production	100	984	98,400
Engineering change orders	10	3425	34,250
			$459,226

Equivalent cost per unit	$9.18
Total unit overhead	$15.68

The general overhead costs for C300 at a production volume of 70,000 units are:

Per Unit	Volume of 70,000 Units		
	Driver Quantities	Cost Driver Rates	$
Supervision	0.15	20	$3
Building	0.5	7	3.50
Total Unit level cost/unit			$6.50

Total Produced			
Work orders	7	3216	$22,512
Bills...	650	80	52,000
Invoices	50	736	36,800
Requisitions	2500	56	190,000
Purchase Orders	90	1216	109,440
Inventory	$5.4 mil	0.0112	600,480
Production...:	125	984	123,000
Engineering change orders	10	3425	34,250
			$628,482
Equivalent cost per unit			$8.98
Total unit overhead			$15.48

Reported Costs:

	50,000		70,000
Material	$40		$40
Labor	9		9
Production overhead	12		12
Support overhead	15.68		15.48
	$76.68		$76.48

The comparison of the three sets of reported costs are:

Single center system	$65/unit
Multiple center system	$71/unit
ABC	
50,000 units	$85.76/unit
70,000 units	$84.25/unit

The shift from one to many cost centers increases reported costs by $6 or just over 9%. The shift to ABC increased costs by another $14 (give or take) or an additional 21.5% of the original reported costs. Volume sensitivity at the 50K and 70K levels is effectively irrelevant. In total, the shift to ABC increased reported costs by nearly 30% which is typical of the results shown in case Exhibit 9.

Q9. Would you implement an ABC at Sentry?

The answer should be yes. The shift in reported product costs shown in case Exhibit 9 and for C300 indicates that the existing system in reporting seriously distorted product costs and moving to a multiple center system does not capture all of the distortion in reported product costs. However, if all products are produced in relatively large volumes, the need to use volume sensitive (i.e. batch and product level) drivers should be investigated.

Q10. What is the profit differential for C300 at $90 and $80 under the old system?

	$90	$80
Selling Price	$90	$80
Reported Cost	65	65
Profit per unit	$25	$25
Volume	50,000	70,000
	$1,250,000	$1,050,000

Q11. What is the contribution differential for C300 at $90 and $80 under the old system?

	$90	$80
Selling Price	$90	$80
Variable Cost (75%)	48.75	48.75
	41.25	31.25
Volume	50,000	70,000
	2,062,500	2,187,500

Q12. What is the profit differential for C300 at $90 and $80 under the new system?

	$90	$80
Selling Price	$90	$80
Reported Cost	76.68	76.48
Profit per unit	$13.32	$13.12
Units sold	50,000	70,000
Total Profit	$666,000	$918,400

The lower price results in a loss for product C300.

Q13. What is the contribution differential for C300 at $90 and $80 under the new system?

This is difficult to answer because the firm has yet to model the avoidability of the costs in the ABC system. However, since the only effect of acknowledging cost avoidability will be to increase the bias in favor of the lower price, for the decision in hand it is a moot point.

The ABC and contribution approach point the firm in the same direction while the fully absorbed cost approach points the firm in the opposite direction. There is no reason a priori to suspect that an ABC approach will always point in the same direction as a contribution approach. For example, in the Schrader Bellows case series the two approaches definitely point in opposite directions. Consensus should be towards selecting the lower price.

Sentry Group: Teaching Note Figures 1 and 2

Sentry Group
Teaching Note
Figure 1
The Direct Labor Portion of The Activity-Based Cost System

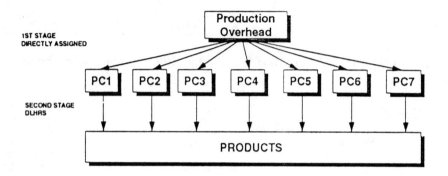

Sentry Group
Teaching Note
Figure 2
The Factory Overhead Portion of The Activity-Based Cost System

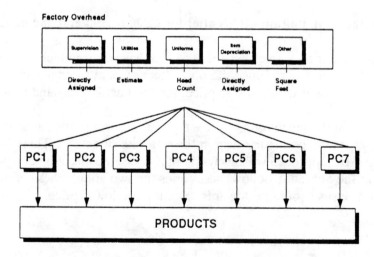

Sentry Group: Teaching Note Figure 3

Sentry Group
Teaching Note

Figure 3
The Support Overhead Portion of The Activity-Based Cost System

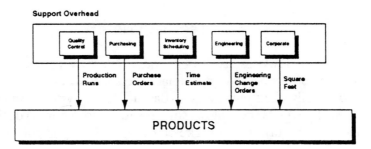

Schrader Bellows

Teaching Note

The Schrader Bellows case series provides students with the opportunity to design and implement their own activity-based cost system. The specially designed software allows students to create, relatively easily, their own Activity-Based Costing system and determine product costs for seven products. The series then allows students to explore how to develop an action plan and observe how and why the firm fails to take advantage of the information provided by the new system.

We teach Schrader-Bellows in up to three or four sessions, providing students with a cradle-to-grave experience of cost systems design (the "grave" metaphor is apt given the outcome revealed in the (F) case). Instructors should order the Schrader Bellows diskette directly from HBS Publishing. The diskette contains the computer programs and data required to design the activity-based cost system based on the interviews in the (B) case, and the data for the (D-1) case. The courseware is an integral part of the case learning experience. Instructors can also order the video-tape that can be used in conjunction with the (B), (D-1) and (E) cases, as described in this teaching note. Instructions on ordering the courseware diskette and the video tape are presented in the introduction to this Instructors Manual. The students may also find the computer model handout (#6-186-049) which comes with the diskette helpful in working with the program.

Since some of the later cases describe outcomes from analysis of earlier sessions, we could not include all the individual Schrader Bellows cases in the book. Instructors teaching the entire Schrader Bellows case series can order copies of:

Schrader Bellows: A Strategic Cost Analysis #9-186-273

from HBS Publishing for each of their students. This packet contains copies of the (C), (D-2), (E), (F), (G), and (H) cases. Of these, the (C) case, and perhaps the (D-2) case are the most

This teaching note was prepared by Professor Robin Cooper as an aid to instructors using the Schrader Bellows cases and case software.

useful (the (E) case has been included in the book already). The principal ideas from the (C) case have been included in this teaching note, either in the text or as an exhibit (Exhibit TN-3). Instructors can review the HBS packet and decide whether they want students to have this material, or whether they feel comfortable teaching the case without handing out these individual cases (which would require that either their school or their students incur extra expenses).

Case Overview

An analysis of the firm's existing cost system shows that it was reporting high gross margins for the low volume items and low gross margins for the high volume items. Marketing, which was isolated from production, was using this information to make long-term strategy decisions. A strategic cost analysis showed that the high volume products were in fact the profit generators and that the low volume products were often selling well below cost.

The case series documents the need for a strategic cost analysis, the cost assignment rules that were selected for support department costs (these include departments such as set up, inventory control, inspection and manufacturing engineering), the development of an action plan to take advantage of the new product cost data, and the reactions of senior management to the study findings.

The actual strategic cost analysis was carried out twice, first in 1983 and again in 1985. This case series documents a mixture of the two studies. The (B), (C) and (D) cases document the 1985 study while the (E), (F), (G) and (H) cases document the 1983 study.

The 1985 study was still ongoing, when we wrote the cases, and we were able to talk to the people actively involved in it. We felt this was much better than trying to document memories about events that were over two years old. Consequently, we wrote the (A)-(D) cases describing the later study. When we wanted to describe management's reactions to the study we used the outcomes from the first study. Management had been exposed to this data for over two years and could not say that its inactions were caused by needing to analyze the data further. Management was forced to acknowledge that little or no action had been taken based upon the study findings.

The two studies were very similar. The major difference between them was the scope of the reallocation. The early study focused almost entirely upon support department costs while the latter study reallocated almost all costs. This difference was in part due to the availability of additional allocation data that Schrader Bellows had collected in the interval between the two studies and to the team's ability to rely upon the early study.

As we were writing the cases it became apparent that Schrader Bellows was going to be a rich but complicated set of cases. We felt that there was a real danger that the allocation cases were going to be so complicated that the students would be unable to cope. This risk was substantially reduced by the decision to limit the case to a description of the reallocation of support department costs. This simplification was justified because an analysis of the 1985 study showed that the reallocation of support department costs accounted for most of the shifts in reported product costs. The issues unique to allocating other cost categories will have to be the focus of other cases.

Computer Courseware

The courseware supporting this case series consists of two computer models and one spreadsheet. To reduce the computational time to a reasonable level, small scale versions of the software developed for the strategic cost analysis were programmed using Lotus 1-2-3 macros. The two computer models consist of the explosion and allocation-implosion routines.

These routines have the ability to cost 7 products that contain about 77 unique sub-components. The development of the data base for the small scale models necessarily involved the modification of the original data. Extreme care was taken to ensure that the resulting swings in reported product costs were typical of the company's findings.

The spreadsheet contains the reported product costs for the 77 products contained in the three product lines that make up the flow control valve group of products. The data have been disguised slightly but the resulting analyses are virtually identical to those produced by the company.

The case series focuses on the Wake Forest facility. Consequently, certain larger strategic issues are omitted from the (A) case. These include:

1.   Schrader Bellows' poor position was aggravated by an even worse position in the cylinder market. Cylinder sales were about 50% of the total sales for the pneumatic industry. Schrader Bellows was a very marginal player in that market and a lot of sales for pneumatic products were driven by cylinder sales. Schrader Bellows was, therefore at a strategic disadvantage. This issue is not brought out in the (A) case because the Wake Forest facility did not produce a significant number of cylinders. It is mentioned in the (F) case videotape, part 2, and the (H) case.

2.   Schrader Bellows' major strategic advantage was its dominance of the mill supply distribution channel. The value of this dominance is brought up in the (F) case videotape, part 2 and the (H) case, in relationship to the sale of the company.

3.   Scovill was acquired in late 1985 by the Belzberg brothers in a leveraged buyout. This forced Scovill into a cash flow predicament that could only be relieved by selling off some of its businesses. This issue is raised in the (F) case videotape and the (H) case.

As the series draws to a close, these previously undisclosed events become revealed. The instructor needs to be aware of them and use them to demonstrate to students the dangers of analyzing a problem at the local level when it has global consequences.

The instructor should consider bringing up these points in the Day 4 discussion to remind students that supplying improved product costs will not lead to immediate management actions. The more accurate ABC costs are a necessary but not sufficient part of the information set that managers require to help select and successfully implement their chosen strategy.

Teaching Plan

DAY 1. The students read the (A) case for company and industry background and the (B) case for the text of the interviews of the support department heads. From these interviews they identify the allocation routines they want to use to assign the costs of the raw material inventory department to the products. The central purpose of this class is to introduce students to the process of designing activity-based cost systems and to set the stage for the rest of the series.

DAY 2. The students read the (B) Computer Model Handout and develop assignment procedures for the setup and quality control departments and use the procedures to produce product costs for seven representative products. A computer model performs the laborious calculations associated with product costing. For students who do not have access to a computer, a special (C-1) version of the (C) case removes the need for the computer (in my opinion the educational value of this day is substantially reduced when (C-1) is used). The students analyze the significance of the product costs reported by the strategic cost analysis. The central purpose of this class is to introduce students to the concepts of the cost of complexity and long-term variable cost. If desired, the (C) case can be handed out at the end of this class. It documents the Scovill solutions.

DAY 3 (optional). The students analyze the data on reported product costs for the 77 flow control valves described in the (D-1) case (the data are on the courseware diskette). Students are expected to analyze the data and prepare a presentation to management about their findings. For executives, or students not familiar with Lotus 1-2-3, the (D-2) case can be handed out with the (D-1) case. It contains a complete analysis of the flow control valve data. The central purpose of this case is to introduce students to the data analysis and presentation problems surrounding the development of new product cost data. If desired, the (D-2) case can be handed out at the end of this class. If only three days is to be spent on the series, the instructor can use the graphical exhibits in the D-2 case to explain the study findings for the flow control valves to students. This presentation requires about twenty minutes and is most effective if the students are asked to comment on the messages portrayed by each exhibit.

DAY 4. The students read the (E) case. It contains the action plan proposed by the firm. Students are asked to critique the plan and comment upon its effectiveness. During the class, the (F) case is handed out. It describes the reactions of senior management to the action plan and plant personnel to the actions taken by senior management. At the end of class, two video segments of the F case can be shown and discussed. The edited text of these videos is captured in the (G) and (H) cases. The central purpose of this class is to sensitize students to the problems of trying to introduce radical change when a crisis is not imminent.

Alternatively, the series can be taught over fewer days by accelerating certain lessons. For example, Day 3 can be replaced by a quick lecture on the findings contained in the D-2 case at the end of Day 2. If there is more freedom to schedule the day 1 session, the students can be asked to undertake a strategic analysis and then design the activity-based costing system for the raw material department before using the computer. This structure allows students to gain an understanding of the design philosophy (i.e., use head count in the first stage and transactions in the second) before using the software.

The suggested assignments for four 80-minute sessions are presented in Appendix A of this teaching note.

Class Discussion

Day 1: (A) & (B) Cases

In the first session, students discuss the strategy and competitive environment of Schrader Bellows, analyze the existing cost system, and begin the design of the activity-based cost system. At the end of the session, students should be aware of the rules that govern the design of activity-based cost systems.

Q1. What caused William Boone to initiate the study?

The (A) case clearly identifies the primary factors that attracted Boone's attention: falling profits. Students should be asked to comment on how seriously they view the degradation in Schrader Bellows' performance. Is this a crisis?

Q2. What is the competitive environment ?

Scovill is a diversified group of light manufacturing companies with 1983 sales of $743 million. Schrader Bellows accounted for about 13% of group sales in 1983. The division, which was a combination of the old Schrader Fluid Power operations and Bellows International, was not performing well and its ROI had fallen from 20% in 1979 to 6.5% in 1983. The main cause of this decline was attributed, by senior division management, to depressed conditions in the fluid power industry. While this undoubtedly contributed to the division's problems it is only part of the story. For the products produced at Wake Forest, Schrader Bellows competed in what amounted to four distinct markets (MRO, FRL, DCV and FCV). In none of these markets was Schrader Bellows the dominant competitor. In fact it was usually third or fourth and in only one, FCV was it the second largest competitor. Thus, while it was the largest producer of pneumatic products in the world, the high returns normally associated with holding dominant position were not achieved because of its weak position in each of the segments.

Schrader Bellows had positioned itself as the industry's full line producer. It competed against different firms in each of several distinct markets. While such a position is, in of itself, of dubious merit the firm compounded the problem by allowing its competitors to capture the majority of the market for high volume products, leaving Schrader Bellows with only a few high- and a hodgepodge of small-volume products.

The strategy that Schrader Bellows is following can best be described as **Everything to everybody** and **You want it, you got it.** This strategy is a direct outcome of the history of the industry and the appeasement of "captive" customers. Captive customers are a double edged sword. While they can be relied upon for business, they have to be kept happy so that they do not worry about being captive. At Schrader Bellows, keeping the customer happy resulted in product proliferation. Every time a customer wanted a variation developed, sales accepted the order and then the product managers were responsible for ensuring that it was manufactured.

Q3. What are the products produced at Wake Forest?

Wake Forest produced over 2,700 products from 20,000 unique parts. These products came from 4 main product groups (FRL, MRO, DCV and FCV) with each group containing a number of distinct product lines. Within a product line there were usually size and function variations. Some of these variations were minor and required minimal change to the production process (for example, using a different O-ring) while others were significant and required the majority of parts be specially machined. The sales volume of products varied widely from several hundred thousand a year to sales of only a few units. This presented an enormous problem for production because the factory was designed for long-run production. Setups required skilled labor and often took many hours. To produce really short runs was obviously economically unsound. Even worse, to provide promised delivery dates of short-run products often required interrupting the manufacture of long-run products.

The case specifically mentions the geographical separation of marketing and production and the perceived lack of communication between them. Students should be asked what are the formal communication systems that firms use to maintain communication between these two departments. One of them is the product costing system. This raises the issue of why the product costing system was failing to communicate the problems. This is the central issue studied in Days 1 and 2.

Q4. What is the production process?

The production processes used by Schrader Bellows were fairly straight forward. Raw material, such as bar stock, was purchased and, as needed, machined to produce subcomponents (machined parts), subcomponents were also purchased (purchased parts) and subassemblies were often manufactured and machined to produce subcomponents. These subcomponents were then assembled to produce a finished part.

Students might not have been asked to cost products that contain several subcomponents and it might be necessary on day 1 to force them to think through the issues. These include:

1. The need to cost the subcomponents not the products. From a product costing perspective Schrader Bellows has 20,000 "products," not 2,700.

2. The loss of cost structure data if materials, labor, and overhead costs of subcomponents become treated as materials costs when subcomponents are used in sub-assemblies and assemblies.

3. The significance of common parts. A low-volume part might be assembled out of components produced in high volumes. A low-volume product produced from common components has very different costs than one that is assembled out of unique subcomponents. This is an important observation as it will be used to explain the results of the Activity-Based Costing analysis in day 2.

4. The need for explosion/implosion routines to convert from products to subcomponents and back again.

Student input should be used to draw a simple five box diagram of the production process on the board. The boxes represent the five production departments; automatic machining, plating, general machining, assembly, and packing. Depending upon the instructor's objective, the path of products through the process can be diagrammed or the diagram left simple so that it can be used later to form the basis for the two-stage diagram of the existing cost system.

Q5. What is the structure of the existing cost system?

Student input should be used to draw a classic two-stage diagram of the existing system. This diagram should show overhead being split into two major sections; production and support department costs. Costs are assigned directly to the departments, both production and support, though undoubtedly, some costs are indirectly assigned. The cost system diagram should illustrate how support department costs reach the products. The costs are first assigned to the production departments, combined with the overhead for those departments, and then assigned to the products using direct labor hours. This treatment of support department costs occurs in all traditional systems. The existing cost system is illustrated in Teaching Note Exhibit 1.

Q6. What is the primary use of reported product costs at Schrader Bellows?

Product mix is set by the customer as part of SB's "you want it, you got it" strategy. Therefore, the only possible use of reported product costs is in setting prices. The production of custom products with no market substitutes clearly requires that prices be set using mechanisms other than market-based. Schrader Bellows uses cost plus pricing. The case provides little evidence that the cost system is used for operational control. Therefore, we would expect and observe a cost systems designed predominantly to report product costs. Evidence that cost plus pricing dominates is provided by the analysis contained in the (D-2) case and should be discussed when that material is presented.

Q7. How do we want to change design of the cost system?

Converting the existing system to activity-based costing can be described in two steps. First, isolate the production department cost system and leave it alone; second, develop independent two-stage procedures to assign the costs of each support department to products. Students should raise some concern about the sole use of direct labor hours in the production cost system. The general machining department is becoming more automated and machine basis diversity is occurring. Students that have completed the **Fisher Technologies** case (in Chapter 2) should be aware of the rules governing a shift to machine hour costing. If students have not been exposed to the principles governing the conversion to machine hour costing, now is probably not the place to do it. There remains much activity-based material to cover in the case.

The key to the design of the Schrader Bellows activity-based system lies in the way the support department costs are assigned to products. In an activity-based system, the costs of the major activities performed in each support department are identified and then assigned to the products. Support department costs do not get assigned to the production departments and then to the products (note: many of the activities are performed in the production departments and may be identified by department, for example, setups in department 203).

Q8. Why is the treatment of the support department costs so critical?

There are three factors that govern the degree of distortion in reported product costs. These are the relative magnitude of the dollars being assigned, the degree and nature of product diversity, and the correlation of the cost drivers with the traditional allocation bases.

All three of these factors are important at Schrader Bellows. Approximately 50% of overhead is associated with the support departments. The products display significant diversity, in particular, production volume diversity. For example, the computer model reports the cost of seven products ranging in production volume from 43,500 to 53 units. The correlation of the support department activities to direct labor hours is low. The support department activities are driven more by the number of batches and different products produced than by the number of units. If students have not been previously exposed to the hierarchy of manufacturing costs (unit level, batch level, product sustaining, and facility sustaining) this is an appropriate time. The hierarchy of operating expenses is discussed in the text material for Chapter 5.

Q9. How did the Scovill team collect data for the design of the new system?

The Scovill design team interviewed the heads of the support departments. The students should be asked to discuss the strengths and weaknesses of the interviewing process.

Strengths

      Relatively fast and inexpensive
      Can capture actual resource consumption
      Involves departmental personnel

Weaknesses

      How well do department heads know what is really going on
      Short-term perspective (answers capture most recent activities not average)
      Fuzzy estimates
      Get political answers

Interview Transcripts

The case contains edited transcripts of the in-depth interviews of the support department heads. The actual interviews had been completed when we were on site and it was necessary to reconstruct them. This was achieved by getting two members of the Scovill team to re-enact the interviews. These interviews were then tape recorded and transcripts prepared. The transcripts were edited to reduce their length and clean up the English. The final transcripts were read by the Scovill team and modified as appropriate.

The interviews were carefully written to focus students' attention on the transactions that cause costs to be incurred in the support departments. The central importance of setups is made very apparent and most students will produce allocation procedures relatively similar to those identified by the design team. This is important; if the students produced totally different allocation schemes there would be a tendency to question the validity of any scheme.[4] The students should be aware that the selection of allocation schemes is to some extent arbitrary but it is not capricious.

It is important at some point in the discussion to make students aware that these transcripts have been cleaned up considerably and that people will not answer the questions anywhere near as lucidly in practice. The real interviews were considerable longer, about ten single spaced pages each, and very difficult to interpret. The design team had to meet with each department head several times to ensure that they had got the facts straight. The Schrader

---

4. The students do not have sufficient information without the interviews to understand the central importance of setups. This focusing of the interviews is required to overcome the lack of other information sources.

Bellows (B) videotape segment shows Pierre Guillaume discussing some of the problems encountered while interviewing.

Q10. How else might the data be collected?

There are several ways to obtain the data required by the Scovill team. These include direct observation, completing time-spent forms for a set time period like two weeks, getting the department heads or support personnel to complete one-time forms, and interviewing all support personnel. The strengths and weaknesses of these approaches should be discussed.

Q11. What was your solution for the Raw Material Inventory Department?

Three different student solutions should be drawn on the board. It is useful to capture the student solutions with the smallest, median, and largest number of cost pools. Capturing the full range of solutions will help the design rules become apparent. Teaching Note Exhibit 2 shows the Scovill solution.

Several design issues should be discussed at this time. First, how many cost pools are appropriate. Second, when transaction versus duration drivers are appropriate. Third, when substitute drivers should be utilized.

The number of cost pools is equivalent to the number of activities identified. Even the simplest product requires numerous activities be performed. Instructors can use setups as an example. The activity "setup" includes the separable activities "picking out the tools", "inserting them in the machine", "locating them", "testing them", "inserting the jig in the machine", "locating it", etc. The skill in designing an activity-based system is to pick the right level of activity definition so that product diversity is captured at a reasonable cost.

The nature of the driver used to assign costs to products depends upon the nature of the activity and the diversity of products. Three different types of drivers should be described. Intensity drivers capture the direct consumption of resources. The most commonly used examples are for "direct" labor and material or the expenses recorded in actual maintenance work orders for specific machines. Intensity drivers capture the actual cost per unit of each resource and the actual quantity consumed by each product of that resource. Duration drivers capture the quantity of the resource consumed but use an average price per unit. For example, the cost per unit of a setup hour is held to be the same for all setups but the length (duration) of setups is allowed to vary each time the activity is performed (e.g., it could vary by product). Transaction drivers capture the number of times an activity is performed. The price per unit of the resource and the quantity consumed of the resource is assumed constant for all occurrences of the activity.

The raw material inventory department can be used to illustrate the difference between duration and transaction drivers. The Scovill solution identifies three activity cost pools. Two of these use the driver "number of shipments received". One captures the number of raw material shipments and the other the number of purchased parts shipments. Students should be asked why two different cost pools are required. The answer is that the cost of processing purchased parts is different from processing raw material shipments. However, the cost of processing a purchased part is relatively independent of the part being processed as is the cost of processing a raw material shipment. Therefore, while there is a need to differentiate between the two types of shipments, there is no need to differentiate within the two types. Therefore, two transaction drivers are sufficient. The same objective could have been achieved by using a duration driver such as processing hours. This would have allowed the different quantities of time for processing raw material and purchased part shipments to be identified. But using processing hours as the driver would require measuring the time spent on every shipment, a considerable increase in data collection cost that would not be offset by the benefit from increased accuracy.

The cost of dispersing raw materials was assigned using a surrogate driver, "number of setups." The most accurate driver would have been hours of dispersement activity. But it seemed reasonable to assume that all dispersement takes the same time so the transaction driver, "number of dispersement," can be substituted. The quantities for this driver, however, were not available. Consequently, the design team used the substitute driver "number of setups" which is equivalent to the number of production runs. The quantities for this driver were readily available. But this driver could not capture the 20% of production runs that required multiple dispersement per run.

Q12. What are the design rules that you used to design this system?

These design rules are discussed in the (C) case. They are:

1. Take the total cost of the department and break it into separate overhead pools based on the major activities undertaken by the personnel in that department. Use the time they spent on each activity to determine the portion of cost placed in each pool.

2. Count the managers and supervisors as departmental personnel only when the managers and supervisors are actively involved in a major activity and not just directing other workers.

3. Allocate the pools to the products based on the events that triggered the activities and the number of those events associated with each product.

If the resulting product costs are to be meaningful then the selection of cost pools and drivers must comply with two guidelines:

1. The cost driver must be chosen such that every product that consumes the resources is charged an appropriate amount for that resource. This objective requires that the resources consumed by each activity are virtually identical irrespective of products. That is with respect to the selected activity all products are homogeneous consumers of the resource (cost pool).

2. The cost pools have to be chosen so that a cost driver with the desired homogeneous property can be identified. This generally requires constructing cost pools for every major activity.

In the guideline for the selection of drivers the term "virtually identical" is used instead of identical. This is because product costing is necessarily inexact. The specification that the products are perfectly homogeneous with respect to the activities, and hence drivers, would be excessive. A cost system designed to meet this specification would consist of a very large number of cost pools. Relaxing this specification to a reasonable extent can substantially reduce the number of cost pools required without significantly affecting the product costs produced. However, the resulting product costs will be misleading if too many cost pools are combined.

Unfortunately, there are no theories to guide the level of aggregation of cost pools. The appropriate level of combination is a judgmental issue that the designer must wrestle with. This discussion emphasizes that designing cost systems is an art not a science, though good design rules can still be taught and learned; it is not a random, unguided process.

Day 2: (B) Case and (B) Computer Model Handout

The purpose of day 2 is to allow the students to put their allocation routines into operation, calculate the resulting product costs for seven flow control valves and then analyze why they are different from the costs reported by the existing standard cost system. To complete their assignments the students require the (B) computer model handout and the Schrader Bellows diskette.

At the end of this session the solution in the (C) case can be handed out. It documents the logic used by the Scovill team and the actual allocation bases and equations they used. Its use is optional. The instructor might want to create a set of transparencies from Exhibit TN-3 and show them in class instead of handing out the (C) case. If computers are not available or the instructor wants to complete the series without using the computer, then Exhibit TN-3 can be distributed in lieu of the computer model handout and diskette.

Computer Models

There are two major benefits to using the computer models. First, any students that have not fully understood the two stage tracing process will now be forced to work it out. Second, they allow the students to gain insights into the processes followed by the Scovill team and the magnitude of the task.

The first model contains the parts explosion. It has been designed to be user friendly so that students with only minimal exposure to 1-2-3 can run it. The student simply enters the volume of production of each product and then selects the explode option. The model takes the bills of material for each of the seven products, multiplies them by the number of products to be manufactured and them sums the common subcomponents. The output of the model is a list of the desired quantities of the 77 subcomponents that are required to produce the 7 products. This list is the information that would normally be transmitted to an assignment routine. In the Schrader Bellows software there is no connection between the two explosion and assignment modules. The assigned-implosion routines will run even if the explosion routine is ignored. I developed the parts explosion routine to allow students to understand what it is and how it works. Also, if we used the output of the explosion routine to supply desired quantities to the allocation-implosion routine, we would have to develop a mechanism to adjust the entire allocation data base to changes in demand volume. At the moment, it can only report product costs for the actual quantities.

The second model contains the cost assignment and implosion routines. Again, even a student with only minimal exposure to 1-2-3 should be able to run it. The student defines the number of cost pools for each support department and then defines the allocation equations that are to be used for each cost pool. When all of the allocation equations have been specified, the student selects the ALLOCATE option and the model undertakes the laborious calculations required to cost the subcomponents. When the assignment routine is completed, the student selects IMPLODE to aggregate the calculated component costs into final-product costs.

(C-1) Case

The C-1 case consists of a brief description of the allocation rules used by the Scovill team and three exhibits. The first exhibit documents the product costs for seven flow control valves as reported by the existing strategic cost system, the second the product costs for the same seven valves as reported by the strategic cost analysis, and the third consists of bills of material for the seven valves. The second and third exhibits, of the C-1 case are identical to exhibits 1 and 2 of the computer model handout.

The (C-1) case does obviate the need for the PC, but at a real cost to the students. The computer forces the student into a hands-on role that requires they develop a deep comprehension of the two stage tracing process. There is no guarantee that this comprehension will be achieved with the (C-1) case.

The "solution" for Schrader Bellows is documented in Exhibit TN-3. It lists the allocation routines selected by the Scovill team. Student solutions tend to be relatively similar because of the highly focused nature of the interviews. The Scovill solution should be compared to the existing conventional cost accounting systems at the Wake Forest plant where support departments costs were either allocated to the manufacturing departments on the basis of direct labor hours (or some modification thereof) or on the basis of workload. These support department costs were then allocated to the products as part of the manufacturing departments' overhead on the basis of direct labor hours.

It is sometimes difficult to unravel exactly what a cost accounting system is doing. The traditional Schrader Bellows system is effectively saying that in each manufacturing department the consumption of the resources provided by the support departments is homogeneous with respect to direct labor hours. This is only true if every lot that requires twice as many direct labor hours as another lot to complete also consumes twice the amount of support department resources. For the support departments whose costs are allocated to the manufacturing departments on the basis of direct labor hours, the existing cost system is also saying that the consumption of support department resources is the same per hour in all of the manufacturing departments (for a proof of this contention see the solution to question 3 of Mayers Tap Inc (B)).

The Scovill analysis tells a completely different story. The consumption of support department resources is driven by the number of transactions that each product causes. Some, but by no means all, of these transactions occur in the manufacturing departments. The cost of each transaction differs between manufacturing departments and also within some of the departments (for example, the cost of a conventional setup in department 201 is different from the setup cost in departments 203 and 214, and both of these costs differ from the cost of an NC setup in departments 203 and 214).

Q1. What was your solution for the Setup Department?

Three student solutions should be documented and discussed. Several important issues should arise. First, the department contains only 13 people but costs over $1.5 million. Clearly there are substantial non-people costs consumed by the department. The Scovill rules assume either that people are the primary cost or that all resources are consumed in the approximate proportion to the number of people involved in the activity. This assumption made sense for the raw material department but it is not clear that it makes sense for the setup one. Second, the use of number of setup hours versus setups as the cost driver should be discussed. The cost driver quantities in the Computer Model Handout clearly identify setup diversity. However, these hours are suspect as the measurements are out of date. Students should discuss whether they believe that the out of date hours are superior to the number of hours which is clearly wrong. One advantage of using the number of hours is it will create a pressure to get the hours right, while the number of hours will not.

Q2. What was your solution for the Quality Control Department?

Again three solutions should be documented and discussed. The quality control department is quite complex to analyze. Student solutions typically range from a minimum of 2-4 pools to a maximum of 10-12. The class learns a lot from this range of solutions. It is more convincing to hear a peer describe a 12 pool system than read about it. The discussion should focus on what is an appropriate number of cost pools for this department. Arguments that should be raised include:

1.   How stable is the solution. As the number of cost pools increases, the chance that the activity mix will change and render it obsolete increases.
2.   The inherent accuracy of interview data. Does it support a 12 cost pools design?
3.   The minimum dollar size of a cost pool. Why bother with pools under say $100 thousand.
4.   The relationship of the design of the setup department system to this one. The setup department is $1.5 million and has 4 cost pools, this department is $0.5 million does it need 12?
5.   The individual differences in interviewees. Some might give very detailed answers compared to others. Does the simplicity of the setup solution versus the quality control one reflect an interview bias?

These are important issues that should be discussed if students are to gain insights into the practicalities of the design process.

Q3. What were the reported product costs for the 7 products using your design?

Five student solutions should be documented. It is instructional to pick three at random and then get the highest and lowest reported costs for product 10400. Typically, the reported costs for that product will range from about $75 to $85.

The product costs as reported by the existing cost system are shown in Exhibit TN-4 (this is the same as Exhibit 1 of Schrader Bellows (C-1) and Exhibit 1 of the (B) computer model handout) and by the strategic cost analysis in Exhibit TN-5 (this is the same as Exhibit 2, Schrader Bellows (C-1). The material and direct labor costs are identical. In the two exhibits, the only change is in the overhead costs. The breakdown of overhead in the strategic cost analysis is shown in Exhibit TN-6 (this Exhibit is the same as Exhibit 2 (continued) of Schrader Bellows (C-1). This Exhibit shows that the only overhead charge that has changed is the support department costs. All other costs have been held constant.

Q4. Does the analysis make a difference?

This is tongue-in-cheek question. The answer is obviously yes. The point is to bring out the magnitude of the shifts in reported product costs. Small for some, huge for others.

Q5. What patterns can be seen in the reported costs?

The analysis of the products show the following patterns:

PART NUMBER	TYPE OF VALVE	SALES VOLUME	COMPOSITION
10000	1 INCH--FCV	HIGH	HIGH VOLUME COMPONENTS
10200	1 INCH--FCV	LOW	LOW VOLUME COMPONENTS
10400	3 INCH--FCV	LOW	LOW VOLUME COMPONENTS
10600	3 INCH--FCV	LOW	LOW VOLUME COMPONENTS
10900	3 INCH--FCV	MEDIUM	MEDIUM VOLUME COMPONENTS
11200	1 INCH--FCV	HIGH	HIGH VOLUME COMPONENTS
11600	1 INCH--FCV	LOW	HIGH VOLUME COMPONENTS

There are two types of FCV in the sample: 1 inch and 3 inch. The sales volumes vary from very high (43,000 units) to very low (53 units).

A comparison of the two sets of reported product costs provides valuable insights into the errors inherent in the product costs reported by the existing cost system.

PART #	TYPE	COMPONENT VOL	MFG COST PER UNIT OLD	MFG COST PER UNIT NEW	%DIFF	GROSS PROFIT PER UNIT OLD	GROSS PROFIT PER UNIT NEW
10000	1"	HIGH	$7.85	$7.17	30%	$5.51	$6.19
10200	1"	LOW	8.74	15.44	35%	3.76	(2.94)
10400	3"	LOW	12.15	82.50	81%	10.89	(62.48)
10600	3"	LOW	13.63	24.51	30%	4.91	(5.97)
10900	3"	MED	12.40	19.99	20%	7.95	0.36
11200	1"	HIGH	8.04	7.96	-15%	5.49	5.57
11600	1"	HIGH	8.47	6.93	-31%	3.74	5.28

Certain trends are visible from this analysis:

1.   At high (low) sales and hence component production volumes the product costs reported by the strategic cost analysis are lower (higher) than those reported by the existing system.

2.   The three inch valves have lower volume sales than the one inch and overall are less profitable using the strategic cost analysis data but more profitable using the existing cost system data.

3.   The difference in product costs vary from -31% to +81%. The asymmetry in the range is a necessary outcome of product costing. The two systems are trying to spread the same amount of costs over the productive output of the firm. At low volumes of production it is possible for the existing system to be out by a huge amount, this is not the case for high volume products.

The next step is to analyze the overhead.

| PART | COMPONENT | DIRECT | OVERHEAD PER UNIT | |
#	VOL	LABOR $	OLD	NEW
10000	HIGH	1.10	$5.44	$4.76
10200	LOW	1.18	6.15	12.85
10400	LOW	1.62	7.30	77.66
10600	LOW	1.55	8.88	19.76
10900	MED	1.48	7.58	15.17
11200	HIGH	1.11	5.34	5.27
11600	LOW	1.14	5.92	4.39

The insights provided by this analysis include:

1.   The relationship between component volumes and profit is repeated in the overhead analysis (this is both necessary and obvious).

2.   The burden rate is fairly constant in the existing system (average $5.07 and standard deviation 0.35) but highly varied under the new system (average $13.54 and standard deviation 14.43). This demonstrates the smoothing effect inherent in conventional cost systems design.

3.   The higher average burden rate (and total overhead costs) in the strategic cost analysis data is not an error. This is simply the effect of looking at a subset of the total output of the factory. The seven flow control valves actually consumed more support department costs than the existing system assigned to them.

The relationship between component volume and profit (and overhead) is driven by the switch from unit-based to activity-based costing. The existing system spreads the support department costs on the basis of direct labor hours, a long-run product is therefore assumed to consume a lot of support department costs. The apparent consumption of these resources is virtually directly proportional to the lot size (the setup time stops this relationship being exactly proportional). The strategic analysis overcomes this simplification by assigning costs at the unit batch and product levels not just the unit level.

The cost system then takes the sum of the total cost of production for each product and divides it by the number of units produced by that product to calculate unit costs. For large-run items the unit costs dominate and hence, the reported costs drop. For the small-run items the batch and product-sustaining costs dominate and hence the reported cost increase.

Q6.   Why does 11600 break the rules? It is a low volume product that appears more profitable under the Activity-Based Costing systems than the traditional one.

The bills of material have to be analyzed to show that 11600 is a composite of the two high volume products. Product 11600 is produced using components also used in 10000 and 11200, both high volume products. Therefore, the components are high volume components. Thus, other than the assembly operation, the key elements in this product are produced in high volumes. The activity-based system captures the benefits of common components while the traditional system does not. This observation is very important and should be reinforced. The ability to reflect the economics of common components is one of activity-based costing's great advantages over traditional systems.

To make the significance of this observation clear, instructors might want to discuss the difference between Wendy's and McDonalds strategy. Wendy's inventories work-in-process while McDonalds inventories finished goods. Wendy's builds the burger "your way" by asking a series of 8 binary questions (onions?, pickles?, lettuce?...). The condiments are added (or not) as the person answers the questions. This production process allows Wendy's to produce 256 different variations of burger at little extra cost over McDonalds. When single, double, and triple burgers are considered, Wendy's can produce 768 different burgers to order by producing the basic product in a continuous-flow high volume process, with customizing occurring at the final production stage. If McDonalds tried to emulate this product mix with its production process, the results would be disastrous. Schrader Bellows is trying to follow a Wendy's strategy using a McDonalds production process and the traditional cost system cannot warn managers of the errors of their ways.

The instructor can now, if desired, hand out the (C) case (or a copy of Exhibit TN-3).

(C) Case

The (C) case consists of the allocation bases and equations used by the Scovill team and a brief description of why they were selected. The (C) case is designed to provide closure on the first two days. It confirms the approaches discussed in class and outlines the theory behind the Scovill solution. Its use is optional.

Q7. How confident in these numbers are you?

The range of solutions, especially for 10400, is a little unsettling to some. But the central message remains the same despite variation in individuals' cost estimates: Product 10400 it is a very unprofitable product. The sensitivity of the reported costs for that product reflect the tiny number of units involved. The other products show much less sensitivity. Other concerns that should be raised include the range of design choices illustrated earlier in class and the inherent inaccuracy of the interview process. Overall. students should be confident that the story the numbers tell is the right one and that the old system was reporting highly misleading product costs.

Q8. Is the Scovill solution too complex?

If the instructor has handed out the (C) case or has shown the Scovill solution in its entirety by transparency, this is a good question to end the day.

Day 3: (D-1) and (D-2) Cases

The first two days are spent on the technical aspects of product costing. The students at this point should have gained some understanding of how to apply two stage assignment procedure to support departments, how to design an activity-based cost system from interview data, and how to analyze the output from a new product costing system.

The next two days force the student to take a broader perspective. The students are asked to analyze the reported product costs of the flow control valve (FCV) group of products produced at Wake Forest. This group was selected because it was fairly representative of all of the product groups. The analysis of the FCV group can safely be generalized to the other Wake Forest product lines.

The purpose of day 3 is to get students to analyze the new product costs of the FCV group. To complete the analysis students require the Schrader Bellows spreadsheet (SCHRADD). This consists of the sales and cost data for the 77 products that constitute the three product lines that together form the FCV product group. The video tape for the (D-1) case highlights some of the data problems the Scovill team faced and indicates how long it took to get the programs operational.

Spreadsheet

The spreadsheet has no macro functions other than the title screen. The students are expected to develop their own analytical routines. At a minimum they should produce gross and operating profits and return on investment figures. The spreadsheet includes capital invested information and suggests a pre-tax interest rate so there is nothing stopping the students from producing residual income (RI) figures. These calculations are shown in Exhibit 2, case D-2.

The analysis of the data in (D-1) produces some fascinating insights:

1. 32 (42%) out of 77 products have a positive gross profit.

2. 24 (31%) out of 77 products have a positive operating profit and hence a positive ROI.

3. 5 (6%) have gross margins over 45% and 16 (21%) have margins over 40% (extra manipulations are required to generate these statistics).

4. The highest ROI is 110% (however, this product and the next are somewhat anomalous and possibly should be ignored) and the third is 36%. The lowest ROI is nearly (6000%)!!! and (100%) or greater is achieved by 23 (70%) of products.

5. Both ROI and RI tell essentially the same story. Does this provide some insight into why ROI is still popular?

6. The majority of the positive ROI products (58%) have sales above $100,000 while only 1 (2%) of the negative ROI products has sales above that amount.

7. The majority of negative ROI products (73%) have sales below $10,000 while only 7 (29%) of the negative ROI products are below that amount.

The story told by the above analysis is truly startling. The profits of Schrader Bellows are being bled away by the low profitability low sales products. The cost of being a full-line producer is staggering. This is not to say that it is the incorrect strategy but it certainly makes you wonder.

It is easier to see what is going on by analyzing the cumulative data. These calculations are shown, after ranking by ROI, in Exhibit 3 case D-2. The analysis obviously tells the same story but more persuasively:

1.   The RI of the FCV group is negative. The group is not producing enough income to cover the resources it is consuming.

2.   The operating profits generated by the 24 profitable products are $481 thousand. This falls to $159 thousand when all 77 products are sold. In other words the unprofitable products cost the firm $322 thousand or just over 200% of profits!!

3.   The RI generated by the 23 positive RI products is $164 thousand. This falls to $(280) thousand when all 77 products are sold.

4.   The profitable products account for $3.8 million of sales. This is 86% of group sales.

5.   The profitable products utilize $1.5 million of net invested capital. This is 71% of group capital.

The cumulative analyses really drive the message home. The cost of the unprofitable products is really huge. The firm could be considerably more profitable if it could just sell the high volume products.

This raises the question of what can be done. It is obviously (?) not possible to drop all of the unprofitable products, but dropping a few of the real dogs would help. This point can be demonstrated by pointing out to students that the bottom 25 products have a negative operating profit of nearly $(125,000) on sales of $75,000 and at the top end it takes sales of nearly $350,000 to recoup this loss. The points discussed above can be demonstrated graphically (see graphical Exhibits in the (D-2) case) for the entire product group and the individual product lines.

An important part of the lesson to be learned about the strategic analysis is the difficulty of "cleaning up" the data. All too often we make it seem so easy to collect the data and then use them. To undertake an analysis such as the one in Schrader Bellows requires an enormous amount of time be spent removing the flaws from the data. The (B) videotape segment discusses the cleanup process in more depth. Most companies' production data are so full of errors that it is amazing that anything can be manufactured. Computers do not help the situation; in fact, they probably make it worse. In manual systems, the person in charge of maintaining the data at least has some intuitive understanding of what makes sense. In computerized systems, this individual is often isolated from the data and consequently the quality of the data can be much worse before it becomes apparent.

(D-2) Case

The (D-2) case contains the analysis of the FCV data. It consists of several spreadsheets and numerous graphs. If the students are Lotus 1-2-3 proficient and the instructor wants them to explore the data themselves, the use of (D-2) is optional. It can be handed out at the end of Day 3 or after the students have spent a couple of hours analyzing the FCV data. If the students are not proficient in Lotus 1-2-3 or the instructor does not want them to explore the FCV data, then the (D-2) case can be handed out instead of analyzing the spreadsheet data for the (D-1) case.

To use the D cases for an 80 minute session, get two or three students to prepare and present their own 15 to 20 minute summaries to the class. Such presentations are a useful learning experience for the students. They should contain, at a minimum, a brief overview of the theory of Activity-based costing, a brief description of the procedures used to design the Activity-based costing, a summary of findings about flow control valves, and a preliminary action plan.

The rest of the class can be spent using the D-2 graphical Exhibits and generating an action plan. The following questions should be discussed:

Q1. What actions would you suggest for the flow control valve product line?
Q2. Why not drop all unprofitable products?
Q3. Who should develop the action plan, Scovill or Schrader Bellows personnel?
Q4. How would you validate your action plans before implementing them?

Day 4: (E) and (F) Cases

The purpose of Day 4 is to get the students to understand:

1.   The procedures required to develop an action plan and obtain commitment to it.
2.   The logic required to identify a "safe" product and the steps required to drop it successfully.
3.   The problems encountered when the actions proposed are threatening to senior management but the organization is not in crisis.

The timing for this day's discussion is crucial. The following breakdown has proved to be effective. If the video portions will be used, then time must be left for them. The (E) and (F) discussions have to be controlled and focused.

1. Discuss (E) case	35 mins
2. Read (F) case	5 mins
3. Discuss (F) case	15 mins
4. Watch (F-1) Video	10 mins
5. Discuss (F-1) Video	5 mins
6. Watch (F-2) Video	5 mins
7. Discuss (F-2) Video	5 mins

(E) Case

The (E) case contains a description of the steps the Scovill team took to develop their action plan and gain commitment to the steps envisioned. The Scovill action plan is a very good example of detailed analytic work leading to a concrete recommendation. At all stages, the relevant people are kept informed and their consensus built. The most interesting aspect of the plan is the ease with which the product managers appear to have accepted the concept of dropping products. They agreed to drop just under 800 products (Exhibit 2 of the (E) case). Students should be cautioned to answer questions with respect to the phase of the study being discussed.

Q1. What were the choices presented to the Product Managers?

The choices identified in the case should be written on the broad and discussed. The concept of residual income being zero at the product level should be brought to the students attention.

The residual income equals zero rule is theoretically flawed given the definition of residual income. If the capital charge was correct, then economic theory suggests that the "average" firm should achieve zero residual income and that only a superior performer should be able to charge Ricardian rents. If all products with a negative residual income are dropped or their price raised to achieve zero residual income, then, assuming that all of the costs associated with the dropped products can be avoided, the firm will have a positive residual income from flow control valves alone of some $150,000 and profits will have been increased by about $300,000 from modifications to the Flow Control Valve Group alone! Thus the options given the product managers were, in fact, highly restrictive and demanded that the firm move from a mediocre performance to an outstanding one by simply dropping products and raising prices.

Q2. What were the results of the analysis?

The product managers recommendations should be added to the list on the broad and discussed. The predominance of the drop the product and reprice options are obvious as are the is the virtual omission of the others. The bias towards dropping products is shown by calculating the percentage of products that the product managers assigned to each option:

Option	Action	%
A	Drop product	46
B	Raise price	27
C	Set up change	3
D	No change	19
E	Question data	3
F	Reduce cost	0
G	Buy out	2

Q3. Are these choices comprehensive, are any options ignored?

The list is very thorough. However, it focuses on the individual product. No global process improvements are considered. This focus leads to the outcomes recommended by the product managers - drop or reprice products. It is useful to draw student attention to issues such as 1) the ordering of the list (is it a coincidence that the first two options are the most favored), 2) the amazingly few products that are recommended for redesign, 3) the politics of using a multiple choice approach, 4) the linear structure of the list, the decision tree is much more complicated than suggested by the list and certainly does not begin with drop the product.

Q4. Are the Product Mangers the right people to ask?

The (A) case describes the product managers. They are all 20+ year veterans of the production process. They are not marketing oriented. Their job has historically been to manage the introduction of new products, not to maintain a balanced product offering. They lack the strategic knowledge required to understand the implications of their recommendations.

They were asked whether the firm should continue to manufacture products that were making a loss and naturally answered no. I am surprised at how rarely they suggested raising prices instead of dropping prices and suspect that the rule, to raise prices until residual income is zero, is too severe. They might have gone with intermediate price increases for the short term with a second or additional price increases over time to reach the desired objective.

Students should be asked to discuss what choice manufacturing and marketing would prefer. This question helps highlight the separation that has developed between the various functions. I suspect that manufacturing would either prefer to drop products (blame the unprofitable product on marketing) or re-engineer them, while marketing would re-engineer them (blame the unprofitable product on engineering or manufacturing).

Q5. Would you follow the product managers recommendations?

There should be little support for the product managers' recommendations. The analysis lacks a revenue model (the impact on revenues of the action plan) and a spending model (what cost savings could be achieved under the action plan). In addition, dropping nearly 800 products and repricing nearly 500 more would have an enormous impact on the strategy of the firm. There is insufficient evidence to suggest that the overall impact would be positive. The product managers' recommendations indicate how little they understand the big picture.

Q6. What are Safe Products?

When the management of Wake Forest was included in the decision process, a more conservative and practical approach was adopted. The concept of a safe product was used to identify the 250 products to consider dropping. The five rules used to identify safe products appear in the (E) case. These rules are powerful and should be specifically drawn to the students' attention. They appear to produce a list of products that no rational individual could defend keeping. Once these criteria were established, further meetings with the product managers were held to determine which products were to be dropped. Eventually 250 such product were identified.

Q7. Is this a good list? What is its purpose?

After the merits of the list has been discussed, its purpose can be explored. The safe product list is effectively a revenue model. It captures the relationship between the drop products decision and revenue effects.

Q8. Why is it necessary to determine the savings?

This question highlights the difference between the cost system that reports on resource consumption and a spending model. The savings analysis is a spending model for the decision to drop the 250 safe products. On the surface, the definition of a safe produce would appear to suggest that there is little value in dropping them as they are effectively irrelevant (low volume), and this is exactly what a conventional cost system suggests (small profit or loss). The strategic cost analysis, however, strongly supports dropping these products. The estimated realizable savings from dropping these products are documented in Exhibits 3 and 4 of Schrader Bellows (E)).:

	$(000)
Sales	(1,178)
Direct costs	645
Factory indirect costs	189
Factory overhead	546
Pension costs	426
Fixed costs	67
	$1,873
Operating profit	695
Cost of capital	154
	$ 849

In other words, dropping the safe products and achieving the savings contracted by the department heads would increase the profitability by over $800,000. This is a significant amount (an additional 4% profit margin) to a facility that is making products that account for annual sales of $20 million.

At this point, the concept of dropping products appears to dominate the action plan, and the option of raising prices has slipped out of sight. In my opinion, this is a major weakness of the plan because:

1. Dropping products is a very permanent step. If competitors fill the gap, Wake Forest may not be able to regain the share. Also, customers might be forced to change equipment and hence destroy the market. Thus, dropping products requires very high confidence that it is the right thing to do. If senior management is uncertain to any extent that the strategic cost analysis is the correct, they will tend to procrastinate.

2. When you drop products, the sales go away almost immediately, but the costs associated with them do not. This means that the bad news arrives first. It is difficult to sell senior management on projects that have this unfortunate timing property.

Q9. If the 250 products are dropped will the savings be achieved?

As part of the confirmation of the savings, the plant controller was asked to prepare a savings estimate based upon the existing cost system. These savings are documented in Exhibit 5 of Schrader Bellows (E). This exhibit is virtually incomprehensible. I wrote the memo to try and help students understand it. The value of the exhibit is twofold. First, it identifies potential savings of $761,000 ($730K + $31K) which is close enough to the strategic savings to induce confidence. Second, the terminology is so difficult to understand that it helps explain why managers fail to understand the cost systems they interact with. Compared to the strategic cost system, the conventional system does nothing to shed light on how the savings will be realized.

Students' attention should be drawn to the actions required to drop products. It is a non-trivial decision to drop products, and the (E) case documents some of the actions required to ensure that a dropped product remains dropped. The drastic nature of step 7 (burn the drawings) shows how difficult the Scovill team felt it was to succeed in dropping a product and keeping it dropped. The reason it is so difficult to keep products dropped is because the old cost system is still operating. These products were earning a high (reported) profit, and, as such, if somebody wanted to order them, it made sense to make them. The strategic analysis showed how flawed this perspective was. However, until the old cost system replaced with a new one, it is necessary to adopt very creative measures to keep product proliferation under control.

Q10. Would you drop the safe products?

Students sometimes have different perspectives about whether they would drop the products. A rich discussion usually follows. Questions such as "Does dropping these products make a strategic statement?" and "What can possible be wrong in dropping these products?" will add fuel to the discussion. If it looks like the students are opting to inaction, the instructor should subtly bias the students in favor of dropping the safe products by asking questions like "What more evidence do you want?" and have you heard of "Strategic paralysis?"

The instructor should now hand out the (F) Case.

(F) Case

The division management's actions as documented in the (F) case are surprising. I would have expected at least 50% of the safe products to have been dropped. The fact that only 20 products were dropped is significant. (How many additional new products were added in the past two years?) The inaction means that division management never really accepted the logic underlying the strategic cost analysis.

Q11. Why did nothing happen?

The students' attention should be drawn to two statements that highlight the logic that is driving division management's actions. These are:

You cannot cherry-pick the line without opening yourself up to problems with distribution. Distributors want to offer a full line.

. . . when products are dropped, the sales go away but the costs do not and there is no improvement in profitability.

The first statement is easily tested. Paul Bauer went to the distributors and some of the customers and asked directly about the issue. There was no resistance to the concept of dropping products. In fact, many people were surprised rationalization had not occurred already. Schrader Bellows still sold a number of Bellows products that were identical to Schrader products. The second statement is more difficult to test a priori. In defense of the Scovill team, the Wake Forest management had committed to produce the savings. So there is a high probability that overall profits would have improved.

Q12. Would you fire anyone?

This question often leads to a lively discussion. I ask students to vote on the future of the various players.

The power of the (F) case lies in the demonstration of the ability of the two untested statements to demolish the end product of months of very rigorous analysis. It provides a fascinating insight into the management process. The (F) videotape segments continue the story.

(F) Case Videotape, Part 1

The (F) case videotape, part 1, deals with the reasons that Bill Boone thinks nothing happened. These include:

1. The outcome of the study. Higher <u>profits</u> from fewer resources with less work <u>is</u> counter-intuitive and <u>requires</u> a lot of energy to overcome the intuition.

2. Disbelief that the overhead costs <u>can be got rid of;</u> that it is possible to slim the organization down without removing critical capabilities.

3. The real message was too dismal to be accepted. 70% of Schrader Bellows' products were losers and should be eliminated. Wrapping the pill in the sugar coating of "safe products" was not sufficient to hide the real problem. If management dropped 250 products, the next time it would be another 250, and so on.

4. You realistically cannot ask managers to give up their turf to the extent suggested by the analysis. It requires firing too many people and losing too much face -- it requires a real crisis or change in environment to bring this about. Boone concludes by observing that it is worth "prewiring" the organization with such analyses so that when the crisis or change occurs, the organization has the data ready to take advantage of the insights provided by the strategic cost analysis.

These are very powerful lessons and different from those we typically teach in our cost and managerial accounting classes. It requires a very patient long-term approach to the concept of strategic planning to "prewire" an organization so that when a crisis finally hits, the analysis can be used to guide actions.

Having shown the tape, I ask for student comments on Boone's position.

(F) Case Videotape, Part 2

The (F) case videotape, part 2, draws the series to a close. It covers the following points:

1. The conventional cost system allowed Schrader Bellows to follow a disastrous strategy.

2. You cannot easily recover from the effects of such a strategy.

3. Often, the only option is to sell the company to someone who can take advantage of what is there.

4. Selling a company is one of the events that can allow the analysis to be used.

5.   A strategic analysis might have saved Schrader Bellows if it had been done 5-10 years earlier.

A short discussion is useful to end the series. The students have been exposed to a rich case series that puts cost accounting in a strategic light and shows it to be critical to the survival of the firm. The technical and organizational issues that the case brings up are really background to the central lesson of the series that poor product costing can cause a firm to get into very deep trouble over a number of years without management understanding what is really going on.

Schrader Bellows TN
Appendix A

Assignment Questions

The Schrader Bellows case series provides you with the opportunity to undertake a strategic cost analysis, analyze the resulting product costs, develop an action plan to reprice or drop products, and then evaluate the company's subsequent progress. The series will be taught over four days.

Day 1

Read the (A) and (B) cases. The (A) case provides background for the rest of the series. The (B) case describes the procedures undertaken by the Scovill team to obtain the data required for a strategic cost analysis.

Use the information contained in the interviews of the five support department heads to identify the bases you want to use to allocate the support department costs to the products.

Prepare a 20 minute presentation to management describing the allocation procedures you developed and the general principles behind your allocation schemes.

You might find it helpful to read the SCHRADER BELLOWS (B) Computer Model Handout. It contains a description of 32 potential allocation bases. You need not limit yourselves to these bases today but will be forced to tomorrow when you use the computer model.

Day 2

Using the SCHRADER BELLOWS (B) COMPUTER MODEL, determine the reported product costs of seven products using your allocation procedures. Compare them to the costs reported by the firm's existing system--how consistent are they? Prepare a 20 minute presentation to management explaining the significance of your findings. In particular, cover the following topics:

1.   What causes a product to be profitable?

2.   Why does the existing cost system produce different product costs from the strategic cost analysis?

3.   The implication of your findings to the firm's strategy.

Day 3 (optional)

Read the (D-1) case and analyze the data in Lotus 1-2-3 form in the SCHRADER BELLOWS (D) COURSEWARE TEMPLATE.

Prepare a 20-minute presentation to management covering the following topics:

1.   What do you think is the relevant measure to use in determining if a product is "earning its keep?"
2.   An analysis of the Flow Control product group.
3.   Any concerns you have about the validity of the Scovill data.
4.   The implication of your findings to the strategy of the firm.
5.   A step-by-step action plan to identify which products should be dropped or repriced, the types of repricing options that might be considered and any other actions you believe the firm should take.

Day 4

Read the (E) case. It contains a description of the actions taken by the Scovill team. Evaluate their action plan. What are its strengths and weaknesses? How would you improve upon it? What do you think will happen next? Why?

Schrader Bellows
Teaching Note
Exhibit TN1

The Structure of a Traditional Cost System

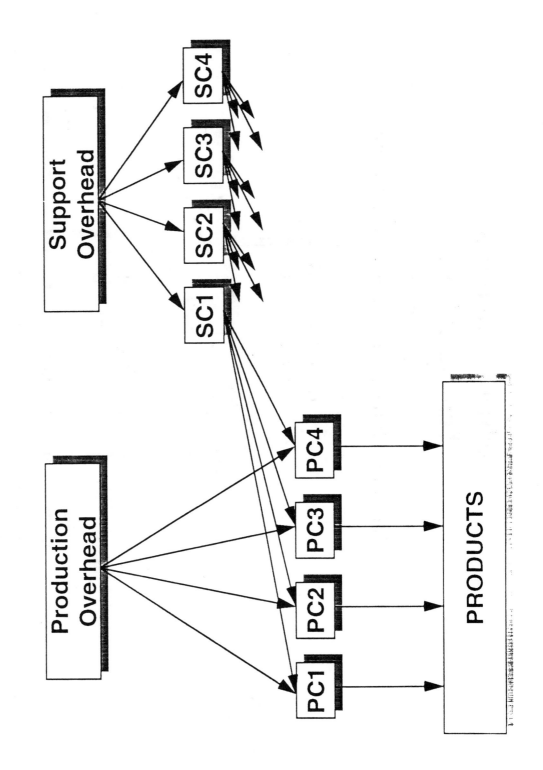

Schrader Bellows
Teaching Note

Exhibit TN2
The Raw Material Inventory Department

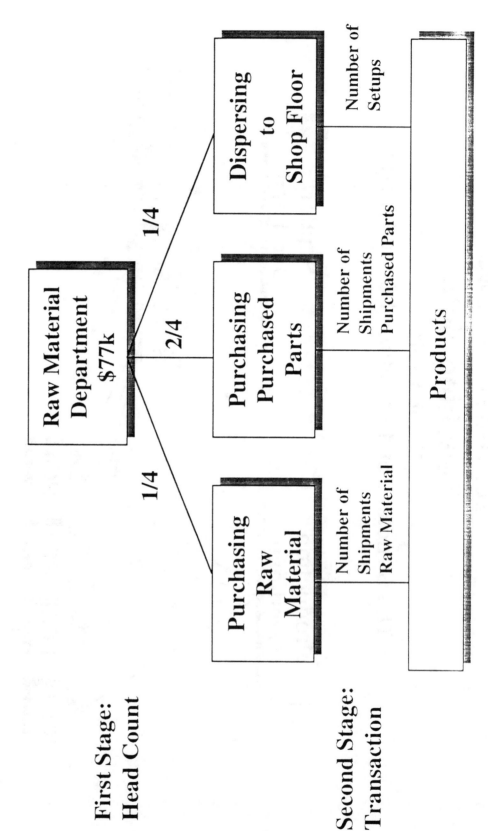

First Stage:
Head Count

Second Stage:
Transaction

Exhibit TN-3

Summary of Allocation Bases Used

Activity

o   Setup hours (201, 203, 205, 214, and NC)
o   The number of setups (201, 203, 205, 214, and NC)
o   The average dollar value of WIP
o   The number of times direct labor was reported in the assembly
    department (201)
o   Sales in dollars and units
o   Direct labor in a department (201, 203, 205, 213, 214)
o   Standard direct labor
o   COGS (total, automotive, manufactured and component item, flow control
    products, coupler)

Material Flow

o   The number of shipments received of purchased parts
o   The number of shipments received of raw materials
o   The number of shipments made
o   The number of parts purchased and produced

Orders

o   The number of customer orders
o   The number of purchase orders sent
o   The number of orders for supplies
o   The number of purchase orders received

Exhibit TN-3 (Con't)

Raw Material Inventory Department (239)

o 2/4 based on the number of shipments received of purchased parts (items that went directly into WIP)

o 1/4 based on the number of shipments of raw material received

o 1/4 based on the number of setups in departments 203 & 214

Work in Progress Inventory Department (230)

o 1.5/6 based on the number of setups in departments 203 & 214 plus the number of shipments of purchased parts

o 40% of 4.5/6 based on the average dollar value of WIP

o 60% of 4.5/6 based on the number of times direct labor is reported in department 201

Finished Goods Stockroom (231)

o 1/8 based on the number of times direct labor is reported in department 201

o 40% of 3/8 based on the sales dollars

o 60% of 3/8 based on the number of customer orders

o 50% of 4/8 based on sales dollars

o 50% of 4/8 based on the number of shipments made

Production Control Department (234)

o 4/12 based on the number of setups in departments 203 and 214

o 5/12 based on the number of all setups

o 3/12 based on the number of setups in department 201

Purchasing Department (235)

o 80% based on the number of purchase orders

o 20% based on the number of orders for supplies

Setup Department (240)

Exhibit TN-3 (Con't)

o   5/13 of the setup hours in department 203 & 214   excluding NC machines

o   2/13 of the setup hours of NC machines

o   4/13 of the setup hours in department 201

o   2/13 of the setup hours in the automotive cylinder and robotics
    departments

Quality Control Department (250)

o   3/15 of the number of setups in departments 203 & 214

o   1/15 of the number of setups in the automotive department

o   7/15 of the number of all setups

o   20% of 2/15 based on the number of setups in the assembly department

o   80% of 2/15 based on the number of purchase orders received

o   30% of 2/15 based on COGS for automotive products

o   15% of 2/15 based on setups in department 203

o   15% of 2/15 based on setups in department 214

o   30% of 2/15 based on setups in department 201

o   10% of 2/15 based on COGS for manufactured and component's items

Manufacturing Engineering Department (260)

o   60% of 6/28 based on the number of parts purchased and produced

o   13.33% of 6/28 based on all direct labor in department 203

o   13.33% of 6/28 based on all direct labor in department 214

o   13.33% of 6/28 based on direct labor in all other departments

o   60% of 3/28 based on setups in departments 203 & 214

o   40% of 3/28 based on standard direct labor (does not include
    direct labor of support departments)

o   80% of 13/28 based on setups in departments 203 & 214

o   20% of 13/28 based on COGS for all departments

Exhibit TN-3 (Con't)

o   2/28 of the number of NC machine setups

o   37% of 4/28 based on COGS for automotive products

o   22% of 4/28 based on COGS for flow control products

o   6% of 4/28 based on COGS for couplers

o   35% of 4/28 based on COGS for all products

Exhibit TN-4   Seven Product Costs: Existing System

Sales Data and Standard Costs of Seven Flow Control Valves
(as Reported by the Existing Cost System)

Part Number	Sales Units	Sales Dollar	Material Costs	Direct Labor Costs	Overhead Cost	TOTAL COST	Total Gross Profit
10000	43,562	$581,988	$56,927	$48,077	$236,958	$341,962	$240,026
10200	500	6,250	707	588	3,073	4,368	1,882
10400	53	1,221	171	86	387	644	577
10600	2,079	38,545	6,654	3,231	18,457	28,333	10,212
10900	5,670	115,385	18,918	8,406	42,960	70,284	45,101
11200	11,196	151,482	17,809	12,391	59,836	90,036	61,446
11600	423	5,165	594	481	2,506	3,581	1,584
TOTALS	63,483	$900,036	$101,771	$73,260	$364,177	$539,208	$360,828

Total Product Cost

Unit Product Costs

Part Number	Unit Price	Material Costs	Direct Labor Costs	Overhead Cost	TOTAL COST	Profit per Unit
10000	$13.36	1.31	1.10	5.44	7.85	$ 5.51
10200	12.50	1.41	1.18	6.15	8.74	3.76
10400	23.04	3.23	1.62	7.30	12.15	10.89
10600	18.54	3.20	1.55	8.88	13.63	4.91
10900	20.35	3.34	1.48	7.58	12.40	7.95
11200	13.53	1.59	1.11	5.34	8.04	5.49
11600	12.21	1.40	1.14	5.92	8.47	3.74

Exhibit TN-5   Seven Product Costs: Activity-Based System

Reported Costs of Seven Flow Control Valves
(Strategic Cost Analysis)

| Part Number | Sales | | Total Product Cost | | | | Total Gross Profit |
	Units	Dollar	Material Costs	Direct Labor Costs	Overhead Cost	TOTAL COST	
10000	43,562	$581,988	$56,927	$48,077	$207,247	$312,251	$269,737
10200	500	6,250	707	588	6,428	7,723	(1,43)
10400	53	1,221	171	86	4,115	4,372	(3,151)
10600	2,079	38,545	6,645	3,231	41,072	50,947	(12,403)
10900	5,670	115,385	18,918	8,406	86,030	113,354	2,031
11200	11,196	151,482	17,809	12,391	58,937	89,137	62,345
11600	423	5,165	594	481	1,855	2,930	2,234
TOTALS	63,483	$900,036	$101,771	$73,260	$405,684	$580,714	$319,323

| Part Number | Unit Price | Unit Product Costs | | | | Gross Profit per Unit |
		Material Costs	Direct Labor Costs	Overhead Cost	TOTAL COST	
10000	$13.36	$1.31	$1.10	$4.76	$7.17	$ 6.19
10200	12.50	1.41	1.18	12.86	15.45	(2.95)
10400	23.04	3.23	1.62	77.64	82.49	(59.45)
10600	18.54	3.20	1.55	19.76	24.51	(5.97)
10900	20.35	3.34	1.48	15.17	19.99	0.36
11200	13.53	1.59	1.11	5.26	7.96	5.57
11600	12.21	1.40	1.14	4.39	6.93	5.28

Exhibit TN-6

Breakdown of Overhead Costs

Reported Costs of Seven Flow Control Valves
Breakdown of Overhead Costs
(Strategic Cost Analysis)

Total Costs

Part Number	Manufacturing Department Costs	Support Department Costs	Factory Costs	Total Overhead Cost
10000	$112,448	$ 64,768	$30,031	$207,247
10200	1,216	4,877	335	6,428
10400	263	3,517	335	4,115
10600	10,452	18,131	12,489	41,072
10900	28,454	21,329	36,247	86,030
11200	24,749	25,062	9,126	58,937
11600	750	806	299	1,855
TOTAL	$178,332	$138,490	$88,862	$405,684

Unit Costs

Part Number	Manufacturing Department Costs	Support Department Costs	Factory Costs	Unit Overhead Cost
10000	$2.58	$1.49	$0.69	4.76
10200	2.43	9.75	0.67	12.85
10400	4.97	66.37	6.32	77.66
10600	5.03	8.72	6.01	19.76
10900	5.02	3.76	6.39	15.17
11200	2.21	2.24	0.82	5.27
11600	1.77	1.91	0.71	4.39

Using Activity-Based Cost Systems
To Influence Behavior

The cases in Chapter 6 show how electronics companies have begun to implement activity-based costing to support their drive to become "world-class manufacturers." The cases illustrate companies' shift in manufacturing strategy to implement continuous improvement programs including total quality management, just-in-time and design-for-manufacturability. The companies find, however, that their efforts to improve manufacturing processes are inhibited by their traditional standard cost systems. The introduction of relatively simple ABC systems must be viewed in the context of supporting the new manufacturing strategies of these companies.

Tektronix: Portable Instruments Division (A) provides an excellent introduction to this chapter. The company, under threat from the Japanese, is completely changing its design and production processes. But the JIT and DFM initiatives are not being supported by the financial system, which still stresses efficiencies of direct labor, and extensive variance analysis and inventory vouchering. Tektronix (A) can be used for two important purposes. First, it shows how traditional systems requiring extensive bookkeeping and vouchering can be replaced (and, indeed, must be replaced) with far simpler systems if the company is successful in its JIT program. Second, it shows how an ABC system was designed explicitly to influence the behavior of design engineers. Unlike the cases in Chapter 5, Tektronix's system was designed not to capture accurately the economics of production but to influence the way engineers designed products; i.e., use more common parts. *Tektronix: PID (B)* extends the system described in the (A) case so that production overhead will be applied based on cycle time, rather than on direct labor hours. This innovation gives students a good opportunity to discuss the differences between a cycle time and a direct labor hour system, as well as the strengths and weaknesses of using cycle time to assign conversion expenses to products. A *Tektronix: PID (C)* case (#9-188-144) can be ordered from HBS Publishing. It contains a discussion with managers at Tektronix about implementation issues with the new systems.

Hewlett-Packard: Roseville Networks Division describes the evolution of one of the earliest ABC systems at Hewlett Packard. Some of the issues raised in the Tektronix case appear again in HP: RND, but this case also shows the dynamic evolution of the ABC system at Roseville. The case illustrates the interplay between an informal costing system, developed by engineers when they lost faith in the traditional financial system, and the ongoing design efforts for the new ABC system. Under close scrutiny, students may realize that the initial innovation at HP: RND was not that radical, since the new cost drivers used in the system were all unit-based. Only in later design stages were product-level drivers introduced.

Zytec (B) describes a situation where a company explicitly designed its cost system to enhance continuous improvement activities. The new system used drivers like cycle time and supplier lead time to highlight the importance of reducing total lead times to customers. The system eventually was rejected, however, because of the weak correlations between the selected cost drivers and the consumption of overhead resources.

Hewlett-Packard: Queensferry Telecommunications Division is a good concluding case for this sequence. The HP: QTD case describes a system very similar to that in the HP: RND case. Rather than focus on design issues, therefore, the QTD case focuses on implementation and use. The division, like other HP divisions, uses its cost-driver (ABC) system not only for product costing but also for performance measurement. Consequently large volume and spending variances occur each month that must be explained. Apart from trying to reconcile between the ABC resource consumption framework and the spending orientation of monthly performance reports, the case allows for an extensive discussion of incremental costing for special contracts.

The Foster-Horngren reading, "Cost Accounting and Cost Management in a JIT Environment," at the end of the chapter should be assigned with the Tektronix (A) case, particularly if the instructor wants to emphasize how cost systems change under JIT. The remaining articles at the end of the chapter cover two types of behavioral issues. Hiromoto's article, "Another Hidden Edge -- Japanese Management Accounting," describes how Japanese companies use cost systems to influence the behavior of managers, a theme that pervades the Tektronix, Hewlett-Packard, and Zytec cases. The Lammert- Ehrsam and the Shields-Young articles describe the organizational and behavioral issues that must be addressed if a new cost system is to be successfully introduced (these are issues that can arise when discussing implementation failures like Zytec). Some students (and even faculty) think that installing a new cost system just involves transferring new software to a computer. Our experience is that introducing a new way of measuring and costing requires a profound change in organizations; much defensive behavior and organizational resistance must be overcome. These two articles allow the organizational and people problems to surface in the class discussion.

In addition to the readings included in the book, several other articles descre the introduction of the new cost systems in technology-based companies. Instructors might wish to review these articles, either for their own class preparation or as additional supplementary readings for students. The relevant articles include:

R. Hunt, L. Garrett, and C. M. Merz, "Direct Labor Cost Not Always Relevant at HP," Management Accounting (February 1985).

James M. Patell, "Cost Accounting, Process Control, and Product Design: A Case Study of the Hewlett-Packard Personal Office Computer Division," The Accounting Review (October 1987), 808-839.

In R. S. Kaplan, (ed.), Measures for Manufacturing Excellence (HBS Press, 1990):

George Foster and Mahendra Gupta, "Activity Accounting: An Electronics Industry Implementation," Chapter 8, 225-268.

Robin Cooper and Peter B. B. Turney, "Internally Focused Activity-Based Cost Systems," Chapter 10, 269-290.

Debbie Berlant, Reese Browning, and George Foster, "How Hewlett-Packard Gets Numbers It Can Trust," Harvard Business Review (January-February 1990), 178-183 [this article describes the situation captured in the HP: RND case].

Tektronix: Portable Instruments Division (A) and (B)

Teaching Note

The Tektronix: Portable Instruments Division (PID) series describes the decisions a company faced when it evolved from its traditional batch manufacturing process to a just-in-time process. Its traditional cost accounting system would have been costly, inaccurate, and dysfunctional in the new production environment. In addition, the series introduces students to the use of activity-based systems to modify the behavior of product engineers. The PID (A) case explores the use of "number of part numbers" as a cost driver and the (B) case "cycle time". A video of the Tektronix production process can be ordered.

The objectives of this case are to teach the students to:

1) be aware of the degree of simplification of cost system design that can be achieved in a JIT environment.

2) consider the relationship between strategy and cost system design.

3) think about the behavioral consequences of the choice of cost driver in an activity-based cost system.

4) Consider whether a cost system is an appropriate vehicle for motivating behavioral change.

The Foster-Horngren article, "Cost Accounting and Cost Management in a JIT Environment," in this chapter (pp. 433-444) would be an excellent reading to assign along with the (A) case. Other relevant articles include:

Hunt, Rick, Linda Garrett and C. Mike Merz, "Direct Labor Cost Not Always Relevant at H-P," Management Accounting (February 1985), pp. 58-62.

This teaching note was prepared by Professor Robin Cooper and Professor Robert S. Kaplan as an aid to instructors using the Tektronix: Portable Instruments Division (A-C) cases (188-142/3/4).

Exhibit TN-6

Breakdown of Overhead Costs

Reported Costs of Seven Flow Control Valves
Breakdown of Overhead Costs
(Strategic Cost Analysis)

Total Costs

Part Number	Manufacturing Department Costs	Support Department Costs	Factory Costs	Total Overhead Cost
10000	$112,448	$ 64,768	$30,031	$207,247
10200	1,216	4,877	335	6,428
10400	263	3,517	335	4,115
10600	10,452	18,131	12,489	41,072
10900	28,454	21,329	36,247	86,030
11200	24,749	25,062	9,126	58,937
11600	750	806	299	1,855
TOTAL	$178,332	$138,490	$88,862	$405,684

Unit Costs

Part Number	Manufacturing Department Costs	Support Department Costs	Factory Costs	Unit Overhead Cost
10000	$2.58	$1.49	$0.69	4.76
10200	2.43	9.75	0.67	12.85
10400	4.97	66.37	6.32	77.66
10600	5.03	8.72	6.01	19.76
10900	5.02	3.76	6.39	15.17
11200	2.21	2.24	0.82	5.27
11600	1.77	1.91	0.71	4.39

Jonez, John and Michael A. Wright, "Material Burdening: Management Accounting <u>Can</u> Support Competitive Strategy," <u>Management Accounting</u> (August 1987), pp. 27-31. (This article specifically describes the Tektronix system presented in the case.)

The instructor might find it valuable to read:

Cooper, Robin and Peter Turney, "Using Activity-based Cost Systems to Modify Behavior," in Robert S. Kaplan, ed. <u>Measuring Manufacturing Performance</u> (Boston: HBS Press, 1990).

This teaching note outlines two 80 minute teaching plans.

Suggested Assignments:

Day 1

1. Identify the limitations of the direct labor cost system in PID's new JIT production environment.

2. What changes would enable PID to reduce the number of monthly labor transactions from 35,000 to less than 100?

3. Consider two products P and Q. Each uses two types of raw materials. Product P uses one unit of material A and one unit of B. Product Q uses two units of B and one unit of C (see below):

	P	Q
Annual Volume	1,000 units	2,000 units
Number of Batches	10	10
Materials $ per unit	$ 50	$ 150
Bill of Materials	1 A	2 B
	1 B	1 C

Annual Materials Overhead equals $30,000.

Calculate the materials overhead assigned to products P and Q using:

- Materials Dollar Burdening
- Number of Parts Burdening
- Number of Part Numbers Burdening

4. Given the impact of part number burdening on reported product costs, would you recommend staying with the existing system, adopting the part number system, or designing a multi-driver system along the lines of Schrader Bellows and John Deere Component Works?

Day 2

1. Evaluate the cycle time burdening system proposed by PID. What are its strengths and weaknesses?

2. Determine the impact of cycle time burdening on reported product costs.

3. Given the impact of cycle time burdening on reported product costs, would you recommend adopting the cycle time system?

Class Discussion

Day 1

Q1.   Describe the Competitive Environment faced by PID prior to the entry of the Japanese.

Until the early 1980s, Tektronix Portable Instruments Division (PID) was the high-quality, high-price leader in its field. The company had the most advanced designs and features, and offered its product at premium prices. Competitors would study newly issued PID products, break them down, reverse engineer them, and eventually produce similar products, offered at significantly lower prices. But by the time the clone products came to market, PID would have already designed and delivered the next generation of products. Thus, PID's strategy was driven by engineering excellence.

Q2.   What is the culture at PID and which function dominates?

In Tektronix, the primacy of design engineers created a culture where each product was designed almost entirely from new components. The culture emphasized continual new designs, and discouraged use of components or sub-assemblies used in older instruments; e.g., "Real engineers design from the ground up." This design philosophy eventually led to very high material support expenses to purchase, stock and keep track of all the different items used in the existing product line.

Q3.   Does the firm's strategy make sense?

The engineering dominated culture was a direct outcome of the firm's strategy of being the leader in state-of-the-art functionality at a premium price. This strategy was extremely successful for a number of years. The firm developed a strong reputation and an engineering expertise second to none in the industry. Unfortunately, the strategy had its achilles heel which the Japanese found and exploited. They could manufacture, or at a minimum were willing to sell, their products at a substantial discount to PID's. Their new products also contained almost the same functionality as PID's latest products. The large price discount and excellent product performance was sufficient to overcome the functional advantages of the latest PID designs. PID's customers despite years of loyalty switched in alarming numbers to the Japanese products.

Q4.   How did the firm react to the new competitive environment?

PID made a major commitment to adopting Japanese manufacturing innovations (Just-in-Time (JIT), Total Quality Control (TQC), and People Involvement (PI)). These efforts, combined with the increasing automation of electronics assembly processes (through automated insertion technology, among others) led to direct labor becoming an extremely small fraction of total manufacturing costs (less than 5%; see opening quotation of the case).

Q5.   What was identified as the final barrier to becoming cost competitive with the Japanese?

The old strategy of designing from the ground up created a barrier for PID to becoming fully competitive with the Japanese. The cost to manage and source the very large number of distinct components that PID's products contained was significant. Management believed that to become more competitive, the number of distinct components used in products had to be reduced. The cost system was to be a mechanism to achieve this objective.

Q6.   Describe the existing cost system.

The Portable Instruments Plant had more than 100 cost centers, including about 25 production cost centers. The 2400 line was produced in seven of these production cost centers. The existing system allocated overhead based on direct labor hours, with a separate rate calculated for each manufacturing cost center. Determining the burden rates required calculating frozen standard hours (FSH) and current standard hours (CSH) for each product in each production cost center. Per unit FSH was the average of the actual number of direct labor hours consumed by a product over a period of a week or more. It was calculated once a year at the end of the fiscal year, and was set equal to the most recent CSH at that time. CSH was updated frequently, often weekly, to reflect reported labor efficiencies.

Production cost center overhead consisted of direct and indirect costs. Direct costs were incurred within or were directly traceable to the cost center. Indirect manufacturing costs were allocated among the cost centers using budgeted FSH.

The system costed products by determining the cost of a single FSH hour in each production cost center. This was calculated by dividing a quarter's actual direct and indirect overhead in the cost center by the total number of FSH earned in that center during the previous quarter. Earned FSH was calculated by summing the number of products manufactured multiplied by each product's FSH per unit. The rate was updated each quarter.

The CSH system was designed to report on the efficiency of the direct labor force. The highly detailed labor efficiency reports were prepared on a daily and monthly basis. Efficiency was measured at the cost center level, for each major step in the production process, and for each individual employee.

Three types of efficiency variance were calculated at the cost center level each month: the method change variance, the volume variance, and the efficiency variance. The method change variance reflected the over- or under- absorption of labor and overhead resulting from changes in the production process (standard labor and overhead rate multiplied by the difference between the center's frozen earned standard hours and the current earned standard hours). The volume variance reflected over- or under- absorption of labor and overhead resulting from differences between planned and actual production (standard labor and overhead rate multiplied by the difference between planned and actual FSH). The efficiency variance measured the over- or under- absorbed labor and overhead resulting from differences between current standard hours and the actual hours paid (standard labor and overhead rate multiplied by the difference between CSH and the actual hours paid). These three variances were calculated for each of the seven cost centers, generating 21 different variances per month. Efficiency variances were not broken down by product.

An efficiency rating was calculated for each major step in the production process. Efficiency was calculated for a large number of operations including sequencing, IC insertion, axial component insertion, and radial component insertion in the machine insertion department and hand insertion, flow soldering, additional hand insertion, testing (several tests were separately measured), assembly (several steps were separately measured), burn in, and final testing.

In addition to these functional efficiency measures, the cost system also reported on the efficiency of each individual employee daily. In departments where the operations were of short duration, such as in hand insertion, employees could make over 50 entries a day, often requiring about 20 minutes a day to complete the reports. Most employees chose to complete these reports at the end of the day rather than on an on-going basis.

Each employee was expected to fill in the quantity produced and the amount of time required to produce it. These data were then used to compute an efficiency measure that formed the basis for the employee's performance evaluation. While these production numbers were policed, employees tended to overestimate the number produced. These optimistic estimates could snowball, because to show improved efficiency against a standard that was updated weekly, an employee would have to report even higher output to compensate for the overestimation in the previous reports.

The structure of the existing system is illustrated in Figure TN-1.

Q7.   What is wrong with the existing system for assigning overhead costs to products?

The decision to use a separate overhead pool for material support expenses (purchasing, scheduling deliveries, receiving, inspection, paying, handling) has become common. Without a separate pool, material support expenses would be included in the conversion overhead rate (applied by direct labor or machine hours), making internal fabrication of parts, sub-assemblies, and products appear very expensive. Should the company decide to out-source some of these labor or machine-intense products, labor and machine hours will drop, materials support expenses will increase, and the burden rate on labor or machine hours will grow even higher, further penalizing in-house production. In addition, the direct labor hour system does not penalize products that contain a large number of unique low volume components. The failure of traditional systems to reward common components was illustrated in the Schrader Bellows case series in Chapter 5.

The quantity of data collected and its poor quality produced many problems. Employees complained about the amount of reporting they had to undertake and the first line managers grumbled about the amount they had to review. The inventory group was unhappy about the accuracy of the records and the impact the optimistic reporting had on inventory valuation. In particular, they cited the shop floor misreporting output as the major cause of the semi-annual write downs that were required when the physical-to-book comparisons were made. Accountants and line managers had similar complaints because they were expected to reconcile the reported hours to paid hours and these rarely agreed. The accounting staff was displeased about the burden of correcting the numerous errors, as well as having to process over 35,000 labor transactions and 25,000 inventory transactions per month. About 18 months were needed to train a new individual to use the system; moreover, it was not clear that anyone fully understood it.

Instructors may wish to follow the following detour that uses the existing cost system at PID to show how traditional cost systems fail in a modern manufacturing JIT environment.

QD1:   Why were 25,000 inventory transactions occurring each month?

The situation described in the case provides a perfect opportunity to discuss the failings of traditional cost systems in a modern manufacturing environment. The instructor can pull in information from the Foster-Horngren reading, from chapters 8 and 9 of Relevance Lost, or from the early chapters of Kaplan, Measures for Manufacturing Excellence. Vouchering inventory at each value-added stage of the production process may have made sense when WIP was large: long delays occurred between successive production stages, and the company wanted a perpetual inventory system so that WIP would be correctly valued no matter when an end of an accounting period might strike. In a JIT environment, where materials flow continually through the production process, there is really no need to account for WIP. First the materials do not stop long enough to make any vouchering system accurate. But, more importantly, there is no need to value WIP when it becomes a small fraction of the throughput of the facility each period. This would be a good time for instructors to describe the two-vouchering point backflushing system that companies implementing JIT processes have introduced (see Foster-Horngren paper, plus others written by Hewlett Packard and Tektronix managers). The backflushing technique applies all labor and overhead (with the two categories perhaps lumped together as "conversion costs") to finished goods production each month. This keeps raw materials purchased in a separate account (RIP - raw and in-process) until a unit is completed, at which time the standard materials cost for a finished good is "backflushed" out of the RIP account. This simplified procedure works well when WIP is minimal, and when no losses due to bad quality, rework and scrap occur. In a traditional production environment, such a simple procedure usually leads to large negative year end variances.

QD2. OK, I think I understand how to stop all the inventory recording transactions that used to occur. How do I deal with the 35,000 labor transactions occurring each month as well?

Again, the demand for excessive measurement of direct labor is an anachronism from production processes earlier in this century. Not only is direct labor efficiency not very important for reducing production costs, the measurements themselves may encourage dysfunctional behavior and sabotage the effort to implement total quality management and just-in-time production processes. By measuring efficiencies at each direct labor station and each machine cell, workers are encouraged to keep busy and produce inventory. Unless the work station is a bottleneck, however, producing more output does not increase throughput; it just produces more inventory. And the excess production of inventory requires more handling and storage and introduces more delay in production processes. It also provides incentives for workers to overlook marginal or off-spec materials and production, and to pass them through to the next stage so that they can show good utilization reports.

The shop floor discipline and the reduction in work-in-process inventory levels associated with JIT production allows direct labor vouchering procedures to be discontinued. The focus of a JIT production process is not to keep the labor work force busy, the focus of the old labor recording system, but to keep the products flowing smoothly on demand. It is not unusual for labor efficiency, as reported by a traditional system to decrease, while output increases. Keeping labor busy ceases to be the objective of a JIT system because production is driven by demand pull. The rate of production at each cell has to be such that the next cell in the process is not kept waiting. If a cell is kept waiting it becomes a highly visible event that is subject to scrutiny. Thus, generating pressure on the workforce to maintain local efficiency measures will undermine the JIT discipline.

In a JIT setting, operators have only limited storage available for inputs to their production process and for the outputs from their production process. If either their input buffer is empty or their output buffer is full, then they should stop work immediately. A problem has occurred either earlier in the production process that has halted throughput to their work station or subsequently which has caused the output previously produced to be processed by the next stage. The JIT discipline has the worker, with either an empty input buffer or a full output buffer, finding where the problem has arisen and helping to be part of the solution. But following this discipline will lower the reported efficiency of the worker and unless this measurement has been terminated, the worker will find ways to keep busy (with a private supply of input materials, or special places to stash output until the output buffer becomes depleted) without solving the problem that has halted factory throughput. If the plant can identify the bottleneck resources, then it can put efficiency measures on those resources; otherwise, efficiency should be measured as the quantity of completed good items (throughput) from the entire production process, and not from individual stations.

The other traditional cost accounting measure that must be terminated is the volume variance. Rewarding production managers for favorable volume variances (perhaps producing in longer runs and in greater quantity than demanded or planned) encourages inventory buildups and long cycle times. Conversely, penalizing managers, with an unfavorable volume variance, for producing just what was needed, when it was needed, will undermine the JIT discipline just as surely as encouraging workers to optimize their individual labor efficiency variances.

QD3.   Suppose I stop measuring labor and machine efficiencies, and volume variances. Are there better measurements that I should be looking at daily, weekly, or monthly?

The TQM and JIT performance measures that companies like Tektronix are using instead of traditional cost accounting measures include measures of:

- Total cycle time
- Ratio of Process Time to Actual Cycle Time
- First pass yields (% of items that make it through the production process with no rework performed)
- On time delivery percentages
- Part per million (PPM) defect rates
- Linearity (uniformity of rate of completed production)
- Inventory turns
- Total spending for each JIT production line
- Total daily (or weekly) output of completed production, by JIT line

Some of these measures will have been discussed in the Analog Devices case (in Chapter 4). Instructors should finish this segment by getting students to realize that just as JIT simplifies the production environment, JIT should also simplify the accounting environment. Companies, such as Tektronix and Hewlett Packard, have been able to reduce the number of monthly accounting transactions from more than 100,000 to only several hundred. Also, the performance measures should be derived from today's production processes, not from the cost accounting for factories of 80 years ago.

Instructors, having covered changes in the financial reporting and operational control systems, can now make a transition back to the proposed materials burdening system that will provide better information for product designers.

Q8.   What cost drivers were considered for assigning materials support expenses to products?

The designers explored three potential cost drivers for the materials burden cost pool: material dollars, number of parts, and number of part numbers. These three methods can be illustrated with a simple numerical example. Consider two products P and Q that each uses two types of raw materials. Product P uses one unit of material A and one unit of B. Product Q uses two units of B and one unit of C (see below):

	P	Q
Annual Volume	1,000 units	2,000 units
Number of Batches	10	10
Materials $ per unit	$ 50	$ 150
Bill of Materials	1 A	2 B
	1 B	1 C

Annual Materials Overhead equals $30,000.

Cost Driver 1: % Markup on Materials Dollars

$$\text{Percentage Markup} = \frac{\text{Materials Overhead}}{\text{Total Material Dollars}}$$

$$= \frac{\$30,000}{[1,000 * \$50 + 2,000 * \$150]}$$

$$= 8.57\%$$

Product P gets a materials overhead charge of $50 * 8.57% = $4.28 per unit and Q gets a charge of $150 * 8.57% = $12.86 per unit. Product Q gets three times the materials overhead charge because its materials cost three times as much. The total material burden costs assigned to P and Q are $4,280 and $25,720 respectively.

Method 2: Materials Overhead based on number of parts

$$\text{Overhead cost per unit part} = \frac{30,000}{[1,000 * 2 + 2,000 * 3]}$$

$$= \$3.75 \text{ per part.}$$

Product P gets a charge of 2*3.75 = $7.50 per unit; Product Q gets a materials overhead charge of 3*3.75 = $11.25 per unit. Product Q gets a 50% higher charge because it has 50% more parts than P. In total, P gets assigned $7,500 and Q $22,500.

Method 3: Materials Overhead based on number of different parts

$$\text{Compute cost per unique product part} = \frac{30,000}{3}$$

$$= \$10,000 \text{ per unique product part.}$$

Compute unit cost for each unique part:

A: $[10,000/(1,000*1)]$ = $10 per unit of A used

B: $[10,000/(1,000*1+2,000*2)]$ = $2 per unit of B used

C: $[10,000/(2,000*2)]$ = $5 per unit of C used.

Product P gets a materials overhead charge of $10 + $2 = $12 per unit, and Q gets a charge of 2*$2+$5 = $9 per unit. Product P is more expensive since it uses the low volume component A, while Q is less expensive since it makes greater use of a high-volume component, B. The assignment of costs to products P and Q for component B is necessarily an allocation not an attribution. As before, dropping only one of the two products will not decrease the materials support resources for component B. That requires dropping both products.

Under all approaches, the total materials overhead cost of $30,000 will be absorbed by the expected production of products P and Q. But the charges to the individual products is quite different under the various approaches.

Q9. What changes to the existing system were proposed? .

The firm chose to drive materials support expenses to products using the assignment base: number of part numbers. The structure of the new system is illustrated in Figure TN-2.

Getting to this point usually requires all 80 minutes. I then direct the students to identify how the product designers behavior would change under each of the different approaches as part of their next day's preparation.

Day 2

Q1. What behavior would be induced by the three methods of assigning material burden to products?

The types of behavior identified for each approach include:

Material $

The primary objective of the designers will be to reduce the material dollar content of the products. The cost system reports product costs as the sum of direct labor, direct material, direct labor overhead, and material dollar overhead. Product designs that decrease material dollar content but increase labor content will have lower reported product costs only if the sum of the reduced direct material and its associated material overhead is less than the direct labor increase plus its associated overhead. For designs that reduce material content but increase overhead, the decision rule is more complex. First, the material reduction will show immediately while the overhead increase will only be reflected when the burden rates are recalculated. Second, if the increase in overhead, either labor or material based, is greater than the reduction in material costs, the burden rates will increase but this increase will be smeared over all products. Therefore, the designer will only see a fraction of the total increase in overhead, and the designer has little incentive to appropriately trade-off material cost for overhead.

With this approach, each dollar of materials acquisition spending absorbs the same percentage of overhead costs. Therefore, small but expensive parts will have much higher materials overhead applied than bulky, infrequently ordered but inexpensive raw materials. The designers will be encouraged to avoid expensive parts and try and replace them with less expensive parts even if there are more of them. Thus, this system will tend to encourage the number of parts in each product to increase and the number of part numbers overall to increase.

The latest technology will often be more expensive than older technology. Therefore, this approach will tend to create a barrier against the introduction of new technology. In addition, with integrated circuits, the number of components tends to decrease therefore, the number of parts in each product will not decrease as fast as it might have.

Subassemblies produced externally will be viewed as all material, while if they were produced internally then would be viewed as a mixture of material, labor, and overhead. Therefore, this approach will tend to favor insourcing subassemblies. Note, the old direct labor system encouraged outsourcing of subassemblies. Thus, the cheapest apparent way to source subassemblies is dependent, in part, upon the direct material to direct labor ratio of the subassemblies.

Cheaper components will be favored. This risks decreasing the quality of the final products, increasing the level of inspections, and failure rates, both internal and external. It will also tend to increase the number of vendors, as the designers identify components by vendor instead of just by characteristics. Alternatively, another way to reduce component costs is to buy in bulk. If designers take this route, they will shift towards common components and single vendors. Reducing the number of vendors will probably increase quality control and hence reduce the required level of inspection and failures. Thus, the exact outcome of shifting to cheaper materials is not obvious. The way the designers choose to reduce material costs will define whether the overall product quality increases or decreases.

Reducing product functionality will also reduce material content. The systems will therefore factor simpler products. The designers might achieve these "savings" by increasing the number of different products offered. The cost system will report that each product costs less, but overall overhead will increase as the product mix becomes more complex.

Number of Parts

The primary objective of the designers will be to reduce the number of parts in their designs. The cost system reports product costs as the sum of direct labor, direct material, direct labor overhead, and material dollar overhead. Product designs that decrease the number of parts but increase material and/ or labor content will have lower reported product costs only if the reduced material overhead is greater than the sum of the increased direct material and direct labor plus its associated overhead. Typically this will be unlikely. Therefore, most of the behavior observed will be to reduce the number of parts by increasing overhead. Again, the decision rules for when a design change looks beneficial will be difficult to gauge and it is unlikely that the incentives on the designers to make trade-offs is optimal.

With this approach, each part absorbs the same percentage of overhead costs. Therefore, small but expensive parts will have the same materials overhead applied as bulky, infrequently ordered but inexpensive raw materials. The designers will have no incentive to consider the size, frequency of ordering, or volume of usage of components. Thus, this system will tend to encourage the number of parts in each product to decrease but the total number of part numbers to increase.

One obvious way to reduce the number of parts in a product is to outsource subassemblies, the part count for a subassembly being one. Therefore, this system will tend to encourage the designing products that have a modular construction and where the modules can be outsourced. Thus, this system will re-enforce the outsourcing pressure created by the direct labor portion of the system. In the limit, the entire product can be outsourced reducing the parts count to one.

The number of parts can also be reduced by using more complex components that replace numerous simpler components. This trend might increase material costs requiring a trade-off that will depend upon the relative costs and the burden rates. In general, each designer will tend to use complex components to reduce part count but unfortunately, the ability to share these components across designs will be limited. Thus, this system will tend to increase the number of low volume parts as well as the total number of part numbers.

Another way to reduce component count is to reduce the functionality of new products. This reduction will tend to increase the number of different products required to satisfy customer demands. This trend will increase both the number of low volume products and hence parts and the total number of part numbers.

Number of Part Numbers

The number of parts numbers is different from the other two drivers because it operates at the component not the product level. Therefore, it creates pressure for behavioral changes at the component as well as at the product level. This pressure will be to utilize as many common components as possible. To achieve this objective, the designers will have to talk to each other in order to design circuits that can take advantage of common components.

The switch to common components will tend to reduce the number of part numbers used in future products. Thus, this driver is the only one that achieves the primary objective of the new strategy. This explains why it was chosen by the cost system design team.

The focus on common components risks creating a barrier to the introduction of new technology. The first product that used a new component would bear a high cost until other products that used that component were developed. The system thus generates a pressure against innovation. Some companies have mitigated this effect by having design engineers meet periodically to discuss which components should be included on a "preferred parts list" encouraging designers to use preferred parts in multiple product designs.

The quality of the products would probably increase because of the reduction in the number of vendors associated with a shift to common components. The firm would have an increased ability to ensure that only very high quality components were received.

The number of parts in each product would probably increase. In order to use common components, the product engineers might use several units of a high volume component versus one low volume one (for example, using two 1K resistors and one 0.5K resistor in series rather than a single 2.5K resistor).

The range of functionality across the product lines might decrease as the use of common components and circuits increased. This might not be beneficial to the success of the firm as the existing strategy depends upon high product functionality.

Q2. How does the activity level of the driver effect the behavioral consequences?

This is a complicated question to answer. Changing the level of the driver does not change the focus of the cost reduction activity but it does alter the way the designers think about volume. Both batch and product level report reduced **unit** product costs as the volume of production increases. As such these approaches foster communication among designers.

Q3. Does a single driver capture all the activities related to material? Identify activities captured by methods and levels.

The answer is no. The materials burden cost pool contains the costs of many different activities. Each of the three drivers at each level captures the behavior of different types of activities. For example:

Driver	Level	Activity
Material Dollars	Unit	incoming freight
Material Dollars	Batch	receiving inspection
Material Dollars	Product	no idea
Number of Parts	Unit	inspection of every part
Number of Parts	Batch	first part inspection
Number of Parts	Product	maintaining bill of material
Number of Part Numbers	Batch	first part inspection
Number of Part Numbers	Product	vendor certification

At least one of the driver-level combinations does not have easily identifiable activities associated with it and for some of the others, the relationships are tenuous. However, it is clear that no one driver can accurately capture the cost behavior associated with materials burden.

Q4. Why choose only one driver?

There are at least two possibilities. First, the distortion introduced into reported product costs is small (the computations of product costs for the five oscilloscopes will test this possibility) therefore, the costs of additional drivers outweigh the benefits. Second, the behavioral consequences of focusing attention on only one driver as opposed to two or more are so positive that any costs associated with lost accuracy are irrelevant. It is extremely difficult to estimate the behavioral benefits associated with a particular system design. The Hewlett Packard: Roseville Networks Division case provides an alternative perspective on the behavioral trade off.

Q5. What is the risk of using only one driver for materials overhead?

There are at least three risks. One is the system will fail to capture the underlying economics. If this failure becomes apparent to the designers, they might lose confidence in the system and start ignoring it. Second, the reported product costs will be too distorted. Third, the behavior induced will be based on the assumption that the cost per unit of the driver is higher than actual. The behavior induced will therefore not be optimal. The designers will reduce the chosen driver quantity more than appropriate.

Q6. Which of the three choices best reinforces the new strategy?

The answer is clearly the one they chose, the number of part numbers. PID managers opted for this approach because they were greatly concerned with the enormous proliferation of part numbers that had occurred and wanted to get the immediate attention of product designers to stop this proliferation unless necessary for the functionality of the new instrument. It is important to note that this decision was not made because managers felt that all material overhead costs were **caused** by the number of different parts in the system. The managers knew that total material overhead costs did not vary solely with the number of different part numbers. But they wanted to modify the design behavior of product engineers and they used the cost system to affect this behavior. This choice is quite different from the cost system design used in

John Deere (A), where the analyst attempted to design an accurate system, with the strategy for product mix, pricing, and process improvements to be determined after the system had been designed. At Tek, the managers already knew what strategy (or behavior) they wanted to achieve (simpler designs with more common parts). They used the cost system to motivate the strategy or behavior already decided upon.

Q7. What will happen over time to the effectiveness of this system?

When such a behavioral approach is used, the system will likely have to be modified within a couple of years. After driving the desired behavior for a while, designers may overshoot by resisting use of newly developed technology and not building enough functionality into new products, which remains Tek's competitive advantage in the marketplace. Also, belief in the cost system will deteriorate as engineers notice that large reductions in number of part numbers may not be matched by proportional reductions in material overhead costs. At that time, cost system designers attempting to develop a more accurate cost system will likely have to add new drivers for materials overhead costs or perhaps switch to a different driver entirely. The company risks totally confusing its most critical resource - product design engineers - by such actions.

Q8. Does changing drivers every few years or adding new ones make sense?

This is an interesting question. Clearly, changing drivers will draw attention to the new drivers. However, there are risks. First, the optimum point to change drivers might be hard to detect. Changing too early or too late may be very damaging. Using multiple drivers avoids this timing problem. Second, if the individual responsible for the cost system moves on, then the change process might be forgotten. Third, the behavior induced by the first driver might be reversed by the new driver. Fourth, unless the motivation for the change can be defended, the change may be poorly received. Finally, if reported product costs change too dramatically, managers will lose faith in them. This will be especially true if a "success" product gets turned into a "failure" product or vice versa. Again, the decision to stick with one or more drivers or change them periodically requires a complex cost benefit trade off.

Q9. Why shift to cycle time?

The discussion on cycle time can follow a similar approach to the one on number of part numbers. Direct labor was still being used to allocate the overhead that remained after removing materials-related overhead. Thus, conversion costs were still being applied to product based on their direct labor content. With direct labor no longer representing an important part of total manufacturing costs, cost system designers searched for other bases for applying conversion costs to products. Machine time would be possible but runs the risk of encouraging engineers to speed up individual machines, or reduce the time a product has to spend on an individual machine, neither of which may reduce the total production time if queues or bottlenecks occur at other stages of the production process. In a well-functioning JIT environment, work is evenly paced through a JIT line. The process can be speeded up not by reducing the time spent at any individual station but by increasing the total throughput of the line. The cycle time basis for assigning conversion costs to products encourages product and process improvements to reduce the total time, from raw material release (or order) to shipment to customer. The JIT cell has been configured to supply hours of processing time (i.e., the basic activity is providing hours of processing time in the cell); products will be costed based on the amount of time they spend within the cell. Since no inventory buildup is possible, any production delays within the cell halt the production of all other products.

Q10. What is the structure of new system?

The cost system has now been completely simplified. It contains two cost pools one relating to cycle time the other to material. The costs are assigned to the products using two drivers, cycle time (at the unit level), and number of part numbers (at the product level). The new system is illustrated in Figure TN-3.

Q11. Is cycle time a good driver?

Cycle time measurement could be expensive, as a new measurement must be made for the calculation. The measurement cost could be minimal, however, if the production line is already under computer control, or if the job release and job completion is triggered by a computerized production control system such as MRP. Also, uniform bar coding of products and remote sensors can collect such data easily and inexpensively. A second concern arises from the erratic cycle time measurements from batch to batch. Instructors should be able to sustain a lively discussion as students speculate about the advantages and disadvantages of using direct labor time, individual machine time, or cycle time for assigning conversion costs to products. Attempt to have students present the behavioral influences from using any method they propose or critique.

If the products being processed by a JIT line are not very different from each other, then applying the conversion cost on a unit produced basis will be accurate and simple (IBM is using this approach with its focused JIT manufacturing cells). Variations in product complexity can be handled by computing a complexity index for different products; that is, a product requiring about 20% more attention or effort would be assigned a complexity value of 120 and receive 20% more conversion costs per unit than the standard product (whose complexity index is 100). Another possibility is to compute the Material Dollar Days for each product. For each material ordered, compute the unit price and the number of days the material is in the plant until it is shipped to a customer inside a finished product. Compute the total number of Material Dollar Days in a year (comparable to calculating the total number of cycle units) and assign overhead costs to products based on the material dollar days of parts contained in the product. This calculation combines both aspects of cycle time reduction as well as materials costs. It emphasizes the essential message of JIT production: individual labor and machine efficiencies are not nearly as important as materials efficiencies. The goal is to keep materials moving once they arrive at the factory.

Q12. Compute product costs under each system.

The case provides students with the reported product costs under the number of part number system. To determine the reported costs under the original labor hour approach requires adding the material overhead pool back into the labor overhead pool. With the data in the case, there are only two ways that this can be achieved. First, by assuming that the material overhead was originally assigned to the products in the same ratio as the remaining labor overhead or second, by assuming that it was assigned on the basis of direct labor dollars (dollars instead of hours have to be used because hours are not reported in the case. This substitution will usually introduce negligible distortion).

The calculation of reported product costs under these two scenarios is relatively simple. Under the first assumption, the sum of the total material burden of $1,640k and the total LOH of $2,529.5k is divided by the total LOH of $2,529.5k to give the LOH multiplier of 1.648. Multiplying this factor by the individual LOH figures for each product gives:

	A	B	C	D	E
MOH	$150	$160	$320	$ 650	$700
LOH	$300	$360	$250	$ 500	$540
SUM	$450	$520	$570	$1150	$1240
ADJ LOH	$494	$593	$412	$ 824	$890
DIFFERENCE	$ 44	$ 73	($158)	($ 326)	($ 350)
% TOTAL COST	1.5%	2.1%	(3.4%)	(5.4%)	(5.6%)

Under the second scenario, the total MOH of $1,640K is divided by the total LABOR cost of $2,039k to give the LABOR factor of 0.804. This when multiplied by the labor cost of each product gives the additional LOH:

	A	B	C	D	E
LABOR	$250	$260	$320	$380	$390
ADJ LOH	$201	$209	$257	$305	$314
MOH	$150	$160	$320	$650	$700
DIFFERENCE	$ 51	$ 49	($ 63)	($345)	($386)
% TOTAL COST	1.8%	1.4%	(1.4%)	(5.7%)	(6.1%)

The difference between the two solutions is effectively irrelevant. The small shifts in reported product costs (from 1.8% to (6.1%)) are probably also irrelevant.

The product costs reported by the cycle time system can be determined by dividing the sum of the total LABOR of $2,039K and LOH of $2,529.5K by the total number of cycle time hours of 786.5k to give a burden rate of $5.81 per cycle time hour. The total number of cycle time hours is determined by multiplying the volume of each product by its average cycle time hours. This gives:

Product	Cycle Time Hours	Units	Total Hours
A	100	3,000	300,000
B	105	3,000	315,000
C	110	750	82,500
D	125	400	50,000
E	130	300	39,000
Total			786,500

Using the $5.81 rate gives reported cycle time costs for the five products of:

	A	B	C	D	E
LABOR	$250	$260	$320	$380	$390
LOH	$300	$360	$250	$500	$540
Total	$550	$720	$570	$880	$930
Cycle Hrs	100	105	110	125	130
Cycle Cost	$581	$610	$639	$726	$755
Difference	$ 31	($110)	$ 69	($154)	($175)
% TOTAL COST	1.1%	(3.2%)	1.5%	(2.5%)	(2.8%)

Again, the changes are relatively small and may be insignificant.

Q13. If it doesn't make a difference why bother?

The only motivation can be the behavioral consequence: the choice of driver effecting the way the engineers think about the economics of product design.

Q14. Is cost system a good vehicle for behavioral modification?

This is a difficult question which the students are probably not ready to answer. The rest of the cases in the module will help students decide. An open ended discussion is appropriate at this time.

Q15. Can you avoid the behavioral consequences?

This question is designed to ensure that students that answer no to the question above realize that if the choice of cost driver does induce behavioral change, then behavioral issues are unavoidable and must be taken into account when designing cost systems and in particular, when selecting cost drivers.

Tektronix: Portable Instruments Division

Teaching Note

Figure 1

The Direct Labor Burdening System

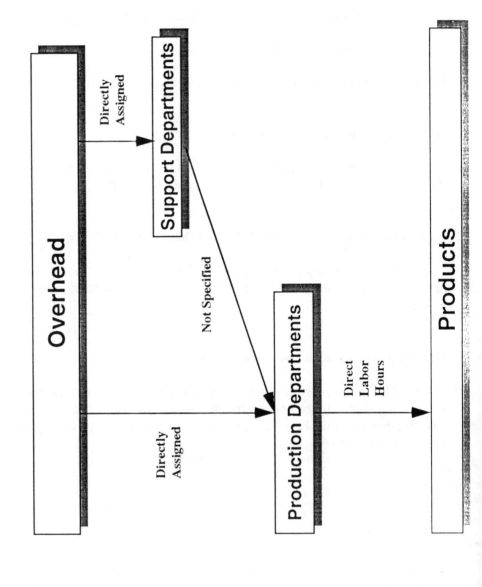

Tektronix: Portable Instruments Division
Teaching Note
Figure 2
The Labor Hour and Material Burdening System

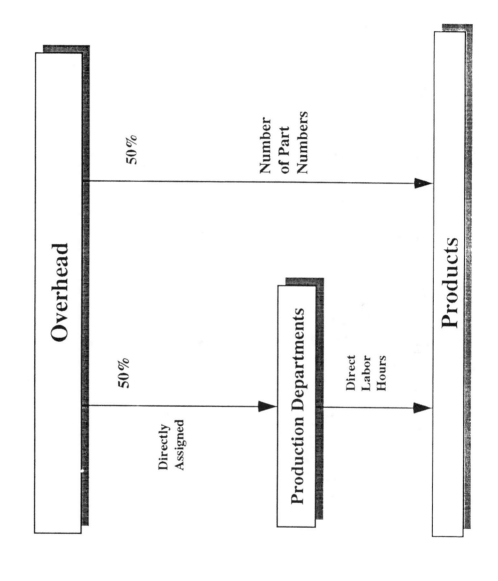

Tektronix: Portable Instruments Division
Teaching Note
Figure 3
The Cycle time and Material Burdening System

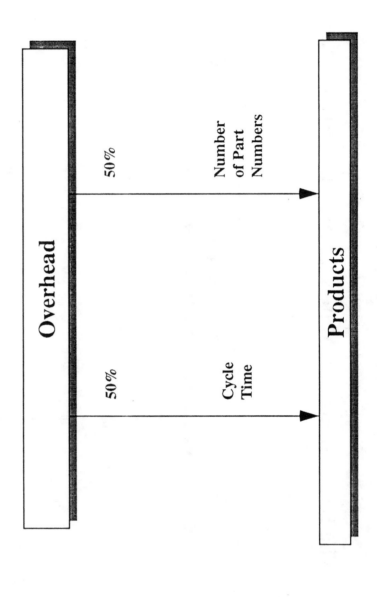

Hewlett Packard: Roseville Networks Division

Teaching Note

The Roseville Networks Division (RND) case illustrates the following issues:

1. The design of cost systems to influence the behavior of product engineers,

2. An incremental implementation of a cost system,

3. The emergence of unofficial cost systems,

4. Hewlett Packard's cost driver accounting approach, and

5. A successful implementation of a new cost system.

This teaching note outlines an 80 minute teaching plan.

Suggested Assignments:

1. What concerns do you have about the way the engineers are using the cost system to design the products?

2. Do you think the Roseville Networks Division system is too complex or too simple? Why?

3. Is a sequential implementation of a cost system appropriate?

    a. Under what conditions would you use sequential implementation?

    b. When would you not use it?

This teaching note was written by Professor Robin Cooper as an aid to instructors using Hewlett Packard: Roseville Networks Division (189-117).

Class Discussion

Q1. What is the competitive environment faced by RND?

The RND division competed in the computer-to-computer, or computer-to-peripheral communications market place. This market was characterized by a diverse mix of products with very short life cycles that were getting shorter every year. With several hundred products and life cycles below two years, RND was introducing a new product on average every month, and implementing a production change to existing products on average once a day. The short life cycles of the products should be emphasized, as this fact will play an important role in the design of the new CDA.

Q2. What is the production process at RND?

RND uses a typical through-the-hole board manufacturing process. Axial, radial and DIP components are automatically inserted into empty boards, the components that cannot be inserted automatically or whose use is too low for automatic insertions are manually inserted using Royonics machines. The next stage is to wave solder the board. The soldered boards are then moved to final assembly, where components that cannot be wave soldered (due to heat or water sensitivity) or because they require field replacement are manually inserted. Finally, the boards are tested and then packed for shipping.

The production process consists of a limited number of distinct production processes. All products require the same processes and pass through the same machines. Different equipment is used only in the testing department.

Q3. What is the structure of the existing cost system?

The existing system was a single direct labor burden rate system. This system had become obsolete because the direct labor content of the products had fallen to very low levels, often below 1% of total product costs. This reduction in direct labor had lead to very high burden rates, the validity of which management had begun to question.

Q4. What is the MAKE model?

The MAKE (manufacturing knowledge expert) is a system designed to help product engineers design lower cost products. The MAKE model has a broader set of objectives than a cost system because it can make trade-offs between alternative components, and suggestions about their use to the designers. The cost model upon which MAKE was designed was not direct labor based. The engineers had rejected the official system as a source of cost information. The design engineers had developed the MAKE model as an unofficial cost system.

Q5. What is CDA and what is its relationship to MAKE?

The CDA is the "official" version of the MAKE cost system. The MAKE model was the test bed for CDA. Engineering, manufacturing, and accounting can use MAKE to explore new cost systems designs and if they are effective, subsequently implement them into CDA.

Q6. What are the objectives of CDA?

The primary stated objective of CDA is to help the designers think about cost so that they would not go for elegance every time. However, it is not clear that MAKE has not already achieved this objective. A second objective is to provide feedback from manufacturing to product engineering that the MAKE model is accurate. By keeping the structure of the MAKE and CDA compatible, the 'actual' reported product costs are comparable to the MAKE reported costs. A third objective is more accurate product costs: the CDA system should report more accurate product costs than the existing system, as it better captures the economics of production. A fourth objective is enhanced cost control. Observing that driver rates are increasing or higher than expected provides an impetus for management to try and reduce driver rates.

The relationship between design objective and the cost control objective can be explored by using the fundamental cost equation, $C = P * Q$. The engineers have two ways of reducing costs either by changing the process required to manufacture a product (i.e., changing the mix of activities required by the production process) so that its total cost is lower (i.e. change $P * Q$ to $P' * Q'$) or by reducing the number of times an activity has to be performed in order to manufacture the product (i.e. change Q). In contrast, manufacturing has control over the resources consumed by each activity (i.e. change P). Thus, engineering can design a product that requires fewer manual insertions but higher automatic ones, trading off between activities. Alternatively, they can select a single automatically inserted component that replaces multiple automatic inserted ones, trading off materials cost for insertion cost. In contrast, production can find ways to insert more efficiently by increasing the component storage capacity of the automatic machines thus reducing the labor consumed in loading them.

Q7. How did CDA evolve over time?

Figure TN-1 shows the evolution of CDA. The instructor should get a student or students to provide the information required to draw Figure TN-1 on the board.

Q8. Why was the CDA continuously changed?

The success of the MAKE model and CDA system is evidenced by their continuous evolution. The firm was learning about the economics of production, and as MAKE and CDA were updated, additional insights were gained and subsequently incorporated into the two systems.

The adoption of the cost driver, number of tests, and its subsequent replacement by the cost driver, test hours, is illustrative of the learning process. The original design relied entirely on transaction cost drivers (i.e. drivers that capture the number of times activities are performed). Such drivers worked well for insertions but were inadequate for the testing process. The duration driver, test hours, was more accurate and was adopted once the limitations of the transaction driver was apparent.

Q9. If, as seems likely, the duration of all automatic insertions is the same why use number of insertions instead of machine hours?

This is a critical question. The answer provides an important insight into the design theory underlying the CDA system. If the number of insertions and machine hours are strictly proportional, then the product costs reported by the two drivers will be identical. In effect, the CDA produces product costs identical to those that would be produced under a pure machine hours system. Thus, the initial CDA is just the HP version of the Fisher Technologies case (in Chapter 2) which substituted a new unit level driver (machine hours) for a previous unit level driver (direct labor hours). The advantage of the number of insertions is that it is in the <u>language</u> of the product engineers. It is much easier for an engineer to compare two different designs when the cost driver rates are stated in terms of the number of insertions, than when it is stated in machine hours. Thus, if the objective of a cost system is to influence behavior, then ceteris paribus it is better to pick drivers that are easier for the user to understand, and that focus attention on the desired behavior.

Q10. Why is product design so critical at RND?

The rationale behind the CDA system at RND can now be explored. The short life cycles of the products make it difficult to significantly re-engineer products once they are introduced. In many cases, it will be more economic to continue making a high cost product rather than to re-engineer it. To ensure that high cost designs are never authorized for manufacture in the first place, requires the product engineers design products that can be manufactured at a low cost. Thus, as product life cycle decreases, the initial design becomes more important. In some industries, once a product is designed, no attempt is made to reduce its costs; thus, 100% of costs are "designed in." In other industries, especially those with long life cycle products, the final production cost of a product can be as low as 60% of the original production cost.

Q11. What level in the hierarchy of activities are the various drivers in the CDA?

The drivers are all unit level. The CDA is not a full implementation of activity-based cost principles, rather, it is a partial implementation. There are grounds for arguing that the CDA is simply a traditional system that uses "funny" allocation bases. Students should be asked to identify the minimum criteria that establish an activity-based cost system. They should consider the identification of activities, the creation of homogeneous activity cost pools, the use of a full hierarchy of drivers, if appropriate, and the treatment of facility sustaining costs.

Q12. What is slot costing?

Slot costing is the first emergence of a non-unit level cost driver at RND. Slot costing is a product level driver. The instructor should illustrate how slot costing will function by getting students to work the following example.

Assume the DIP automatic insertion costs are $200,000 every six months. The number of automatic insertions in a six month period is 2,000,000, what is the cost per automatic insertion? The answer is of course $0.10 per insertion.

If the three cost pools for slot costing are:

Name	$	Driver	Driver Quantity
Board Handling	$30,000	# assemblies	10,000
Insertion	$100,000	# inserts	2,000,000
Slot	$70,000	# slots	100
	$200,000		

The driver rates are:
$3 per assembly
$0.05 per insertion
$700 per slot

To explore the effect on reported product costs of the two cost systems requires four pieces of additional information. First, the production volume of the product (i.e., the number of assemblies), the number of insertions required by each assembly, the number of each different components required, and their volume of usage across all products.

Product 1

Six month production volume	50 assemblies
# insertions/assembly	100
# different components	10A, 20B, 30C, 20D, 20E
component volume	A B C D E
	10k 5k 20k 5k 5k

Product 2

Same as product 1 except component volume

Component volume	A	B	C	D	E
	1,000k	500k	2,000k	500k	500k

The reported component volume cost of Products 1 and 2 under number of insertion system are the same at:

# of insertions per unit =	100
Cost per insertion =	$0.10
Reported cost of automatic insertion =	$10

The reported insertion cost of Product 1 under the slot costing system is:

Total Cost of Assemblies	(50 x $3) =	$150
Total Cost of Insertion	(50 x 100 x $0.05) =	$250
Total Cost of Slots		
A 700/10k x (50 x 10) =		$ 35
B 700/5k x (50 x 20) =		$ 140

C 700/20k x (50 x 30) =	$52.50
D 700/5k x (50 x 20) =	$ 140
E 700/5k x (50 x 20) =	$ 140
Total Reported Product Cost	$ 907.50
Unit Reported Cost	$ 18.15

The reported cost of Product 2 under the slot costing system is:

Total cost of Assemblies	$150
Total cost of Insertion	$250
A 700/1,000 x (50 x 10) =	0.35
B 700/ 500k x (50 x 20) =	1.40
C 700/2,000k x (50 x 30) =	0.52
D 7,000/500k x (50 x 20) =	1.40
E 7,000/500k x (50 x 20) =	1.40
Total Reported Cost	$405
Unit Reported Cost	$ 8.09

The product that relies upon the very high volume components has considerably lower reported costs in the slot costing system than the product that uses low volume products. In contrast, in the number of insertions system they both have the same reported costs.

Q13. How will the slot costing system shed light on the utilization of DIP machine capacity?

This is a complicated question to answer. The slot capacity systems will cause product engineers to question the appropriate number of different components that should be inserted by the DIP machines. However, it cannot capture the cost of the capacity freed by going from a single four in-line machine layout to two sets of two in-line machines layout. To capture the costs of that extra capacity requires developing estimates of the number of products that can flow through the two sets of two machines versus the one set of four machines. Such estimates cannot be determined from the CDA.

Q14. Where do the designers' heuristic rules come from?

Rules 1, 2 and 4 are derived directly from the MAKE model and CDA systems. The insertion rates are direct outputs of that model and system. The other rules are derived from other sources. Students should question whether these rules require a system as complex as CDA to deserve them. A one time study should be sufficient to set the rules. This observation strengthens the earlier discussion on the role of the CDA as a feedback mechanism.

Q15. What are the limitations of the MAKE model and CDA systems that the engineers are referring to?

1.   The MAKE model and CDA systems are all consumption models. As such they do not predict very well changes in spending levels associated with different product designs.

2.   The accounting model cannot capture complex trade-offs like the DIP capacity problem or the quality and reliability of different designs.

Q16. What is the fundamental difference between the design philosophy underlying the Tektronix: Portable Instruments Division design and that at RND?

The PID design is based upon the premise of using a very limited number of cost drivers and focusing the product engineers' attention solely on those drivers. The assumption underlying the system is that the firm is better off focusing on a limited number of issues than developing a more balanced view of the economics of production. There are two opposing views to the validity of the PID approach:

1.   It treats the engineers as stupid. The assumption is that they cannot make their own trade-offs between multiple objectives.

2.   The engineers cannot adequately see the significant advantages of reducing the number of different components in the products.

The RND approach assumes that the engineers can handle as many trade-off as they are willing to build into the design of the MAKE model and CDA system. Therefore, they are primarily responsible for the design of the CDA, though all design decisions are shared between engineering, productions, and accounting.

Q17. Since its inception, the CDA system has grown in complexity. Is there a limit to how complex it should become?

The obvious answer to this question is yes. When will RND know when it has reached the limit? There are several factors that should be taken into account when deciding upon the upper level of complexity. These factors include:

1.   The cost of measurement. Each additional cost driver requires measurement for every product or component. Thus, as the CDA becomes more complex the cost of measurement increases.

2.   The ease of comprehension. Each additional cost driver makes it more difficult for a first time user to understand the system. Presumably, there is a point at which the system becomes too complex to understand or takes too long to internalize. However, it is not clear that this point has been reached yet.

3.   Accuracy. Each additional cost driver presumably increases the accuracy of the CDA system. While there may be diminishing returns, the engineer presumably will only be interested in additional cost drivers that shed light on economics of production.

4.   Behavior. Each additional driver focuses attention on another set of behaviors. For example, shifting to slot costing will focus attention on the number of different part numbers used in the products.

5. Process change. Over time, the production processes will change. These changes will require the introduction of new cost drivers and the retirement of others. For example, surface mount technology avoids insertion, therefore, the number of insertions is zero.

While the optimum number of cost drivers is uncertain, pressures to stop proliferating drivers has already appeared at RND. The emergence of these pressures suggests that the optimum is close to the current design. A number of firms who have gained experience with ABC implementation have identified 10-20 as the appropriate number of cost drivers for a plant. The CDA is currently in the middle of that range and indeed may be reaching maturity.

Q18. What risks are there in letting the product engineers design the MAKE model and hence the CDA?

There is a risk that the product engineers will design the MAKE model so that certain products are preferentially costed. For example, they might design the system to favor new technology introduction more than is appropriate. The appropriate role for the accounting function is to monitor the design process and ensure that the system is being designed to provide insights into the economics of production, not achieve hidden objectives of the product engineers.

Q19. Why not implement in a single step?

The RND case is the only case that captures an incremental implementation of a cost system. General experience suggests that ABC system designs typically change in the first few years as users obtain experience and learn to design better systems. However, it is unusual to see such a steady evolution of a system every six months. The rationale behind the steady evolution is grounded in the product engineers learning about the economics of production. Each incremental design is the outcome of the engineers discovering more about the economics of production. The process could have been quickened by immediately introducing a multi-driver system but only at the risk of the engineers losing ownership and comprehension. There is no way to determine whether a one-step versus a multi-step implementation would have been less expensive, but clearly the multi-step approach adopted at RND did lead to a sophisticated system which is "owned" by product engineers, production, and accounting.

Q20. The Schrader Bellows system failed while the RND system succeeded. What factors do you think lead to success at RND?

Several factors can be identified that probably played a critical role in the success at RND.

1. Engineers had ownership from day 1,
2. Corporate culture was one of change,
3. Accounting supported the change but did not lead it,
4. MAKE model used the data,
5. Management supported change.

Hewlett Packard: Roseville Network Division
Teaching Note

Figure 1

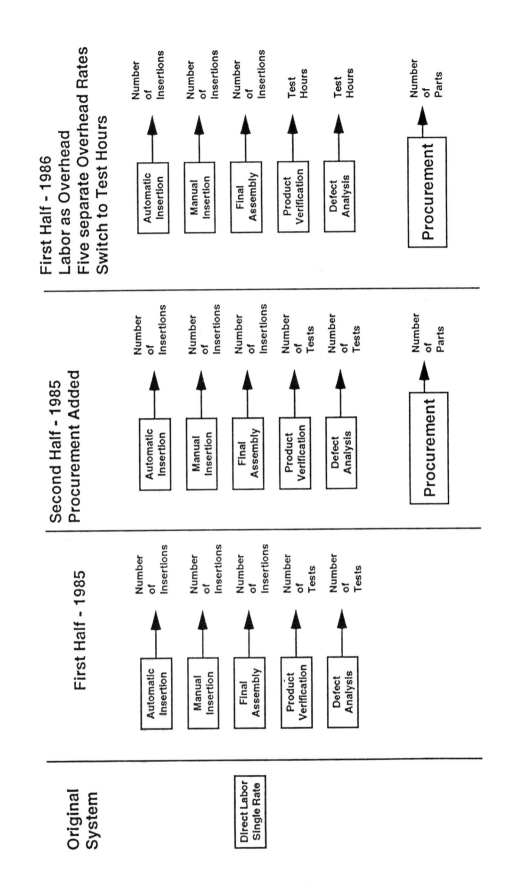

Figure 1 (continued)

Second Half - 1986
Automatic Insertion Split
Final Assembly Split
Kitting and Shipping

First Half - 1987
Procurement Split

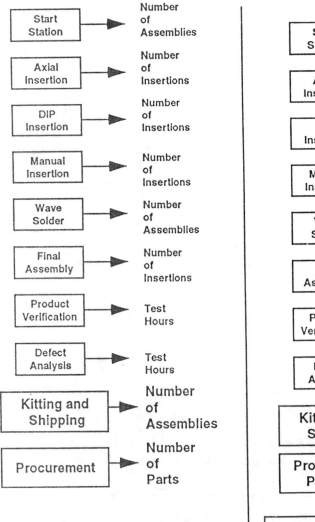

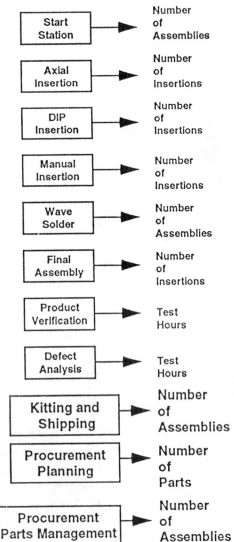

Figure 1 (continued)

First Half - 1988
Final Assembly Split
Radial Insertion Added

Last Half - 1988
Introduction of Slot Costing?

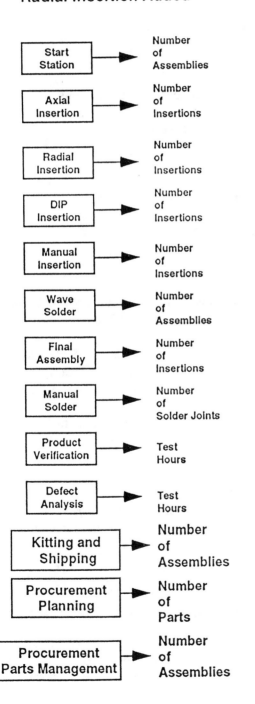

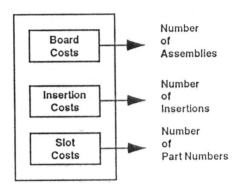

Insertion Process

Zytec Corporation (B)

Teaching Note

The Zytec case series illustrates the following issues:

1. The relationship between the cost and performance measurement systems,

2. The calculation of product costs using different cost drivers,

3. Designing cost systems to modify behavior,

4. The properties of a good cost driver in an activity-based cost system.

This teaching note outlines an 80 minute teaching plan.

Suggested Assignments:

1a. For the Sample Company determine the product costs reported by the proposed supplier lead time and cycle time system for products 401, 402, 403, 404.

   a.   Supplier lead time costs for all eight productive cells equals $282,000.
   b.   Cycle time related overhead costs (excluding direct labor costs) for the productive cell in which the series 400 products are produced are $150,000.

1b. For the Sample Company determine the unit product costs reported by the existing direct material dollar and labor dollar system for products 401, 402, 403, 404.

   a.   Direct material dollar burden rate is 17%.
   b.   Labor related overhead costs (excluding direct labor costs) for the productive cell in which the series 400 products are produced are $150,000.
   c.   Total material and labor costs for the 400 series products are:

This teaching note was written by Professor Robin Cooper as an aid to instructors using the Zytec Corporation cases (190-066/077).

Note: The following information is required to answer question 1.

PRODUCT #	MATERIAL $	STANDARD DIRECT LABOR $
401	152,000	2,400
402	91,000	800
403	45,000	3,600
404	137,000	8,200

2a. What types of products will the proposed system favor compared to the existing one?

b.   What types of behavior will be rewarded and penalized under the proposed and existing systems?

c.   What are the characteristics of a good cost driver? Evaluate the four drivers considered by the design team.

d.   Would you have included the yield and linearity cost drivers in your design?

3.   Evaluate the proposed cost system. In your discussion be sure to include:

   a.   A critique of the existing system.
   b.   A critique of the proposed system.
   c.   An analysis of which of the two systems provides better cost information.
   d.   Any problems you would expect to encounter if you implement the proposed system.
   e.   A recommendation about whether to implement the proposed system.

4.   If you do not believe that either the existing or proposed cost systems is totally appropriate, give a brief description of the system you would implement.

The case has been used as a final examination for the second year elective "The Measurement and Management of Product Costs". The case worked well as an examination; the balance between numerical and essay questions was 30:70. The percentage scores associated with each assignment were: 1 = 30 points; 2 = 30 points; 3 = 30 points; 4 = 10 points.

Classroom Discussion

Q1. What is the competitive environment faced by Zytec?

The power supply market is highly fragmented with over 400 U.S. and offshore companies competing for a $4 billion market. Zytec ranked number 6 but only had 1% of total market shares at $60 million in sales. In recent years, the Japanese had entered the market with high quality and low price products. Zytec had lost a lot of market shares and to recapture it had embarked upon an aggressive campaign to become more efficient. Management introduced J-I-T production, T.Q.M., continuous improvement, and a performance measurement system.

Q2. What is the structure of the performance measurement system?

The PM system contains six objectives. These objectives are:

Improve Total Quality Commitment
Reduce Total Cycle Time
Improve Zytec's Service to Customers
Improve Profitability and Financial Stability
Improve Housekeeping and Safety
Increase Employee Involvement

Departments were expected to identify improvement targets for each of these six objectives. The program appears to be successful; the case gives an example of a product whose overhead costs were reduced from $530 to $325.

Q3. What is the structure of the existing cost system?

The existing cost system relies upon two allocation bases to assign costs to products. These bases are direct labor dollars and material dollars. Material burden is assigned to all products at the same rate. In contrast, direct labor burden is assigned using a number of different rates. This is a relatively typical traditional system. All costs are assigned at the unit level using bases that captured characteristics of the product unit. Management is dissatisfied with this system because they do not believe that all products consume the same burden per direct material dollar or that direct labor captures the consumption of production overhead by products.

Q4. What types of products are encouraged by the old system?

The old system will encourage products that have low labor and low material content. These products will have relatively little overhead assigned to them.

Q5. What type of behavior will the old system induce in the product engineers?

The system will create incentives for the product engineers to design products that have low labor and material content. They will also tend to outsource the labor intensive production steps. The trend will therefore be towards simple products. Whether this trend will be sufficient to shift the strategy of the firms, depends upon the other controls in place and pressures in the market place.

Q6. What are the reported costs for products 401, 402, 403, and 404 under the original system?

The calculations of reported product costs are relatively straight forward given the information supplied in the assignments. The calculations are shown in Exhibit TN-1. The reported costs are:

Product Number	Reported Cost
401	340.40
402	288.18
403	307.50
404	500.98

Q7. What drivers were considered for the new activity-based cost system?

Four drivers were considered, Linearity, Cycle Time, Supplier Lead Time, and Yield, as described in the case (p. 423).

Q8. Why did they pick these drivers?

These drivers were picked to reinforce the continuous improvement program and performance measurement system. At least two of these drivers, cycle time and yield were taken directly from the management by objectives program. A third, supplier lead time was already being measured and its reduction was probably used as an objective by the materials acquisition function. Linearity was not currently an objective though the case suggests that it soon will be.

Q9. Are these drivers independent?

At least two of the four drivers, if not three, are interdependent in the eyes of management. For example, management at Zytec believes, not unreasonably, that to reduce cycle time requires increasing production yields. Low yields make low cycle times impossible because of the disruption rejects cause in the production process and hence increase cycle time. Similarly, the plant manager believes that if cycle time can be reduced, linearity will follow. When drivers (and performance measures for that matter) are interdependent, there is a risk that one or more of them are redundant. For example, if low cycle times requires high linearity and yield, what is the benefit of creating incentives to increase linearity and yields in addition to creating incentives to achieve low cycle times? There probably is no benefit if everyone that is concerned with cycle time is also concerned with linearity and/or yields. However, if some individuals are concerned with linearity and/or yields but not with reduced cycle times, then using multiple measures probably makes sense.

Q10. What is the structure of the New System?

The new system is very similar to the existing system except material dollars has been replaced by supplier lead time and direct labor dollars by cycle time. All of the costs are assigned to the product unit. Some students might be confused and think that supplier lead time is a product level cost driver. However, the computation of reported product costs will demonstrate how the new system at Zytec is a totally unit-based system.

Q11. Why did they not use the yield and linearity drivers?

The case indicates that the system designers "were unable to come up with formulae for linearity and yields that represented saleable correlations with cost". This is an important observation. While, any quantifiable attribute of a product can be converted into a cost drivers only some of them can be causally related to the consumption of resources. Linearity for example can be computed, as shown in the case, by taking the modulus of the difference between the planned production and the actual production. Summing the linearity of all products passing through a production process gives the total quantity of the linearity drivers and dividing that total into the dollars in the linearity related cost pool gives the linearity burden rate. Multiplying this rate by the linearity factor for each product gives the linearity cost of the product. Similarly, by developing a yield factor, yield related costs can be assigned to products. Thus, the problem does not lie with assigning costs but in the credibility of the assignment process. While the design team could justify the use of cycle time and supplier lead time, they apparently could not justify the linearity and yield stories.

Q12. What types of products will the new system encourage?

The new system will encourage products that have low supplier lead times, which suggests low parts count and simple to manufacture.

Q13. What behavior will the new system induce in the product engineers?

The new system will reward designs that have low supplier lead times and cycle times. Thus, the designer will have incentives to use commodity components as opposed to custom components, simple designs instead of complex ones, and to outsource the long cycle time subassemblies. The labor content of the products will be almost irrelevant to the cost of the product. Again, whether the incentives will be strong enough to cause a shift in strategy will depend upon a number of factors.

The system clearly will reward low supplier lead time and cycle time products. The question is whether the through-put time is dependent upon the design of the product or the management of the production process. Both factors are probably important. The performance measurement system is already rewarding short cycle time. However, it probably functions most effectively on the shop floor. The benefit of having a cost system that rewards short cycle time lies in its influence on designer behavior. However, if the performance measurement system creates adequate incentives to reduce cycle times both at the shop floor and product engineer levels, the student should question the benefit of a duplicate system.

A perverse incentive will emerge if too much attention is focused on cycle time. One of the major causes of interruption to the steady flow of products is the introduction of new products. Thus, one way to reduce cycle time is to reduce the number of new product introductions. This action is clearly not in the best interest of the firm. Students should consider how to ensure that the rate of new product introduction is kept at the appropriate level.

Q14. What are the reported costs for products 401, 402, 403, and 404 under the new system?

The calculations of reported product costs are slightly more complicated for the new system than the old one. Using the information supplied in the assignments, the calculations are shown in Exhibit TN-2. The reported costs are:

Product Number	Reported Cost
401	439.79
402	345.68
403	162.72
404	427.03

The two systems clearly report different product costs. The ratio of the new to old costs for the four products are:

Product Number	Ratio of Reported Costs
401	1.29
402	1.20
403	0.53
404	0.85

The magnitude of these shifts is quite large and clearly significant compared to product profitability.

Q15. Which of the two systems is more accurate?

This is a difficult question to answer. It is not clear that the new system is any more accurate than the old system. The new system was eventually rejected by management because they felt that it was not superior to the old one on a number of dimensions including accuracy. The accuracy problem can be demonstrated by comparing the reported labor content of the four products under the two systems. The old system measured direct labor costs directly and reported them separately. In contrast, the new system assigned direct labor costs as overhead via cycle time. A comparison of the two sets of reported labor costs highlights the effect of the difference between the way the two systems assign labor costs to products. The reported direct labor costs under the two systems are:

Product Number	Old System Reported Labor Content	New System Reported Labor Content
401	$ 4.00	$ 8.39
402	$ 2.00	$ 5.59
403	$12.00	$ 9.79
404	$16.40	$12.58

Assuming the old system more accurately captures the consumption of direct labor by products, which all things considered is likely, the new system is introducing quite significant distortion into the direct labor costs. While admittedly, these are small compared to other costs, it is not obvious that the cycle time system is better. Similarly, the supplier lead time is not intuitively a good driver especially at the unit level. The material overhead costs presumably contain a fair degree of batch and vendor level costs , yet the new system forces them to all be assigned using a single unit-level driver that does not appear to capture well the underlying cause of the overhead.

Q16. What was management's reaction to the new system?

At this point, the instructor can describe management's reaction to the new cost system.[1] The controller stated:

> The initial reaction to the cycle time portion of the new system was dominated by confusion. Everybody wanted to compare the old and new numbers and have us explain the differences. Unfortunately, we could not satisfy them about the causes of the differences. We never got to discuss what the products actually cost or what were the appropriate allocation bases. It was very frustrating.

> Reaction to the supplier lead time system was even more negative. In particular, the purchasing manager argued that supplier lead time was not under his control. He could not see any way to change his behavior to reduce supplier lead time. He felt unable to react to the new system.

Within a few months of its introduction, the new cost system was modified. Material burdening was treated as a period cost and only manufacturing burden was allocated to the products. Then, one of the firm's major customers refused to accept the cycle time system as a basis for determining product costs and hence selling prices. This customer demanded that Zytec return to its existing cost system for calculating the costs for its contracts.

Thus, the basic system was rejected. Students should be asked why the new system was not accepted. They should soon realize that the problem lay in the choice of cost drivers.

Q17. What are the properties of a good cost driver?

The inability of the design team to sell the linearity and yield drivers helps focus attention on what are the properties of a good cost drivers. These properties include:

1. a clear causal relation to the underlying activities whose costs are being assigned.
2. driver quantities or prices that are controllable.
3. the ability to induce beneficial behavior.

---

1. A one page case describing management's reaction can be ordered from HBS Publishing and handed out to the class: HBS # 9-190-077, Rev. 03/20/91. (If you order the case, don't get confused by the name of the supplementary case which is also called Zytec (B); the Zytec cases were repackaged after the book went to press so the case presented in the book as Zytec (B) now exists in the HBS system as Zytec (A)).

4. low cost of measurement.
5. the quantities consumed by a given product should be relatively stable.
6. difficult to game.
7. relatively independent of other cost drivers.
8. interpretable to the user; i.e., stated in their language.

The Zytec system failed because the drivers selected failed to satisfy one or more of the above criteria. First, neither driver had a clear causal relation to activities. While, empirically, costs do go down if cycle time is reduced, there is no simple activity story to tie the consumption of overhead to cycle time. In order to reduce cycle time, the production process must become more streamlined. Events that disrupt the steady flow of products must be avoided. The expenses that are reduced by decreasing cycle times are not all overhead but only the production overhead associated with turbulence. The same argument holds true of the supplier lead time driver. That driver also suffered from a lack of linkage to activity expenses and controllability and was therefore rejected.

Exhibit TN-1 Reported Product Costs Under the Original Cost System

Material Cost[2]	Material Burden[3]	Labor[4]	Labor Burden[5]	Reported Cost
$152,000	$25,840	$2,400	$24,000	$204,240
$ 91,000	$15,470	$800	$8,000	$115,270
$ 45,000	$7,650	$3,600	$36,000	$92,250
$137,000	$23,290	$8,200	$82,000	$250,490

2. Taken from Assignment 1.
3. 17% of Material Cost.
4. Taken from Assignment 1.
5. Labor Burden is 10 times Labor Cost ($150,000 to $15,000). Therefore, this column is 10 times the prior column.

Exhibit TN-2   Reported Product Costs Under the New Cost System

Material Cost[6]	Cycle Time[7]	Units Shipped[8]	Total Cycle Time[9]	Cycle Time Burden[10]	% Supplier Lead Time Factor[11]	Supplier Lead Time Burden[12]	Reported Cost
$152,000	3	600	1800	$50,338.98	21.82	$61,532	$263,871
$ 91,000	2	400	800	$22,372.88	8.83	$24,901	$138,273
$ 45,000	3.5	300	1050	$29,364.40	2.48	$6,994	$81,358
$137,000	4.5	500	2250	$62,923.72	4.82	$13,592	$213,516

6. Taken from Assignment 1.
7. Taken from Case Exhibit 2.
8. Taken from Case Exhibit 2.
9. Cycle time x units shipped.
10. Total of column 4 is 5900. Burden rate for cycle time is $27.97/cycle time day ($165,000/5900).
11. Taken from Case Exhibit 2.
12. Assignment 1 gives total supplier lead time costs as $282,000. This figure times % factors in the prior column gives burden.

Hewlett Packard: Queensferry Telecommunications Division

Teaching Note

The Hewlett Packard Queensferry Telecommunications case (QTD) was designed to complete a module on designing cost systems to modify the behavior of product engineers. The case can also be used to illustrate capacity costing issues.

The QTD case illustrates the following issues:

1. The application of variance analysis in a cost driver accounting system.

2. The factors to consider when determining cost driver rates.

3. The appropriate way to cost incremental business in an activity-based cost system.

4. The tensions that arise when designing cost systems for multiple purposes (see pp. 398-400 in text).

5. The effects of ignoring capacity utilization when determining reported product costs.

This teaching note outlines an 80 minute teaching plan.

Suggested Assignments:

1. Is the cost driver accounting system an activity-based cost system?

2. Should the cost driver rates for the 2nd half of 1990 reflect the lower production volumes due to the postponement of the British Telecomm contract?

3A. The actual results for the three assembly and test areas for the second half of 1990 were:

This teaching note was written by Professor Robin Cooper as an aid to instructors using Hewlett Packard: Queensferry Telecommunications Division (191-067).

	SPENDING ($000)			VOLUME (000)		
	A	B	C	A	B	C
Assembly:	450	200	220	8	2.5	5
Test:	900	670	550	10	5	13

Calculate the spending and volume variances for the three units separately and collectively.

3B.   Should the three assembly and test production units be treated as separate cost centers?

4.   Should the cost of the British Telecomm Contract be determined using the cost driver rates established for the entire firm (as per Exhibit 2) or for just the contract (as per Exhibit 6)?

5.   A product designer has developed two alternative designs for a module. One design relies heavily upon expensive integrated circuits, the other design contains a large number of inexpensive components. Functionally, the two designs are equivalent. Cost to manufacture is the primary factor to choose between them. Determine which design you would recommend:

First Design		Second Design	
Material	$325	Material	$220
	#opns		#opns
Auto	150	Auto	600
Pre	50	Pre	400
Post	10	Post	25
Auto Test	100	Auto Test	250
Ass	0.5	Ass	0.5
Test	0.5	Test	0.5

Class Discussion

Q1. What is the competitive environment?

The QTD division sold products to the major European telecommunications firms. The recent shift from analog to digital circuitry caused led to both reduced product life cycles and an increased number of competitors as firms with digital circuitry design experience could now enter the telecommunications market. The division from inception was dedicated to high quality. High quality is important in the telecommunications industry where uninterrupted service is critical. The emphasis on high quality led to a higher than usual degree of vertical integration in the electronics industry. Finally, one customer, British Telecomm (B-T), represented a significant portion of business (3-12%) and was viewed by some as incremental business. The way the new cost system reported product costs depended significantly on the overall level of business, and how the B-T contract was treated, either as incremental or normal business.

Q2. What were the objectives of the new CDA system?

The objectives are laid out in the case. They are:

1. Encourage design for manufacturability.

2. Improve QTD's understanding of its true cost structure, thereby facilitating manufacturing cost reduction.

3. Encourage management to support Total Quality Control methodology, and eliminate waste.

4. Provide improved information to monitor production performance.

5. Provide improved product cost information to support pricing and other strategic decisions.

Q3. Are these objectives compatible, or will they introduce tensions?

The case focuses on these tensions. The tensions are primarily caused by trying to use the same system for financial reporting and management accounting purposes. Additional tensions are introduced by using the system for monitoring performance measurement as well as modifying the behavior of the product engineers. These tensions will be explored throughout the session, but if students have read the text (pp. 398-400), they will be able to discuss the general tensions that can be expected to emerge.

Q4. What is the structure of the CDA system at QTD?

The system contains 8 drivers, one for each of the 7 major production centers and one for material procurement. These drivers are: number of insertions, number of parts tested, labor hours, test hours, and material cost. Figure TN-1 illustrates the two-stage diagram of the CDA system. There are several properties of this system that should be highlighted. First, all 8 drivers are unit-based. Thus, the system is not a full implementation of activity-based principles. The drivers such as number of insertions and number of parts tested capture the primary activities of the production departments but no attempt is made to identify batch or product level costs and appropriately drive them to the products. Second, too few drivers are used to capture cost behavior appropriately. The procurement activity, for example, is known to require additional cost drivers.

The system is clearly designed primarily to identify the cost of production processes and provide product designers with the ability to explore the implications of different product designs. For students that have studied the Hewlett Packard: Roseville Networks Division case, the lack of a MAKE model should be discussed as should the one-time implementation. While the lessons had to be learned the hard way at Roseville, because it was Hewlett Packard's first implementation, QTD could rely upon the experience gained through multiple implementations. However, students should question whether the designers have had time to internalize and to commit to the system. The two Hewlett Packard cases, when taught back to back, can be used to illustrate how to successfully migrate innovations in cost system design between different divisions. It should be pointed out that by this time, HP had developed considerable experience in implementing CDA systems, and there is no reason to suspect that the CDA system at QTD will fail.

Q5. What is the advantage of using number of insertion instead of machine or labor hours in the insertion departments?

The number of insertions is preferred to machine or labor hours because it is more closely aligned to the *language of the product engineers*. It is far easier for the engineers to consider the cost of the number of insertions rather than the cost of the number of machine hours it takes to produce a design when comparing different designs. Students should question the use of number of insertions to assign costs in the post wave solder department. There, the types of components being inserted are quite different and it is not obvious that every component takes the same time to insert (the central assumption of the transaction driver, number of inserts). In contrast, in the pre-wave solder departments, the relationship between machine and labor hours and number of insertions is probably much tighter since all automatic insertions are basically the same. The potential discrepancy between post wave solder labor hours and number of insertions highlights a design tension. It is easier for the designers to have the cost drivers in "their language" but using that language can reduce the accuracy of the reported product costs.

Q6. How are cost driver rates determined?

This question allows the mechanics of a CDA to be explored. The CDA rates are determined by dividing the budgeted total cost for each production department or procurement by the total budgeted driver quantity. Case Exhibit 1 identifies the cost of each cost pool. Case Exhibit 2 reports the cost driver rates. These two exhibits can be used to determine total cost driver quantities for the second half of fiscal 1990.

Certain elements of Exhibit 1 should be drawn to the students' attention. First, the costs of the support departments such as quality, materials management, and engineering are assigned to the production departments. Thus, the structure of the CDA is more akin to a conventional system than an ABC. Figure TN-2 illustrates a more detailed two-stage diagram than Figure TN-1. The assignment of support department costs to the production centers and then in a subsequent step to the products using unit level drivers will introduce distortion when production volume diversity and other forms of diversity occur. Second, there is no adjustment for capacity utilization. Therefore, the firm risks entering a death spiral if it both relies on the reported product costs to set prices or outsources unprofitable products.

Q7. What do the variances mean?

The spending variances captures changes in the expected level of spending (i.e., it really is a spending variance) and the volume variances captures changes in the level of consumption (i.e., it is a consumption variance).

Q8. What are the variances for the three assembly and test areas?

The numerical solutions are shown in Exhibit TN-1. The calculations are very simple. The spending variance is calculated by simply subtracting the actual costs from the budgeted costs. It identifies how actual spending was different from the unflexed budgeted amount. If the budget could be flexed, the spending variance would change to an efficiency measure. The volume variances are calculated by subtracting actual cost driver volumes from budgeted and then evaluating them at the budgeted cost driver rates. These variances are capturing the cost of the unutilized capacity.

Q9. What do these variances mean?

The volume or consumption variances are quite simple to interpret. The volumes of activity in the three assembly and test areas are larger than expected. The increases in units A and B are probably due to random fluctuations while for unit C it is due to the reactivation of the B-T contract. Unit A shows consumption variances of nearly 11% for assembly and 13% for test. Unit B has nearly 8% higher consumption in assembly and 12% in test. Unit C has consumption variances of nearly 14% and 20% for assemble and test respectively. Thus, the firm is producing more than expected in all three departments in the second half of the year.

The spending variances are more difficult to interpret. The actuals for all three departments are above expectation. The increases are however, less than the consumption increases.

The ratios of the spending and consumption variances are:

	Assembly	Test
Unit A	90%	91%
Unit B	86%	00%
Unit C	18%	22%

As can be seen, the variances in unit A are relatively well matched. The spending and consumption variances appear to be in step. Since Unit A is not effected by the B-T contract, the high ratio of the two variances makes sense. The department is at capacity and any increase in resource consumption has to be funded. For Unit B, capacity utilization is low as a new product is coming up to speed. Therefore, excess capacity is built into the budget to provide the capacity as required. The low ratio for the test department simply indicates that area could increase the consumption of resources with out having to increase spending. In contrast, the assembly area behaves much like the equivalent are of Unit A suggesting that as volume increases additional spending is required. Unit C, which is driven by the B-T contract shows different behavior to the other two units. The ratio is about 20% in each area which suggests that the budget contained significant excess capacity. Excess capacity is likely to be built into a budget when production volume has recently dropped because the lag between spending and consumption is built into the budget. Therefore, as spending reductions lag the decreased consumption, the budget, which is a spending estimate, will automatically contain excess capacity.

Alternative explanations for the imperfect match between changes in the level of resource consumption and spending include more efficient use of the resources, and that spending levels on some costs are not sensitive to production volume. The more efficiently activities are performed, the less resources will be consumed at a given production volume. Thus, if efficiency is improved, the spending variance will be proportionally smaller than the consumption variance. The existence of non unit level activities will cause the spending variance to be smaller than the consumption variance because the non-unit level activities will not increase as fast as the unit level ones. Without a more sophisticated analysis, it is not possible to determine which of the three potential explanations for the slower increase in the spending variance than the consumption variance are operating. However, it is very unlikely that the low ratio observed for unit A is caused predominantly by anything but excess capacity in the budget.

Q10. Should the three units be treated as three separate processes?

This is somewhat of a trick question. To answer it requires first defining the purpose of the analysis being undertaken. For performance evaluation, the answer has to be yes. The three unit managers are each independently responsible for their units. They should not be held responsible for the efficiency levels of others. For product design and product costing purposes, the answer depends upon the reason products are manufactured in a specific unit. If the decision is due to differences in the production processes in the unit and each unit can only service a unique set of products the answer is yes. If all units can service all products the answer is no, and the appropriate design cost is the average for the three units. For example, the rates in unit B are higher than the other two rates because the unit is ramping up a new product. It would be inappropriate to view a product as being more profitable because it is manufactured in unit A rather than unit B at this time. Note, this perspective challenges the validity of the high rates in unit B. Should some of the costs of unit B be treated as an investment in new products? In summary, performing variance analysis using the CDA rates requires splitting the units apart, however for design purposes this may be inappropriate. Another tension between the multiple uses of cost systems has been identified.

Q11. How should the large volume variances be treated?

The large volume variances are caused by a decrease in the consumption of cost drivers without a corresponding decrease in the level of expenditure. The CDA because it is unit-based assumes that 1) each unit of cost driver consumes the same resources and 2) that the level of expenditure is directly proportional to the units produced. The large volume variances created by the loss of the B-T contract indicate that the second assumption is not valid. The level of expenditure does not vary directly with the level of consumption, at least in the short run as evidenced by the low spending:consumption ratio. Thus, these variances are capturing the costs of unutilized capacity.

The treatment of these variances is discussed, in depth, in the cases in the capacity costing module. Briefly, there are two primary ways of treating these costs: as product costs or as period costs. At QTD, these variances should not be reassigned to the products, they are caused by the excess capacity that has emerged with the down turn in business. Excess capacity should only be charged to products when it is unavoidable, i.e., it is required to support the production process.

These excess capacity costs can be viewed as consisting of two elements. The first element is the excess capacity that relates to the unit, batch, and product level activities that are no longer being performed. The second element relates to the under-utilized capacity of the facility, itself. The excess capacity at the unit, batch, and product levels, in theory, can be avoided over time by reducing the level of capacity provided to perform those activities provided. For example, one less inspector can be employed. In contrast, the facility level activities can not be avoided, as easily, since facility level activities are independent of the volume of products produced. The CDA, because it only recognizes unit level behavior, is unable to differentiate between these two types of excess capacity costs.

The pressure to change the driver rates so that large volume variances do not occur in the second half of the year, arises because the cost system is used for financial reporting as well as managerial accounting purposes. The usual treatment of the costs of temporary excess capacity for financial reporting purposes is to write up the products (i.e., treat it as a product cost). However, given the primary objective of the CDA system, to provide insights into the economics of product design, it does not make sense to have the apparent cost of each production process vary every time the expected production volume changes. If the apparent cost of each process is allowed to change because of volume fluctuations, then the designers choice of the most cost efficient way to design products will depend upon the budgeted volume (Assignment 5 illustrates this phenomenon from a slightly different perspective).

Q12. Is the B-T contract incremental business?

Students will have a hard time answering this question, as does QTD management. The B-T contract is different from other contracts due to its large size and high variability. These characteristics suggest it should be viewed as incremental business. On the other hand, the contract repeats almost every year and therefore has properties of core business: B-T is no different from any other customer that does not buy products every year. A few minutes of student discussion will highlight all the relevant issues. Eventually, or with help, the students should begin to question why it matters whether or not the contract is considered incremental business. The apparent profitability of the business will depend upon whether or not it is assigned costs on an incremental basis. If incremental costs are used, the reported profit of the contract will be position while if non-incremental costs are used it will have a negative reported profit.

Q13. If the contract is viewed as incremental business, must it be incrementally costed?

This is the critical question, it raises a number of interesting theoretical issues. In particular, incremental cost is a spending orientation. The CDA being a consumption model is not equipped to provide insights into spending. Therefore, the determination of incremental costs requires a special study. Once this study is completed then the decision to accept the contract of bid at a particular price can be taken. Once the incremental business is accepted, the question becomes "Do we maintain separate cost driver rates for the incremental and core businesses or do we use a single rate?" This approach can be illustrated using a simple example.

A company sells 20,000 units of product 1 at $5.00 per unit. The total cost of manufacture (and delivery) is $80,000. A customer approaches the company and asks management to accept an order for 2,000 units of product 2 at $3.00 per unit. The incremental costs of the product 2 order are $5,000.

If the core business is kept separate from the incremental business, then the core business shows a profit of $20,000 and the incremental business a profit of $1,000. If the two businesses are combined. Then the total revenue is $106,000 and the total costs $85,000 giving an overall profit of $21,000. Assuming that the reported cost of product 1 and 2 are the same per unit, then the reported cost of the core business becomes $77,273 ($85,000/22,000) and its profitability $22,727 and the cost of the incremental business $7,727 (1/10 of the core total) and its profitability $(1,727). The incremental business now looks like it is unprofitable. If the cost system is to maintain effectiveness as an attention focussing device, it should not report losses for the incremental contract. The system is saying "look at this contract it is unprofitable" and yet it is known to be profitable.

The activity-based perspective on incremental business can be illustrated by asking a deceptively simple question.

Q14. If all business is viewed as incremental, what costs will be included and excluded?

In theory, two types of costs should be excluded from the analysis. These costs are:

1. Facility level costs because these are incurred irrespective of the level of production, and

2. Excess capacity costs because these are not consumed by the existing products.

In a full ABC implementation, the costs of the unit, batch, and product level activities will be attributed to the products that cause them. The facility level costs will either be allocated arbitrarily to the products or held at the facility level. Thus, ABC systems adopt, to some extent, an incremental perspective. ABCs do not adopt a total incremental perspective because the incremental cost of a product will be a function of the order in which products are considered. For example, the last product dropped on a particular machine will allow the spending associated with that machine to be avoided. Thus, the incremental cost of the last product will be much higher than earlier products. Yet, the last product can be any product.

To avoid this ordering problem, ABCs adopt a consumption orientation and assign costs to all products using the same driver rates. As noted above, this approach can be used for both core and incremental business, if separate driver rates are established.

Q15. Which of the two designs is superior?

The two designs were chosen so that the lowest cost alternative depends upon the treatment of the B-T contract. The primary purpose of the assignment is to get students to push some numbers and work out how to adjust a cost system for incremental business. The assignment also allows a discussion on the role of other factors besides cost in choosing a preferred design.

The determinations of the reported costs of the two different module designs using the existing driver rates is quite simple. The driver rates (from Exhibit 2) are multiplied by the cost driver quantities associated with each design to give the reported cost of each operation. Summing the operations costs gives reported product costs. These calculations are illustrated in Exhibit TN-2.

The determination of the reported costs for the two designs using the core only driver rates is more complicated. To determine the core only driver rates requires four distinct steps. First, the cost of the core business is determined by subtracting the B-T costs from the total cost of the facility. Step 2 is to determine the total driver quantities in the 2nd half of the year. These are determined by dividing the total cost by the driver rates to give total cost driver quantities.

Step 3 is to subtract the B-T driver quantities from the total driver quantities to give core business driver qualities. Step 4 generates the core only cost driver rates by dividing the core only business costs by the core only driver quantities. This four step procedure is shown in Exhibit TN-3.

Computing the reported cost for the two designs using the core only rates is now easy. The calculations are identical to those used to determine reported product costs using the reported product costs using the total driver rates. Exhibit TN-4 illustrates these calculations.

The two designs have effectively identical reported product costs when the existing driver rates are used. When the core only rates are used, then the first design has a lower reported product cost than the second one. Thus, the first design would probably be chosen if core only rates were used while either design would be picked if existing rates are used.

If the instructor desires, the non-cost factors that should be considered before choosing between the two designs can be discussed. This discussion can be initiated by asking the following question, "If the existing rates are used to report product costs, the two designs are still equivalent; what other factors should we consider?"

The discussion that follows should identify factors such as:

1) Reliability
2) Potential for future cost reduction
3) Potential for use in future designs

Exhibit TN-1   Calculating the Variances for the Three Assembly and Test Units

Assembly	Budget ($000)	Actual ($000)	Spending Variance	% of Budget
A	409.5	450	-40.5	-9.89%
B	187.5	200	-12.5	-6.67%
C	214.5	220	-5.5	-2.56%
	811.5	870	-58.5	-7.21%
Test				
A	802.5	900	-97.5	-12.15%
B	665.7	670	-4.3	-0.65%
C	526.6	550	-23.4	-4.44%
	1994.8	2120	-125.2	-6.28%

Assembly	Driver Quantity Budget ($000)	Actual Quantity ($000)	Driver Quantity Variance	Cost Driver Rate	Volume Variance	% of Budget
A	7.21	8	0.79	56.84	44.9036	10.96%
B	2.32	2.5	0.18	80.94	14.5692	7.76%
C	4.39	5	0.61	48.89	29.8229	13.90%
	13.92	15.5	1.58	58.34	92.1772	11.35%
Test						
A	8.82	10	1.18	91.03	107.4154	13.38%
B	4.47	5	0.53	148.93	78.9329	11.86%
C	10.86	13	2.14	48.51	103.8114	19.71%
	24.15	28	3.85	82.6	318.01	15.94%

Exhibit TN-2   Computing the Reported Cost of the Two Designs Using
          Existing Cost Driver Rates

Design 1

	Existing DVR Rates	Cost Driver Quantity	Reported Cost
Auto Insert	$0.07	150	$10.50
Manual Pre	$0.24	50	$12.00
Manual Post	$0.75	10	$7.50
Auto Test	$0.04	100	$4.00
Assembly	$58.34	0.5	$29.17
Test	$82.60	0.5	$41.30
Fab	$40.88	0	$0.00
Procurement	26.51%	$325.00	$86.16
Total Overhead Cost			$190.63
Material Cost			$325.00
Total Cost			$515.63

Source:	(Exhibit 2) Existing DVR Rates	(Assignment 5) Cost Driver Quantities	(Multiply) Reported Case
Auto Insert	$0.07	600	$42.00
Manual Pre	$0.24	400	$96.00
Manual Post	$0.75	25	$18.75
Auto Test	$0.04	250	$10.00
Assembly	$58.34	0.5	$29.17
Test	$82.60	0.5	$41.30
Fab	$40.88	0	$0.00
Procurement	26.51%	$220.00	$58.32
Total Overhead Cost			$295.54
Material Cost			$220.00
Total Cost			$515.54
Difference (Product 1 Minus 2)			$0.09

Exhibit TN-3   Computing Core Only Cost Driver Rates

How To Calculate the Cost Driver Rates Excluding the B-T Contract

Step 1: Calculate 2nd Half Core Business Costs

	Total Cost	B-T Cost	Core Only Cost
Auto Insert	$248.10	$85.30	$162.80
Manual Pre	$734.70	$46.00	$688.70
Manual Post	$275.40	$18.50	$256.90
Auto Test	$151.90	$82.80	$69.10
Assembly	$811.80	$214.50	$597.30
Test	$1,994.80	$526.80	$1,468.00
Fab	$532.80	$54.20	$478.60
Procurement	$2,247.90	$265.00	$1,982.90
Source	(Exhibit 1)	(Exhibit 6)	(Subtract)

Step 2: Calculate 2nd Half Total Driver Quantities

	Total Cost	DVR Rates	Total Cost Driver Quantities
Auto Insert	$248.10	$0.07	3544.29
Manual Pre	$734.70	$0.24	3061.25
Manual Post	$275.40	$0.75	367.20
Auto Test	$151.90	$0.04	3797.50
Assembly	$811.80	$58.34	13.91
Test	$1,994.80	$82.60	24.15
Fab	$532.80	$40.88	13.03
Procurement	$2,247.90	26.51%	8479.44
Source:	(Exhibit 1)	(Exhibit 2)	(Divide)

Step 3: Calculate 2nd Half Core Driver Quantities

	Total Cost Driver Quantities	B-T Cost Driver Quantities	Core Cost Driver Quantities
Auto Insert	3544.29	1979.20	1747.09
Manual Pre	3061.25	1099.00	1962.25
Manual Post	367.20	53.40	313.80
Auto Test	3797.50	2382.80	1414.70
Assembly	13.91	4.39	9.52
Test	24.15	10.86	13.29
Fab	13.03	1.90	11.13
Procurement	8479.44	2485.00	5994.44
Source:	(Step 2)	(Exhibit 6)	(Subtract)

Exhibit 3 (cont'd)

Step 4: Calculate 2nd Half Core Driver Rates

	Core Only Cost	Core Cost Driver Quantities	Core Cost Driver Rates
Auto Insert	$162.80	1747.09	$0.09
Manual Pre	$688.70	1962.25	$0.35
Manual Post	$256.90	313.80	$0.82
Auto Test	$69.10	1414.70	$0.05
Assembly	$597.30	9.52	$62.71
Test	$1,468.00	13.29	$110.46
Fab	$478.60	11.13	$42.99
Procurement	$1,982.90	5994.44	33.08%
Source:	(Step 1)	(Step 3)	(Divide)

Step 5:   Compare Rates

	Core DVR Rates	2nd Half DVR Rates	Difference
Auto Insert	$0.09	$0.07	$0.02
Manual Pre	$0.35	$0.24	$0.11
Manual Post	$0.82	$0.75	
Auto Test	$0.05	$0.04	$0.01
Assembly	$62.71	$58.34	$4.37
Test	$110.46	$82.60	$28.14
Fab	$42.99	$40.88	$2.11
Procurement	33.08%	26.51%	6.57%
Source:	(Step 4)	(Exhibit 2)	(Subtract)

Exhibit TN-4 Computing the Reported Cost of the Two Designs Using Core Only Cost Driver Rates

	Core DVR Rates	Design 1 Operations	Design 1 Cost
Auto Insert	$0.09	150	$13.98
Manual Pre	$0.35	50	$17.55
Manual Post	$0.82	10	$8.19
Auto Test	$0.05	100	$4.88
Assembly	$62.71	0.5	$31.35
Test	$119.53	0.5	$59.77
Fab	$42.99	0	$0.00
Procurement	33.08%	$325.00	$107.51
Total Overhead Cost			$243.22
Material Cost			$325.00
Total Cost			$568.22

	Core DVR Rates	Design 2 Operations	Design 2 Cost
Auto Insert	$0.09	600	$55.91
Manual Pre	$0.35	400	$140.39
Manual Post	$0.82	25	$20.47
Auto Test	$0.05	250	$12.21
Assembly	$62.71	0.5	$31.35
Test	$110.46	0.5	$55.23
Fab	$42.99	0	$0.00
Procurement	33.08%	$220.00	$72.77
Total Overhead Cost			$388.33
Material Cost			$220.00
Total Cost			$608.33
Difference (Product 1 Minus 2)			(40.11)

Hewlett Packard: Queensferry Telecommunications Division
Teaching Note
Figure 1

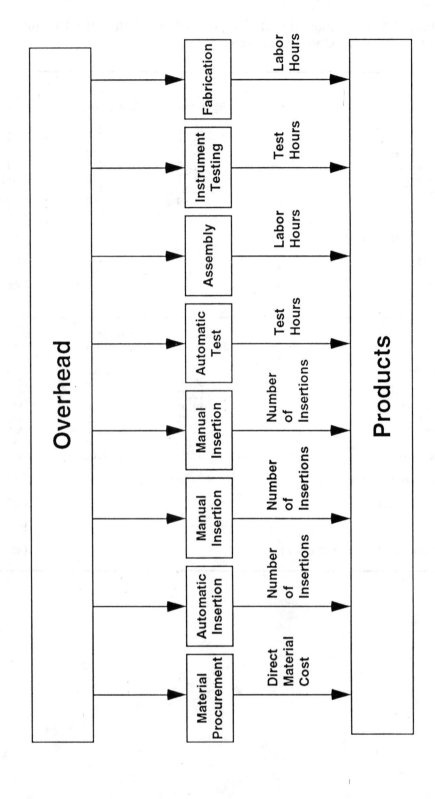

Hewlett Packard: Queensferry Telecommunications Division
Teaching Note
Figure 2

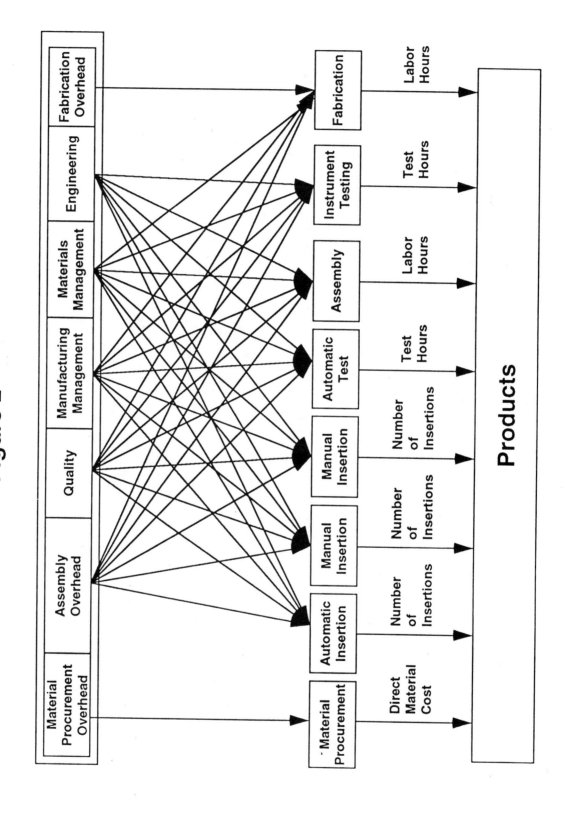

Activity-Based Systems
In Service Organizations and Service Functions

The cases in Chapter 7 demonstrate how the activity-based concepts introduced in Chapters 5 and 6 can be applied both to service companies (health care, financial institutions, transportation companies) and to the selling and administrative activities for manufacturing companies. Instructors may, instead of waiting for the end of the course to cover service organizations, choose to weave some of these cases together with the manufacturing cases to show students how the activity-based concepts apply without modification to service operations.

The *Union Pacific* case series that opens Chapter 7 can also be taught as a bridge case between Chapters 4 and 5. The (A) case describes the development of an elaborate system for spending and operational control, but which provides no information on product costs. As the railroad is thrust into a newly competitive (deregulated) environment, the company must decide how to get new information to help make decisions on pricing, and product and customer mix. The (B) case describes the two new cost systems that were developed for these purposes: the Network Cost System to be used for bidding and pricing, and an ex post "job order cost" system that costs out every carload move. The new cost systems followed activity-based principles by using multiple drivers to assign operating expenses to products. The Union Pacific case is a particularly good case to show why traditional direct costing systems are inadequate for companies whose cost structures are shifting to high percentages of indirect support costs. In Union Pacific's case, the direct costs for a particular carload move are virtually zero, yet the managers in the company felt that a majority of their operating expenses were caused by individual carload moves.

The *Massachusetts Eye and Ear Infirmary* case describes a 1970s application of ABC principles to a health care institution. The application is simple, yet elegant, and would be a reasonable choice to start the entire ABC sequence. By introducing ABC concepts in a health care institutional setting, the concepts that emerged in subsequent cases set in manufacturing companies could be related back to the hospital setting. In this way, the instructor could continually maintain the application of ideas to both manufacturing and service companies. But the Mass Eye and Ear case does fine in its own right, even when deferred to after the manufacturing ABC cases, and permits students to discuss the applicability and extension of the relatively simple model developed for MEEI to more complex comprehensive health care institutions.

American Bank describes the adoption of more accurate product costing procedures for a banking institution facing the pressure of the de-regulated environment of the late 1970s. It is a good introduction to costing transactional accounts (checking and savings accounts) and for showing how to relate bank operating expenses to individual customer accounts. The case should be relatively straightforward to teach. Students likely will have more familiarity with checking and savings accounts than with hydraulic valves, taps, and flexible machining centers. Some instructors have used American Bank as the final exam for their cost management course.

Kanthal (A) demonstrates the applicability of ABC principles to selling expenses. Kanthal shows how selling and administrative expenses can be related to individual customers and customer transactions. The company designed a simple ABC system to highlight the cost of order processing and of handling non-standard products. But even with the simple system, they got dramatic insights. The powerful aspect of the case occurs at the end when the class discusses the actions that can be taken based on the new profitability information. The instructor can reveal (from the (B) case and teaching note) the actions actually taken and the increase in profits experienced.

Winchell Lighting (A) and (B) extends the Kanthal analysis of customer-specific expenses to driving selling and distribution expenses to channels and market segments. The analysis in Winchell (A) shows strong shifts in the perceived profitability of individual distribution channels. The case permits discussion of cost hierarchies for product lines, channels and segments, thereby extending the hierarchical model (illustrated for factory expenses in Chapter 5) to general selling and corporate expenses. The (B) case discusses the actions the company took based on the analysis of the (A) case and allows the class to talk about how to get management to assume ownership of the new marketing profitability study and to act on its findings.

The *Manufacturers Hanover Corporation: Customer Profitability Report* (MHC) case combines the American Bank and Kanthal cases by showing the need for measuring customer profitability in a banking institution. MHC focuses on two key issues: measuring the return on risk-adjusted-equity (the key profitability measure) of individual commercial loans; and devising a reward and recognition system for bank lending officers who market products sold by other units. The two new cost systems developed by MHC--the Loan Pricing Model and the Customer Profitability Report--bear a remarkable resemblance to the two new costing systems developed in the Union Pacific (B) case.

For the readings at the end of Chapter 7, "Why SG&A doesn't always work" can accompany the Kanthal and Winchell cases and "Customer Profitability Analysis" can be used with Kanthal, Winchell, and Manufacturers Hanover. "How Weyerhaeuser Measures Corporate Overhead Costs" describes some excellent procedures for assigning corporate overhead costs to divisions. None of the cases in the book addresses the accurate assignment of corporate overhead expenses, the subject of this reading, so instructors may wish to discuss the article in a separate class. Alternatively, they can assign it with Kanthal, Winchell, or Manufacturers Hanover to stimulate a brief discussion on assigning corporate overhead expenses.

Harvard Business School

5-187-058

rev. 3/20/91

Union Pacific (A) and (B)
Teaching Note

The Union Pacific case series provides a new setting for the study of cost systems. Studying cost systems in a service industry frees us from our traditional thinking in how cost systems should be designed and operated. At a deeper and more subtle level, however, the Union Pacific cases enable us to develop some extremely important concepts that have applicability in manufacturing and other service industries, not just railroading.

The important issues that will emerge by the end of the second session of teaching (the B case) include:

1. The concept of a product in a complex service environment;

2. Operational control and product costing require two completely different systems (this is perhaps the most important lesson from the case series);

3. Long run variable cost is the appropriate cost concept for measuring product costs;

4. Long run variable cost can include no short-term expenses; estimating variable costs may consist entirely of estimates of long-run spending consequences; and

5. Successful introduction of radical new cost systems may only be possible when the industry, or company, experiences major changes in its competitive environment, such as was introduced by the Staggers Act that deregulated the railroad industry in 1980.

The assignment for the first session should be to read the Introduction case and to prepare for discussion of the (A) case.

This teaching note was prepared by Professor Robert S. Kaplan as an aid to instructors in classroom use of cases Union Pacific (Intro.) 9-186-176, (A) 9-186-177 and (B) 9-186-178.

Assignment or Discussion Questions for Union Pacific (A):

1. As of 1965, what systems were likely used by Union Pacific to control operations and measure costs?

2. Evaluate the MCC and COAT systems installed during the 1970s. What functions were done well by these systems and what functions were done poorly or not at all?

3. If you were a member of the senior management group of Union Pacific in 1980 observing the imminent deregulation of the railroads, what new systems or modifications to existing systems would you be advocating?

The series Introduction provides a brief history and description of Union Pacific and the operation of the railroad. I usually start the class by giving a historical perspective to the development of cost systems in railroads. I mention that the railroads, in the mid-nineteenth century, were the largest enterprises yet created by mankind, requiring extensive systems to collect cash, disburse cash, and monitor operations across enormous geographical areas. It is unlikely that the extensive railroad systems could have been created without the simultaneous development of the telegraph which permitted communication and control over vastly larger areas than previously were possible. The railroads thus provided a rich setting for the development of management accounting and control procedures; in fact, leadership in developing accounting procedures shifted from England to America because of the demands created by accounting for railroad operations. Details on this development can be found in Alfred Chandler's, The Visible Hand, for instructors who want to be more confident about discussing this historical context. In any case, one can open the discussion by mentioning that cost accounting in railroads was highly influential on subsequent developments in large manufacturing enterprises such as steel, metal fabricating, and automobiles, and that it is worthwhile to revisit this 150 year old industry to see what new insights we can glean for contemporary cost accounting practice.

After the brief summary of the history of railroads and railroad cost accounting, I ask the class to describe the state of railroad operations around 1965, just before the two new cost systems, MCC and COAT, were developed at Union Pacific. Usually, it is easy to get comments describing the highly regulated rate structure, where prices were a function of what was carried rather than on the cost of transporting commodities. That is, deliberate social and political policies were carried out through the railroad rate structure by charging rates based on the value of the item carried rather than its marginal transportation cost. Thus commodity goods (agricultural products, coal for utilities) were transported at low prices; they were subsidized by the high prices charged for transporting manufacturing goods. One can mention that using prices to execute social and political pressures has a predictable effect. Other transportation forms, such as trucks and air cargo, will carry manufactured goods, leaving low margin bulk commodity goods for the railroads to carry.

The class usually mentions the heavily unionized work force with consequent work rule restrictions. I point out that train crews were still being paid a full day's wages for each 100 mile segment they ran since that distance represented an average day's travel when locomotives were run by steam (some relaxation of this 100 mile limitation is now being attempted by railroads, but the pay for distance feature is still prominent). Thus, with modern, high speed diesel locomotives that can travel more than 400 miles in one day, train crews can receive four days of pay for one day of work. Unionized rules also can cause over-staffing of train crews, such as the provision requiring a fireman to be carried on diesel locomotives where the demand for man-made on-board fires is quite low. But the case really does not depend on discussion of work force issues so I would not spend much time talking about labor problems.

A third characteristic that could be mentioned is the increasing competition from trucks, especially with the government financing of the interstate highway system in the post World War II era. Intermodal (trains combining with other transportation forms, such as trucks and ships) operations has been one response to the increased competition from trucks who offer timeliness, convenience, and dependability (and frequently price) advantages. Students sometimes think, however, that railroads do not compete with each other; that they have a natural monopoly based on rights of ways granted more than a century ago. A quick glance at the map in Exhibit 2 should be sufficient to make the point that shippers in most locations will have a choice of railroads to move commodities to a wide variety of destinations.

After these background remarks, I turn to a discussion of Rail Form A (Exhibits 1, 2 and Appendix A in the (A) case) by asking what cost system was being used up to 1965? Rail Form A was developed more than 50 years ago to serve as a uniform basis for reporting costs so that regulators would have consistent information as they attempted to determine prices. I mention that the thinking behind Rail Form A is quite sophisticated. The variable cost percentages that are shown in some of the Exhibits to the (A) case are based on extensive cross-sectional statistical studies. Regression analyses were performed on railroad operating and cost data long before digital computers and sophisticated software packages became available.

I also show how Rail Form A is an advanced two stage procedure where the second stage allocation uses multiple allocation bases (see Exhibit TNl) . That is, unlike traditional manufacturing cost systems, where the second stage allocation is done just by direct labor hours, the Rail Form A procedure allocates costs to products using multiple allocation bases: gross ton miles, yard/train switching hours, freight-car miles, tons of freight, number of cars, etc. Thus, the Rail Form A allocation procedure is an early version of an activity-based system. It is interesting to observe the sophistication of this procedure, developed more than a half-century ago. One might also ask students to explain why such a complex system was developed long before the cost of information processing made such computations easy. You would like them to realize that measuring costs using just a single basis, such as cost per gross ton mile, would not capture the complexity and diversity of any particular move. Such a discussion would set the stage for a subsequent discussion on the definition of the "product" in a railroad.

While I have the diagram of Rail Form A (Exhibit TNl) on the board, I ask the class how much cost is represented by the three main cost categories (data appear in Exhibits of Introduction case):

Way and Structures (Tracks, Yards)	17 %
Equipment (Locomotives, Freight Cars)	25
Transportation (Train Crews, Fuel, Stations, Yards)	47
Total	89 %

This illustrates that Operations is what railroads are about. Also, students usually observe that labor represents about 60 % of total costs.

Before moving to discussion of the MCC system, I like to have the class think about how railroad operations were controlled before any of the new systems were developed and introduced. Does Rail Form A provide a basis for managing costs? There is not enough information in the case to develop this point well and few if any students have any additional knowledge about railroad operations. You can mention that a key performance measure, in use for more than a century of railroad operations, is the operating ratio: the ratio of operating costs to revenues. Over the years, railroad managers learned that if the operating ratio was in a certain range, say 80 to 85%, they would be profitable. If the operating ratio were over 90%, they were in trouble. In addition, the railroad engineers conducted detailed studies to guide their repair and maintenance activities. Railroad operations are so repetitive that given the number of years they had been in existence, an enormous stock of knowledge had been acquired about life of track, freight cars, locomotives, and the effect of speed, weight, and terrain on wear and tear. Also, simple summary measures such as revenue dollars per gross ton mile, or operating cost per gross ton mile, per locomotive engine minute, or per switching minute were probably collected and monitored.

The Management Cost Control (MCC) System

At this point, I turn to discussion and analysis of the MCC system. I ask, why did this system have to be developed; what is the scope of its reach. Clearly, with 22,000 route miles, 108,000 freight cars, 3,200 locomotives, and switching yards, repair facilities, and stations dispersed over thousands of square miles, it would be difficult to monitor and control costs with aggregate systems such as Rail Form A, or with aggregate performance measures such as the operating ratio or costs per gross ton mile. MCC is a beautiful example of responsibility reporting, with costs collected at 5,000 cost centers using up to 1,500 cost codes.

Because the forms seem complex, I walk the students through Exhibits 3-9. Exhibit 3 shows the cost break down, at the ICC cost code level, for one locomotive repair yard in North Platte, Nebraska. Remind students that there would be 5,000 such reports prepared monthly for each cost center in the railroad. Exhibit 4 presents the same data as in Exhibit 3 but aggregated into broad functional categories: personnel, materials and supplies, purchased services, and miscellaneous that are similar to the four functional categories used in the Introduction case to disaggregate Union Pacific's cost structure. You can remark on the informal variance analysis for each account: actual, % deviation from budget, and % deviation from same month last year; also, same three categories are used to analyze year-to-date expenditures.

Exhibit 5 presents the monthly cost summary for all locomotive repair yards. Note the $21,833 amount for the North Platte Yard. This report would be sent to the manager in charge of locomotive yard repairs, systemwide. The total expense ($94,084) of locomotive repair yards shown in Exhibit 5 is explained in Exhibit 6 by the four main functional categories (note similarity in form between Exhibits 4 and 6). You can mention that reports similar to Exhibits 5 and 6 would be prepared for freight car repair yards, fuel consumption, operations of crew districts, maintenance of track, train stations, and switching yards; that is all major operating units.

Exhibit 7 presents unit costs for all railroad operations. Costs by functional categories, such as fuel cost, locomotive maintenance and freight car maintenance, are normalized by alternative activity measures: power unit miles (a measure of locomotive horsepower used), power unit hours, service locomotive days, hundred freight car miles, thousand gross ton miles, and serviceable car days. This report still is a summary only of the Mechanical Department and would be prepared monthly for the head of Mechanical in Omaha. Similar reports would also be prepared for the heads of Transportation and Way and Structures.

Exhibit 8 shows how one other major expense category - freight crew costs - is collected and summarized by district. This cost is normalized by thousand gross ton miles, the standard activity measure for freight crew output. Note the sophistication of the reporting system in which costs are reported as actual and also net of wage increases.

Exhibit 9 summarizes costs by train symbol. A train symbol designates a regularly scheduled train that runs between two specified points; e.g., Los Angeles and Denver, or Seattle and Portland. A number of key operating performance measures are reported for each train symbol - tons/train, horsepower/train, initial terminal delay (ITD), final terminal delay (FTD) (these represent delays in excess of a predetermined standard in getting a train underway or completing a run; interestingly, train crews are paid bonuses if ITD or FTD exceed the standard, certainly a perverse incentive for efficiency and promptness). If students are not too overwhelmed (or bored) by all these numbers and reports, you might mention the considerable variation in operating characteristics across the different train symbols. Unlike Gertrude Stein's roses, a gross ton mile is not a gross ton mile is not ... .

At this point, students are usually ready to toss in the towel with the MCC system. A typical response to my non-directive question, "Well, what do you think of MCC?" is "lots of numbers and data; no information." After talking them through Exhibits 3-9, it is worth letting the class give comments and talk back and forth without too much instructor guidance. Key points could be summarized on the board as they are made. The usual criticism is that with all the data collected and presented in MCC, there is no information useful for pricing or determining the profitability of different kinds of service. This is an extremely important point; I would note it on the board if it arises naturally from the class discussion but would not push it or elaborate on it at this time.

Before the discussion turns too negative, I attempt to point out that MCC is really a excellent system for spending and expense control. Expenses are collected at responsibility centers, and details of 5,000 cost center reports are aggregated hierarchically for higher levels of management until senior operations executives, in Omaha, can review a one page summary of all activities under their control and responsibility. The data are probably quite meaningful to cost center and operations managers. Some students point out that variances from budget or from last year are not very meaningful; it would be better if a flexible budget were prepared to control for variations in activity at each cost center. This is a reasonable observation; but I reply that many of the activities being reported on are highly discretionary. While in the long run, the amount spent on maintenance and repair varies with activity levels, in the short run the company has enormous discretion to accelerate or, more likely, defer maintenance and even repair activity. Therefore, it would be difficult to obtain activity measures that would predict well the fluctuations in monthly expenses for many of the cost centers. At a senior, and aggregate, level, costs are normalized for activity by dividing by the variety of activity measures - locomotive unit miles, gross ton miles, number of cars, etc.

In summary, MCC seems to me like an excellent expense or operational control system that fits very well into the strong engineering and operations culture that has existed in railroads for more than a century. It requires considerable sophistication in the use of remote information entry and centralized information processing. As some students may have noted, it does not provide much information about product costs. But in the highly regulated railroad environment prior to 1980, there was little payoff to knowing costs for each move. Prices were set by published tariff so the key to success was controlling expenses while providing satisfactory levels of service, timeliness, and reliability. The big leverage item was to keep expenses down (operations accounted for 89% of total costs) and the MCC system provided detailed, comprehensive information for this task.

But what is missing? At this point, the discussion can return to the information not provided by MCC? Anticipating the influence of deregulation, the class will want to think about the product-line and pricing issues that will soon be emerging for Union Pacific. Be provocative; ask how you would use information in MCC to aid the pricing decision or to determine product-line profitability. The answer that easily emerges is that with all the incredible amount of data generated monthly by MCC, there is not a scrap of information useful for measuring costs of particular move (I usually put up a symbolic diagram of MCC - see TN2 to show that the cost of a particular move requires a slice through every single cost category). This is usually the correct time to talk about what a product represents to a railroad. If a railroad is just providing a homogeneous output - say, gross ton miles as the best bet - then couldn't it accumulate all costs, divide by projected gross ton miles, and thus estimate the costs for any particular move as number of gross ton miles in the move multiplied by the standard (or historical actual) cost per gross ton mile? If this were satisfactory, why did the railroad even bother with developing the COAT system?

One hopes that at least some students recognize that not all gross ton miles are alike. The cost of a particular move depends on the number of cars connected together to form a train, the number and power of locomotives used, the route taken, the nature of the terrain, how many switches get made, how long does a switch take, the type of freight car used, etc. (go back to Rail Form A if they have trouble thinking about all the variations associated with a particular move). If all carload moves were identical along each of these dimensions, then a surrogate such as gross ton miles would work fine and the railroad could be thought of as a single product (gross ton mile) producer. But if there is significant variation from move to move along each of these dimensions - as seems more plausible - then each different type of move could represent a different product.

The COAT system is an approximation that computes the cost of a move based on industry-side averages: number of switches per thousand miles, average switching time, average number of cars per train, average speed, average locomotive powering, average frequency of empty returns. It was probably better than what they had before (which was nothing) in estimating profits by product line, geographical area, or for a particular move. But it hardly represented the basis for an aggressive marketing and pricing activity to be competitive in the deregulated, post Staggers Act environment of the 1980s.

After discussing how product costs require slicing across the functional cost categories in the MCC system, I point out that the railroad has virtually a complete separation between the system that generates revenues and the system that generates costs. Revenues are generated by customer orders and tracked by the waybills. Revenues and accounts receivable are triggered by waybills. Costs, on the other hand arise from the operating functions of the railroad: transportation, engineering, maintenance, repair, etc. No costs that are incurred can be traced to a particular waybill. Fuel costs and train crews are associated with an entire collection of cars and therefore still require an allocation to each car within a train. At this time, one can ask the class, why this situation does not occur for traditional manufacturing environments. What links exist that tie costs and revenues closer together in manufacturing than in railroad operation?

I believe that direct labor and direct material provide the linkage between costs incurred and revenues earned in manufacturing. When working on a discrete, identifiable product, we can measure the material and touch labor committed to that product; these are the directly traceable costs. And these direct costs provide the hooks by which other factory costs - overhead - get "attached" to products. The railroad, lacking direct material and labor for its products, which are the individual carload moves, has no "hooks" by which costs can get attached to revenue generating activities. Thus the revenue and the cost systems end up being quite separate systems.

This observation seems worth making for as manufacturing organizations have their factory overhead and marketing and distribution costs increase as a total fraction of total product costs, they will start to look more like a railroad environment with increasing separation between activities that generate revenues and activities that incur costs. Therefore, lessons we learn about how railroads measure total product costs may be relevant for measuring product costs in manufacturing organizations.

I also ask the class to think about what other types of organizations have this almost complete separation between the revenue generating system and the cost system. They usually identify other types of service organizations, especially telecommunications and financial services, as having this characteristic. For telecommunications, there is no direct or incremental cost associated with an individual transfer of voice or data. The costs exist to create and maintain the network that individual messages travel over - much as railroad cars travel over rail lines. In a commercial bank, revenues are earned by the dollar volume of assets (such as loans and mortgages) whereas operating (noninterest) costs are incurred to place or process transactions for these assets that are unrelated to the size of the loan.

Union Pacific (B)

The second day of discussion of the Union Pacific Case Series focuses on the design and introduction of the new product cost systems: CPMS and NCS. The session starts out working through a lot of detail to understand the underlying structure of the systems but it can close with a powerful message about the design of cost systems.

Possible assignment questions include:

1. Evaluate the Consolidated Profit Measurement System (CPMS) and the Network Cost System (NCS). What do you see as the strong and the weak aspects of these two systems?

2. Why are two different systems - CPMS and NCS - needed by Union Pacific?

3. What organizational issues are raised by CPMS and NCS? Where should the Planning & Analysis group be located? What types of linkages are required among existing organizational units?

4. Some of the largest current expenses of the railroad, such as maintenance and repairs, relate more to past traffic than to current traffic. How should these expenses be treated in CPMS and NCS?

5. How should incremental business be costed? For example, what costs should be attributed to the last car to be added to an existing train?

I start the class by asking, "What did CPMS add over the COAT system?" The class should respond that CPMS is a cost system based on the actual car movement and the operating characteristics of the train used, whereas COAT was based on industry averages for car and train movements. The statement in the case that the system was successful 95% of the time in matching a waybill to an actual carload movement in the system is worth noting, given the large number of moves executed each day and the great geographic dispersion in operations over the Union Pacific system. One needs an impressive real time information system in order to reach this 95% success rate. (One might contrast this with the situation at Penn Central when it went bankrupt in 1970; Penn Central often lost track of where its cars were for extended periods of time.)

Specifically, CPMS was based on the actual number and powering of locomotives (locomotives could be added or subtracted from a train based on the load it was carrying), the specific routing used for the carload movement, actual speed, actual gross ton miles, car miles, and number of cars, and whether the movement involved an empty return or not. At the time the case was written, the switching times and initial and final terminal delay were based on historical averages, but a system was being developed to capture and measure these data at each switching yard for each car and train. In summary, CPMS attempts to measure the costs and profits of each individual move. It is analogous to a manufacturing cost system measuring actual costs by individual batches and operations.

One might raise the issue as to why a railroad, with operations covering thousands of square miles can capture actual resource consumption by jobs whereas manufacturing companies do not attempt to capture actual costs even when all jobs are done under a single roof. I suppose the answer is at least twofold: for the railroad, each movement could be unique whereas manufacturing companies with repetitive processing of a narrower product line can rely more on a standard cost system. More important, however, may be that Union Pacific developed its product cost system in the 1980s and therefore exploited all the computer technology of this era; manufacturing companies designed their product cost systems decades ago and most have not reconsidered the opportunities now available for individual part and batch tracking through use of automatic bar code reading and local area networks. Related to this point is that the Union Pacific system builds off the information used for operations control whereas many manufacturing product cost systems do not link closely to existing production control systems in the factory.

After reviewing the goals of CPMS, I turn to Appendix A to walk the class through the costing of an actual car movement. I start on page 500 by showing how locomotive repair costs are computed. One starts with the estimate, made by UP cost analysts, of locomotive repair costs of $.7407 per locomotive unit mile. This number comes from extensive internal statistical and engineering studies relating repair costs to a measure of locomotive activity. The specific measure - locomotive unit mile (LUM) - is an internally generated (and not easily understood or explained) measure of the intensity of use of a locomotive. It would be analogous to a direct labor or machine hour for a manufacturing operation. The cost of each LUM is the same but the number of LUMs demanded will be a function of train size and weight. The railroad can add locomotives as the train size and weight hauled increase. One might mention that the estimate of locomotive repair costs is not based on last month's or last year's experience. It is an average over the past 3 to 5 years. Maintenance and repair expenditures are quite discretionary over short periods of time so that it would be misleading to use experience over a short time period to estimate the relationship between activity levels and maintenance and repair costs.

The particular train, symbol Z200 that ran on Feb. 3, 1985, used 300 locomotive unit miles of activity from the locomotives and pulled cars that totaled 500,000 gross ton miles. The estimated repair cost for this movement, therefore, is 300 x $.7404 = $222.21 and this cost must be shared by the 500,000 GTM of freight carried. This leads to the estimate of $.000444 per gross ton mile for carload on this train. For a particular car on this train, for example car # ABX 003301 (see data at the bottom of page 501) that incurred 27,000 gross ton miles (90 tons of gross car weight carried on 300 miles of track: 100 from A to B, 50 from B to C, and 150 from C to D), the estimated repair cost is 27,000 x $.000444 = $12. This corresponds to the fourth line on the exhibit on page 503, Locomotive repairs $12. The exhibit on page 503 accumulates all the costs for carload ABX 003301. (There is a mild inconsistency in the numbers which a very alert student might notice: strictly speaking, car ABX 003301 was connected to three different trains (Z200, XZ, and Z400) as it moved from city A to city D -see data on page 16: Car Movement Operating Statistics. We estimated the locomotive repair cost assuming it traveled only on train Z200. I have yet to have a student notice this inconsistency, however, and it does not detract from understanding the philosophy of the calculation of locomotive repair costs.)

Having explained the derivation of locomotive repair costs, we now turn to the cost of crew wages for car ABX 003301 . Total train crew wages for the train movement from A to B were $1,050 and this train carried 500,000 GTM of cargo. Thus, the crew wage per GTM for this segment was $.0021 (see second panel on page 502). For car ABX 003301, this segment was 90 Tons x 100 Miles or 9,000 GTM. Thus its share of crew wages is $.0021 x 9,000 = $18.90 . The crew wages to this car for the other two segments can be computed similarly ($7.45 for B-C and $25.65 for C-D) and when added together yield the $52 estimate found as the first entry on the car movement costed history on page 503.

One can demonstrate the calculation of quite a few numbers that appear in the Car Movement Costed History on page 503. Fuel cost of $ 34 is shown in the second panel on page 502. Students may notice that there is no repair or depreciation cost for the freight car itself. This is because this car is not UP owned. From the data, one can infer that this is a leased car with no per diem rental costs but a mileage charge of $0.63 per mile (see entries on the sixth line of the third panel on page 502). Since the car traveled 300 miles, the Car-mileage charge of $189 can be derived. The terminal switching costs - Origin, Destination, and Intermediate - can also be calculated from the data on page 502.

After working through some of the above numbers, you should ask what kinds of costs are being calculated in CPMS? Even though we have actual operating data for each carload - weight, distance, locomotives used, switching terminals, etc. - the unit cost for each cost category is an estimate of variable costs; e.g., repair cost, depreciation cost, overhead cost. Fuel cost, which in principle could be measured at the train level - it's really the only "direct material cost" in the cost of a train move - happens to be estimated based on an engineering model rather than measured directly. Interestingly, the only expenses that is measured accurately at the train level - - the train crew wage expense -- must be allocated to individual cars within the train. All the other expenses represent estimated demands on the railroad's resources, some short-run like fuel, others long-run such as freight car, locomotive, and track maintenance and repair, and hence are causally related to running a loaded freight car down the track. The wages of the train crew, however, are "train-sustaining:" they are incurred to run the train down the track but are independent of the number and weight of the cars carried by the train. Relating back to the cost hierarchy introduced in Chapter 5, train wage expenses are a batch-level expense whereas fuel consumption, and wear and tear on cars, locomotives, track, and railbed are unit-level that vary with the gross-ton miles being run.

I then ask, who gets the CPMS report, what is it used for? There is frequently some confusion about this. Some people claim that it is useful for pricing decisions. Strictly speaking, this is not true. It is an ex post measurement system that evaluates the profitability of moves already made. It is not helpful in future pricing decisions except to indicate how some moves or types of moves made in the past were or were not profitable. CPMS was developed at the request of the chief executive of the railroad who wanted to be able to evaluate how well the marketing department was handling its new freedom in the deregulated environment. He wanted to be able to evaluate long-run profitability by type of commodity carried, by geographic region, or by marketing manager responsibility and the CPMS was designed to provide this information. This helps to explain why, despite the daily updating of the CPMS file, managerial reports were only prepared monthly and were distributed to only a few senior executives.

Either at this point, or perhaps earlier, at the end of the (A) case, you can discuss with the class the major shift in managerial focus between the regulated and deregulated environment. In the old regulated days, when prices were set by the ICC and the ability to enter or leave product markets restricted by regulators, engineering and operating people were the key personnel in the organization. Profits could be earned by providing a higher quality of service and/or by controlling costs. In the deregulated environment, marketing people became critical resources as they searched and bid for new business. Therefore systems that served engineering and operating people well (such as the MCC system) would not be adequate for the marketing function. CPMS was a system to evaluate the performance of the marketing function.

But in order to help the marketing function, not just evaluate it retrospectively, another system, NCS, had to be developed. NCS, while working off the same data base as CPMS, differs from CPMS in important dimensions. At the most obvious level, it provides forecasts of the costs of future moves not estimates of the costs of past actual moves. Therefore, NCS must be based on average statistics of past moves. Where CPMS uses the actual locomotive powering, number of cars, quantity of GTM, routing, and switching locations, the NCS uses averages based on recent (6 month) experiences when estimating the costs of future moves. NCS also provides simulation capabilities so that the effect of altering assumptions on routing, powering, train size and weight, speed, empty return or not, etc. can be evaluated. NCS further provides the capability for rolling costs forward six months or a year or two to forecast the cost of future moves. Finally, Exhibit 2 of the (B) case shows that four different estimates - book value vs. replacement, long term variable vs. fully allocated - are prepared to provide some flexibility to the marketing department for adjusting bids depending on the nature of the demand and competition, and its judgment on how badly it wants a particular type of business.

Once the differences between CPMS and NCS have been articulated, one should turn to the managerial issues involved with NCS. The system may appear straightforward but lots of managerial judgments and decisions have to be made about the design and implementation of the NCS system. I have found that I can not cover all of the relevant issues; the instructor has to make a judgment as to which issues seem most interesting or pertinent to discuss with the class.

On the design front, the treatment of incremental costs is quite interesting. Suppose a train consisting of 30 cars is already in existence and set to run or that the average train size for a given run is 30 cars. The opportunity to bid on business involving a 31st car arises. How should this new business be costed? One possibility is to calculate just the incremental fuel and wear and tear costs from adding the 31st car and price on this basis (the train crew cost would not change by adding a 31st car and hence would not represent an incremental cost). The other possibility, and the one adopted by UP, is to compute the total costs of a 31 car move and then allocate the cost - by GTM, car miles, etc. - across each of the 31 cars. UP's philosophy - at least the philosophy of the Planning & Analysis group who developed and oversee NCS - is that it is dangerous to cost on a short-run incremental business. If too much business comes in on this basis, eventually you start adding new trains. Also, if the class seems to be pushing hard for incremental costing, you can ask how would the cost of the first car be determined under their system. I believe that there is an information processing dimension too. UP is a big company and it needs a system that will work without too much managerial intervention every day. I don't think they want a system where someone has to decide, perhaps daily, which business is normal long-run business that pays average costs and which business is short-run incremental business that should be accepted if it covers short-run incremental costs.

One can ask, Who prepares an NCS estimate? What discipline exists to insure that the assumptions on routing, train size, power, etc. are reasonable? Where is the P&A group located? Where should it be located? Arguments can be made that the NCS serves the marketing function so that the P&A group should report to the senior marketing executive. George Craig, the marketing VP, however, strongly believes that the P&A function has to be in the finance group. It has to provide an independent discipline to cost out projected business without being subject to the pressure to shave cost estimates for new business to help meet marketing goals. Therefore, at least at UP, the P&A function that operates the NCS and CPMS systems exists within the finance group and does not report to marketing executives.

The question still remains as to how this finance group obtains validity checks on its own estimates. At present, the group has senior operating executives review and sign off on the parameters used in the NCS projections. This review is done monthly and helps to give credibility to the operating assumptions built into the NCS projections. This seems to me an extremely important organizational strategy so that the finance group is not viewed as coming up with estimates in isolation and, in effect, "throwing them over the wall" to the marketing people. Some students may also wish to argue that the P&A function should be in the operations department so that the NCS estimates and feedback from CPMS could be tied closely to the people making operating decisions. This is certainly a defensible viewpoint but not the way UP chose to organize its P&A function.

I think the current arrangement is fine: it forces the cost estimating and measurement people (in the P&A group) to be sensitive to the concerns of the marketing and operating departments but to have the independence that stems from being separate from either. I believe the links between the product costing people in P&A and the marketing and operating managers presages the new role for cost accountants in manufacturing organizations. Product costing data for manufactured products need to be made more strategic (the message from Schrader-Bellows) and cost people will have to interact far more with marketing and operating people than they have in the past several decades.

This discussion of organizational issues leads naturally to asking how NCS and CPMS estimates can and should get reconciled. The following flow chart illustrates the process by which carload moves get estimated and performed:

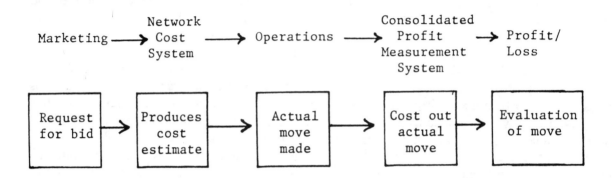

There could be a significant lag between the time when an NCS estimates the cost of a proposed move and when the actual move is made. At the time the case was written, there was no systematic means by which the assumptions used in the NCS estimate were transmitted to Operations to serve as a working guide for the actual move. In practice, some of the P&A people felt that the Operations people were not always as sensitive as they might be on the effect of their operating decisions on the estimated cost of a move. Thus routing or powering decisions may be made for operating convenience rather than to minimize costs. The impact of such decisions would not show up until the CPMS run was made. The marketing person responsible for the business could then discover that a move, thought to be quite profitable, turned out to be only marginally profitable or even unprofitable because of the way the carload was routed, switched, powered, etc. This points out the need for improved communications between the estimates used to prepare NCS and the actual operating decisions. Recall that operating people did review underlying NCS assumptions on a regular basis but this did not extend to having information used to prepare estimates for individual moves transmitted to the operating department.

Another opportunity for reconciliation would attempt to aggregate the cost estimates from CPMS to the actual expenditure data collected by the MCC system (described in the (A) case). Over time, the cost estimates for actual moves should sum to the costs incurred throughout the system. One check on the accuracy of CPMS, for example fuel and train crew costs, would be to sum up the costs estimated in CPMS for all carload moves and see whether this sum corresponded to the actual fuel and crew costs accumulated in the MCC system. Not all categories could be reconciled in this way. Recall that maintenance and repair costs were discretionary in the short- run and were estimated using 3-5 year averages. Therefore, estimated repair and maintenance costs in CPMS would not likely match current maintenance and repair costs. Or alternatively, current maintenance and repair costs relate to past moves and the maintenance and repair bill for current moves would not come due, perhaps, for several years into the future.

One can ask how the computer capacity and programming sophistication existed in UP to develop the train costing systems. One would be hard pressed to start an organization up to produce such extensive online data collection, data processing, and reporting systems as were required for TUCS, CPMS, and NCS. I believe the answer lies in the extensive information processing capabilities already established at UP for its day-to-day operations. Computerized systems had already been established to plan, track, and evaluate all carload and train movements. Therefore, the cost systems could build on both the computing capacity already in existence plus the high degree of sophistication in programming and operating real-time management information systems.

Now we get to one of the most important aspects of the entire case series. Having explained and discussed the details of MCC, CPMS, and NCS, the class may accept the functionality of all these systems. It is time to force them to compare these systems to their previous cost accounting concepts. I point out that NCS and CPMS both assume that most of railroad operating costs are variable. I then ask, "How many of these variable costs represent actual cash outflows associated with a particular carload move? Look at the panel on page 503 where the data estimating the cost of an actual move are presented; how many of these costs are actual cash outflows and how many are estimates of either current or future spending?"

Students should see that with the exception of the car-mileage charge, a charge that arises only because the car is leased and not UP owned, every single cost in the panel is an estimate or an allocation (e.g., the wage cost of $52). Therefore, even though all these costs are considered variable, they do not represent current cash outflows. It is common in cost accounting courses to indicate that only costs that represent changes in spending with respect to particular decisions are relevant. The railroad setting indicates that estimates, even rough estimates of future spending (repairing a locomotive or replacing track perhaps several years later) play a vital role in measuring the resource demands made by individual carload moves (i.e., the railroad's product) since the directly traceable cash outlays for a move could be zero. George Craig, the UP vice president of marketing, put this philosophy very bluntly: "I want to be assured that every time we run a car down the track we're making money, not just polishing rail." In order to determine whether an individual carload move is or is not "making money," the company developed a system to cost out the long-run resource demands made by every carload move.

Finally, if the class is sensitive to organizational issues, I ask how was it possible for CPMS and NCS to be developed, implemented, and accepted in Union Pacific. These systems are radically different from the previous way costs were collected and operations managed at the railroad. Particularly if students have been exposed to the organizational problems that Schrader-Bellows had in accepting the findings from its strategic product costing study, one can ask the class to contrast the entirely different environment at Union Pacific for accepting a new product cost approach. I believe there were two important and related circumstances that led to success at UP. Clearly, there was a degree of top management support for the new system. The CPMS system was instigated at the request of the chairman of the railroad. The quotes from George Craig show his support for having an independent, reliable system to estimate product costs.

Also important, and likely explaining the senior management support for the systems, was the radical change in railroad operating environment triggered by deregulation. The Staggers

Act could be viewed as a major discontinuity that called for major change in thinking and management. If appropriate innovations were not instituted, the organization would soon be in a crisis situation. Schrader-Bellows, on the other hand, was not seeing a strategic crisis. The division was experiencing stagnant sales and declining profitability but it was still showing profits. No obvious change in its operating environment was apparent and, hence, it was less willing to implement the major change in its strategic thinking that the cost studies seemed to indicate. I believe that both factors, enthusiastic support from top management (not just acquiescence) and major change in the operating environment - perhaps a crisis - caused by events such as deregulation or the sudden inroads by formidable overseas competitors like the Japanese, may be necessary for strategic product cost systems to become a central part of an organization's thinking. A third factor explaining the contrast between UP and S-B could be that the UP systems were developed to help the organization grow and prosper in the new environment whereas the S-B cost system indicated that the organization may have to shrink to become more profitable. The growth story will generally win out over the story telling the senior general and marketing managers that they need to reduce their scope of operations.

It is important to leave about five minutes at the end of the class to summarize the major messages from the Union Pacific case series:

1.   The differences between the MCC system and the train costing systems (CPMS and NCS) show that organizations likely need quite different systems for operational control (MCC) and product costing (NCS, CPMS). Even though all the systems operate from the same data base, the aggregations and estimates between these two sets of systems are completely different.

2.   Product costs should be estimated as long-term variable costs. The cost elements in the CPMS estimate shown on page 19 of the (B) case are predominantly long-term variable costs. Many of these costs could not truly be said to be costs that were incremental, in the short-run, with the movement of car ABX 003301. Train crew, fuel, maintenance, repair, overhead costs would not decrease if this car movement did not occur. But just as in integral calculus, where something substantial arises from summing up lots of little things, so do all costs eventually arise from the summation of delivering all the organization's products and services. The goal is to understand the cost drivers that explains the source of long-term cost behavior. For the railroad, Rail Form A helped to identify the multiplicity of cost drivers associated with actual moves: gross ton miles, carload miles, number of switching minutes, etc.

3.   For operational control (MCC), costs that are traceable and measurable at the local cost center level are the ones to measure and report. There is no role for allocating costs to cost center managers to guide their search for short-term efficiency and productivity improving activities.

4.   Direct costing is not helpful for product costing. The railroad provides a vivid example where product costs are considered almost all (about 90%) variable yet for which there may be zero direct (cash) costs. This message also carries over to manufacturing products in highly automated environments where the only direct (out-of-pocket cash) product costs will be materials and minor amounts of energy. Using direct costing to guide product related decisions in these situations would be disastrous. For product costing, you will likely need to estimate long-run spending consequences based on current resource

demands. It is not important that these estimates be performed with a precision of five significant digits. We're trying to be approximately right; to learn how many zeroes should be in the estimate, which digit should be first, and be reasonably close on the second digit.

Outline of Class Discussion for Union Pacific (A) and (B)

I.   Union Pacific (A)

    1.   Background of case, brief historical perspective.
          (5-10 minutes).
    2.   Railroad Environment, circa 1965. (5 minutes)
    3.   Cost structure of railroads; Rail Form A. (10 minutes)
    4.   Discussion of MCC. (20 minutes)
    5.   What's missing from MCC? Product costs; what's a product for the railroad? (10-15 minutes)
    6.   What role does COAT play? What makes it so difficult to measure product costs for a railroad as compared to a manufacturing environment? Separation of revenue and cost systems.
          (10-15 minutes)
    7.   Perspective from (A) case (5-10 minutes)
          ● Compare to manufacturing, particularly in automated environment.
          ● Compare to other service industries: finance,   telecommunications.
          ● Cost control different from product costing.
    8.   What will the future (deregulation) bring? (5 minutes)
          ● Greater emphasis on marketing function: how to create value for customer.
          ● Need to measure costs and profits by product, customer, geographic areas.

II.   Union Pacific (B)

    1.   What did CPMS add over COAT? (10 minutes)
    2.   Illustrate how costs computed by CPMS. (10-15 minutes)
    3.   What is value of CPMS? Who gets this report? (5 minutes)
    4.   Why is NCS needed? How does it work? (10 minutes)
    5.   Design issues in NCS. (20-25 minutes)
          ● Incremental analysis
          ● Where should P&A group be?
          ● How are estimates verified, validated?
          ● Organizational linkages (NCS to CPMS, CPMS to MCC)
    6.   Important characteristics of product costing for the railroad. (10 minutes)
    7.   Summary of (A) and (B) cases. (10 minutes)
          ● Operational control separate from product costing.
          ● Product costs measured as long-run variable costs.
          ● For process control, report locally measurable and traceable costs.
          ● Direct costs not helpful for product costing.
          ● Need senior management commitment and, perhaps, radical change in the marketplace to introduce successfully a new cost system with major shift in strategic focus.

Exhibit TN-1

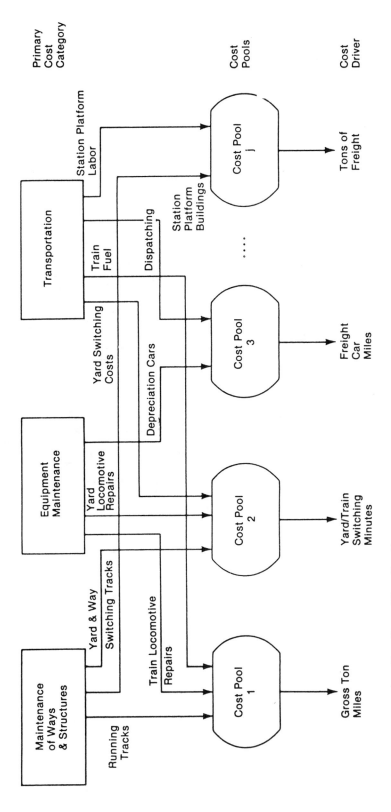

Rail Form A viewed as Two Stage Allocation Process

Exhibit TN-2

Transportation:
    Train Crews

    Switching Yards

    Station Loading

    Diesel Fuel

Mechanical:
    Locomotive Repairs

    Freight Car Repairs

Way & Structures:
    Running Tracks

    Switching Tracks

Accumulation of cost center costs into cost of individual
product: shaded areas represent cost segments that must
be added together to produce the cost of an individual move.

Massachusetts Eye and Ear Infirmary[1]

The Massachusetts Eye and Ear Infirmary case illustrates the application of activity-based costing concepts to a health care institution. Interestingly, the case was written by faculty at the Harvard School of Public Health in the late 1970s, long before ABC systems had begun to appear in manufacturing or industrial companies. This case used to be taught in the MBA program to illustrate the application of the stepdown procedure for allocating service department costs. When we inherited the 2nd year MBA elective course in the mid-1980s, we discovered this case which contained a beautifully simple early example of the power of the ABC approach. For the book, we have suppressed a complex exhibit in the original case that described the stepdown procedure so that students could focus on the *split-cost* accounting system. The class discussion should examine the rationale for and impact of the split-cost accounting system, and, if time permits and the instructor is interested, could conclude with an open-ended discussion of the applicability of the approach to more complex comprehensive health care institutions and hospitals.

Suggested Assignment Questions

1. What problems arose with the old per-diem costing system? How would the new split-cost accounting system remedy these problems? How might it affect patient mix?

2. What would be the difference between the budgeted 1977 routine care cost of a cataract operation under the old accounting method and under the split-cost accounting system? What would the difference be for a tonsillectomy/adenoidectomy procedure, a laryngectomy and radical neck dissection? What accounts for the differences? Are they significant?

3. Using the hypothetical data given by Ms. Arndt, how could a hospital under a per diem reimbursement lose revenue and how much revenue would it lose?

4. How might the MEEI administrators use the information from the split-cost accounting system?

5. How might a split-cost type system be implemented at a less specialized hospital? What kinds of implementation problems do you foresee and how would you avoid them? What importance or relevance do you attach to the distinction between procedures and

---

1. *This teaching note was prepared by Robert S. Kaplan based on an earlier note, HBS # 5-179-506, prepared by Patricia O'Brien and David Young.*

diagnoses? What bearing does this distinction have on the transferability of the MEEI system?

Class Discussion

Q: **What is the environment of MEEI?**

Hospitals are highly regulated institutions. Much of their payment comes from third parties, especially insurance companies and the government. Perhaps the most important influence has been Blue Cross, a private not-for-profit organization, and government reimbursement through the Medicare (over age 65) and Medicaid (indigent) programs. Historically, Blue Cross and the government reimbursed hospitals on the basis of average per-diem cost, calculated as total reimbursable expenses[2] divided by number of patient days. This procedure led to complex systems for calculating and allocating costs in hospitals, and to steady inflation in the cost of health care institutions since higher costs could largely be recovered by higher reimbursements. Commercial insurers paid hospitals on the basis of charges for patient days and special procedures, and self-pay patients also paid charges, based on the institution's published prices. (Anyone who works on the economics of health care institutions soon learns of the critical distinction between costs and charges.)

During the 1970s and accelerating in the 1980s, extensive attempts were made to retard the rapid increase in health care costs. Reimbursement started to shift away from full cost reimbursement and towards various types of incentive schemes, attempting to reward institutions that slowed their rate of cost increases. Problem arise because of the diversity of health care institutions. Some are simple community hospitals performing only routine procedures while others are complex urban teaching institutions that perform highly complex procedures for high-risk patients. Any attempt to set standards for reimbursement must acknowledge the vast diversity in institutional missions and patient mix.

To update the case into the 1980s, Medicare introduced DRGs (Diagnostic Reimbursement Groups, -- known among New Yorkers as "De Revenue's Gone") in which a fixed amount was paid to hospitals each time it treated a patient based on the patient's ailment, i.e., the patient's diagnosis category. Thus the environment was shifting to where health care institutions needed to pay much more attention to their cost structure and systems.

Q.   **What is MEEI's product? Who is the customer?**

The product is apparently delivered health care. The case describes several classifications of the product; e.g., the list in Exhibit 6 of the case describing 10 products offered by MEEI. Alternatively, students might feel the product is patient days; are all patient days sufficiently homogeneous that we feel comfortable describing the delivery of

---

2.   Some categories of expenses such as bad debt expense and the cost of capital might be excluded from reimbursable expenses.

patient days as the product? Or is the delivery of a healthy or at least cured patient the product?

The question of who is the customer is even more interesting. At first glance, the patient might appear to be the customer. But unlike most customers, few patients pay for the product they receive; nor do many of them have much choice as to where they receive their product or from whom they purchase it, or at what price. Thus, insurance companies or other third-party payers (Blue Cross, government) might be considered the customer. But MEEI is not a primary care facility; virtually all of its patients are referrals from physicians. So perhaps doctors are the customers since they provide the primary demand for MEEI. It might be useful to introduce the distinction between the customer (who the institution sells it services to -- perhaps both insurance companies and doctors) and the consumer (who ultimately consumes the service being delivered). The distinction between customer and consumer occurs for any organization that sells products to entities that repackage or retail the product before it is ultimately purchased and consumed. The discussion on the product and the customer is worth having to familiarize students with the special situations of health care institutions but not more than 10 minutes should really be spent on these institutional arrangements since they will likely change over time and vary by country (only the U.S. has such a diverse health care system, with significant amounts of private payments and control).

Q. **Please describe the old cost system. What assumptions did it make?**

The old cost system summed all reimbursable costs (it excluded the costs of specific services such as the use of the operating room, the pharmacy, and the laboratory whose services were billed separately). The total costs were divided by the number of patient days to determine the per diem cost. Occasionally, the hospital attempted to charge for particular activities, such as admissions, but the case indicates these attempts were rarely successful. The fully loaded per diem cost system assumed that all patient days cost the same, independent of patient type, procedure being performed, or length of stay.

Q. **What problems arose from the old cost system?**

Obviously not all patient days have the same cost. In effect hospitals in general, and MEEI in particular, were guilty of the same problems as manufacturing companies who retained a direct labor cost system for determining product costs because it was convenient for regulatory reporting. The per diem system was adequate for cost reimbursement but it suppressed the highly different demands that different patient days made on organizational resources. Patients with short stays but who required extensive nursing support and administrative activities (e.g., admission, billing, and medical records maintenance) were under-costed by the per diem system and patients who required long hospitalization, but who were ambulatory and required minimal nursing attention, were over-costed, probably to a considerable degree. If self-pay and third-party payments were based on the per diem costing system, patients (or their physicians) who had any concern with hospital charges would shift their patients requiring extended hospitalization to facilities that specialized in extended care patients, and increase the use of MEEI for outpatients and short-term stay patients. As this trend continued, MEEI would find its per diem costs skyrocketing, much like manufacturing companies under a direct labor cost system that automated or outsourced all direct labor-intensive products and processes.

Despite pressure from private and public regulators, MEEI administrators would find it difficult to contain its per diem costs, because of the shift in patient mix to short-term high-resource demanding patients.

Q.   What changes were introduced by the split-cost accounting system?

The split-cost accounting system separates the cost of routine services into three different activities:

1.   <u>Hospitalization</u> - admitting and discharging patients[3]

This activity encompassed scheduling patient admissions; admitting patients; creating, maintaining, and updating medical records; preparing a bill; discharging patients; and a portion of plant and administrative overhead (e.g., the readiness to serve costs).

2.   <u>Routine Daily Care</u> - the motel/hotel aspect of the institution; providing room and board

The routine daily care encompassed the cost of supplying the bed and the room, daily meals and other dietary services, laundry and housekeeping, and routine pharmaceutical, medical, and surgical supplies.

3.   <u>Nursing Service,</u> as measured in Clinical Care Units

The nursing care activities are identified in Exhibit 4 of the case. Nursing intensity varied by type of diagnosis and procedure as well as by length of stay (see Exhibit 6).

Q.   Why did MEEI adopt the split-cost accounting system? What advantages did it offer?

Analysis of the activities performed by the personnel at MEEI suggested that three different types of demands generated work for them:

(1) One time activities associated with admitting and discharging patients that were independent of patient type, diagnosis, or length of stay,

(2) Routine daily activities that were incurred every day that a patient was in the facility, independent of the patient type, diagnosis, or treatment, and

(3) Activities that varied depending on the patient type, procedure performed, and severity of the illness.

The split-cost accounting system enabled the total operating expenses of the institution (other than the cost of operating rooms, laboratory, pharmacy, radiology and other specialized resources, whose costs were collected and charged for separately) to be assigned to each of the three identified activities. Once the operating expenses were collected in the three activity pools, the second-stage or activity drivers could be identified

---

3.   Procedures done at MEEI were rarely life-threatening. It is reasonable to assume that all admissions were eventually followed by a discharged patient.

and measured; number of admissions for the *hospitalization* activity, number of patient days for the *routine daily care* activity, and total number of clinical care units for the *nursing intensity* activity (see the calculations in Exhibit 5 of the case). MEEI administrators felt that the split-cost accounting system much better represented the economics of the institution, thereby enabling them to improve decisions on pricing, resource allocation (how many nurses would be required based on forecasted case mix), and cost control (flexible budgeting based on actual demands for resources rather than on patient days).

The impact of the system might occur in several ways. First, the lower costs of long-term patients would enable MEEI to lower the charges for the elderly, generally sicker patients who required extended hospitalization. This would enable MEEI to be more competitive with specialized extended care facilities and keep its primary demand and occupancy rates higher. The actual per diem cost of $34 per day, and charge of $41 per day, is probably competitive with hotel/motel rates and longer term nursing facilities. With a lower per diem charge, MEEI could reduce the need for new construction for facilities that specialize by type of care (e.g., the health-care equivalent of "focused factories.")

The system eliminates the variation in cost caused by shifts in patient (diagnosis) mix -- out-patient versus extended stay patients, simple versus complex procedures. It enables the administrator to forecast the demand for nursing resources based on projected CCU units. Under the per diem system, the administrator might be budgeting a fixed number of nursing hours per patient day. As patient mix shifted toward shorter-stay intensive care patients, and the number of patient days declined, the administrator would be budgeting for fewer required nursing resources even though actual demand for nursing services could be increasing, not decreasing. Also, the demand for admissions and routine care (dietary, laundry, and housekeeping) activities could be better forecasted based on the drivers for the resources performing those activities. The administrator would also be better able to forecast revenues based on changes in volume and mix of patients.

Q.   How does the new system work? What impact will it have on particular procedures?

Exhibit TN-1 shows a comparison among three procedures: cataract extraction, T&A (be careful with this one if your students have seen <u>Chorus Line</u>), and Laryngectomy. The calculations are straight-forward and you should be able to have students supply the calculations for you to put on the board. (If you want to speed up the class, you can prepare an overhead transparency or hand out the solution during class for this and the subsequent calculations.) You can ask the students what factors account for the differences between the old and the new cost system. The principal differences, of course, arise from the large up-front cost for admissions and for the impact of the much lower per-diem cost eventually reducing the cost of procedures with long convalescences and low CCUs to below the per diem costing procedure. Thus with the new procedure, short-term high CCU patients are assigned higher costs, and long-term patients are assigned lower costs.

Q.   Ms. Arndt, the Director of Patient Services, claims that hospitals could lose revenues under a per diem system even as more intensive care is required. How could this happen?

You might encourage students in advance to prepare examples using a spreadsheet program to illustrate the phenomenon described by Ms. Arndt. You need to be careful to be consistent; either doing estimates using the cost numbers or the charge numbers (this is why the discussion is useful at the beginning of the class to distinguish between payers who reimburse based on costs versus payers who reimburse based on charges). Exhibit TN-2 shows some sample calculations.

MEEI could receive less reimbursement than a hospital that remains on a per diem system if MEEI's patient mix shifts to patients requiring less intensity of care. Presumably, in this situation, MEEI administrators could forecast the impact of the case mix shift and start to reduce spending on resources that will be demanded less in the future. This point reinforces the notion that activity-based systems are forecasts of resource **consumption**, that provides predictive information, enabling administrators to reduce future **spending** on resources so that demand and supply are brought into balance. The split-cost accounting system gives administrators the ability to more effectively control institutional costs by knowing where critical changes are occurring and to either expand or contract spending on resources, as necessary.

Q. **We have been talking about the split-cost accounting system as helping administrators develop better costs for determining patient charges and reimbursement, and to facilitate resource planning for the future. Is there any role for the system in operational control, to measure managers' performance?**

This question is designed to get students to think about developing standards and flexible budgets for control. Especially for the per diem and nursing service activities, a flexible budget can be prepared each period to forecast the volume of work authorized based on patient volume and mix. The actual spending in these categories can then be compared to the flexible budget, and significant variances highlighted for attention of the responsible manager. Managers might want to investigate the use of part-time employees, flexible scheduling of employees' worktime, or overtime to allow resource spending to fluctuate within the month based on actual activity demands (e.g., actual CCUs and patient days) during the period. In principle variances could be reported based on:

- input prices
- volume (number of admits, number of patient days)
- efficiency (actual CCUs per procedure versus standard; perhaps segregated by physician)
- case mix (actual procedures versus budgeted)

This discussion might lead to the importance of measuring actual CCUs. The standard CCUs shown in Exhibit 4 of the case are rough estimates and averages. Demands by individual patients might vary significantly from those forecast in Exhibits 4 and 6 based on the age of the patient, complications from other illnesses and symptoms, or unexpected variations in outcomes from the treatment and procedures implemented. If such variation is significant, then MEEI will need to deploy additional resources to measure actual CCUs by patient if the system is to be used for operational control. Measuring actual CCUs will also be important to correct inaccuracies or detect shifts due to changing treatment and technologies if the cost system is to remain representative of actual operations (pun only slightly intended) in the institution.

Q. **Is this system good only for a specialized medical facility like MEEI? What problems would arise in transferring this system to a general, comprehensive-care hospital?**

MEEI, as a specialized facility, can organize its work by procedures rather than by diagnoses. Patients generally show up already pre-screened and selected for particular procedures that the facility does in high volumes. The system would transfer easily to a surgical or radiological facility that also performs well-specified procedures. But it might be more difficult to transfer as is to a general medical facility where patients show up with symptoms rather than with procedures to be performed. In this case, patients must be classified into categories for which the demand for length of stay and nursing units can be reasonably well predicted. This is the objective of the DRG categories introduced in the U.S. in the 1980s. But many hospital administrators and consultants remain skeptical that hospital resource demands can be forecasted sufficiently accurately even within a DRG category to permit a cost system based on patient type and mix to be developed.

I have no direct experience with attempting to implement an activity-based cost system in a general hospital but the complaint that variation exists within categories does not seem to me to be a fatal or decisive criticism, mitigating against attempting to build ABC hospital systems. Such criticisms are an example of the old adage that "perfection is the enemy of the good." If existing cost systems reflect only patient days as a cost driver, then even a rough attempt to split operating expenses into admissions (one-time) expenses, daily expenses, and diagnostic-specific expenses is bound to provide a better approximation to the forecasted demands patients make on organizational resources. The enthusiasm with which Blue Cross greeted MEEI's split cost accounting system suggests that at least one very important group closely involved with monitoring the costs of health care delivery found merit with the innovation.

Exhibit TN-1

	Cataract Extraction	Tonsillectomy & Adenoidectomy	Laryngectomy and Radical Neck Dissection
Hospitalization	$ 201.93	$ 201.93	$ 201.93
Room	172.70[1]	69.08[2]	587.18[3]
CCUs[4]	308.43	143.04	1,095.15
Split Cost Total	$ 683.06	$ 414.04	$1,884.26
Per Diem Total[5]	693.95	277.58	2,359.43
Difference	(10.89)	136.46	(475.17)
Percent Difference	-2%	+49%	-20%

1. 5 days @ $34.54 (count day of admission but not day of discharge)
2. 2 days @ $34.54
3. 17 days @ $34.54
4. $4.47 multiplied by # of CCUs shown on Exhibit 3 of case.
5. Per diem cost computed from Exhibit 6:

   [2,262,652 + 1,864,728 + 3,368,318] / 53,984 = $138.79

Mass Eye and Ear Infirmary: Exhibit TN-2

	Quantity	Cost/Unit	Total Cost	Per Diem Cost @ 99.433	Difference	Percent
Admissions	1,000	201.93	$201,930			
Days of Care	10,000	34.54	345,400			
CCUs	100,000	4.47	447,000	$994,330		
			$994,330	$994,330	$0	0%
Admissions	1,000	201.93	$201,930			
Days of Care	9,000	34.54	310,860			
CCUs	100,000	4.47	447,000	$894,897		
			$959,790	$894,897	$64,893	7%
Admissions	900	201.93	$181,737			
Days of Care	10,000	34.54	345,400			
CCUs	100,000	4.47	447,000	$994,330		
			$974,137	$994,330	($20,193)	-2%
Admissions	1,000	201.93	$201,930			
Days of Care	10,000	34.54	345,400			
CCUs	90,000	4.47	402,300	$994,330		
			$949,630	$994,330	($44,700)	-4%
Admissions	1,000	201.93	$201,930			
Days of Care	9,000	34.54	310,860			
CCUs	90,000	4.47	402,300	$894,897		
			$915,090	$894,897	$20,193	2%
Admissions	900	201.93	$181,737			
Days of Care	9,000	34.54	310,860			
CCUs	90,000	4.47	402,300	$894,897		
			$894,897	$894,897	$0	0%

EXHIBIT TN-2 (cont.)

	Quantity	Cost/Unit	Total Cost	Per Diem Cost @ 99.433	Difference	Percent
Admissions	1,000	201.93	$201,930			
Days of Care	10,000	34.54	345,400			
CCUs	100,000	4.47	447,000	$994,330		
			$994,330	$994,330	$0	0%
Admissions	1,000	201.93	$201,930			
Days of Care	11,000	34.54	379,940			
CCUs	100,000	4.47	447,000	$1,093,763		
			$1,028,870	$1,093,763	($64,893)	-6%
Admissions	1,100	201.93	$222,123			
Days of Care	10,000	34.54	345,400			
CCUs	100,000	4.47	447,000	$994,330		
			$1,014,523	$994,330	$20,193	2%
Admissions	1,000	201.93	$201,930			
Days of Care	10,000	34.54	345,400			
CCUs	110,000	4.47	491,700	$994,330		
			$1,039,030	$994,330	$44,700	4%
Admissions	1,000	201.93	$201,930			
Days of Care	11,000	34.54	379,940			
CCUs	110,000	4.47	491,700	$1,093,763		
			$1,073,570	$1,093,763	($20,193)	-2%
Admissions	1,100	201.93	$222,123			
Days of Care	11,000	34.54	379,940			
CCUs	110,000	4.47	491,700	$1,093,763		
			$1,093,763	$1,093,763	$0	0%

American Bank Teaching Note

The American Bank case provides an opportunity to apply product costing concepts in the context of a familiar service organization, a regional commercial bank. Apart from the specific benefits from understanding and applying generic product costing concepts to one of the most common and familiar service organizations, the case gives students a chance to examine the structure of operations and the summary financial statements of a financial institution. Thus, it could provide some new insights for students whose main previous exposure has been to the balance sheets and income statements of industrial and retailing organizations. The case focuses on the costs of transactions-based liability accounts, not on the costs of developing and maintaining various types of loans in asset accounts, an issue covered in the Manufacturers Hanover Corporation: Customer Profitability Report case also in this chapter.

The case uses the "before and after" approach of most of the ABC cases. The old, highly regulated environment and the cost system that was adequate for that environment are described in some detail. With the challenges from a deregulated environment of more vigorous competition, a more accurate cost system is needed. The case describes the development of the new cost system and closes with a simple numerical example that permits students to explore the value of information from the new system.

Suggested Assignment Questions:

1. What are the strengths and weaknesses of the cost system used at American Bank before 1979?

2. Why was a new system needed?

3. How were the limitations of the existing cost system overcome by the new product costing system? What weaknesses still remain?

4. Should American Bank phase out Passbook Savings Accounts?

This teaching note was prepared by Robert S. Kaplan as an aid to instructors in classroom use of the case, American Bank 187-194.

Organizing the Class Discussion

Question: What was the competitive environment of banking in the 1960s and early 1970s?

As described in the Appendix, banking operations were highly regulated in price (the maximum interest rates that could be paid on demand and time deposits), in product (the nature of products that could be offered and the types of businesses that banks and non-banks could enter), and in market territory (the regions in which banks could establish their presence). Under the regulations in Pennsylvania until the 1980s, banks could establish branches only in counties that were contiguous to their home county. This occasionally led to interesting incorporation decisions such as when Pittsburgh National Bank decided to base itself in Westmoreland County, the county directly to the east of Allegheny County (in which Pittsburgh is located) so that it could branch to counties further towards the center of Pennsylvania.

Funds were raised by a combination of non-interest paying demand deposit (checking) accounts and savings accounts limited to paying 5 to 5 1/4 % interest. They were loaned out at market interest rates, say at 9 percent. Under these conditions, the bank could make money on almost all of its liability and asset accounts. A bank would have to be wildly inefficient not to be profitable under such an arrangement. The pressure for accurate product costing data does not arise until more funds are raised by deposit accounts and securities paying market interest rates, or until large-scale disintermediation occurs - the withdrawal of funds by interest-sensitive depositors to be reinvested in money market instruments paying market rates of return.

American's core depositors did not subject the bank to much disintermediation pressure. The balance sheets in Exhibit 1 show that as recently as 1978, American had almost no purchased funds. Virtually all its assets could be funded by demand, savings, and time deposits. The economics of interest expense of savings and time deposits vs. the interest revenues from loans can be obtained by analyzing the numbers appearing in Exhibits 1 and 2.

Question: How did the existing cost system operate?

The previous system focused on branch profitability, with only a simplistic and likely highly distorted attempt to measure product costs. As described in the case, Central Support Costs are collected in functional categories and then allocated sequentially to operating units and other support departments.

The focus of the case is on operating expenses, not the cost of borrowed or purchased funds. From Exhibit 2, in 1978 the bank had $44.5 million in net interest margin (interest income less income expense). The primary pre-tax deduction from this margin is the $39.6 million in Other Expenses that is the object of the cost system's attention.

The flow of costs is from central support departments, to branches, and then, within branches, to savings and checking accounts based on measures such as the number of each type of account. Exhibit 5, a sample branch profitability report illustrates the system. The branch has accounts with $23.8 million in demand and time deposits. The interest expense for this money is $908,000 (the average interest rate of 5.95% multiplied by the $15.3 million in time deposits). The branch has a total of $2.4 million in outstanding loans (consumer, commercial, mortgage and revolving credit). After subtracting reserve and portfolio requirements, the branch has generated

$13.6 million for the bank to invest in other assets. The branch receives an average interest rate of 9.76% from its own loan portfolio and a credit of 11.27% on the excess funds it provides the rest of the bank.

One can compute the lending spread from these activities. The $2.3 million in interest income represents a 9.7% yield on the total deposits of $23.9 million. The interest expense of $0.9 million is 3.8% of total deposits, leaving an interest spread of almost 6.0 % (600 basis points in banking lingo), a nice comfortable margin.

The costs of operations include $110,000 of personnel expense arising within the branch and $92,000 of other branch operating expense (probably rent, equipment expense, utilities, etc.). The support department allocation exercise generates the $172,000 of pre-tax Charge for Internal Operations.

Exhibit 6 shows a sample product profitability report for demand deposits. An interest credit is applied to funds available for lending (gross deposits less statutory and other reserve requirements). An interest credit of about 10% is applied to these funds and operating expenses of about 6.7% are subtracted, leaving a net margin of 3.4% from these funds. As described in the case, the accuracy of the expenses charged to these accounts - despite their measurement to 4 significant digits - is highly problematic. Apparently, the costs of the demand deposit accounts in each branch - as determined by the arbitrary allocation of branch costs to all its liability accounts - are aggregated together to obtain the $17,281,000 figure shown in Exhibit 6.

Question: Why was the old cost system inadequate for the new competitive environment?

As described in the case, the system did not even measure branch profitability well. Revenues were credited to where the account was established but the operating expenses for servicing accounts could be incurred in other offices. The reserve for delinquent accounts was a company-wide average. The costs of transactions were measured by industry-wide averages, not by the actual experience of American Bank. And, of course, the reported product costs were crude approximations to the actual costs of processing various types of accounts. While such a system may have been adequate in the protected environment of extensive regulations, it would provide little useful information in an environment where:

Interest margins would be squeezed by market forces,
The bank could expand into new areas, and other banks could expand into American's core territory,
New banking products could be offered, and
Extensive automation would replace manual handling and processing.

In principle, new systems for both branch profitability and product costing would have been useful. In practice, American seems only to have introduced a new product costing system. It is interesting to note that during the system's development, the branch and product profitability reports were suspended, providing additional evidence of management's lack of faith in the existing cost system.

Question: How was the new cost system developed?

The Peat Marwick consultants helped American hire three new people who would do the actual work for the system. This is a good approach for successful implementation of any new system by building more commitment and in-house expertise. The specific procedures used to perform the analysis are deliberately vague since I did not want to bog the students or the class down in detailed descriptions of various industrial engineering techniques. At some point, I hope that a summary technical note or reading on this subject will be prepared that can provide more detail for interested students.

The objective of the analysis is to produce the Unit Cost of an activity. The Unit Cost is computed as the product of the Unit Time to perform the activity multiplied by the Hourly Cost of the activity. The Hourly Cost is estimated as the ratio of Line Item Expenses of a Department (or activity) divided by the Practical Capacity (number of effective hours available) from the Department or activity. The use of practical capacity rather than actual utilization is a key design decision. Terry Troupe's concerns with the full product costs from the old system reflected the distortions introduced by spreading capacity costs to actual volumes. His desire for "standard costs" was to avoid cost fluctuations induced by changes in the volume of activity. This goal mirrors the message on assigning capacity-based expenses (see cases in Chapter 3).

The key measure, the Unit Time to perform an activity, equals the ratio of the total time spent on a task divided by the volume of items processed during that time. This calculation is complicated by the seasonal nature of retail banking business. Mondays and Fridays are much busier than the other three weekdays. Most banks have under-capacity on busy days, when people are paid and before or after weekends and holidays, and over capacity on the remaining days. Observing work on a random basis would not provide an accurate measure of times required to accomplish a given task. At American Bank, the standard Unit Times were obtained by multiplying the monthly average times by 80% to control for peak and idle periods of work. Thus standard unit times were below the average actuals.

The entries in Exhibit 7 show the Unit Cost estimates for all the activities required to open, maintain, process, and close Passbook Savings Accounts. After unit costs have been obtained for each activity, they can be summed to yield the total costs to process transactions and the costs of individual products. Local overhead is assigned, based on estimated effort, to various branch products and applied to these products as a percentage mark-up to individual product costs. This will be accurate for product-lines with only a single product but likely not a good method for distributing local overhead among various products within a product class.

More problematic is the practice of allocating corporate overhead (about 25 percent of operating expenses) to products based on total product expenses. This practice remains a current point of disagreement between Greg Nolan (of PMM), the American Bank system's designer, and myself. Greg feels that corporate expenses are "below the line." They are not controllable at the local level so that we should not be more scientific in charging corporate overhead to products. Charging at a uniform rate makes it clear that branch and support department managers should manage their local, traceable operating expenses and not be overly concerned with the corporate overhead tax being applied to all products.

My point is that product costing information should not be used to evaluate managers of operating centers. Applying corporate overhead as a flat markup over operating expenses prevents us from understanding the functions that corporate overhead performs. Many people feel that corporate overhead is a "fixed" expense so that we should not attempt to allocate it accurately to products. I argue, in return, that if corporate overhead were indeed "fixed," then all banks in the country, regardless of size and complexity of products and operations, would have the same absolute level of corporate overhead. Since banking corporate overhead seems to consistently average 20 to 25 percent of total operating expenses across all kinds of banks, the overhead must be performing functions that vary with the size and complexity of banking operations. The goal of a good product costing system should be to understand the activities being performed by overhead resources and to assign the costs of these resources to the branches, product lines, or operating activities that require or benefit from these corporate overhead resources. If time permits, you can explore both sides of this issue with the class.

Another point of controversy is whether it is worth measuring the unit costs and volumes of activities to the five or six significant digits shown in Exhibits 7 and 8. Some students remark that PMM and American must have invested too much effort in obtaining the precision shown in these exhibits. Perhaps if unit costs were only measured to two significant digits, the cost study could have been done with simpler, faster, and less costly procedures than the extensive industrial engineering techniques that were actually performed. This highlights the difference in precision required for a cost system used for measuring product and customer profitability (as in the case) versus that required for operational control and performance measurement (a goal that the PMM system designers also wanted to accomplish with the system).

Question: What should American Bank do about Passbook Savings Accounts?

Now that we have explored the theory and design of the new system, we can turn to the controversy on Passbook Savings Accounts as an example of the types of issues that can be examined better with the new information. There were several such issues that I could have illustrated in the case. This one seemed to capture the relevant concepts in a context that should be familiar to all students.

If you are not rushed for time at this point, you can have the class contrast the difference between Passbook and Statement Savings Accounts:

Passbook	Statement
Labor intensive	Back-Office (computer) intensive
Loyal, older customers	Higher account activity
Low account activity	More technologically sophisticated
Higher account balance	

I have found the most convenient calculation to illustrate the relative profitability of the two accounts is to compute the break-even level of balances. The calculation is shown below:

	Passbook	Savings
Avg. Funds Yield[6]	12.2%	.88* 12.2 = 10.74%
Operating Cost	1.5	1.5
Net Yield	10.7%	9.24%
Interest Expense	4.5	5.0
Net Margin	6.2%	4.24%
Annual Operating Cost	$34.60[7]	$36.80
Breakeven Account Balance	$ 558	$ 868

Thus, despite the higher unit costs of activities for the Passbook Account (see data in Exhibit 8), the Passbook Account is less expensive because of the considerably lower number of monthly transactions per account when compared to the Statement Savings Accounts. Also its interest rate and reserve requirements are lower. Like most service organizations, revenues are earned by completely different activities from those that cause costs to be incurred. In this case, revenues are earned based on the size of the account, and expenses are incurred by the number of transactions. The cost of individual transactions is independent of the size of the transaction being processed.

Based on this analysis, the Bank actually raised the interest rate on Passbook accounts to insure retention of its loyal customers who maintained high balances in these accounts. Operating data several years later revealed that the aggregate dollars were about the same in both Passbook and Statement Savings Accounts. But there were 60% more Statement Savings Accounts so that the average account balance was about 60% higher in Passbook Accounts. The assigned operating expenses were more than twice as high for all Statement Savings accounts as for Passbook accounts. The bottom line was that the calculated return on assets for Passbook accounts was almost 2.5 times that calculated for Statement accounts.

Several additional comments can be made about the above calculations and results. First the breakeven analysis (which mirrored the actual calculation performed by the bank) understates the breakeven account balance. The calculation assumes that the mortgage and general lending activities (yielding an average return of 12.2%) could only be performed by funds provided by the savings accounts. Alternatively, the bank could purchase funds, at money market interest rates, for its lending opportunities. Therefore, a more accurate calculation would compare the interest and operating cost of the savings accounts with the cost of the higher money market rates plus the operating cost of raising money market funds.

Second, even though Passbook Savings Accounts as a whole seem both absolutely profitable (the average account balance is close to $3,000) and relatively more profitable than Statement Savings Accounts, a more detailed analysis could reveal that most Passbook accounts have quite low balances (less than $100) with a few accounts having quite large balances - in excess of $10,000. Such an analysis shows that product costing is only the start of analysis for

---

6. 4*11% + .6*13% = 12.2% . Multiply funds yield for statement accounts by .88 because 12% of these balances must be held as ATM facilities usage reserve.

7. The monthly cost of doughnuts and coffee could be added as a direct marketing expense for this product category.

service enterprises. Profitability must be determined by taking many slices or aggregations of the data: by customer, by socio-economic or demographic status of customer, by region, by account size, or by any meaningful segmentation of product line and customers.

Apart from the decision on Passbook Savings Accounts, the management of American Bank used the new product cost system as the basis for raising prices on fee services for demand deposit accounts, especially NOW accounts, to reflect the costs of handling different types of transactions (overdrafts, stop payments, etc.). The bank stayed away from certain new products introduced by their competitors, such as a $25 bond. And, in general, it used the information from the system to design new products and services.

Kanthal (A)
Teaching Note

The Kanthal case provides a simple illustration of the application of activity-based costing (ABC) to selling and administrative expenses. The case is particularly dramatic because the new system was installed at the specific request of the President and Chief Financial Officer of the company. The case allows a discussion of marketing and customer strategies. Thus the class raises a different set of discussion issues than the typical shop-floor level issues of manufacturing cost systems. The Kanthal (B) case (#9-190-003) is a brief postscript to the (A) case. Instructors can order this case directly from HBS Publishing for their own information in closing the class, or can order sufficient copies (or get approval to reproduce locally) to hand out to the class.
The Dudick and Bellis-Jones articles at the end of the chapter provide background reading for the case.

Suggested Discussion Questions

1. Why have selling and administrative costs not traditionally been traced to individual products and customers?

2. Evaluate the approach taken at Kanthal to compute the profit of individual orderlines, including assigning S&A costs to each customer order. How were the costs of customer orders and of producing non-stocked items estimated?

3. Consider a product-line with 50% gross margins (after subtracting volume-related expenses from prices). The cost for handling an individual customer order is SEK 750, and the extra cost to handle a production order for a non-stocked item is SEK 2,250.

    (a). Compare the operating profits and profit margins of two small orders, both for SEK 2,000. One order is for a stocked item, and the other order is for a non-stocked item.

This teaching note was prepared by Robert S. Kaplan as an aid to instructors in classroom use of the case Kanthal (A) 190-002.

(b). Compare the operating profits and profit margins for two large customers. Customers A and B both purchased SEK 160,000 worth of products this year. Customer A placed just three orders, for three different non-stocked items. Customer B placed 28 orders; 6 for stocked items and 22 for non-stocked items.

4. What should Ridderstrale do about the large number of unprofitable customers revealed by the account management system? Should salespersons be allowed to accept an unprofitable order from a customer?

Discussion

Q: **What was the President, Ridderstråle, trying to accomplish with the Kanthal 90 Account Management System?**

The Kanthal 90 goals called for significant increases in worldwide sales. How could these increased sales be achieved without requiring corresponding increases in corporate support staff?

The new system was to provide signals to salesmen about customers' behavior that led to unprofitable or profitable orders. Currently, the company had a huge variety of products and customers. A new system was needed to direct attention to the most profitable product-customer combinations and to be able to transform unprofitable combinations into profitable ones.

Ridderstråle, as a new President, coming in from outside the company, wanted a new system to change the culture of the organization and to establish the context in which his strategic vision could be implemented.

Q: **The case refers to high profit and low profit customers. What are the characteristics of high profit and low profit customers?**

High Profit Customers
    High order size
    Order high margin products

    Order predictably, no changes

    Order standard items
    Require low sales & technical support

Low Profit Customers
    Small orders
    Order low margin items
    Demand heavy discounts
    Erratic order patter
    Change delivery requests
    Order non-stocked items
    Demand high amount of sales and technical support

Q: **Why were the differences between high and low profit customers not revealed by the existing cost system?**

The traditional cost system (see TN Exhibit 1) assigned manufacturing costs to products using traditional allocation bases, such as direct labor hours. Selling, general and administrative (SG&A) expenses were not attributed to products or customers; they were considered period expenses and written off each period.

The treatment of SG&A expenses as period, not product costs, likely arose about 60-80 years ago when financial accounting conventions began to intrude on cost accounting practices.[8] Standard setters had to decide which operating expenses could be inventoried and which were to be expensed as incurred. These deliberations concluded that SG&A costs were not to be considered product-related costs. After this convention had been adopted, cost and management accountants lost interest in analyzing SG&A costs. Consequently, little attention was devoted to analyzing them or attributing them to the activities that caused these expenses to be incurred.

Another contributing factor was that many decades ago, SG&A expenses were likely a small fraction of the organization's total expenses. With information processing technology either expensive or unavailable, it was not worth devoting much attention to a minor expense category. Refer students back to the quote in the case:

1885	1985
10 Blacksmiths	3 Blacksmiths
1 Bookkeeper	8 Bookkeepers

In Kanthal, in 1987, Selling & Administrative expenses had grown to 34% of total expenses (see Exhibit 2 of the case), a magnitude comparable to manufacturing conversion costs and therefore worthy of considerable attention. The "Willie Sutton" rule leads us to look at Selling & Administrative Expenses as a category deserving attention (Willie Sutton, a bankrobber in the 1950s, was asked when finally apprehended why he robbed banks. "That's where the money is," he replied logically. Cost systems designers, like Willie Sutton, should focus their attention "where the money is" since that where they will get the high payoffs from their efforts.)

A final reason given by students is that SG&A expenses tend to look like fixed expenses, so that their assignment to products would be arbitrary. A different version of this statement is that the SG&A expenses are joint or common to a wide range of activities. You cannot link salesmen to the activities they perform in the same way that industrial engineers could develop work standards for direct labor employees.

The second concern with the existing cost system is that it did not highlight the added expenses associated with producing non-stocked items. The production organization produced to stock the 20% of the products that were inventoried. When an order for a non-stocked item was received, additional effort would be required to order the special materials, schedule the production order, and manage the order through the production process. As a consequence, the expenses associated with producing a given volume of a non-stocked product were much higher than the expenses of producing the same volume of a stocked product. The added expenses of producing an order for a non-stocked product were independent of the size of the order; they related to having to process the order--from materials ordering, production scheduling, and through customer shipment--but not to the size of the order.

Q: **What new features were added by the Kanthal 90 account management cost system?**

---

8.   See Chapter 6 in T. Johnson and R. Kaplan, <u>Relevance Lost: The Rise and Fall of Management Accounting</u> (HBS Press, Boston, 1987).

The analysts at Kanthal, after a preliminary investigation, decided to add two new cost drivers; one related to the costs of handling individual customer orders, and the second to the costs of producing a non-stocked product. This approach is much less elaborate than the analysis conducted at the John Deere Component Works or at Schrader Bellows, and is closer in philosophy to the systems installed at Siemens Electric Motor Works and Tektronix where analysts deliberately chose simple systems that would be easy to develop, install, and explain. The challenge when designing these simpler systems is to be sure that the few new cost drivers chosen correspond to real economic activities within the firm and that these activities have a high impact on firm profitability. As we see in Kanthal, the choices met both these criteria.

The SG&A expenses were investigated in detail to determine which expenses related to handling individual customer orders and which did not (see Case Exhibit 3). The expenses that were not attributable to handling individual customer orders were assigned to individual orders based on standard manufacturing costs. In effect, these expenses were not analyzed closely; they were just globbed onto other expenses assumed to vary with the volume of production.

Similarly, the Production Overhead expenses that were attributable to handling orders for non-stocked products were isolated in a separate cost pool, and the remaining expenses (including, for example, the setup costs for stocked products) remained to be allocated to products using direct labor hour bases. Thus the system was designed by isolating one pool each of directly attributable expenses in the production overhead category and in the SG&A category, and assigning each of these new expense pools to products or customers with a new activity-based driver (see TN Exhibit 2).

For a numerical example, you can assume that Production Overhead expenses are 6,000,000 and the SG&A expenses are 5,000,000. The analysis identifies 1,000,000 of the Production Overhead as being incurred to produce non-stocked items, and 2,000,000 of the SG&A for handling individual customer orders. The two new cost pools are assigned to products and customers as shown in Case Exhibit 4, and the remaining indirect expenses are globbed onto the products based on their standard costs.

Q: **Why were the two new cost pools analyzed so carefully (assigned to the "Order-Related Work" in Case Exhibit 3), whereas the remaining expenses were treated so casually and allocated proportional to the product's unit-related costs.**

The previous system was all volume-based so that people would likely not question expenses that were allocated proportional to volume with both the old and the new cost system. The innovative features of the Account Management system were the two new cost pools. If people were unhappy or disbelieving of the numbers from the new system, they would question the procedures used to estimate the costs of individual customer orders and of producing non-stocked items. Therefore, it was important that these numbers be "hard" or defensible. If the results from the new system were to be believed, accepted and acted upon, the proponents of the new system would have to be able to point to specific activities that are undertaken to handle individual customer orders and to produce non-stocked items.

Q: **How does the new cost system work?**

I would work through the answer to discussion question # 3 at this point just to make sure the class understands the principles of the Account Management system. The answer to the two parts of this question are presented below.

(a).

	Order # 1	Order # 2
Sales	2,000	2,000
Cost of Sales	1,000	1,000
Gross Margin	1,000	1,000
Order Cost	750	750
Non-stocked item cost	--	2,250
Profit	250	(2,000)
Profit percentage	12.5%	-100%

The comparison of the two small orders is designed to capture the information in customers S001 and S013 in Case Exhibit 5. Kanthal can be profitable with small orders (SEK 2,000 is about $150) but small orders better be for stocked items. With an order handling cost of 750 and a cost of producing a non-stocked item of 2,250, it is impossible for a small order for a non-stocked item to be profitable even if its manufacturing costs were zero.

The information contained in the profitability analysis of an individual customer order provides the data base for a wide range of profitability studies. At the end of a period (a month, quarter, or year) individual orders could be aggregated by product or product-line to show total profitability of each product (for example the bottom line in Exhibit 6, showing the total profitability of SEK 411,422 for Finished Wire N). The orders could also be aggregated by geographic regions to show the total profitability in each region or country where Kanthal operates. And, most relevant for this case, the information could be aggregated across products and regions to calculate the profitability of individual customers.

(b).

	Customer A	Customer B
Sales	160,000	160,000
Cost of Sales	80,000	80,000
Gross Margin	80,000	80,000
Order Cost	2,250	21,000
Non-stocked item cost	6,750	49,500
Profit	71,000	9,500
Profit percentage	44.4%	5.9%

The comparison of these two somewhat high volume customers is similar to customers 33518 and 33537 in Case Exhibit 6. The two customers have similar sales volumes and the products they order have similar gross margins. But the pattern of ordering is completely different. Customer A placed only three large orders during the year. Even though each order was for a non-stocked item, the size of the order overwhelmed the additional expense of producing the product to order. The overall profitability of A is very high. Customer B, however, achieved the 160,000 in sales volume by ordering 28 times during the year. Of these 28 orders, 22 were for non-stocked items (presumably different non-stocked items; if all 22 were for the same item, Kanthal would likely have figured out to start stocking that item for Customer B when it ordered the item every other week).

In fact the typical order for Customer B could be for an invoiced value of about 5,700 [160,000/28]. This produces a gross margin of 2,850 which is not high enough to cover the expenses of 3,000 [750 + 2,250] of handling and producing an order for a non-stocked item. Thus, perhaps most of Customer B orders could have been unprofitable. This example prepares students for the analysis of Exhibit 7 in the case, where large customers can be breakeven or even unprofitable if they order non-stocked items in small lots. Salesmen and sales managers, however, rewarded on gross sales volume would be indifferent between the pattern of orderings of Customers A and B in the above example.

I would try to cover this much of the analysis in about 40-50 minutes of an 80 minute class, leaving the remaining time to discuss Exhibit 7 and its implications, and to describe what Kanthal actually did.

Exhibit 7 is the heart of the case. Instead of starting with Exhibit 7, the teacher could display TN Exhibit 3 where the profitability of individual customers (rather than cumulative profitability) is graphed, starting from the most profitable on the left and proceeding to the least profitable on the right. It is important to emphasize the statement in the case that the two most unprofitable customers were among the top three in sales volume. At first this should seem surprising; the activity-based analysis usually shows that high volumes are more profitable and small volumes are less profitable than reported by traditional cost systems. I usually point out, in explanation of the actual results in Exhibit 7, that it is difficult to lose large amounts of money with small customers. It takes really perverse behavior by large customers for a customer to be that unprofitable.

Exhibit 7 and TN Exhibit 3 both illustrate the Pareto rule that a few things (20%) generate most of the benefits; in this case about 225 % of the total profits. Here we see that 30% of the customers make 250% of total profits, 40% of the customers break-even, and 30% of the customers lose 150% of the profits, leaving us with a net of 100% of profits. And the least profitable 10% of customers lose more than 100% of the profits.

Q: What makes a large volume customer unprofitable? What must be its order pattern?

By understanding the structure of the new Account Management cost system (see TN Exhibit 2), it should be obvious what makes a customer unprofitable: lots of small orders, and a high fraction of small orders for non-stocked items. In fact, we learn in the case that one of the large, unprofitable customers had switched to just-in-time ordering, placing orders every week or perhaps twice a week. Another customer (recalling Customer B in the numerical example above) was using Kanthal for small orders of non-stocked items, while placing large orders for standard products with its regular supplier.

Q: OK, I think we understand what gives rise to Exhibit 7, what should Ridderstråle and Kanthal do once they have seen the numbers in this exhibit?

Exhibit 7 is the end of the cost accounting story. What comes next must be a managerial story not an accounting one. This case provides a superb opportunity for collaborative teaching.

I had the best experience in teaching this case when I was able to enlist a marketing professor to join me in the classroom. He sat mostly quiet through the first 40-50 minutes of discussion, scowling occasionally and looking genuinely annoyed at having to participate in an accounting analysis of sales and marketing activities. As students started to volunteer various proposals for dealing with unprofitable customers, I eventually claimed ignorance about this set of issues and asked my marketing colleague to conduct the discussion. He started with comments like the following:

"I bet you're wondering what could get me to attend a cost accounting class. The accountants have really gone too far now. They weren't satisfied to mess up factory accounting and product costs. Now they're going after the one place in the company that really makes money. What do you mean by unprofitable customers? Are you going out in the field to a salesmen and tell him not to take an order for a product from one of our best customers; a product that we all agree has a 50% profit margin?"

Even when I have to teach the case alone (a distinctly inferior solution), I have simulated the switch in roles by attempting to act out how a marketing manager might behave; even better than the instructor attempting to role play, why not call on a student to take the role of a marketing manager who has been confronted with the information in Exhibit 7 (but without having had the benefit of the discussion that preceded Exhibit 7 or any of the activity-based cases that preceded Kanthal)?

Suggestions that get made to the marketing manager include:

Raise prices for small orders or apply a surcharge for non-stocked items (making sure this is legal; staying consistent with Robinson-Patman if you're in the U.S. market);

Introduce a minimum order quantity, or volume discounts for large orders;

Attempt to trim the product line, avoid unnecessary product proliferation;

Form a distributor, let the distributor stock and handle items that Kanthal does not wish to stock;

Change the compensation plan of the salespersons or the sales manager to emphasize profitability, not volume;

Deny this is a marketing or sales problem, it's a production and back office problem. Have them get their act together;

Lower the prices to customers who order predictably, especially stocked products in large quantities.

Special discussion should be focused on the large customer who adopted just-in-time. Should Kanthal approach this customer and say that it doesn't want to work with the customer in this manner; that the customer has to place less frequent orders for larger quantities? In today's competitive environment, such an approach is a good way to lose important customers. Alternatives include: have an open order with the customer so that separate orders do not have to be written each time a small order is placed; order predictably and only for stocked items--knowing what the customer is making should enable Kanthal to stock items for this customer rather than scrambling to handle a non-stocked production order.

The solution actually taken by Kanthal (as described in the (B) case which could be handed out at this time) was to give a present to this large customer: a computer terminal, though with a string attached; actually a wire, with the other end of the wire going into Kanthal's home office. By using computer technology, the cost of handling individual orders (the approximate SEK 750) was virtually eliminated. By integrating the information systems of the two companies, great savings could be realized by both sides (the computer terminal would reduce the customer's costs of placing orders) thereby creating a win-win solution.

While seemingly a simple and obvious solution, the message is an important one. Many organizations have found it difficult to justify financially additional investments in information technology. One of the principal benefits of information technology, both in the office and in the factory, is to greatly lower the cost of handling small, customized orders. But traditional cost systems do not identify how expensive it is, using conventional manufacturing and order processing procedures, to handle small, customized orders. Therefore, attempts to justify investments in such equipment usually founder. The activity-based analysis provides a much more favorable environment for understanding the substantial benefits that can be realized from successful implementation of information technology.

The (B) case and the remaining exhibits at the end of this note give the outcomes from actions taken by the company after seeing the results from the Account Management cost system. The bottom line is given in the last paragraph of (B): on a sales increase of 20% (which includes selective price increases), profits increase by 45% and total employment drops by 1%. In fact, over a four year period Kanthal was using fewer staff people to support a sales level 25% higher. Ridderstråle estimated that at least one-third of Kanthal's increased profits could be directly attributed to actions taken as a result of the new Account Management system.

Perhaps the most interesting example of what is possible with the new Account Management system is the Anders Drackenberg sales story. Anders was the salesman for customer # 199 in TN Exhibit 3, the high volume but highly unprofitable customer. Anders took pride in having built that customer to its present high volume level over a fifteen year period. Needless to say Anders was crushed by the Account Management report of his customer's massive unprofitability. Initially, he denied the validity of the analysis, but the senior management stood firmly behind the message from the system and Harry eventually decided to probe the system more deeply. It took several weeks, but Anders finally understood and, more importantly, accepted the message as well. He went back to his customer, shared the analysis with the customer, and through a combination of changed behavior (fewer orders and on a more focused set of products, price discounts for large orders for standard products, and price increases on small, customized orders) was able to transform a reported SEK 132,000 loss into a SEK 46,000 profit within one year.

Exhibit TN-1

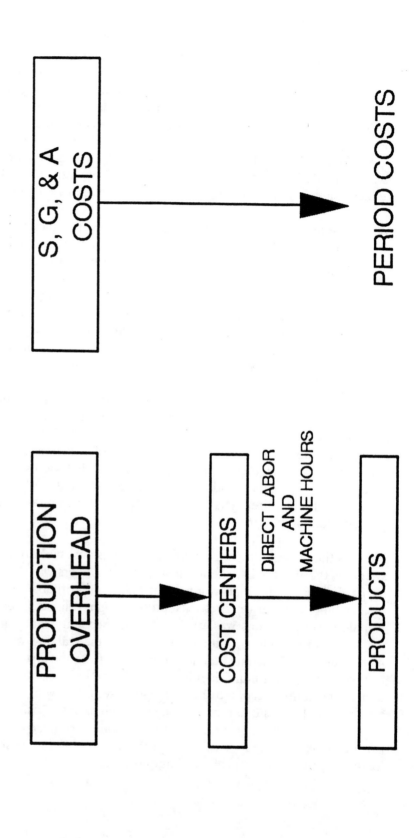

KANTHAL
UNIT-BASED COST SYSTEM

S, G, & A
COSTS

PERIOD COSTS

PRODUCTION
OVERHEAD

COST CENTERS

DIRECT LABOR
AND
MACHINE HOURS

PRODUCTS

Exhibit TN-2

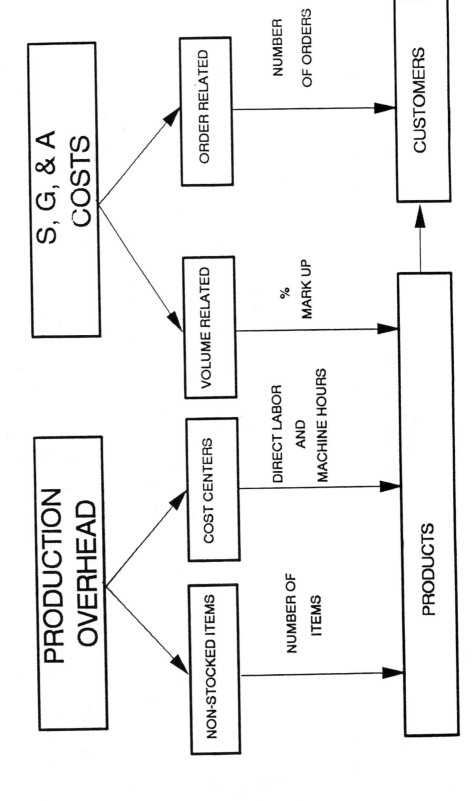

KANTHAL
ACTIVITY-BASED COST SYSTEM

Exhibit TN-3

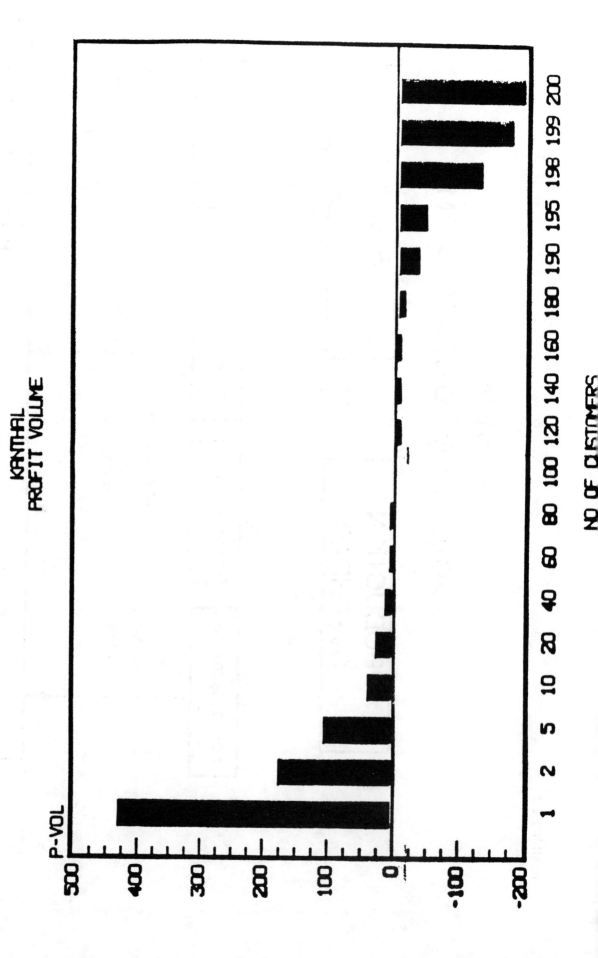

KANTHAL
PROFIT VOLUME

NO OF CUSTOMERS

Winchell Lighting, Inc. (A) and (B) Teaching Note

Winchell Lighting provides an example of the role for activity-based costing to assign marketing and distribution expenses to customer channels. The Kanthal case identifies customer ordering costs for individual customer transactions. Winchell extends this approach by looking at expenses that can be attributed to aggregate collections of customers: market segments, channels, and product lines. If not previously read with Kanthal, the "Why SG&A doesn't work," and "Customer Profitability Analysis" articles at the end of the chapter can be read in conjunction with the Winchell cases.

Winchell is a heavily disguised case setting. After writing the case, the president of the division felt that the case provided too much insight on the division's competitive strategy. In order to retain the case, we shifted the product line to lighting fixtures where we could illustrate the principal points of measuring profitability in multiple distribution channels. Gertrude Winchell, a lighting consultant in Boston, helped us on many institutional details for the new setting, but if students claim that some aspect of the case do not correspond to reality, we recommend conceding that the case was not originally written about a company making lighting fixtures and get on with the discussion.

Assignment Questions

Winchell (A)

1. Why has it become important for Winchell Lighting to assign its marketing and distribution expenses to product lines, channels, and market segments?

2. Evaluate the approach taken at Winchell Lighting to trace marketing and distribution expenses to product lines and channels.

3. Based on the new information in the Channel Profitability Report (Exhibit 4), what changes might Winchell consider?

This teaching note was prepared by Professor Robert S. Kaplan as an aid to instructors using the Winchell Lighting (A) and (B) cases (9-187-074 and 9-189-075).

Winchell (B)

1. Did the new strategic marketing cost analysis make a difference in how Winchell's thought about its business operations?

2. Was the information from the strategic marketing cost analysis accepted by management?

Winchell (A)

Class Discussion

Q: What is the competitive environment of Winchell Lighting?

Winchell competes in both the consumer and commercial lighting segments, selling both incandescent and florescent fixtures. Exhibit 2 shows that Winchell is the only company to compete in both the fluorescent and incandescent consumer market, but does not dominate in either line or for any distribution channel. Winchell receives 15% of its sales from the consumer market, which is highly competitive and cost-sensitive.

The commercial market accounts for 85% of Winchell sales. Apparently, there are four full-line competitors, and two specialty producers. A different company is the market leader for each product line. Winchell, is not the market leader for any particular segment (except for the small External Fixture segment) and is the only company in both consumer and commercial markets.

Q: Is Winchell in a good competitive position?

Winchell is spread across the entire lighting fixture segment. While it is the largest producer overall, it does not really dominate any particular segment. Consequently, Winchell will not enjoy the normal advantages of a market leader to determine or strongly influence strategy in the marketplace. Winchell's apparent strategy, "Everything to everyone," undoes many of the economies of scale normally enjoyed by the largest producer.

Some students will note that the different channels make very different demands on Winchell's sales force: the Contract channel requires extensive technical and sales support to keep contractors up to date on recent innovations and applications. The mass merchandising market emphasizes low price offerings, high availability of a limited range of products, and special allowances for promotions and quantity purchases. Offsetting these apparent dis-economies of scope, the multiple channels provide some diversification of business lines in a highly cyclical business, that enables Winchell to absorb demand fluctuations in individual channels and reduce production variability for its factories.

Q: Is there any synergy across these different distribution channels?

Apparently not; the lack of leadership across the different lines, and the different leaders in each segment suggests that the channels are quite independent. Perhaps there is a spillover effect from contractors to industrial suppliers.

Q: **What is the structure of the existing cost system?**

Winchell uses a very traditional financial system. Factory expenses are collected by major functional categories: materials, labor, and overhead. Likely, Winchell could have benefited from performing an ABC analysis to its factory expenses but that is not the focus of this case.

As in all conventional systems, selling, general, and administrative expenses are treated as "below the [gross margin] line" expenses. Expenses in these categories are aggregated together and expensed as period costs in the financial statements. While perfectly acceptable for financial reporting, this treatment gives no insight as to the source or cause of selling and administrative expenses.[9] Thus the financial reporting treatment provides virtually no guidance for management decisions or control.

Q: **How do we know it may be beneficial to undertake an activity-based analysis of marketing and distribution expenses?**

The Willie Sutton rule would lead us to focus on Winchell's below the line expenses. Marketing expenses are 15% of sales revenue and General and Administrative expenses are another 10% of sales. In fact, astute students should identify that marketing expenses are almost three times direct labor expense. You can be sure that direct labor is measured and monitored with great care, while the much larger marketing expenses are barely accounted for.

Also leading to a focus on marketing expenses is the **diversity** in the company's product lines, distribution channels, and market segments. In fact, the actual company had 14, not 6, different distribution channels. The situation was simplified for case presentation and class discussion. The combination of high diversity and high expenses suggests that the study described in the Winchell cases will yield significant insights to the company.

Q: **What is the risk of operating with the old cost system?**

By not assigning marketing expenses to customers or channels (or by assigning it uniformly across all channels, such as using % of sales dollars as the allocation base), marketing people are encouraged to seek high margin business regardless of the marketing, distribution, and service costs associated with the new business. The system ignores the "cost to serve" component of costs.

Basically, the existing system signals either that marketing and general expenses are independent of sales (that only gross margin matters), or, if below the line expenses are

---

9.   The article on Weyerhaeuser at the end of Chapter 7 gives instructors an opportunity to discuss an ABC analysis of corporate overhead (i.e., "general") expenses.

spread to products based on sales revenue, that every $1 of sales "costs" the company $0.25 of SG&A expenses.

Following the strategy of seeking high gross margin business will lead to Winchell getting business with heavy customer demands. Such business could require lots of advertising and promotion expenses, extensive technical support and expertise, generous discount, return, and credit policies, and, in general, lots of handholding by sales and marketing personnel. Low margin gross margin business, that may have low cost to serve (e.g., government, OEM) will be discouraged. We can also expect channel proliferation as marketing people continually search for new outlets for the company's product line. This proliferation could also feed back to increased complexity in the factory to meet specialized customer and channel needs. Basically, managers are unable to assess the trade-offs between marketing and other types of expenditures such as product design, manufacturing, and logistics.

Q: **Why have cost systems not typically focused on accurate assignment of sales, marketing and distribution expenses?**

Traditional cost systems have a product focus to satisfy financial reporting requirements to allocate factory expenses to all items produced. Selling and marketing expenses could not be "inventoried" so to do a more accurate assignment of expenses would require a system separate from that used for financial reporting. This was not a high priority task in an environment where marketing expenses might have been relatively small and information collection and processing costs were high. Also, marketing expenses would not have been under the control of a plant manager. Companies may want plant managers to focus on product costs that they could manage and control.

Also, marketing expenses seem somewhat "fixed" and joint with respect to all products. Many of them will have no obvious linkage between selling more products and generating higher costs. And these expenses may tie more naturally to customers and channels than to individual products.

Q: **OK, we now see the opportunity for a more accurate analysis of marketing expenses. How did the project team at Winchell accomplish this?**

The case is actually quite specific in describing the procedures used to identify various categories of marketing expenses to their causes or sources. Instructors should not have to spend much time on the details of the procedure but should be prepared to have a discussion on any particular aspect. We generally display the procedure by drawing the diagram of marketing expense hierarchy, shown in Exhibit TN-1, and identifying at which level in the hierarchy the expenses could be accurately assigned.

Marketing Expense Category	Traced to:
Commissions	Product Lines
Catalogs	Channels
Trade Advertising	Business Segments
Cooperative Advertising	Channels
Sales Promotion	Products & Product Lines
Warranty Expenses	Products & Product Lines
Customer Service	Channels
Marketing Management	Segments and Channels
Sales Policy	Channels
Marketing Travel & Entmt.	Channels
Postage	Channels
Admin. Travel & Entmt.	Channels
Warehousing	Product Lines
Meetings	Segments and Channels
Fixed Expenses	Segments and Channels
Cash Discounts	Channels

Several factors are interesting in the analysis. First, unlike Kanthal, none of the expenses seemed to be traced to individual customers. This undoubtedly reflected the preferences of Winchell's design team who wished to inform management about the profitability at the distribution channel level, not the individual customers. The team felt that action should be taken at the channel level, not by managing individual customers within the channel.

Second, many expenses could only be segregated by channels, and not by product lines sold within the channel. The design team wanted a full-allocation of marketing expenses to product-lines. In order to get channel level expenses to product-lines (or segment expenses to channels), the team allocated expenses downward using sales $. We now recognize that this is an arbitrary allocation that does not contribute to understanding product-line profitability. Anytime a design team finds itself driving expenses to products or customers using a basis like sales dollars, it is getting a powerful signal that it does not have a good causal basis for assigning those expenses to that level. Rather than arbitrarily allocating these expenses (which we can call channel-sustaining or segment-sustaining expenses) to customers or products, it may be preferable to aggregate the operating margins earned by products and customers upward in the hierarchy and calculate channel profitability by subtracting channel-sustaining expenses from the margins earned by selling products to customers within that channel.

Q: What did the new strategic marketing analysis reveal?

Exhibit 4 shows how the traditional system measured channel profitability. Each channel was evaluated by the gross margins earned by products sold within that channel. This perspective indicated that the Industrial Suppliers and Contract channels were the most profitable; and that the government and OEM channels were below the 34% return-on-sales average profitability for the company. The $31,814 of SG&A expenses were treated as a lump sum subtraction from the gross margins earned from selling through all channels.

Exhibit 9 of the case shows the new perspective from the marketing cost analysis.[10] Industrial Suppliers are still the most profitable channel but now Government and OEM are seen to be as profitable (as measured by net return on sales) as the Contract channel. In fact, if net invested capital is assigned based on actual demands for working capital and equipment utilized, the Government and OEM channels show a higher ROI than the Contract channel, a major reversal from the profitability rankings shown by the traditional system. The more detailed look at the individual marketing expense categories shows that many activities are not performed at all for the Government and OEM channels. These channels select vendors on the basis of product design and price, and are not influenced by advertising, catalogs, and special promotions. By assigning the expenses of those activities to those channels that require or benefit from the activities, we learn that OEM and Government are attractive channels despite the lower gross margins earned by selling to customers in those channels.

Exhibit 9 also shows that the newly re-entered Consumer channels were even more unprofitable than had been previously shown. These channels not only had lower gross margins (because of price concessions and discounting) but also demanded higher than average marketing and sales support. While Contract and Industrial Suppliers had 24% of sales in marketing expenses (and Government and OEM only 20 and 18%, respectively), the Consumer channels had marketing expenses that were 34% of sales revenues. Thus the strategy of getting the Consumer channels to at least breakeven operations is signaled with greater urgency by the marketing cost analysis in Exhibit 9.

Winchell (B)

Class Discussion

Winchell (B) is a short case. Instructors can incorporate the Johnson-Loewe Weyerhaeuser article (at the end of Chapter 7) on assigning corporate overhead expenses into the day's class discussion to fill an 80 minute teaching period.

I would start the class by re-drawing Exhibit TN-1 from the (A) class discussion to review the hierarchy of marketing expenses.

Q.   **Can we trace all marketing expenses to products as the Winchell Lighting analysts wished to do?**

The discussion in the (A) case makes clear that many marketing expenses had to be allocated to product-lines and products. Anytime the analysts said that they had to allocate channel expenses to product lines based on the sales volume of the individual product lines, students should recognize that this is truly an allocation. The expenses being allocated are not "caused" by the product line, nor are the resources in the channel

---

10.   In Exhibit 9, the company's General & Administrative expenses are allocated to the six channels based on sales revenues. In practice, a separate study had been performed to generate a more accurate assignment of these expenses to channels. For simplicity, we ignored this separate analysis and spread the G&A expenses as had been done under the traditional system.

or market segment in any sense consumed by the different product lines. The expenses are incurred in order to operate within a given channel but are independent of the volume and mix of products and product lines sold through that channel. Thus the expenses are channel-sustaining, that is traceable to individual channels, but not caused by the volume or mix of activity within the channel. They are avoidable only by shutting the channel down, not by making decisions at the product or product-line level. This insight likely invalidates the stated goal in the (A) case to calculate costs at the "product-channel" level.

Q.   **What kind of presentation makes sense to summarize the relevant information from the strategic marketing analysis?**

Certainly the information at the channel level (see Exhibits 1 and 2 in the (B) case) captures the economics of each channel quite well, with few allocations required. The sales and contribution margins of all products sold within each of the six channels are calculated and the expenses of sustaining each channel are subtracted from the product contribution margins. This yields a reasonably accurate picture of the operating profit of each of the six channels, before assignment of General & Administrative expenses (see Figure 7.1 on page 471). If senior managers insist on allocating all marketing expenses down to the product level, then we would suggest separating expenses specifically attributable to making the products and selling them in channels to customers from the marketing and G&A expenses that have been **allocated** to the products, using drivers such as sales dollars or units sold.

Q.   **How can we tell when an expense has been allocated to a product?**

The general rule we use is that anytime a unit-level driver like sales dollars, units sold, or manufacturing costs is used to assign an expense to a product (or customer), we have a pretty good clue that the product or customer has received an allocation. A few expenses, such as commissions, may be driven by sales dollars but most selling and administrative resources are not consumed proportional to sales dollars or units sold. These allocation bases are typically used as a default, when no causal relation can be identified. Therefore, managers should be suspicious of marketing and G&A expenses that have been assigned based on unit-level drivers like sales dollars. If managers insist on seeing fully-burdened product or product-line costs, then perhaps we should present the allocated costs separately, below a contribution margin line or in a different color, to show that the allocated costs are not causally related to the individual product.

Q.   **Did the marketing study make a difference?**

Apparently the study did make a difference. It focused attention on the poor performing products through the Low ROI Products Report and helped to create the climate for action. Managers had started to shed some of their losing products. It also encouraged them to take actions to improve operating margins. The discount structure was changed and period expenses were capped to stem operating losses in unprofitable channels such as mass merchandising. Other products, such as fluorescent fixture line, were re-engineered to reduce manufacturing costs and increase margins. Certain segments, revealed to be highly attractive, were defended. Also, certain niches -- such as OEM business and government -- that were revealed much more profitable than had been thought became the focus of aggressive marketing activities. A new niche, the 100 largest builders, that had characteristics similar to the OEM channel, was being developed. And new product lines, such as the budget recessed fixture line, had been introduced.

On the other hand, the managers seem to be ambivalent about the particular role played by the marketing study. As the conversations continued, they claimed that many of the above actions were underway already. Perhaps they would have been done without the marketing study. Also, the managers started to identify barriers to change; they felt limited by the external environment (it is difficult to shed an "everything to everybody" strategy in the short run -- recall the Schrader Bellows (F) case) and by the actions of their competitors. Winchell continued to sell loss products to maintain a full-line offering. Thus after finishing reading the (B) case, the evidence on the impact of the study is not decisive.

Q.   **Was the marketing study accepted by management?**

At one level, yes, the study was accepted. Managers spoke favorably of the study and felt it confirmed what they thought they knew was happening in the marketplace. On the other hand, they didn't follow a naive strategy based solely on the numbers in the study. The kept poor performers to maintain their commitment to offer a full product line. They talked about the need to "go slow," to wait a few years recognizing that poor results in any given year could have been caused by external considerations rather than any fundamental flaw in product or market strategy. Students can debate whether they believe the managers are experienced and wise or simply being defensive and unwilling to challenge the company's long-held strategy of being everything to everybody.

Q.   **Well, several years from now, will we be able to tell whether the marketing cost analysis has made a difference?**

We might look for whether the company has achieved more focus in its product line offerings or the channels in which it sells. Have the number of channels been reduced, or are products and channels still being proliferated?

We could examine whether aggressive repricing has occurred in some of the low-volume, low margin business. Significant price increases might enable Winchell to continue to offer a full product line, and also to test its theory that customers truly value a product line that offers highly specialized niche products. Also, we might look to see whether Winchell has reduced pricing, or offered more services, to defend segments revealed by the marketing cost study to be highly attractive. An observable consequence of both these actions would be for reduced dispersion in the profit margins across segments and product-lines calculated in subsequent marketing cost studies. For example, in the 1982 study shown in Exhibit 1, the maximum dispersion is the -19% in the Mass Merchandise channel to the +22% in the Industrial Supplier channel, a range of 41 percentage points. In 1985, the dispersion goes from -15% in Mass Merchandise to +17% in Industrial Supplier, a range of 32 percentage points. This analysis can be extended by driving it down to the product line level.

The instructor can conclude the discussion by summarizing the actions that seemed to follow the marketing cost analysis.

- Shifted management focus from gross margins to profit margins

- Developed marketing strategies based on more accurate knowledge of business economics

    - Product-line coverage
    - Distribution channel presence
    - Competitive moves
    - Long-term perspectives for developing distribution channels

- Developed tactical moves based on newly revealed information

    - Pricing and discount structure
    - Advertising
    - Redesign products to reduce manufacturing costs
    - Focus management attention of poor performing products and channels

Exhibit TN-1

Winchell Lighting Inc.
Teaching Note
Figure 1

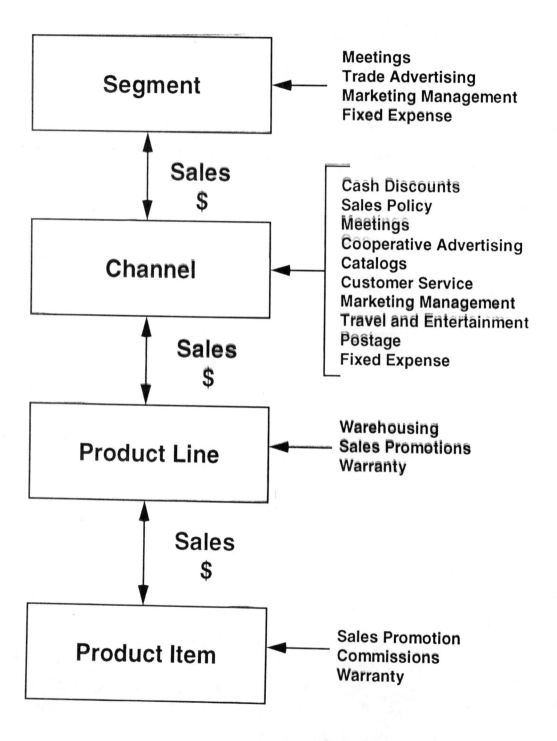

Manufacturers Hanover Corporation: Customer Profitability Report

Teaching Note

The Manufacturers Hanover Corporation (MHC) case is an advanced case on measuring customer profitability in a financial institution. It should generally be taught after the American Bank case has been used to introduce the application of activity-based cost concepts to measuring the cost and profitability of customers' transactions accounts (checking and savings accounts). Many of the terms, especially the different types of lending facilities, in MHC may be unfamiliar to students. I would recommend telling the students not to get bogged down in the details of how to calculate Risk-Adjusted-Assets (RAA) and to focus on the big picture of what the company is trying to accomplish with the Loan Pricing Model and Customer Profitability Report (CPR). The CPR described in the case is still in transition; the case therefore provides a snapshot of a large financial institution evolving into a new measuring and reporting environment.

The case can be taught from two perspectives. I have used the case in a program for general managers to introduce the notion of customer profitability; in this situation, I try to generalize the motivation and procedures used by MHC to all types of companies, not just banks. Taught to a group more interested in the particular problems of financial institutions, I might suppress some of the general questions to focus on the particular environment of banks in the early 1990s.

Assignment Questions:

1.   What forces drive the need for companies to measure customer profitability?

2.   What were the basic measurement issues that had to be solved for the Loan Pricing Model?

This teaching note was prepared by Professor Robert S. Kaplan as an aid to instructors in classroom use of the case, Manufacturers Hanover Corporation: Customer Profitability Report N9-191-068.

3.   Why were two systems needed: the Loan Pricing Model and the Customer Profitability Report?

4.   What actions were influenced by the Customer Profitability Report?

5.   How should the bank give credit to the lending officer for other business done by the bank with the officer's customer? What are the strengths and weaknesses of the alternative proposals?

Teaching Strategy:

Q: What drives the need for a customer profitability report? Why does a senior bank group executive come to work one day and decide that he really wants his staff to develop a customer profitability report?

Several forces were at work in the 1980s that caused Herb Aspbury to desire a new reporting mechanism. First, there had been a substantial decline in the profitability from the bank's (more particularly, his division's) main product line - commercial lending. With the loss of attractive margins, the division was showing low profitability, yet was still contributing to overall bank profitability through access to and relationships with customers.

Second, the bank had proliferated the products and services it could offer, and the regions in which these products were delivered to customers. If all these products and services were offered through the domestic commercial lending division, then the profit report of the lending division would still give an accurate picture of the profitability of the complete relationship. But many of the new products and services were being offered and booked in other division -- either product divisions, such as treasury and trading, and investment banking, or geographic divisions, such as Europe and Asia.

The proliferation of products and regions also was accompanied by considerable diversity in the use of interest-rate sensitive services and fee-based services, as well as the demands by customers for support in non-priced services (customer calls, advice, lending officers learning of the full range of customer needs).

At the same time, the customers themselves were getting more sophisticated, evaluating the full range of services they were receiving from each bank, issuing report cards to the banks, and demanding attractive pricing when they did extensive business with a single institution. Thus, MHC's relationship with some of its large and sophisticated multi-national customers mirrored the increased attention that companies like IBM must pay to the full range of products and services it offers to customers around the world, and that decentralized consumer packaged goods companies (Johnson & Johnson, Procter and Gamble) must devote to their increasingly concentrated retail customers (e.g., Walmart). Many observers have noted that for the 1990s, companies must shift from a product focus to a customer or market focus. If this trend is accurate (and it does seem that way), then new measurement and reporting systems must be developed to reflect the performance, not on a product basis, but on a customer and market basis. Thus MHC's development of the CPR is not unique to banking. Likely, many companies will need to develop customer profitability reports to identify how well they are doing by individual customers and markets.

Finally, but perhaps at least as important as any of the above forces, MHC was operating under severe resource constraints. Because of loan loss write-offs and increased regulatory scrutiny, MHC had to ration its equity base across all the products it offered. Therefore return on risk-adjusted-equity had become an extremely important performance measure. In the good old days of the 1970s, when lending margins were much higher, any loan that did not default would likely generate highly attractive returns. With equity now extremely scarce and razor-thin lending margins, the bank could not afford to carry loans whose return on RAE was below the cost of capital (calculated at 16%) unless it was getting attractive profits from other bank products. A CPR was therefore needed to determine whether the entree provided by commercial lending was being used to market other, and more profitable, banking products.

Q: **Consider the existing financial system for the North American Markets (NAM) Group. Did it at least measure profitability by product?**

Not really, the existing system measured all the income and expenses booked into the NAM group, but did not break it out by letters of credit, revolving loans, terms loans, etc.

Q: **Well what was measured in NAM's existing financial system?**

The existing system measured profitability by the organizational unit. Apart from limitations on not measuring the revenues from the full range of services generated by lending officers, it did at least provide information on departmental spending, interest and fee revenues, and interest and loan expenses on business booked by the unit. It remained adequate for spending control, but was only adequate for evaluating the performance of the unit when most of the business was booked within the unit.

Q: **What role does the Loan Pricing Model (LPM) serve?**

The LPM is used to estimate the profitability of proposed lending transactions. It identifies the projected revenues (fees, interest income) and expenses for proposed loans. The lending officer can use the model to vary the pricing of various features of the loan, recognize how much value might be destroyed for an aggressively priced loan so that it could be compared with the profits earned from the same customer in other banking transactions, and negotiate with the customer on the magnitude of the loan, pricing, and utilization.

Q: **Does the LPM have a counterpart in other organizations?**

If students have studied the Union Pacific case series, they should be able to identify the exact similarity between the LPM and the Network Cost System of the railroad for estimating the cost of proposed carload moves. For a manufacturing company, the LPM is like a bidding or pricing model for customized products. The marketing person would estimate the parameters of the proposed job (direct materials, labor, machine time, and demands for support resources) and plug these into a model that would estimate the costs of the resources consumed by the job. This cost estimate could then be used as the basis for pricing the job. Health care and insurance organizations might want to enter the parameters of the population they are bidding to service so that they can estimate the projected costs of serving that population. An LPM is useful when the company offers highly customized products or services. It will not be needed if the company offers standard products whose differential utilization by individual customers does not affect the demands on the company's resources.

Q: **Why was an LPM not needed before by the bank?**

The need for an LPM becomes more obvious when not all loans are profitable. In the old 3-5-3 banking days (borrow at 3%, lend at 5%, and be on the golf course by 3 P.M.), all loans were profitable. The more loans you made the more money you earned. Managers did not need a complicated analytic model to tell them they were making money on each (non-defaulted) loan they could market.

Q **What were the key features incorporated into the LPM?**

The key driver was return on risk-adjusted-equity (RAE) leading to the calculation of value added/destroyed when returns were above or below the bank's 16% cost of capital. RAE was the scarcest resource in the bank, so the LPM calculation of return on RAE provided a clear focus for the profitability measurement system.

The calculation started with the Risk-Adjusted-Assets (RAA). The risk adjustment was necessary so that lending officers could not increase loan income by writing riskier loans. As the case identifies, risk increases with the tenor (length) of the loan and with the type of loan. You might point out that the bank has to reserve some RAE even when facilities are not used; many companies obtain a standby letter-of-credit that is only used when they run out of money from their normal cash management activities. Thus a standby letter, even if not currently being used, has some risk since customers will use such a credit line when other financing and cash generating alternatives have been exhausted.

The RAA figure is used for several subsequent calculations. First, a percentage, varying by the risk classification of the customer, is applied to calculate the RAE for the facility. Second, the loan loss reserve is determined by applying another percentage to the facility's RAA. And third, the RAA was used to allocate departmental operating expenses. Why was RAA used for this purpose? As noted in the case, the lending officers objected vigorously to filling in detailed time sheets, especially when they saw the limitations and inadequacies of the early CPR's. The RAA calculation was devised by Bill Maass to defuse the hostility to the time reporting sheets, so that the project could progress and not be killed in its infancy. Using RAA to allocate department operating expenses assumes that the effort expended by the loan officer is proportional to the magnitude and risk of the loan. The LPM had a feature that allowed the officer to indicate whether the proposed facility had more or less effort required than the RAA allocation assumed. The RAA allocation was clearly a short-run compromise and likely will be revisited by the bank once the CPR gains greater visibility and acceptance.

Q: **The Risk-Adjusted-Asset (RAA) calculation clearly plays a central role in the bank's LPM and customer profitability report. Is there a counterpart to RAA in other organizations?**

I am trying with this question to get the students to identify other forms of customer-specific assets. Accounts receivable, particularly with customer-specific loan loss provisions, is a direct counterpart to the bank's RAA for a loan. Other examples could include specific tooling, software, or equipment that can be identified to individual customers. Dedicated inventory (including consignments), reserved capacity, and peak-load capacity for specific customers are other examples. This brief discussion is good for getting students to realize that many of a company's assets can be traced accurately to individual customers, and therefore must be part of any customer profitability measurement system.

Q: **Are there any other features of the LPM that are worthy of note?**

This question allows the instructor to cycle back to the LPM and pick up any additional issues he/she or the class wishes to discuss. If it has not come up earlier in the discussion, working through the logic of the value added/destroyed calculation might be worthwhile here. It is interesting to note that the bank is willing to sell off part of a low return loan, decreasing further the return on RAE for the loan, but, more importantly, reducing the equity required by the loan and therefore lowering the shareholder value destroyed.

Q: **Okay, I think I understand what the LPM is and what it does. Why then was the customer profitability report (CPR) needed?**

The CPR provided two additional and critical functions. At the level of the individual loan or facility, the LPM helped bank officers bid for and price loans based on projected interest rates, fees, and utilization. The CPR was an ex post measurement system that reported actual profitability using actual interest rate spreads, payments, fees, and utilization. The CPR is an exact counterpart to the CPMS (Cost and Profitability Measurement System) described in the Union Pacific (B) case. (The parallels between the completely independently developed measurement systems for the two service organizations is quite striking.) For a manufacturing organization, the counterpart to the CPR is a job cost accounting system that would record the actual labor, materials, and support resources used to design, produce and deliver the job.

The second critical function is to bring together, for every individual customer, the profitability on all MHC products used by the customer. Thus the CPR must measure the actual profitability on every banking product used by customers, and be able to identify and capture all the products that each individual customer used.

Q: **Do other companies also have this linkage issue?**

Formerly decentralized product-focused companies have had to learn how to identify all the transactions they have with a given customer, across different product groups and around the world. This is far from an easy task, as the case describes. Customer ID codes will likely vary in each product division's and geographical unit's computer system. Therefore, either recoding of customers has to occur throughout the organization, or an extensive glossary and set of table must be developed that enables all transactions to be aggregated by customers.

Q: What other problems had to be solved for the CPR?

MHC had to have solved the set of issues raised in American Bank (calculating the cost and profitability of individual liability accounts - demand and time deposits) for all banking products, including cash management, corporate trust, stock transfers, pension work, etc. It also needed to know, by individual customer, the utilization of each of these products. In MHC, these calculations were in the domain of the GEOSERVE organization which, for purposes of the case and, as far as I know, could indeed calculate the cost and profitability of each transaction-based banking product.

Q: How was the CPR being used? What actions were being taken?

The actions taken by the NAM group mirrored those done by the manufacturing companies we studied who implemented activity-based cost systems (see, for example, John Deere, Siemens, and Kanthal). Officers tried to raise the price to marginal customers to make their return on RAE more attractive. When pricing improvements were not possible, the bank dropped many low-return customers (and followed through to capture the savings by making significant reductions in its lending staff). As in Kanthal, lending officers worked to change the behavior of customers, requesting them to reduce their use of products that made heavy demands on RAE and to increase their use of fee-based products that required little additional RAE. Also, lending officers reduced the amount of time they spent supporting low return customers.

The CPR enabled the bank to manage a complete customer relationship. An officer would be willing to make low margin loans to a customer that was a heavy user of other, and more profitable, bank products, but could to refuse to grant price concessions when such other business was not available. Also, lending officers could be rewarded for bringing new business into MHC even when the new business was booked in a group other than NAM.

Q: How should the bank calculate the contribution that a lending officer should receive for helping to market a product booked in another banking unit?

Herb Aspbury has advocated the double counting procedure in which the lending officer receives full credit for revenues no matter where the transaction is booked.

Advantages:

Lending officer is motivated to generate profitable business for the global bank, independent of which unit actually books the business

No turf battles, or time devoted attempting to sort out the relative contribution of each officer to a transactions

Lending officer more willing to serve as the customer's "relationship manager," making sure the customer is happy with the banking relationship and each transaction

Disadvantages:

With double counting, each organizational unit can look profitable when the entire company is unprofitable

Booking revenues into the marketing officer's unit doesn't reflect the operating expenses of the product group or other geographical unit that delivered the product. Thus the profitability of the transaction is over-stated. Could MHC get an effort-reporting system so that operating expenses can be assigned to each transaction? Not likely at this time.

Lack of real credibility to organizational unit profit measurement. People won't believe the results since the organizational units' profitabilities can't be aggregated into the company's financial figures. As a consequence, the double-counting procedure may not provide a basis for a formal incentive compensation plan.

Copeland has proposed the fee-splitting plan, in which the revenues from a transaction are divided between the marketing and the product groups.

Advantages:

Revenues are only counted once. It is a simple, consistent plan where unit profitabilities will sum to the organizational results.

Provides objective "real" basis for incentive compensation and other recognition and reward plans.

By splitting revenues, no need to assign expenses to individual transactions and transfer these to the marketing unit.

Disadvantages:

Lending officer may not provide full effort if she only receives 20% of the fee. Less incentive for marketing officer to be the key company relationship manager -- who will fix things when a customer has a problem with the bank?

The fee-splitting arrangement can lead to continuing arguments about the "fairness" of the fee-splitting percentages.

The lending officer may try to perform the complete transaction herself rather than bring in someone from a product group who might receive a large percentage of the fee.

One company executive who manages her company's different banking relationships told me:

"We have experienced difficulties with banks who have gone to the revenue-splitting approach. Typically the calling officer has a grandiose title but little authority over

the backroom or product guys who actually do the work. If the dollar split is defined in advance, whenever a problem occurs or a special service is requested in the course of a transaction, the guys actually doing the work figure they are not getting paid for the extra effort. Problems or special requests don't occur very often, but when they do, an efficient resolution of the issue will be important to the customer. Occasionally the lending officer reports the product/backroom problem to his/her supervisor and the issue eventually its way up to my Banking Director who calls his counterpart. If that doesn't work, I have to call the primary calling officer but, based on past experience, the 'solutions' within that person's authority tend to be limited.

I understand the dangers of double-counting profits, but would suggest that unless it is clear that the officer w\serving as the primary relationship contact is given the authority to ensure that all necessary resources are delivered to the customer, it is important to keep the incentives in line with the goal of customer service."

These questions and issues should provide ample opportunity for a 75-90 minute class discussion. The instructor may wish to reserve time at the end for a brief update. At the time of writing this teaching note (March 1991), MHC had adopted the fee-splitting approach (much to the chagrin of several executives in the most recent class where I taught this case). Fee-splitting percentages for 1991 had been defined for 15 standard products. At the end of the year, the results from this arrangement will be evaluated by the bank. For transactions where the fee exceeds $500,000, the reward percentages will be individually determined with conflicts resolved at the Group Executive level, chaired by Tom Johnson.

Tom Johnson will be receiving CPR's on the personal computer in his office. The visibility of this report in the President's office will likely create added incentive for banking units to participate in and be actively involved in the system. The actual CPR shown as Exhibit 5 of the case is being revised during 1991 to become a more comprehensible report. Also, Herb Aspbury had recently been appointed as Group Executive for the International Group, providing additional support for the international operations to be fully incorporated in the CPR. Some form of effort reporting (less detailed and onerous than the original time sheets) was also being investigated so that operating expenses could be assigned more accurately to customers.